More Than a Native Speaker

An Introduction to Teaching English Abroad

REVISED EDITION

DON SNOW

TESOL Teachers of English to Speakers of Other Languages, Inc.

Typeset in Avenir and New Baskerville
by Capitol Communication Systems, Inc., Crofton, Maryland USA
Printed by Kirby Lithographic Company, Inc., Arlington, Virginia USA

Teachers of English to Speakers of Other Languages, Inc.
700 South Washington Street, Suite 200
Alexandria, Virginia 22314 USA
Tel 703-836-0774 • Fax 703-836-6447 • E-mail tesol@tesol.org • http://www.tesol.org/

Publishing Manager: Carol Edwards
Copy Editor: Ellen Garshick
Additional Reader: Kelly Graham
Cover Design: Tomiko Chapman

ISBN 9781931185325
Library of Congress Control No. 2006901938

Table of Contents

Introduction

It was at the Taipei YMCA in 1979 that I first stood before a class as an English teacher, wondering how to survive the period with my dignity intact. I was assured of my command of English, but much less confident that I would even understand a jargon-laden question about English grammar rules, let alone be able to answer it.

I was also distinctly aware that knowing how to speak English was not the same as knowing how to teach English. What few vague ideas I had about language teaching dated from painful experiences in high school and college foreign language classes. These experiences had convinced me that there had to be a better way to teach language than lecturing on the finer points of grammar, but they had not shown me what that better way might be. Thus, in that first class period, my attention was focused much more on my need not to make a fool of myself than on effective pedagogy, and my primary goal was to hear the bell ring before I had run out of things to say.

Over the next two years, as my skills improved and I became more confident, I became less worried about getting through a class period. In this stage of my development, I tended to judge the success of a class period largely on whether or not students seemed to like a lesson, and I rarely persisted in any activity to which students did not quickly respond. As a result, my courses evolved into a series of "greatest hits" activities that entertained reasonably well and generated quite a bit of language practice, but did not have much continuity. Only after considerable trial and error—and a graduate program in language teaching—was I able to move from a standard of "Do my students like this activity?" to one of "Is this activity really going to help them learn?"

This is not to say that the English courses I taught during my earlier years were a waste of students' time; I no doubt provided the students with good practice opportunities and valuable language knowledge, and may have enhanced their interest in language learning by making it more enjoyable than it might otherwise have been. However, as I studied the rudiments of the language teaching craft, I learned not only how to teach language lessons more effectively but also how to help students learn to structure more productive language learning experiences.

Every year, thousands of men and women from English-speaking nations go abroad as volunteer English teachers through organizations such as the Peace Corps, Voluntary Service Overseas, and myriad other government, church, and academic organizations. Many others locate English teaching jobs on their own, through the Internet, through personal connections, or simply by appearing in a city and asking around. These novice language teachers face problems similar to those I confronted, and, over time, many novices learn to be good language teachers. To a large extent, success in teaching is based on qualities such as diligence, patience, and common sense, which many nonprofessionals possess in abundance, and many novice teachers make a significant educational contribution to their host nations in spite of their lack of professional training. However, learning the craft of language teaching by trial and error can take a long time and involve considerable emotional wear and tear on both teachers and students. The purpose of this book is to accelerate the process by providing a nontechnical introduction to English teaching that is geared toward the special needs of native-English-speaking teachers working abroad.

Strictly speaking, not all such teachers are volunteers in the sense that they work without pay; in fact, the great majority are paid for their services (though often less than what they might make if they were working in their home countries). However, for a great many, the decision to look for English teaching jobs abroad is driven partially or largely by nonfinancial considerations, such as a desire to make a positive contribution to the host society and to learn more about the people and culture of the host country. I wish to both recognize and encourage such kinds of motivation; also, at times my discussion of how teachers should teach and even live in the host country will even assume such motivation, particularly that teachers are genuinely interested in learning more from students about the host country. Therefore, throughout this book I refer to my target audience as *volunteer (English) teachers* (VTs).

The Volunteer Teaching Experience

Because teaching English as a VT in a foreign country is quite different from teaching as a trained teacher in an English-speaking country, the assumptions and emphases of this book are different from those of most introductions to English teaching in several ways:

1. Most VTs have some experience with language learning as a result of high school or college foreign language courses, have a native or near-native knowledge of English, and have a native understanding of at least one English-speaking culture. However, most VTs do not have professional training or experience in language teaching and are not necessarily interested in making a career of it. Therefore, this book is a practical introduction to the range of issues involved in learning to teach English abroad rather than a scholarly introduction to the language teaching profession as a whole. The book is not unprofessional; to the contrary, it is based firmly on current English teaching thought and research as well as on my experience as a language teacher and language learner. However, I assume that what a VT needs most is a readily intelligible distillation of English teaching theory and practice, explained with a minimum of technical jargon. I also assume that readers are less likely to have the opportunity to follow up on academic footnotes than to be interested in buying a few books on English teaching, so I have restricted my references to a relatively small list of readily available books and resources that VTs might purchase for a small, portable teaching reference library.

2. In contrast to English teachers in English-speaking countries, VTs abroad are almost by definition working in an environment that is culturally alien to them. This means that the task facing them involves not only learning how to teach English, but also learning about and adapting to the expectations, goals, methods, and resources of an unfamiliar educational system and culture. Note that, in addition to posing challenges, this situation has distinct advantages, one being that it provides an excellent opportunity for genuine communication; students are experts in the culture about which the teacher is trying to learn, so many activities can involve students in talking and writing about their culture in order to help educate the teacher.

3. VTs abroad are trying to cope with teaching while simultaneously undergoing the exciting but difficult process of adapting to life in a foreign culture. While this adaptation process may seem to be outside the range of topics normally considered in a book on language teaching, I have chosen to discuss it because it not only has a significant impact on the life of VTs abroad but can also affect their teaching, especially their effectiveness in teaching explicit or implicit lessons about culture and intercultural communication.

The Typical VT Environment

Teaching situations abroad can differ significantly according to the culture of the host country, students' skill levels, the resources available, class size, and a host of other variables. While I have tried to address as broad a range of situations as possible in this book, the teaching setting that I most often assume is a country that is non-Western culturally and less economically developed than most Western nations. To be more specific, I assume that VTs will work in a setting that has many of the following characteristics:

1. **equipment:** There will probably be at least chalk and a blackboard, or some equivalent. Tape recorders, videotape and DVD players, and other types of equipment may also be available, but access might be limited, and VTs cannot take their availability in classrooms for granted.

2. **materials:** A textbook will probably be available for most English courses, though in some cases only the teacher may have a copy. Some supplementary reading and listening material in English is available outside the classroom, but the range is probably limited. VTs are sometimes confronted with the problem of adapting existing material and sometimes of creating new material.

3. **students:** The age range of students VTs might teach is quite broad, with the low end consisting of preschool children and the high end including retired adults. However, most VTs work with adolescents (especially the higher levels of secondary school) or young adults (especially university students or young working people).

4. **class size:** VTs often teach classes with thirty or more students, and classes of fifty or more are not unusual. This means that teaching methods that require individual attention to students may not always be realistic.

5. **skill level:** VTs teach students at every skill level; some students are brushing up their command of the terminology of nuclear physics, and others still don't understand "How are you?" However, volunteers usually face students lying somewhere

between these two extremes, who have adequate English skills for rudimentary communication with a foreign English teacher in class but who cannot yet communicate fluently. In many countries, students can read more than they can say or understand in conversation.

6. **program:** VTs often teach in situations within an already established program (i.e., with goals, curricula, expectations, evaluation systems), but by design or default most programs still leave considerable room for innovation and decision making on the teacher's part. Teachers thus need to adapt to the existing program and are faced with deciding when to conform and when to innovate, a decision that can be tricky in an unfamiliar cultural environment.

7. **school:** VTs often work in the host country's formal education system, teaching in primary, secondary, or tertiary institutions. However, some teach in night schools, adult education classes, intensive English programs, courses that prepare students to take the Test of English as a Foreign Language (TOEFL), or various English clubs.

8. **language environment:** Most volunteers teach in places where English is not widely used outside the classroom. This not only limits students' opportunity for practice but also means that goals and motivation are more problematic than they are for students studying English for survival in an English-speaking country. For example, in many countries, students study primarily to get high scores on examinations; consequently, they study in ways that prepare them for tests but do not help them develop usable English skills. This, in turn, means that they may lose interest in English study once they no longer have tests to pass. Therefore, VTs need to be aware of the vital importance their classes have in giving meaning and life to English study. It is often in classes with native-English-speaking volunteers that students first experience English as a tool for communication, not just an obstacle to examination success.

9. **culture:** Many volunteers teach in relatively traditional societies, that is, societies that look more to their past for values and practices than most Western societies do. In some of these societies, attitudes toward English teaching have been influenced by traditional methods for learning to read a prestige language, such as classical Chinese in China and Arabic in many Islamic countries (languages that play a role similar to that which Latin played in premodern Europe). Such societies tend to value the authority of the printed word and of the teacher, see language learning as knowledge acquisition rather than skill development, and emphasize study of texts (grammar, vocabulary, and reading) more than speaking and listening skills. In these societies, grammar books and dictionaries usually have a very high degree of authority, and woe be to the unsuspecting innocent who contradicts them. As a result, VTs' assumptions about how one should teach and learn language may differ considerably from those of their students and colleagues.

10. **relationship to the West:** The position of economic, military, and cultural dominance that English-speaking nations have occupied over the past two centuries allows a few generalizations about the relationship between the VT's culture and that of the host country. First, most (but not all) volunteers teach in nations that are not as wealthy as the volunteers' home countries. Second, the wealth, technology, markets, and cultural power of English-speaking nations often inspire considerable admiration (and much of the motivation for English study) in the host country. These feelings of admiration are,

however, often complicated by feelings of bitterness toward ex-colonial and imperial powers, and by resentment of the host country's relative poverty (which may stand in glaring contrast to a more glorious past). In many nations, therefore, VTs need to be sensitive and cautious as they teach about their nations. Students may have very mixed feelings about the English-speaking nations of the West, and many volunteers have been surprised at the speed with which a class of students who seemed very enthusiastic about the West becomes defensive or even hostile.

Theoretical Assumptions

In this book I operate primarily from the theoretical assumptions of an approach called *communicative language teaching* (CLT); in other words, I stress the idea that language is a tool for communication and that communicative activity should play a major role in the language classroom. I take this stance not only because it is a dominant trend in current thinking about language teaching, but also because most VTs find it instinctively appealing and comfortable to work with. At times, however, I also discuss teaching methods, such as text memorization, that are associated with other theoretical approaches. This is partly because I share the belief of many scholars that currently no single theory of language teaching can be taken as authoritative (see Bowen, Madsen, and Hilferty 1985, 4–5; Richards 1990, 36; Omaggio Hadley 2001, 80; Brown 2002, 10–11). It is also partly because VTs often teach in environments where noncommunicative methods may be the norm, and whether or not volunteers choose to use such methods, they need to be familiar with them. Given the tendency of many Westerners to be highly critical of traditional or outdated approaches—and the distinct possibility that their host colleagues will use these methods—VTs need to be able to see that there are reasons these methods are used and that they are not without merit. Without this bit of empathy, volunteers may end up alienating both their colleagues and their students.

As language teaching professionals increasingly recognize, the English classroom is often not the most important focus of activity for many students. In many cases, students' success in learning a language depends more on the effectiveness of their strategies outside class than on the skill of the language teacher in class. This is especially true for the many students who are not studying English in full-time programs that allow them several hours a day of language class, and whose success depends on the work they do outside class or after the English course ends. It is also especially true for students whose native language is not closely related to English and whose acquisition of English is not speeded by the vocabulary, grammatical, or cultural similarities that accelerate the English study of many European students. Consequently, I do not limit my discussion to classroom teaching techniques; I also discuss study methods and ways for students to plan their own study programs.

I organize my discussion of language teaching in a rather traditional way, approaching listening, speaking, reading, writing, grammar, vocabulary, and culture separately rather than organizing discussion in a way that is more obviously compatible with whole-language approaches. Again, this is a deliberate choice. Without ignoring their interrelatedness, I organize discussion around traditional categories because such divisions are likely familiar to VTs as a result of experience in foreign language classes. Also, many of the schools and students with whom VTs will work tend to think in terms of these categories, and volunteers who are learning a new craft in a new environment would be wise to begin from what is familiar to both them and the students.

In sequencing the topics in this book, I roughly follow the order in which a VT is likely to need the information. As suggested previously, in my experience, beginning language teachers go through an English teacher version of Maslow's Hierarchy of Needs that looks something like this:

- **level 1:** need to make it through the classroom hour without running out of material

- **level 2:** need for positive student response to one's lessons (or at least no overt expression of boredom and displeasure)

- **level 3:** need to feel that one's lessons actually help students develop English skills

The first section of the book, Preparing to Teach (chapters 1–6), is devoted to issues of classroom survival: basic principles of language learning and teaching, and course and lesson planning. The second section, Aspects of English Teaching (chapters 7–14) discusses the various aspects of language teaching in more detail. Finally, chapter 15 addresses adaptation to life in the host country, and chapter 16 suggests future paths for volunteers who become interested in being professional language teachers.

Changes in the Revised Edition

Readers familiar with the first edition of *More Than a Native Speaker* will find a number of significant changes in this revised edition:

1. The discussion of student-directed language learning in chapter 3 has been expanded. I also introduce the term *language learning projects* for language learning efforts designed and carried out by students either as a part of their work for a language course or as entirely independent language learning efforts. Examples of such projects are provided at the ends of chapters 7–12.

2. Each chapter ends with a section entitled For Thought, Discussion, and Action. These activities are intended to serve as a workbook in settings where *More Than a Native Speaker* is being used as a textbook for a course; however, they can also be valuable to readers who are studying the book on their own.

3. The brief list of culture-based discussion topics in appendix B of the first edition has been greatly expanded and renamed Culture-Topic Activity Ideas for Oral Skills Classes. Many more activities are provided than in the first edition, and they are more fully fleshed out. The material in this section can be used as supplementary activities for English courses, especially oral skills courses, or even as the core material for an entire course.

Additionally, I have updated some references and tidied up parts of the first edition that I felt needed an additional layer of polish.

Additional Notes

This book is intended for VTs from any English-speaking nation, but I find that I am more convincing and accurate if I draw primarily on my own U.S. background for language and culture examples. Asia in general and China in particular are overgenerously represented in my choice of examples; again, this is because much of my language teaching experience has been in the East. Finally, I beg your indulgence for my occasional use of *Westerners* to refer to people from countries where English is spoken by most people as their first language. It is simply too much of a mouthful to consistently refer to *Americans, Canadians, British, Irish, Australians, New Zealanders, and others*.

As much as possible, I have tried to use normal English rather than jargon and abbreviations. The few exceptions are as follows: *English as a foreign language* (EFL) refers to teaching English in a country where English is not widely used. This is in contrast to *English as a second language* (ESL), teaching English to non-English-speaking people in an English-speaking area.[1] As mentioned earlier, CLT refers to *communicative language teaching*. And for the sake of convenience, I also allow myself the new acronym VT—*volunteer (English) teacher*—to refer to native speakers of English who are serving as volunteer teachers of English abroad.

Acknowledgments

Working on the first edition of this book, I was fortunate to receive assistance from a number of friends and colleagues. I wish to express my gratitude to Kate Parry and Shelly Chase for truly sacrificial efforts in reading over entire early drafts, to Clifford Hill for suggestions on evaluation methods, and to the anonymous TESOL reviewers for their generous gifts of expertise and time. Thanks also go to John Garoutte, Alexis Albion, Fred Elting, Chris Blankenship, and Jim Kwong for their feedback on various portions of the draft.

For comments and suggestions on the second edition, I thank Brad Baurain, Andy Cheely, Carl Jacobson, Anne Kavanagh, Mick Kavanagh, Hans Klar, Mary Beth Maher, Kitty Purgason, Lisa Reshad, and Kim Strong; special thanks go to Brad Baurain and May Shih for suggestions on useful Web sites. I also thank all the English teachers who patiently filled out forms and answered my questions as I compiled the list of books in appendix C. Thanks are also due to Alice Renouf and the Colorado China Council for the opportunity to try out the revised edition in their new teacher training program in summer 2005 and to Charley Kelly for helping me spot typos. Finally, I am particularly thankful to the two anonymous TESOL reviewers, who gave me a number of excellent suggestions and even made some revisions for me. Of course, as always, ultimate responsibility for any nonsense remaining in the final product lies with me.

---

[1] Many recent books on English use a more sophisticated set of divisions in which nations are divided into three categories: (1) *Inner Circle* nations, in which English is spoken as the first—and often only—language by the majority of the population (e.g., Australia, the United Kingdom, the United States); (2) *Outer Circle* nations, in which English is not the first language of most of the population but has some official role, for example, in education, and is sometimes used for internal communication (e.g., India, Singapore; most of these are ex-colonies of the British Empire); and (3) *Expanding Circle* nations, where English is taught and used only as a foreign language and is generally used only for interaction with people from other countries (e.g., China, Japan). My use of the term *EFL contexts* corresponds to the Expanding Circle category, the context in which VTs are most likely to live and work. (Relatively few VTs go to Outer Circle countries.)

I retain the older EFL/ESL distinction in part because it is familiar to many people and because I feel the phrase *English as a foreign language* better captures how teachers and students in Expanding Circle nations view English; for example, the Chinese term *waiyu* and Japanese term *gaigokugo* both literally mean *outsider* (i.e., foreign) *language*. I also wish to avoid any suggestion that English necessarily spreads like expanding circles on a pond, with Expanding Circle countries inevitably on the road to becoming Outer Circle countries. As noted, virtually all Outer Circle countries share the historical experience of once being part of the British Empire, and, in that sense, their history is distinctly different from that of many Expanding Circle countries.

PART I

Preparing to Teach

The chapters in this section address the issue of planning for language teaching. Chapter 1 discusses some basic principles of language teaching and learning. Chapter 2 then suggests ways in which you can gather information before planning your courses. Chapters 3 and 4 consider the basic elements of a language course, essentially a formula consisting of *goals + materials + methods + evaluation*. Chapter 5 discusses the practical issues involved in planning a successful lesson, and chapter 6 wraps up this section with some examples of how all of this is put together into typical language courses and lessons.

Chapter 1

Principles of Language Learning and the Role of the Teacher

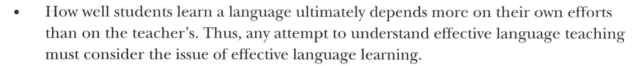

- How well students learn a language ultimately depends more on their own efforts than on the teacher's. Thus, any attempt to understand effective language teaching must consider the issue of effective language learning.

- Four basic realities of language learning are that a language is a tool for communication, that learning a language involves mastery of both knowledge and skill, that the struggle to learn a language is a battle of the heart as well as of the mind, and that learners vary considerably in their preferred approaches to language learning.

- The language teacher is not simply a transmitter of knowledge; like a coach, the language teacher needs to assist students in understanding the task before them, staying motivated, building discipline, and learning how to pursue the task on their own.

- The assumptions stated above may not be shared by students or colleagues in your host country, so it is important to make your assumptions explicit to the students and to make sure that there is not too large a gap between your expectations and the students'.

What is a language teacher? Perhaps the first image that occurs to you is of a tidily dressed woman or man standing in front of an attentive class, explaining a grammar point or a new word. Then he or she checks whether or not students understand the point by asking each one a question or two, patiently correcting any mistakes they make. Most people have seen this model of teaching in films and on television, and many have been in language classes that were taught largely in this fashion; it would therefore be easy to let this model shape the way in which you set out to teach your own classes.

In this chapter, my purpose is to challenge some of the assumptions underlying this language teaching model, to introduce a number of basic principles of language learning, and to suggest a different model of the language teacher.

Students at the Center

Even though this is a book about language teaching, any discussion of teaching needs to start with students. In recent years, more and more books on language teaching are placing students rather than teachers at center stage. This shift is due to a growing recognition that whether or not students succeed in learning a language depends more on their own efforts than on the teacher's and that a good program of instruction therefore needs to be student centered instead of teacher centered.

One reason it is important to view language learning as student centered is that students are individuals who differ in significant ways. First, students differ in their language knowledge and skills; one student may read well and have a broad vocabulary but be almost incapable of speech, while another student may have exactly the opposite profile of skills. Second, students differ in their learning styles and strengths; a study method that is intolerably boring, confusing, or intimidating for one student may prove comfortable and effective for another. Finally, students differ greatly in their levels of motivation, their attitudes toward study in general, and their feelings toward English study in particular. One student is quite diligent but resents Western cultural influence in her country; another thinks the West is appealing but has little love for study; a third doesn't care one way or another about English but would like to get a good grade on the final exam. Consequently, the reasons for a student's successes or failures have to be sought at a variety of different levels and differ greatly from person to person; inevitably, no teacher-designed, one-size-fits-all lesson or program will meet the needs or suit the styles of all of the students in a class. Instead, as much as possible, students need to take charge of their own learning, choosing goals that fit their needs and strategies that work for them.

A second argument for student-centered approaches is that students learn more effectively if they are active participants than if they only passively follow the teacher's instructions. This is true if for no other reason than that much language study and practice takes place when the teacher is not around to give instructions or to check up on students; students who view homework or small-group conversations as a welcome chance to develop their skills make much better use of these opportunities than students who merely consider them a chore to cope with as quickly as possible.

The final reason that language learning needs to focus on students is that few EFL programs of English study are long enough to guarantee that students will have mastered English by the time they leave the program. In many countries, English is offered in middle school and even primary school—often as a required subject—but students study English only a few hours a week and have little opportunity to practice what they learn. Even the few students who complete a university major in English still usually have gaps in their English skills when they graduate, and students who are not English majors or who study in a night school have even less English training and practice. Thus, if a high level of proficiency is the goal, students will probably have to continue studying English long after they leave the educational system, and the students most likely to keep making progress toward mastery of English are those who are already accustomed to designing and carrying out their own language study plans.

Language Teacher as Language Learner

For the reasons stated above, the focus of this book is frequently on language learning as much as on language teaching per se. To become increasingly effective as a language teacher, you must understand as much as possible about how the process of language learning works and what it feels like. Therefore, as you embark on your career as a language teacher, you also need to either begin or continue your career as a language learner. Given that this point is not normally emphasized in books on language teaching, I make this argument in some detail here. I suggest that there are at least four main reasons why language teachers should also be language learners.

The first and perhaps most obvious reason is that the more experience you have as a language learner, the more you will know about what does and doesn't work in language learning. Decisions you as a language teacher make about what you require of students will have a significant impact on how students invest their study and practice time, so you must be sure that what you ask students to do will actually enhance their language learning. One of the best ways to know this is by having tried out a given method yourself to see how effective it is. Granted, what works for one person may not always be effective for another, so your personal experience as a language learner does not provide a perfect guide for what will benefit students, but it certainly provides a very good start. Furthermore, as you try different approaches and methods in your own language learning, your bag of language learning ideas and tricks will gradually fill, and you will have more alternatives to offer to students when whatever they are doing does not seem to be working and they need to try something new.

A second reason your ongoing experience as a language learner will enhance your language teaching is that it will deepen your understanding of what it feels like to try to learn a new language. As I argue below, language learning is a battle of the heart as much as of the mind, and your ability to empathize with students—to know how they feel—is the first step toward knowing how to more effectively encourage and motivate them (not to mention knowing how to avoid overwhelming them).

Let me tentatively suggest that a third important benefit of language study has do with the level of conviction underlying your teaching. Volunteer teachers (VTs) from Western nations often have only limited experience with foreign language study, and many have never achieved a significant level of proficiency in a foreign language. In fact, the main thing that many VTs have learned in high school or college foreign languages classes is that language study can be hard work. Rubin and Thompson (1994) make the interesting observation that "if an individual's first experiences with a foreign language were not particularly pleasant or successful, he or she will tend to expect the next language learning experience to be just as stressful and unfruitful as the first" (p. 8). It would seem reasonable to assume that these negative experiences would color one's language teaching as well as language learning. Teachers who have never experienced success or reward in language study may find it difficult to be emotionally convinced that such success is possible, and they may not really expect students to achieve a high degree of proficiency. These teachers may, in turn, communicate this lack of expectation to students through teaching practices that focus more on the rules students have to play by to get a good grade than on proficiency itself. I do not mean to suggest that someone who does not speak a foreign language cannot be a good English teacher. I do suggest, however, that language teachers for whom rewards and success in language learning are not an emotional reality may not have as much enthusiasm or as strong a proficiency orientation as those who are at least beginning to experience those rewards and success in their own language study.

A final reason for you to be a language learner has to do with the symbolic message your choice to study the local language sends to your host community. Presumably, one motivation for teaching English lies in a desire to build bridges of understanding between people of different nations and cultures, and the growing role of English as the world's international language makes its mastery especially important in a world brought ever closer together by globalization. However, the same dominant role of English and its close association with globalization can make it a threat—symbolic or real—to other nations, languages, and cultures. English may be seen as a symbol of world homogenization or of the growing power of English-speaking nations (particularly the United States), and to some degree even serves as one of the engines driving these processes.

My own belief is that this issue is not a reason to abandon the teaching of English—command of English simply offers the people of host countries too many benefits, and lack of access to English places them at a disadvantage in too many ways. However, I believe this problem makes it imperative for English teachers to be not merely advocates of the English language and Western culture but rather ambassadors who believe in the value of all languages and cultures and who promote the value of language and culture learning in general. If this is a message that you as a teacher wish to symbolize in a convincing way, it is one you must practice as well as preach, and one of the most convincing ways to demonstrate respect for the value of languages other than English is by actively making the effort to learn the language (and culture) of the host country. One additional symbolic advantage of such an effort is that it changes the nature of your relationship with your host. If you arrive in your host country solely as a knower and giver of the English language, your presence suggests an unequal exchange in which you have gifts to bring but need nothing that the host country has to offer. If, on the other hand, you arrive with the desire to learn as much as to teach, your presence suggests a more equal exchange, a mutual need to both teach and learn.

While the primary function of this book is to introduce you to the teaching of English, my hope is that you also read it as a language learner, perhaps one about to embark on the study of a language you have not had much previous experience with. Read the following section for ideas that will help you become a better language (and even culture) learner as well as a better English teacher.

Basic Principles of Language Learning

Of the great many points one could make about language learning, I have chosen to focus on four that deserve special attention because they are central to communicative language teaching (CLT) and because they are points that learners in EFL settings can easily lose sight of: (1) language is a tool for communication, (2) learning a language involves mastery of both skill and knowledge, (3) learners need to give serious consideration to the impact of feelings on language study, and (4) learners vary considerably in their preferred approaches to learning.

LANGUAGE AS COMMUNICATION

Perhaps the most fundamental reality of language learning is that language is a tool for communication. As obvious as this point may seem, its implications are not always as clear to students as they should be. Remember that many students' experience of English learning trains them to see English as anything but a communication tool. The daily reality of English study for many students is one of memorizing words and rules in preparation for a test and rarely involves using English for communicative purposes. After years of this kind of study, it is only to be expected that students come to see language learning as an exercise that is primarily geared toward formal accuracy, especially on tests.[1] Such noncommunicative approaches to English study tend to focus students' attention on form to the exclusion of use and to undermine student interest; few students are excited by grammar and vocabulary study per se.

The study of English is potentially more appealing when English is presented as a key for establishing communication with a new world. This communication can take a variety of forms; it can mean sharing ideas face to face with someone from a foreign country or gaining access to the knowledge embedded in the world's vast library of material published in English. In either case, learning English means developing the ability to understand and interact with a universe that is largely inaccessible to those who don't know English. Here it is worth pointing out that although learning any language opens new doors, learning English particularly does so because of its growing role as an international language; English is now the language of publishing and speech for most international communication and is often used even by people from non-English-speaking countries when they need to interact with people from other nations.[2]

There are other reasons to focus on communication in class, one being that such a focus may make language learning easier. Brown (1991, 36) notes that in learning their first language, children tend to focus on communication before accuracy and suggests that this order of priority should also apply to learners of a second language. Taylor (1987, 46) also suggests that a communicative approach to language learning helps students learn grammar more effectively.

If students are to view the study of English as the learning of a tool for communication and to begin to taste the thrill of discovery that mastery of a new language can entail, they must actually experience language as communication as early as possible in their learning. In an English class, this means using speaking or writing practice as an opportunity for students to share what they really think, feel, or believe. It also means that when students say or write something, you should respond to the ideas expressed rather than only to the accuracy of the language.

LANGUAGE AS KNOWLEDGE AND SKILL

A second important truth of language learning is that it is mastery of a skill as much as acquisition of knowledge. In other words, it is not enough for students to know word meanings and structure rules; students need to be able to apply this knowledge quickly, even automatically, in order to express themselves smoothly in speech or writing, read at a reasonable rate, or comprehend spoken English rapidly enough to keep pace with the speaker. In order to build these skills, practice is necessary; study alone will not suffice.

Again, this point might seem obvious, but remember the unintended lessons that many approaches to language teaching leave students with. For many students, learning language has always been about learning grammar rules and memorizing vocabulary in order to be able to successfully figure out true/false, matching, and fill-in-the-blank puzzles on tests. Many students have had little training in speaking-listening skills that require speed and automaticity and can only be learned through repeated practice. Naturally, students' perceptions of what is and is

---

[1] While these assumptions are held by students in many parts of the world, especially Asia, they are not universal. Some students (especially those from Latin America, Africa, and the Middle East) may go to the opposite extreme, striving for communication with relatively low regard for accuracy.

[2] For example, Crystal (1997, 102–05) points out that 70–90 percent of scientific journal articles and roughly 80 percent of the world's electronically stored information are in English.

not important in language learning are shaped by their experience in language classes, and it is not surprising if students do not fully appreciate the skill component in language use and are inclined to neglect practice in favor of study.

The fact that language use has a heavy skill component, which demands that the user perform complex operations accurately and quickly, has some important implications for the ways in which students must learn:

1. Language learners need a lot of practice. In order to learn to speak well, students need to spend a great deal of time speaking; in order to learn to read quickly and effectively, they need to spend a lot of time reading, and so forth. Almost all teachers would assent to this principle in theory, but in many English classrooms the teacher still talks most of the time. Sometimes this is because teachers feel they need to dominate in order to maintain control in class; sometimes it is because teachers feel that if they aren't "teaching," they aren't really earning their pay. For whatever reasons, stepping off the podium and giving students a chance to speak (read, write, etc.) is more problematic than it may initially seem.

2. Language learners need repeated practice. One important concept related to language learning is *automaticity*. The idea here is that many language skills require a student to do many different things at the same time; for example, speaking involves choosing words, applying grammar rules, and attending to pronunciation and intonation—all while trying to decide what to say. A speaker cannot consciously pay attention to all of these operations at the same time, so some of them must be practiced often enough that they can be performed automatically. The point is that it generally takes more than one practice opportunity to learn to perform any skill smoothly and automatically, and language learning is no exception (for further discussion of automaticity, see Brown 2001, 55–56; Omaggio Hadley 2001, 65).

This point is important because students and teachers often unconsciously assume that what they are supposed to do in class is cover the material in the book; in other words, the teacher should explain the material, and the students should do any related exercises. Part of this unconscious assumption is that each point should only be covered one time and that, once the material is covered, students should know it. (Among students who have internalized this view of language learning, the protest that "We've done this already" is expected to effectively veto an activity whether or not they have really learned the skill in question.) The problem, of course, is that covering material in a textbook is often not enough to allow learners to build necessary skills in using the material, and you may need to repeat activities several times before students can use the new material automatically.

LANGUAGE LEARNING AS A BATTLE OF THE HEART

A third fundamental reality of language learning is that feelings play a major role in language study and need to be taken seriously in planning a successful language learning campaign. As Oxford (1990) puts it, "The affective side of the learner is probably one of the very biggest influences on language learning success or failure" (p. 140). Learners who have a strong desire to learn and who feel good about their progress are far more likely to continue working hard over the long haul required in learning a language.

One reason emotions play such an important role in language learning is the long haul just mentioned. Learning a foreign language well involves a great deal of effort over a long period of time. The basic rules of English grammar and a survival vocabulary can be learned within a few months, but mastering the language takes much longer. Students need considerable practice to develop effective skills in listening and speaking, not to mention reading and writing. It also takes a long time to amass a sufficient vocabulary for reading texts and listening to speech (e.g., radio, television) intended for native speakers. Finally, students can benefit from a good understanding of the cultures of English. All of this is particularly difficult for students in an EFL environment to achieve because they have fewer opportunities for practice and contact with Western culture than do students in an ESL setting. The problem is especially severe for students of English in places such as Asia, the Middle East, and Africa, whose native languages, writing systems, and cultures have little in common with those of the English-speaking world and whose English study thus entails far more learning.

Some students are surprised by the amount of time and effort required to learn a language. Thinking back on my days as a beginning-level Russian student, I remember noticing in my college catalogue that the third-year Russian courses were literature courses. I therefore foolishly assumed that if I was going to read literature in the third year, the first two years would be sufficient to teach me daily Russian.[3] Most language students are probably not quite this naïve, but unreasonable expectations are not rare. As Scarcella and Oxford (1992) point out, "Students are often unrealistic in what they believe they can and should accomplish in a given period of time, so their self-esteem suffers" (p. 58). Students who feel bad about their language learning are particularly vulnerable to discouragement and the temptation to quit.

Even students who recognize that language study is emotionally demanding often fail to account for this problem in their study plans. Too many students assume that being a good student means toughing it out, slugging away at a language until it finally gives in. Again drawing on my own experience, I remember fantasizing that if I could just read one big Russian novel—even if it meant shoveling my way through the book word by word with a dictionary—I would conquer the Russian reading problem forever. The strategy may well have worked if I had been able to keep at it, but I never could.[4] This tendency to try to take a language by frontal assault, of course, often reflects the way languages are taught, with inadequate attention to learners' emotional needs.

Another problem arises from a peculiarity of the language learning process: the further students go, the more their rate of progress seems to slow. To some extent this peculiarity is due to a phenomenon known as *plateaus,* which are often experienced by intermediate- and advanced-level learners. For reasons no one quite understands, many learners tend to make progress in spurts more than in a neat, step-by-step progression, and between those spurts students often feel that they are making no progress; they have hit a plateau. These plateaus, however, are generally temporary and therefore do not pose a serious threat to students who know that such periods are a common feature of language learning. (The best thing for a student to do is either just keep on studying or lighten up for a short break before plunging back in.)

A more serious problem arises from the fact that the more students learn of a language, the less visible impact each additional day of study makes on their skills; progress therefore becomes harder and harder to discern. The analogy of a river emerging from a mountain gorge onto a broad plain may be helpful in understanding this phenomenon: as its channel widens, the river

---

[3]Within a few months I was disabused of the notion that one learned spoken Russian in two years of college courses, but the need to complete a language requirement kept me going. Sheer perversity pushed me into a third year, and I then learned that reading Russian in third-year courses meant slowly decoding texts with a dictionary.

[4]This suggestion may sound a bit bizarre, but I am not the only language learner it has ever occurred to. For example, Farber (1991) seriously suggests this approach for beginning-level readers, using newspapers instead of novels. Granted, to his credit, he makes it very clear that this approach is not for the fainthearted.

appears to slow down, although the same amount of water is moving over the same distance in the same time. Likewise, beginning-level language students can see their progress very clearly because they are making progress on a narrow front. Between lesson one and lesson two in a text-book, their knowledge of English doubles, and every new word they learn significantly increases their ability to communicate. However, as they reach more advanced skill levels, their progress becomes less apparent; successful completion of lesson seventy-four does not make as obvious an impact on students' English skill level as completion of lesson six did, and learning lower frequency words like *manual* and *tome* doesn't enhance their ability to communicate as much as mastering earlier words like *book* did. This means that students in the intermediate stages of language learning are especially vulnerable to discouragement because they often have relatively little sense that they are making progress.

A final reason English study can be emotionally demanding is that the first years of English study in an EFL setting generally offer few rewards. Reaching a level of English skill that allows students to actually use English for practical or personally rewarding purposes provides a reward that helps sustain interest in continued use and study of the language. For example, students who can finally follow a radio news broadcast in English no longer need a sense of daily progress to keep them going. However, students in the middle stages of language learning, whose progress seems to be slowing but who cannot yet do much with their English, may find it very difficult to resist the temptation to chuck the books and go fishing. It may take years for students to develop their speaking to the point where they can converse with an English speaker or learn to read well enough to comfortably read an English newspaper or book, and even when they attain a sufficient level of skill, they may find few English speakers to speak with or few newspapers to read. It is hard in such circumstances to sustain much enthusiasm for language study.

Brown (1991) sums up the importance of affective factors in language learning: "The emotions are the foundation on which all your learning strategies, techniques, and gimmicks will stand or fall . . . . Without that emotional foundation, you are fighting an uphill battle at best" (p. 73). It thus makes sense to structure programs of language study in a way that gives students the maximum sense of progress and reward and encourages them not to abandon the effort halfway.

DIFFERENCES BETWEEN THE LEARNING STYLES OF LANGUAGE LEARNERS

The final point to be made about language learning is that learners vary considerably from one person to the next in their *learning styles,* that is, the ways they go about learning. One contrasting set of learning styles that has received much attention has to do with learners' sensory preferences, and based on these learners are categorized into four groups:

1. **visual learners:** those who tend to learn best by seeing

2. **auditory learners:** those who learn best by hearing

3. **kinesthetic learners:** those who learn best by moving and doing things

4. **tactile learners:** those who learn best through feel and touch

Another set of learning-style categories has to do with learners' personality types, and in this area some learning-style contrasts that have been suggested include distinctions between

1. **extroverted versus introverted learners:** This one is fairly self-explanatory.

2. **thinking versus feeling learners:** This is a distinction between learners who are more cognitively oriented and those who are more affectively oriented. For example, in a discussion, thinking-oriented students would generally be more interested in the factual

content of the discussion, while feeling-oriented learners would be more attentive to the feelings and emotional needs of others in the discussion.

3. **closure-oriented and judging learners versus open and perceiving learners:** The former would strive for clarity, results, and closure; the latter are more comfortable with ambiguity for longer periods and feel less internal pressure to resolve questions any time soon (for more categories, see Oxford 2001, 360–62).

Of course, no learner is a pure example of any of these categories, and most learners have elements of most or all of the above in their approaches to learning. However, a learner often leans in one direction or another, favoring some styles over others, and will presumably be more successful in a classroom where the teaching approaches favored by the teacher match the learner's favored learning styles.

Obviously, it is not possible for each student to have a teacher and classroom situation tailored precisely to his or her preferred learning styles; this can't happen even in small classes, let alone the large classes that are common in EFL settings. However, teachers can do two important things to accommodate students' varied learning styles. The first is to use a reasonably broad and rich variety of teaching techniques, so that each learner has a greater chance of experiencing a method that is relatively good match for his or her style for at least part of the class period. The second involves encouraging learners to explore different approaches to language learning so that they find study and practice methods that suit their style. This is one of the most important reasons any consideration of language teaching needs to start with a look at the learners.

The Role of the Language Teacher

As suggested at the beginning of this chapter, many people are accustomed to a model of language teaching that is heavily teacher centered. To my mind (influenced no doubt by many years in China), this teacher-centered approach calls up images of the great sage Confucius sitting amidst his disciples, explaining the Way and occasionally asking questions to check his disciples' comprehension; hence, I refer to this approach as the *Sage model* of teaching. The Sage owes his exalted position to the fact that he knows more than his students do, and his primary task is to transfer his knowledge to his students. Once the students understand what the Sage is trying to explain, the teaching task has been successfully completed.

It is not surprising that the Sage model is influential in shaping VTs' ideas about the language teacher's role. As noted, this may be the model that you saw in your own high school or university language classes. It may well be the predominant teaching model in your host country and thus the role that students and colleagues will expect you to play. However, there are also more subtle reasons behind the influence exerted by this model. One is that it is a natural role for VTs because it places a premium on expertise in knowledge of the subject. The primary qualification for Sage status is knowing more than the disciples; the VT's primary qualification as a language teacher is superior knowledge of English. Another attraction of the Sage model is that it places the teacher in firm control of the classroom, with the power to steer away from uncertain or uncomfortable waters and to maintain the appearance of an orderly class.

A certain amount of the Sage is virtually inevitable in your teaching life, and it is not necessarily bad. You do in fact know far more about English than the students do, and one of your roles as language teacher is to convey as much of that knowledge as possible to the students. However, I would suggest that excessive reliance on this model has serious drawbacks. One is that it can be hard to play the Sage role well. For example, setting yourself up as the final authority on English can result in very uncomfortable situations, particularly if you are not a master at explaining the intricacies of English grammar. While students' command of the rules of English is generally faulty, they often have more explicit knowledge of grammar rules (and the vocabulary used to discuss them) than VTs do. This can prove rather awkward when students ask questions that you can't answer or even test your grammar knowledge in order to show off at your expense.

Even for VTs who become proficient in explaining obscure points of grammar, the Sage model still presents problems, one of which lies in the model's teacher-centered nature. In this model, teachers are personally responsible not only for transmitting most of the knowledge students are to learn, but also for deciding what is to be learned and how. One (usually unintended) side effect of this approach is that students learn to be passive, to do what they are told rather than actively finding ways to enhance their own learning. Another unfortunate side effect is that, as suggested earlier, the teacher's role may degenerate into one of covering material during class (i.e., explaining or simply mentioning it briefly), reducing class to a formalistic exercise in which the teacher skims over material primarily so that students can be held responsible for it on the final exam.

A second flaw of the Sage model is that it is often classroom centered; in other words, it assumes that most learning takes place in the classroom and downplays the importance of work students do on their own. Of course, homework is also assigned, but in the minds of the teacher and students, the homework is simply rehearsal for the main show. The subtle message of this assumption for students is that real learning requires the teacher; the temptation for teachers is to measure success by the polish of their classroom performances rather than by student progress.

A final problem with the Sage model is that it assumes that learning a language is essentially the accumulation of knowledge and that the battle is won once students understand what the teacher is trying to explain. Unfortunately, as I have tried to show, this assumption isn't true. Acquisition of knowledge plays an important part in language learning, but it is not enough—learning a language is also mastering a set of skills, and skills are not learned via explanation. Explanation is generally only the beginning of the learning process, and the teacher who plays the Sage role often puts on an impressive show but leaves students to face the real battle alone.

A better model for a language teacher is that of the athletic coach or piano teacher, a model that I will call the Coach.[5] The main advantage of this model is that it assumes that most of the learning process takes place during practice away from the teacher's watchful eye, and that success or failure in the learning process depends much more on what students do outside class than on what teachers do in class. A coach certainly has some tips on how a basketball player should make jump shots, but it is the player's hours of practice shots that teach the skill. Likewise, a piano teacher cannot teach a student digital dexterity by explaining it; a student must practice scales many times before they can be played smoothly.

Of course, one duty of the Coach is to share knowledge of the subject, but equally important parts of the Coach's role are (1) helping students better understand the learning process, (2) encouraging students and cultivating motivation, (3) helping students build discipline through accountability, and (4) guiding them toward taking initiative and responsibility for their own learning. These are not the only possible roles that VTs could adopt, but they are vitally important ones that are worthy of further discussion. In the following sections of this chapter, I consider these four aspects of the Coach's role and the way they relate to basic principles of language learning and teaching.

---

[5] I am hardly the first to suggest this analogy. See, for example, McKay (1987, xii) and Stevick (1988, 202).

HELPING STUDENTS UNDERSTAND LANGUAGE LEARNING

One of your first tasks as a language teacher is to help students understand some of the concepts discussed above. In part you do this by talking with the students about these principles, and you should certainly do so as often as you have the chance. However, if your views are going to have much impact on the students, what you say about language learning must be backed up by the way you teach your courses. In other words, if you stress the idea that students should take responsibility for their own language learning, you need to find ways to structure room for student initiative into your courses. If you argue that language is a tool for communication, you must as often as possible allow students to use language for genuine communication in your courses. If you emphasize that mastery of English involves developing language skills through practice, you need to give students ample opportunities to practice in class. Finally, if you urge students to attend to the affective side of language learning, you need to show similar concern for the issue in the way you structure class exercises and practice. Students will often learn more about the nature of language and language learning from what you do in your classes than from what you say.

Another important aspect of helping students understand language learning is teaching them to think through their goals and methods. This is especially important for students who have generally been passive participants in the language learning process because, without a clear sense of goal, it is difficult to decide what methods will be most effective. When I lecture on English study, one of the questions students ask most often is "How can I improve my English?" My first response is usually to suggest that the questioner study hard, but this invariably brings a groan from the audience and a demand that I stop avoiding the question. I then ask the questioner to be more precise about his or her goal—is it to build a better reading vocabulary, improve oral fluency, or what? Unfortunately, the questioner often has no clear idea of what he or she wants to achieve beyond "improving English" and doesn't seem to realize that I can't be more specific in my directions unless I have a clearer idea of where the inquirer wants to go. Teaching students to consider the question of goals and methods is a big first step toward helping them become better language learners. (See chapter 3 for further discussion.)

A final way to help students become better language learners is to help them explore different methods and strategies for language learning. (As noted previously, this is one reason why your own engagement in language learning is so important.) In part this involves sharing what you know about language learning from your own experiences, both positive and negative. However, it is equally important to encourage students to explore new methods on their own and share with each other what works and what does not. Often the mere fact that you raise this issue from time to time for class discussion expands students' horizons and serves as a useful stimulus, prodding them to get out of an old study routine that may have outlived its usefulness for them.

ENCOURAGING AND MOTIVATING STUDENTS

In EFL settings where opportunities to use English are relatively few and far between, one of the main challenges faced by English teachers is how to motivate students in their English study. While many students are initially interested in learning English, it is not unusual for their enthusiasm to disappear over time, partly because learning a foreign language involves lots of hard work, partly because English doesn't seem immediately useful or relevant to their lives, and partly because they rarely get a chance to use the skills they learn. Indeed, they generally need to persist in studying English for years before they reach a skill level that allows them to comfortably watch a film, read a book, or chat with a foreigner in English.

For many students in EFL settings, to the extent that they are motivated to study English at all, their primary motivation is what researchers call *extrinsic motivation,* in other words, motivation

SOME EXTRINSIC REWARDS

- Good test scores
- Increased range of education opportunities
- Better job opportunities (wider range, better pay, more promotion opportunities, opportunity to travel)
- Ability to interact with people from other countries (for practical purposes)
- Access to professional information in English (e.g., books, journals, Web sites, lectures)
- Access to wider range of information about the world and world events
- Easier travel
- Praise from teacher, parents, and others[6]

SOME INTRINSIC REWARDS

- Sense of accomplishment (pride, self-respect)
- Sense of confidence in one's ability to handle a wider range of situations
- Opportunity to pursue a wider range of interests (e.g., through reading books or watching films one likes in English)
- Sense of understanding the world better, being more in touch with the international scene, being a "world citizen"
- Opportunity to develop friendships with people from other countries (out of a personal desire to do so)

based on a reward that comes from outside the learner (see the box). Examples of extrinsic motivation would include the desire to get a good score on a test or to get a good job. Such rewards can have significant power in motivating students to study and learn, but they are also problematic in some ways. For example, students who are motivated primarily by a desire to do well on tests may study only what they need to in order to pass the test, and once the test is over, they may lose interest in English study. Similarly, the motivating force of job opportunities may be weakened if the prospect of a job is years in the future; a reward that seems too distant may not have much power to motivate students to study today.

Rather than relying exclusively on extrinsic rewards to motivate students, many researchers who study language learning argue that English teachers should also try to build their students' *intrinsic motivation* (see the box) by encouraging students to consider rewards that come from within themselves, such as a sense of accomplishment, the love of learning new things, the love of creating, or the desire to pursue their curiosity and interests. In fact, many researchers suggest that intrinsic motivation is a more powerful driving force than extrinsic motivation (Brown 2001, 76–77). One reason intrinsic rewards tend to be especially effective as motivators is that, coming from within the learner, they are always there to drive one's study—they are not years away, and they don't disappear when the test ends.

One way you can help motivate students to engage actively in English study is simply to make your class as lively and interesting as possible; on the whole, students tend to learn more about

---

[6] This reward is something of an anomaly in that praise from people whom one respects tends to act more like intrinsic than extrinsic motivation, even though it comes from outside the learner. See Brown (2001, 77).

something they like and find interesting than about something that holds no appeal for them (Scarcella and Oxford 1992, 33). A class that is lively and enjoyable is—all other things being equal—usually better than one that is boring or tense. It is also helpful if students find you encouraging and friendly, and if the class environment is as nonthreatening as possible (Littlewood 1984, 58–59).

A second way to arouse and maintain student interest in English study is to make your courses as genuinely communicative as possible. Most people enjoy talking about themselves and learning about others, which provides a natural opportunity for speaking and even writing practice—and is certainly more interesting than rewriting sentences or parroting a memorized dialogue. Many students are also interested in the world beyond the borders of their town or country, and learning about this broader world provides an excellent excuse for reading and listening. In fact, as a foreigner in your host country, you have a powerful advantage as a teacher because your presence in the classroom creates a natural *information gap*. In other words, you know many things that the students don't, and vice versa, so you have a great deal to talk to each other about without having to manufacture a topic.

The two other important factors in the sustaining of student motivation are ones I have already mentioned, a sense of progress and feeling of reward, and are covered in more detail in chapter 3, where I discuss how to structure language study plans. Here, suffice it to say that praise from the teacher and a good time in class will not go far if students do not feel that they are making progress or that their study has any purpose.

A final way you can be a source of encouragement for students is by serving as a role model (Dörnyei 2001, 33). Students often have great respect for a teacher who has mastered a foreign language, and this respect may make them more eager to follow the teacher's example. However, it by no means follows that a good language teacher must be a great language learner; in fact, those rare individuals who seem to absorb languages effortlessly are often quite discouraging for struggling students to be around, and such individuals may not make very good language teachers because they don't understand the difficulties that mere mortals face. To be a good role model, what is perhaps most important is for you to make a serious effort to learn what you can and for students to see you practicing what you preach. Your effort to learn the language of your host country will make your life there easier and richer, give you a much better idea of the difficulties that the students face, and increase your ability to empathize with them. In general, students tend to work harder for a teacher who they feel understands them and identifies with them than one who doesn't seem to share their burdens. (See further discussion of learning the host language in chapter 15.)

BUILDING ACCOUNTABILITY AND DISCIPLINE

When it comes right down to it, one of the greatest advantages of taking a language course (as opposed to studying a language on your own) is that it provides someone who holds you accountable for how much and how well you learn. In other words, when you take a course, you must study because tomorrow there might be a quiz, a test, a discussion covering tonight's reading assignment, or at least a teacher who will be disappointed if you don't do what you are supposed to. Thus, as long as human beings are naturally inclined toward procrastination and laziness, a third important role of the language teacher will be to see that students put in the many hard hours of work necessary to master a language and to help them learn the discipline necessary to keep them working diligently when there is no longer a teacher around.

Many of the ways in which teachers hold students accountable come under the heading of assessment and evaluation, discussed in chapter 4, but I note here that accountability is not only a matter of quizzes, tests, graded homework assignments, and other measures that students often view as more akin to the stick than the carrot. Accountability also includes praise, encouragement for work well done, and almost any other response that recognizes students' efforts. In fact, research in psychology indicates that rewards affect behavior more than punishment does (Brown 1991, 42; 2001, 76), and positive reinforcement often has more impact on students than negative.

The basic idea of accountability is that you consider students' efforts important and care whether or not they did their work. Some students will work only if threatened; others only need a gentle reminder. Most, however, are a little more likely to work if they know that they will be held responsible for doing so. As Littlewood (1984) notes, while excessive anxiety in a situation can hinder learning, "a certain amount of it can stimulate a learner to invest more energy in the task" (p. 59).

ENCOURAGING STUDENTS TO TAKE COMMAND

A final role of the language teacher is to move students toward taking charge of their own language learning—setting their own goals, making their own study plans, and then holding themselves to their plans—because it is self-starters who are most likely to reach the final goal. As Brown (2001) notes,

> All too often, language teachers are so consumed with the "delivery" of language to their students that they neglect to spend some effort preparing learners to "receive" the language. And students, mostly unaware of the tricks of successful language learning, simply do whatever the teacher tells them to do, having no means to question the wisdom thereof. In an effort to fill class hours with fascinating material, teachers might overlook their mission of enabling learners to eventually become *independent* of classrooms—that is, to be autonomous learners. (p. 208)

Even as you plan out your course, then, you need to think about ways in which you can encourage students to take initiative. There are an endless number of ways to do this: have students keep their own vocabulary list, let them choose their own books for reading practice, have them choose topics for writing or discussions, ask them to tape their own listening material (e.g., off the radio), or even have them design and carry out their own study plan as a component of your course. The important thing is for students to get into the habit of taking charge of their own study programs as much as possible.

One aspect of helping students take control of their own learning is exposing them to different learning strategies. As mentioned above, students are individuals who differ in their learning styles as well as in their English skill levels. Some students learn language best through careful analysis, and others may rely more on instinct; some thrive in freewheeling group discussion, and others in quiet conversations with a partner; and so on. However, in many countries, students are only familiar with a narrow range of study methods that are recommended—or required—by teachers, classmates, or tradition, and may use methods unsuitable to their personalities or skills simply because they are not aware of alternatives. One of your roles as a teacher is thus to suggest approaches to language learning that students might not have previously considered. Of course, this is easier if you have had experience with a broad range of study methods and strategies, but generally you can still make a valuable contribution simply by calling students' attention to the issue—many students have never consciously asked themselves what study methods are best suited to them. The fact that you are from a different culture also means that you are probably familiar with a somewhat different range of study methods than those normally used by students in your host country, and this creates the possibility for useful and interesting cross-fertilization.[7]

A second aspect of encouraging students to take control of their own language learning involves encouraging or requiring students to undertake what I refer to as *language learning projects*

---

[7] A growing body of literature in the TESOL field emphasizes the teaching of learning strategies. See, for example, Oxford (1990) and Cohen (1998).

(LLPs). In the framework of your course, an LLP is a separate, additional project in which students choose their own goals, methods, and study plans. While doing an LLP may be a required part of your course, students are expected to take as much responsibility as possible for all aspects of the project—including evaluation. The virtue of such projects is that, in addition to helping students learn a little more English, they help students become more independent and autonomous as language learners; the hope is that by helping students become accustomed to taking as much responsibility as possible for their own language learning, you are helping prepare them for the day when they no longer have teachers and ready-made courses on which they can rely to drive their further language study. (See chapter 3 for more on LLPs.)

Getting students to take charge of their own language study is often more easily said than done. Many students no doubt have no real desire to learn English and only long for the day when they complete their requirement and can kiss the whole thing good-bye. However, there are other students whose whole attitude toward language study will change if you carefully but firmly hand the reins over to them.

Making Your Assumptions Explicit

The assumptions about language teaching presented above are basic tenets of CLT and would not raise many eyebrows in the Western English teaching world. However, they would not all be taken for granted in many of the nations to which you are likely to go as a VT. In fact, some very different assumptions may shape the approaches of your host-country colleagues and students. Here are a few examples:

1. **focus on the student as learner:** In many societies, the teacher's social role is much closer to that of the Sage than that of the Coach; teachers are respected in the community primarily for their knowledge of their field, and their word is not to be challenged. In such a society, a teacher-centered approach to education fits the culture better than the student-centered approach I have argued for.

2. **emphasis on the individuality of each student:** The emphasis on the student as a unique individual with a distinct learning style may seem rather foreign and Western in some societies. In comparison with the United States, for example, many societies are somewhat more culturally uniform, have a more standardized education system, and encourage individualism less.

3. **language as communication skill:** In many host countries, teachers do not emphasize the idea of language as communication, and it might work against their interests to teach language in this way. Some of your host-country colleagues may have had little opportunity to develop their English skills, particularly spoken fluency; in contrast, they may be very familiar with the formal features of English, especially grammar and vocabulary. They may also tend to give lectures that stick closely to the text because this allows them to prepare a limited body of material. This text-centered, grammar-analysis approach to teaching plays to their strengths; a highly communicative teaching approach that plays to the strengths of a native-English-speaking VT might be unfamiliar and very difficult for some of your colleagues to adopt.

Note that for many students who are in educational systems in which test results determine their academic futures and careers, learning how to communicate is not the primary goal; the primary goal is to score well on examinations. In such situations, while adding as much of a communication skill element as possible to a course is no doubt desirable, it would be irresponsible for the teacher to fail to prepare students for tests, and traditional methods may well be as effective in preparing students for examinations as communicative methods are—or more so.

My point is not to undermine all of the principles that I have argued for in this chapter; those CLT principles are sound and provide a good foundation for your language teaching. However, it is important not to arrive in your host country with the attitude that your colleagues and students are backward and that your job is to reform their English teaching system. A more generous and fairer way to look at the situation is to recognize that all approaches to teaching have advantages and disadvantages, and that in many ways the teaching methods I have described as traditional may be very efficacious within their context. However, they also have weaknesses, and your different approaches to teaching can help round out the diet of language learning approaches offered to the students.

I would make two suggestions for helping students deal with discrepancies between your language teaching approaches and their language learning expectations:

1. You cannot assume that students share your assumptions, so be sure to explicitly communicate them to the students. Students should know what to expect in your class and how you perceive your role as teacher. You may sometimes also need to modify your assumptions so that you are more in tune with your class.[8]

2. You need not explicitly or implicitly criticize other approaches to teaching. Instead, present your assumptions as just that—your assumptions—rather than as the only acceptable approach to language teaching. As suggested previously, some of these ideas have a Western flavor, and you might present them as an alternative approach that you are adopting in class because it suits your teaching strengths and because it is a part of the culture from which you come.

By approaching your teaching in this way, you are less likely to come into conflict with the culture in which you will teach and live, and it will be easier for you to maintain an open mind when considering the weak and strong points of other approaches to teaching.

A Concluding Thought

When all is said and done, your most important role may be an unintended one, related more to who you are than what you do. Many schools like having VTs less because of their expertise in language teaching than because they are natives of an English-speaking country, and your presence has a number of advantages for an English program. First, as Dörnyei (2001, 124) notes, the presence of foreigners brings a sense of authenticity and reality to the classroom—you are living proof that there is a place where real people use the peculiar sounds and symbols of English for real communication. Second, your presence forces students—possibly for the first time—to use English as the medium for real communication. Unlike your host-country colleagues, you probably can't speak to students in any language other than English, and success even in limited communication with you is evidence to students that they have in fact learned something that has a purpose going beyond examinations. This realization can be a boost to students' self-confidence. Finally, the opportunity

---

[8] Nunan (1989) notes that this may even be necessary in classes in English-speaking countries: "It is not uncommon in adult ESL classes for the teacher to see herself as a guide and catalyst for classroom communication while the learners see her as someone who should be providing explicit instruction and modelling the target language" (p. 84). In such cases, Nunan recommends negotiation.

to meet and get to know a native of an English-speaking country often does a great deal to raise students' level of interest in English study. As Rubin and Thompson (1994) point out, "Research has shown a definite relationship between attitudes and success when foreign language learners have an opportunity to know people who speak the language they are studying. Such positive attitudes usually help learners maintain their interest long enough to achieve their goals" (p. 6).

The implication of these realities for you is that the professional polish of your teaching is not the only yardstick by which your contribution will be measured. Certainly, you should still strive to make your teaching as professional as possible, but you should also bear in mind that, simply by offering your presence and your efforts, you may be making a far greater contribution than you would have imagined.

For Thought, Discussion, and Action

1. **a look back:** Look back at your own foreign language learning experience to date, and list lessons you have learned about what does and does not seem to work in foreign language learning. Compare your ideas with classmates', and discuss.

2. **feelings in language learning:** Think back to your experience learning a foreign language, and try to remember the role feelings played in the process. List ways in which feelings entered the experience and the impact they had on your learning.

3. **language learning survey:** Ask several friends or classmates to talk with you about their language learning experiences. What are the best language learning experiences they had, and why were they good? What experiences were more difficult, and why?

4. **skill learning:** Think back on your experience learning a skill (e.g., playing a sport, doing a craft, playing a musical instrument). Describe the process, and compare it with your foreign language learning experiences. In what ways were the processes similar, and how did they differ?

5. **past language teachers:** Think back on positive and negative examples of language teachers you have had. Who would you like to be like, and why? Who would you not like to be like, and why?

6. **description of a language learning experience:** Think of a successful language learning experience you had, and prepare a detailed description involving everything you can remember that might be relevant. Then share your experience—and any lessons learned—with a friend or classmate. Include answers to questions like these:
   - What was your skill level at the time?
   - What was your goal?
   - Why did you do what you did? What motivated you?
   - What exactly did you do? (Describe what you did in detail.)
   - What materials did you use?
   - What role did a teacher play?
   - What influence did classmates have?
   - What was the environment in which you learned/studied like?
   - Why did it work?

7. **legacies:** Ask a friend from the host country to talk with you about the history—both good and bad—of relations between the host country and your country. Ask what

impact—if any—the historical legacy or current relations might have on the students' attitudes toward studying English.

8. **host-country learning culture:** Ask someone from your host country to tell you about the normal language teaching and learning practices there. Talk with that person about the learning and teaching assumptions discussed in this chapter, and find out how similar to or different they are from the assumptions commonly held in the host country.

9. **communicative language teaching (CLT):** Talk with an English teacher from your host country about CLT. Find out what he or she knows about it, whether or not it is promoted or accepted in the host country, and what he or she thinks about it.

10. **choices in language learning:** One of the most important strategies for helping students become more independent and autonomous as language learners is to give them as much choice as possible in their own study. The more they make their own choices, the more they are likely to take responsibility for their own English study. Consider a typical English course in your country, and make a list of ways you could give students some choice in their English study (e.g., with regard to goals, homework, activities). Be as specific as possible.

11. **intrinsic motivation:** Brown (2001) argues that teachers should try to build students' intrinsic motivation as much as possible, and he provides the following checklist of criteria that can be applied to a language teaching technique (activity, etc.) to determine whether it promotes intrinsic motivation. Analyze each of Brown's criteria, and explain how or why it would contribute to intrinsic motivation:

- Does the technique appeal to the genuine interests of the students? Is it relevant to their lives?
- Do you present the technique in a positive, enthusiastic manner?
- Are students clearly aware of the purpose of the technique?
- Do students have some choice in choosing some aspect of the technique and determining how they go about fulfilling the goals of the technique?
- Does the technique encourage students to discover for themselves certain principles or rules (rather than simply being told)?
- Does it encourage students in some way to develop or use effective strategies of learning and communication?
- Does it contribute—at least to some extent—to students' ultimate autonomy and independence (from you)?
- Does it foster cooperative negotiation with other students in the class? Is it truly interactive?
- Does the technique present a reasonable challenge?
- Do students receive sufficient feedback on their performance (from each other or from you)? (p. 80)

12. **genuine communication:** This chapter suggests that one way to motivate students is to include as much genuine communication as possible in English courses. Make a checklist (like Brown's checklist above) for assessing whether or not an activity is genuinely communicative.

Chapter 2

Getting the Lay of the Land

- *Flexibility* is the key word in preparation before you leave your own country.

- Before beginning to make detailed plans for your courses, try to find out as much as possible about your teaching environment and the students' goals, needs, and expectations.

- Think of the first few days of class as an excellent opportunity to find out more about the students and their English skills.

Volunteer teachers (VTs) often arrive in a new city only days—or even hours—before the first day of class, which puts them under considerable pressure to sit down at the first possible moment to begin pulling together lesson plans. The problem with these early plans is that they often have to be scrapped within a few days because they don't quite fit the situation. Perhaps the students' levels are higher than you thought, or the students passively but firmly refuse to go along with one of your planned teaching methods, or you discover that the students' listening comprehension is so poor that they don't understand your instructions.

You can avoid many false starts if you take time before the first day of class to find out as much as possible about the students, school, and new teaching environment. You are entering a culture in which many aspects of life—including education—are likely to be unfamiliar, and it makes sense to allow yourself some orientation to your new situation. This chapter discusses ways to lay good groundwork for your course planning before leaving your home country, after arrival in your host country, and during the first few days of class.

Before Leaving Home

While you are still at home, you can prepare for a stint teaching abroad in a number of ways. One is to find and talk with people who have lived in your host country, especially those who have served as teachers there. Through a local university you can often locate either citizens of your host country or foreigners who have lived there. You might even try going to your local host-country restaurant and asking around; people who have an interest in your host country may gather there and be known to the staff. It is also a good idea to begin looking for books about the culture and history of your new host country before you leave home.[1] You may find such books readily available once you reach the host country, but the range available in the host country in English may be limited; also, such books may be geared more toward presenting visitors with a positive view of the country than toward providing deeper, more critical analysis.

Another valuable form of predeparture preparation is English teaching experience. Many community organizations and churches run volunteer-taught English classes for immigrants and refugees, and an experience of this kind will help you get your feet wet. One option is to volunteer to take responsibility for a course on your own, which will obviously give you a healthy dose of first-hand teaching experience. Another option to consider is offering to serve as an apprentice to an experienced teacher who is open to having a little extra help. An apprentice-type arrangement has the advantage of allowing you to observe an experienced teacher before you try teaching yourself and makes it easier for you to get useful feedback on days when you take over the class for a while. (Another practical advantage is that an apprenticeship may be easier to work into a busy schedule because you do not necessarily need to commit to being in class every time it meets.)

Granted, teaching an immigrant—or even a small class of immigrants—in an English-speaking country is very different from teaching an English class abroad. Students in an English-speaking environment not only have access to a much richer range of practice opportunities but often also have much clearer goals and sense of motivation; after all, their ability to find a job and survive may depend on their ability to learn English. However, even a brief teaching experience is still useful for the insight it provides as well as for the practice it gives you in learning how to communicate with people whose native language is not English. One of the most important skills a language teacher needs is the ability to make instructions understood even by students whose

---

[1] See Kohls (2001, 167–79) for a list of resources covering a large range of countries. One useful resource is the Interacts series published by Intercultural Press, which offers books introducing the cultures of many of the places to which VTs most frequently go, including Africa, Arabia, China, East Europe, Israel, Japan, Korea, Mexico, the Philippines, Russia, Spain, and Thailand.

English skills are very minimal, and teaching practice in your home country will help you begin to hone that skill. Another way in which a volunteer teaching experience may be enlightening is that it puts you in contact with people who are undergoing the often difficult adjustments of adapting to life in a new culture. An understanding of the culture-shock experience may help you as you adjust to life in your host country, and you may need to prepare some of your future students for similar adjustments if they should ever go abroad. (See chapter 15 for further discussion.)

A final way you should prepare is by collecting teaching resources to either mail or take with you. The problem here is that you often have little idea what to prepare for. Of course, your school or sending agency might have sent you a brief description of your new teaching situation and perhaps even a list of courses that you will teach, but this information is rarely complete, and teachers sometimes arrive in the host country and discover that, for any number of reasons, the information they were given bears only minimal resemblance to the actual job. I have known more than one teacher who hauled a heavy collection of literature anthologies across an ocean, expecting to teach a literature course, only to find that (1) the materials were completely inappropriate for the students' level, (2) the host institution already had the books, (3) the institution couldn't efficiently duplicate material in the books for student use, (4) the course had a required text geared toward a national standardized examination, or (5) the course assignment had been changed. This, of course, leads to more frustration and bad feeling than would have been the case if the teacher had packed the suitcase with pleasure reading and a few favorite snack foods.

Given this reality, the key word in predeparture preparation should be *flexibility;* unless you are absolutely certain about courses to prepare for, it makes more sense to prepare for a variety of eventualities than to put all your eggs in one basket. Appendix C contains suggestions for specific books you might take with you as a small reference library, but in general the types of materials I would consider highest priority for VTs would include

1. **one or more texts on language teaching:** Bring some to help you continue to improve your teaching skills and as a source of teaching ideas.

2. **a grammar book:** Choose one that you find easy to understand so that you can learn about grammar as you teach it.

3. **a writing text:** Look for one that contains ideas for assignments and on how to structure a writing class.

4. **a book of speaking and listening activities:** Bring at least a good list of topic or activity ideas; once you have an idea, you can modify it to fit your class.

5. **a book of cultural information about your country:** Choose one to use when teaching culture lessons.

6. **pictures of your hometown, family, and country:** Bring some to use as conversation starters.

As you choose teaching resources, ask yourself how flexible they are. To be more specific, can the materials be adapted for students at different skill levels? Can they be used for large classes as well as small? Can they be used without audiovisual or duplication equipment, which may not be available? If the answer to these questions is yes, you have good candidates.

I have not included any reading texts in my list of suggestions because such texts generally need to be duplicated in order to be useful, and getting materials copied in the host country may be difficult and time-consuming. In some countries, of course, duplication is not a problem, but most VTs work in countries where teaching plans that are heavily dependent on duplication facilities are a recipe for frustration for both the VT and the host institution. Relations between more than a few VTs and their schools have been poisoned by running battles over what can be copied on the (expensive but quick) copier and what has to be produced by cheaper, slower, and less effective methods. My suggestion is to rely on locally available reading materials if at all possible, or, as an alternate plan, mail yourself lots of secondhand paperbacks.[2]

After Arrival, before the First Day of Class

During the first days after arrival in your host country, you will probably be busy setting up your new home, becoming familiar with the surroundings, and sleeping off the effects of jet lag. You will also likely be worried about your first day of class, and the temptation will be to focus on preparing for your classes rather than becoming familiar with the situation in general. However, I would argue that no matter how much you want to jump right into preparing those first few lesson plans, it is invaluable to first devote a day or so to getting the lay of the land; time invested in learning about the general situation will rapidly pay off in terms of more effective preparation.

ASKING THE RIGHT QUESTIONS

Below I suggest some questions you might investigate as part of your self-orientation. This questionnaire may seem a bit excessive, but I have chosen to be thorough at the risk of seeming a touch fanatic. The questions are divided into three sections: questions concerning the goals of your courses, those related to methodology and resources, and those concerning your role in the teaching community.

Questionnaire

GOALS

1. **Why are the students learning English?**

   requirements?

   jobs?

   educational advancement?

   desire to go abroad?

   social polish or prestige?

   recreation or social needs?

   test?

   - This question is very important because goals will determine what skills students need most and how hard they are willing to study.
   - Finding out what kinds of English tests students need to take, how important they are, and what they are like is also very important. In many countries, English tests play a major role in determining which students will be admitted to graduate programs, university, or even middle school.
   - Not many English programs explicitly advertise themselves as meeting social or recreational needs, but I can assure you that such classes exist and that the social nature of students' goals affects how the class needs to be taught.

---

[2] In many countries, there are special low rates for mailing printed matter. For example, in the United States books can be mailed quite inexpensively by M-bag (mailbag). Check the local post office for current information.

2. **What are reasonable expectations for the progress of the students in English?**
   - Consider the time and energy students will have to devote to your course, especially to homework. Find out the demands placed on students by other courses, and by other duties and responsibilities the students have at school, at home, or elsewhere.
   - Learn about the local norms for what is considered a reasonable amount of homework; these differ greatly from culture to culture and school to school.
   - Investigate how motivated students are to study English—this will have a great impact on progress. Is English required, or did the students choose to study it? Have their previous courses generally been boring? How do they feel about English speakers? About people from your country? About foreigners in general?

3. **What are the students' goals? Your school's?**
   - Your goals don't need to be exactly the same as the students', but if your goals are radically different, you may well meet resistance or at least confusion about what you are trying to achieve. Knowledge of the students' expectations will help you explain why you choose the goals you do and help you avoid trying to upset too many apple carts at once.
   - In addition to finding out what expectations others have, you should try to find out how strong those expectations are. Some schools may give you considerable freedom to set your own agenda; in others, even small deviations from orthodoxy may upset your superiors.

METHODS AND RESOURCES

1. **What teaching methods is a teacher expected to use?**
   - As suggested in chapter 1, the prevailing teaching mode in many host countries is more teacher centered and traditional than the methods you might find more suitable. If there is a discrepancy between your methods and those the students expect, you will need to be especially careful to explain why you are doing what you are doing.

2. **What learning strategies and styles are students in the host country accustomed to?**
   - The students' study approaches might be quite different from those you are familiar with, and you may need to teach students how you want them to study.

3. **What kinds of texts, tapes, and other teaching or study materials are available?**
   - Find out who has access to such resources and under what conditions; it is not safe to assume that their existence means that you can use them. For example, in countries where resources are scarce, access is much more likely to be tightly controlled in order to protect them (or protect the person responsible for them).
   - Check what materials students can get in local bookstores; this has a significant impact on what kinds of self-study are possible.
   - Resources may not be kept where you would expect to find them, so learn where to look. For example, in China, books related to English learning and teaching are often kept in the English department resource room rather than in the school library.

4. **What kinds of teaching equipment (e.g., blackboards, overhead projectors, slide projectors, videotape/DVD players) are available?**
   - As with teaching and study materials, find out not only what exists but also how much access you have. Teaching plans may have to work around the availability of a staff member as well as of the machine.
   - Remember that reliability is another important factor. Lesson plans built around an overhead projector are very vulnerable to blown-out bulbs or electricity stoppages,

and you need to know how likely such problems are and how quickly they can be remedied.

5. **How readily can materials be duplicated? How long does it take? How expensive is it? How high is the quality?**

- In the West, many teachers take regular use of photocopying machines for granted and assume that if the host school has a photocopying machine, there is no reason not to sail on as usual. This is a very dangerous assumption. The reliance placed on copiers in Western countries is only possible because there are several in each building (at least one or two usually out of order) and a repair shop nearby. Your host school may have fewer machines and much more difficulty getting them serviced; hence, their use may be reserved for a few high-priority items rather than for bulk copying of a *Reader's Digest* article for the adult education English class. Bulk copying may be handled via processes more like mimeographing than like photocopying.

- When asked about copying, your school may well give you an answer that tends toward the optimistic. Such answers, often intended to be more polite and helpful than precise, can have the unfortunate effect of setting unrealistic expectations. What you need to find out—either from experience or by asking other teachers—is the normal amount of time, expense, and difficulty involved in getting copies made.

6. **What is available in the classroom (e.g., blackboards or an equivalent, movable chairs or desks, electric outlets)?**

- Go and look rather than making assumptions.

7. **How many students will be in your classes? (Regular students? Auditors?)**

- Remember that in many countries, language classes have many more students than most language classes in the West do. Class size, of course, has a significant impact on methods.

- Try to discover what policies your school has about additional students sitting in on your course. In many host countries, a foreign teacher is a rare attraction, and many people may show up in your class for the sheer thrill of seeing and hearing a native speaker. You need to know who is supposed to be in your class and who is not; you should also know what to do about guests.

THE ROLE OF THE TEACHER

Most cultures have distinct expectations as to the teacher's role; even in the relatively easygoing United States it is not common to see a teacher wearing shorts in class, and there is at least a moderate social taboo against teachers dating students. Many other cultures have more numerous and stronger expectations, and your failure to conform to these could undermine your effectiveness before you have a chance to prove yourself. If the members of the host community view your behavior as inappropriate, it might diminish how seriously they take you as a teacher and affect their respect and affection for you as a person.

My point is not that you must conform to all expectations; in fact, as a foreigner and a guest, you will probably have more leeway in your adherence to cultural norms than a teacher from the host country has. However, it is still wise to know what cultural expectations exist so that you do not unwittingly fritter away the fund of goodwill usually extended to a guest. Also, as a novice teacher, you will probably find that anything you can do to ensure respect and cordiality will help. If wearing nice leather shoes earns you a little more control in the classroom, do it.

1. **How much are teachers expected to know?**
   - In some cultures, teachers are expected to know everything, and you may run into some initial problems if you are straightforward about admitting your ignorance when you don't know the answer to a question. While I encourage you to be relatively open with students rather than trying to bluff, it is be good to know how much turbulence you can expect while students are adjusting to your style.

2. **How are teachers supposed to behave in class?**
   - One main issue is formality. Western VTs are likely to be less formal than teachers in many countries, and while students may find this relaxed style refreshing, they may also see it as inappropriate or as indicating a lack of professionalism. If your level of formality differs from the host-country norm, you may need to explain why you have chosen your particular style. (This might be an opening for an interesting discussion of cultural differences, though you should also point out that level of formality often results from individual choices and styles.)
   - Students may be accustomed to addressing teachers in rather formally (e.g., Mr. . . ., Miss . . . , or even Teacher . . .). Find out how students normally address teachers and vice versa. If you want to be addressed by your first name, you might also explain the cultural reasons underlying your choice.
   - In some countries, students are expected to stand when speaking to the teacher in class, or to rise when the teacher enters or leaves a classroom. If you want to change this habit, explain your reasons. Otherwise, enjoy it, but try to not let it go to your head.

3. **How are teachers expected to dress?**
   - Many VTs are more comfortable in jeans and T-shirts than in suits but teach in countries where shirts, slacks, skirts, and leather shoes are the norm for teachers. The real potential for trouble comes from the fact that many Westerners—especially those whose previous experience has been almost entirely in student roles—are not very attuned to how seriously dress is taken in many cultures (including professional circles in Western countries).

4. **What expectations exist about teacher-student relationships?**
   - Teacher-student friendships are often a big part of the life of VTs. In fact, VTs may find most of their new friends in the host country among students; this is natural because students are the group of people VTs are in closest contact with. However, teacher-student friendships can be tricky in any country because it is hard to balance the friend role with the power inherent in the teacher role (mainly due to your power to grade), and the issue is even more slippery when you and the students don't share a common set of cultural norms. In many countries, students interpret friendship from a teacher as a sign of favoritism and an invitation to take advantage of that favor. Far be it from me to suggest that you avoid making friends with students; I would, however, advise you to be alert to the possibility of misinterpretation or role conflicts.
   - VTs in a new country are often lonely, close in age to their students, and not necessarily card-carrying ascetics. Romantic and sexual attraction to students is thus as natural as it is problematic. However, in many cultures romantic relationships between teachers and students are at least frowned on if not highly taboo, and a good argument can be made that it is questionable ethically to date someone over whom you have the power of the grade. Note also that in many cultures male-female friendships are rare or unknown, and friendly overtures from a teacher to a student of the opposite sex would almost inevitably be interpreted as romantic or sexual interest.

FINDING ANSWERS

Having been presented with a formidable list of questions, you might well ask where to go for answers. If you are going abroad through an agency that provides an orientation program, no doubt some of these issues will be addressed before you reach your new school. However, no matter how good an orientation is, many things you hear about a new country and culture won't make much impact until you have actually been there and seen it, especially if the orientation occurs predeparture, while you are also worrying about making travel arrangements, packing, finding out what shots to get, and so on. Much of what you hear before you leave is likely to go in one ear and out the other, or be half-remembered at best.

Orientation meetings provided by your school after arrival in the host country are another useful opportunity to gather information. However, the person who serves as your informant will often also be acting as a host, and in most cultures dragging the dirty laundry out is not a normal part of welcoming a guest. As a result, you get a picture of the teaching situation that is often biased toward the optimistic, and you will need to check what you learn against other sources. Another problem is that your host may not know exactly what kinds of information a foreigner needs. Every culture has many unwritten, taken-for-granted rules and practices, and it is not unusual for a host national to assume that everyone knows and follows them. For example, a host national may assume you know it is improper to teach in sandals that have no ankle strap but okay to teach in those that do, or that teachers should hand out very few grades above 90 percent (both lessons I learned the hard way in southern China). It is therefore important to take an active role in your orientation by being ready to ask the questions that will get you the information you need rather than relying too heavily on the ability of others to guess what you need.

Veteran foreign teachers can also be an invaluable source of information, but their advice needs to be taken with a certain amount of caution. Not all expatriates adapt well to life in their host country, so when seeking advice, be alert for bias. Many veterans are helpful and insightful, but there are others whose primary interest in orienting you is an opportunity to get back at the host country. In judging how seriously to take a veteran's evaluation, be careful of someone who is consistently negative, has not spent much more time in the host country than you have, or shows little evidence of successful cultural adaptation. On the other hand, veterans whose evaluations seem objective and fair, who have made progress in understanding the host culture, and who have established a good working relationship with their hosts may well be your best sources of insight.

Other people who should be part of your orientation often aren't unless you seek them out. The support staff at your institution (e.g., secretaries, librarians) are very helpful people to know, and dropping by to ask them a few questions can provide a good excuse for you to meet them under nice circumstances rather than only after a problem has arisen. In most institutions, the office staff are wonderful sources of information, and their goodwill is vital to your well-being, so take advantage of your early days to make the best impression possible. Also, while students are not usually included in orientations, they are often among your best and most important sources of information. If you have an opportunity to speak with students before your first day of class, you can learn more about their English learning experiences and get a better idea of the level of their communication skills. After the semester begins, you can continue to learn much from them inside and outside class. In fact, by bringing real questions into the classroom, you provide students with an opportunity to use their English skills for a genuine communicative purpose.

The First Days of Class

Professionalism in English teaching does not necessarily mean having the whole semester's plans laid out in detail before the first day of class. In fact, I generally find that it is wise to leave a fair degree of flexibility in your plans until you have actually met with the students; often, you can make good decisions about specific goals and methods only after you have had some contact with the students.

Consequently, your investigation of your English teaching situation should not end the day classes start; in fact, the first few class periods are an important part of your information-gathering process. Of course, it is a good idea to spend time during the first classes getting to know the students' names, where they are from, and so forth. But equally important is that you get a sense of what their English skill levels are, what attitudes they have toward English study, and how easy they will be to work with. To this end, spending a portion of the first few class periods informally assessing the students is generally helpful. This chapter concludes with a brief discussion of activities for your first few days of class.

INTRODUCTIONS

Traditionally, the first day of a VT's English class consists of each student standing up, announcing his or her name, presenting a bare-bones biography, and sitting back down. While not a complete waste of time, this activity is boring in classes where students already know each other, and often not much more interesting even when they don't because students spend most of the class period waiting for others to stumble through awkward little speeches. This activity can be improved in a number of ways:

1. In classes where students know each other, ask students to mention something a little unusual in addition to their names. For example, ask them about their favorite food, favorite time of year, or another personal preference that other students in the class might find new, interesting, or amusing. This makes the introductions a little more memorable and enjoyable, and increases the chance that students will listen to each other.

2. In classes where students don't know each other, have them interview each other and then introduce their partners. This livens the class up by giving students opportunities to talk and to meet at least one other person in the class. As in number 1 above, you might suggest one or two interesting or amusing questions to add to the standard biographical inquiries.

3. If your primary goal is to gather basic information about the students, have them write it down on a card rather than spending a class hour presenting the information orally. Such cards are very useful for reviewing students' names and give you a written database about each student that often comes in handy later in the semester. When possible, having students give you pictures is also a good way to help you match student names and faces. (By taking the pictures yourself, you can add a festive touch to your class.)

LISTENING COMPREHENSION EXERCISES

Quickly finding out how well students understand what you say is very useful because you need to know whether they will understand explanations and classroom instructions. A simple way to do this is an activity in which students take notes while you orally introduce yourself briefly or tell a brief story. After the presentation, ask the students to write as detailed a summary of what you said as possible. As a formal test, this exercise is problematic because it relies on both listening comprehension and writing skills, but if the exercise is used as a quick probe, its dual listening-writing nature actually becomes an advantage, allowing you to quickly get a rough sense of students' listening, writing, grammar, and vocabulary skills.

WRITING EXERCISES

One of the main advantages of doing a writing exercise early in the course is that, in addition to giving you some idea of students' writing skills, it is an opportunity for you to learn other kinds of information. Rather than having students write about "My Summer Vacation," ask them to write about something related to English learning or their education in general. Here are some topic ideas to get you started:

- Why I Am Taking This Course (if the students have a choice)

- How I Learned English

- My Best (Past) English Teacher

- Why English Study Is/Is Not Useful

- My Experience with Foreigners (e.g., Americans, Canadians)

- How (Americans, British, etc.) Are Different from Us

SMALL GROUPS

Small-group and pair work are an important part of oral English lessons, so it is usually a good idea to try these approaches out in order to see how well students take to them. Students may function very well in groups or pairs, or they may never have done this before and feel very awkward about it. One way to try these methods out is to break students into pairs or groups of three or four, give them a topic, and ask each group to discuss the question and write down a response. (For topic and activity ideas, see appendix B, especially the Getting to Know You activities in the Daily Life module.) A group leader could then present the response orally, or you could circulate among the groups and see what they have written. An exercise like this helps you quickly discover how willing students are to work together in pairs or groups, allows you to hear them speaking in a relatively low-pressure setting, and again may produce some interesting insights about their approach to language learning.

INDIVIDUAL INTERVIEWS

Individual interviews allow you to get a very clear sense of students' oral skills as well as learn more about the students and begin to establish some rapport with them. For this reason, interviewing deserves serious consideration as an activity for the first week or so of class.

Granted, interviewing involves some challenges, one being that students may be absolutely petrified at the idea of confronting the teacher—a foreigner to boot—in a one-to-one setting, and you may learn less about how well they speak than about the grit and determination with which they would face a firing squad. Obviously, anything you can do to put students at ease will help. Suggestions include

- starting with light conversation

- opening with very easy questions

- meeting in relatively informal surroundings and perhaps even offering tea or cookies (though these well-intended attempts to create an informal atmosphere may be more confusing than reassuring in some cultures)

The other problem with individual interviews is that they are very time-consuming. In order to have anything resembling a conversation, you need to spend at least five to ten minutes per interview. You may also need to take a minute or two after each interview to make notes. You can interview more students in a limited time by interviewing in pairs or groups, and if your purpose is primarily to establish rapport and get a sense of the general skill level of the class, this is a very viable alternative. (See chapter 8 for further discussion of interview technique.)

Conclusion

The most important message of this chapter is that you don't need to finalize your class preparations before getting on the plane or even before the first day of class. Remember that you are not only embarking on a new kind of job; you are also entering a new country and culture about which there is much that you don't know. While course preparation is certainly useful, it is vitally important to first learn as much as you can about what you are preparing for. As suggested in this chapter, the shape of the task before you may finally become clear only during the first days of class. Take time to scout out the lay of the land; time invested in investigation of the situation will pay rich dividends in terms of more effective preparation.

For Thought, Discussion, and Action

1. **questionnaire task A (predeparture):** Look over the questionnaire in this chapter, and list the questions to which you don't yet know the answers. Then locate several people from your future host country, especially international students who have arrived in your country fairly recently, and ask them the questions.

2. **questionnaire task B (predeparture):** Locate one or more people from your country who have had experience teaching in your future host country, and ask questions from the questionnaire in this chapter. Also ask your informants to recommend good books about the host country.

3. **Internet search (predeparture):** Do an Internet or library search for materials about your future host country.

4. **campus tour task A (postarrival):** Ask your hosts to give you a tour of your campus. Before the tour, make a list of important questions you want to ask, and use the tour as an opportunity to explore these questions. In addition to asking about things you don't yet know anything about, check information you were given predeparture.

5. **campus tour task B (postarrival):** Find and meet some students from your host school (not necessarily students from the classes you will teach), and ask them to give you an informal campus tour. Use this as an opportunity to get a student perspective on questions from the questionnaire in this chapter. (What you learn will overlap to some extent with what you learn on a more official campus tour conducted by staff from your school, but you will probably also learn much new information.)

6. **department visit (postarrival):** After an official tour conducted by staff from your department, go back on your own to explore further, reviewing what you learned on the official tour and trying to strike up conversations with people you were (briefly) introduced to. Make a point of trying to meet staff and teachers other than department leaders or those with official responsibilities related to you.

7. **first-week activities (postarrival):** Choose one or more of the activities suggested in this chapter for the first day of class, and try them out during your first week of class.

Chapter 3

Planning Your Course

- A course needs to have a long-term plan because plans made day-to-day can leave students feeling that the course lacks direction.

- The key elements of a course plan are goals, materials, methods, and evaluation measures.

- Students must learn to make and take responsibility for their own language learning plans. Hence, one of the goals of a course should be to help students learn to design and carry out language learning projects (LLPs).

When it comes to planning courses, English teachers may fall into two common traps. One is planning the course one day or lesson at a time, the "I wonder what will work in class tomorrow?" syndrome. This approach often arises from a well-intended desire to keep students interested and often results in the teacher's picking through the course textbook or other materials daily to find something that will work—that is, something students will respond well to. This approach to lesson planning is not entirely without merit. Its primary virtue is that it may result in quite a few fun lessons, but it can also be unsatisfying if it leaves students with little sense of direction and progress.

The other trap lies in simply sticking to the book. While most volunteer teachers (VTs) are disinclined toward such a lockstep approach, they may be drawn into it because they often teach in situations where texts and programs have already been decided, and the easiest way to adapt to a preexisting program and feel secure in an unfamiliar environment is to go along with the program. Again, this approach has its strong points and is especially important if students will face a standardized examination based on standardized textbooks. However, simply moving through a text drill by drill tends to be boring, and it trains teachers and students to be passive recipients of direction rather than active creators of their own plans. (For a more detailed discussion of these two traps, see Abbott and Wingard 1981, 248; Bowen, Madsen, and Hilferty 1985, 345.)

In this chapter, I suggest two main points to consider in your course planning. First and most obviously, you should have a plan that gives direction and coherence to your course. Such a plan will improve your teaching as well as give students a sense of direction and confidence. Naturally, your initial course plans will probably be rather general because you are most likely not yet in a position to lay out your daily lesson plans for a whole semester. Even for experienced teachers, real life does not work out so neatly, and planning is never really completed. However, having at least an initial set of goals and plans for materials, methods, and evaluation measures will go a long way toward ensuring that both you and the students know where you are going.

Second, one of your goals in any course should be to lead students toward taking responsibility for planning their own language study. By learning to actively consider their goals and methods, students are more likely to focus their study efforts in a way that will suit their styles, take advantage of their strengths, compensate for their weaknesses, and meet their personal needs. Students who study in this way will probably do better in their course work and be better prepared to continue their study once their days in English classes end.

If you have had the chance to take some of the steps suggested in chapter 2, by now you should know something about students' needs, skill levels, study habits, and expectations. You should also have some idea of what limitations—in materials, facilities, equipment, and institutional guidelines and expectations—you will have to work within. In this chapter I discuss the basic elements of a course plan: course goals, materials, and methods. (Other important aspects of course planning—evaluation and grading—are considered in chapter 4.)

Goals

Goal setting will vary considerably according to the situation. Consider the following examples.

CASE ONE

You are teaching a general English course for high school seniors who later in the year will face a nationwide standardized examination that determines whether they will have the opportunity for further education.

Given the importance of the upcoming examination, you have little freedom in setting goals. Obviously, the primary goal is to help students do as well as possible on the examination, so your teaching should be tailored to its demands. A secondary goal would be to enhance students' interest in English so that some of them choose to continue studying English even after they have completed the exam.

CASE TWO

You are teaching a course for middle-aged scholars who are preparing to go abroad for research in a Western country. The class consists mostly of people who have considerable experience reading and translating English but very marginal speaking and listening skills.

This group needs a heavy diet of listening practice, especially practice understanding the kinds of English they might hear in daily life. Lack of listening comprehension skills will effectively isolate these people from even the simplest social contact—far more so than will inability to speak—so these skills should be the overriding concern. A secondary goal should be helping students improve their speaking skills so that they can cope with survival needs and simple social situations. Finally, survival cultural knowledge would be of benefit.

CASE THREE

You are teaching a general English course in a college where all first-year students are required to take one year of English. They have had two years of high school English and can read simple texts and handle simple conversation. You must use the assigned text, but the only tests students need to take are the ones you give.

In this situation, you have considerable freedom of action. The main problem is that, because the students are required to take the course, you cannot assume that they have any other reason for being there. The first goal might therefore be to enhance their interest in English study. A second important goal is getting students started in designing and carrying out their own study programs; there is a limit to how high a skill level they are likely to reach in one year, and unless they become genuinely interested in English study, their efforts to learn English will probably grind to a halt at the end of your course, leaving them little to show for their effort. As to what English skills to emphasize, you might decide based on the skills that seem to interest the students or that offer the most promise of being useful in the future. However, you would be wise to focus students' efforts to some degree rather than simply doing a little bit of everything; if students can see and feel progress in one skill area, it is more likely that they will be encouraged to continue working on English after the course ends.

In some cases you will know why students are learning English and what they will eventually do with it; you can then set goals based on the types of skills and knowledge that will best serve students in their later use of English. Unfortunately, in other situations, students' needs will be neither clear nor uniform. Students in the same class, especially voluntary adult classes, may have utterly different needs or goals; one student may be in your course because she needs to improve her grammar for writing business letters while another wants to improve his oral fluency for striking up conversations with tourists. School settings may also be problematic because few or none of the students have any clear reason for studying English other than that it is required.[1] Thus tailoring the goals of an English course specifically to students' future needs is often difficult.

As should be clear from the examples given, goals need to be set within a specific context; different situations call for very different kinds of goals. The discussion here thus addresses only a

---

[1] Abbott and Wingard (1981, 12) have a wonderful acronym for this type of situation: TENOR (teaching English for no obvious reason).

few of the main issues involved in goal setting. (Goals for the various language skills are dealt with in chapters 7–12. See also appendix A.)

HEALTHY BALANCE OF SKILLS

When you cannot tailor instruction to a particular set of needs, it is generally best to help students develop a balanced, general set of English skills and knowledge. In ideal situations, developing all the language skills to a high level is no doubt desirable, but time limitations often demand that you choose what to stress in your classes and that students choose what skills to give the highest priority to. The following observations may be useful as you think through the problem of prioritizing goals:

1. **listening over speaking:** Usually it is best if students' listening skills are somewhat more advanced than their speaking skills. Even native speakers of a language can generally understand more than they can say, and many situations (e.g., watching TV, listening to the radio, listening to lectures) depend entirely on listening skills.[2]

2. **reading over writing:** Students are far more likely to need to read than write, if only because it is through reading that students gain so much of their vocabulary in EFL settings. Again, even native speakers generally read better and more often than they write.

3. **communication over accuracy:** In most situations, communication is more important than accuracy. Although in some situations (such as tests or formal writing) accuracy is very important, in general an English user's primary need is to understand and be understood.

4. **vocabulary over grammar:** For listening and reading, an extensive vocabulary is more important than a thorough knowledge of English grammar (see Lewis 1993, 33, for development of this argument).

Given these general features of a good balance, one way to decide where to focus your efforts is to assess the students' levels and then to emphasize those areas in which students need improvement to reach a good balance.

BASIC SKILLS AND KNOWLEDGE

A second all-purpose suggestion is that it is often best to emphasize fundamental knowledge and skills rather than situation-specific knowledge or skills, for example, stressing general speaking and listening skills over the fine points of job interviews, grammatical accuracy in writing over the art of the memo, or reading speed over skills in literary criticism. One obvious problem with situation-specific skills is that they are of limited value to students who never find themselves in the right situation. Another problem is that the speed of change in the modern world means that a situation for which you prepare students may no longer exist by the time they graduate. I am reminded of a class of Chinese university students I taught who were being prepared to work in trade companies. Because of their future job needs, the department wanted me to teach the class telex writing (a request that I ignored mainly because I didn't know how to write telexes). Despite the apparently uniform job needs of these students, when I interviewed them a year after gradu-

---

[2] Scarcella and Oxford (1992) claim, "Listening in almost any setting is the most frequently used language skill" (p. 139). This statement may be less true for English learners outside English-speaking countries—where learners may read more often than they listen—than for those in English-speaking countries, but the emphasis on the importance of listening skills is still well taken. See also Hedge (2000, 228–29) and Morley (2001, 70).

ation, I found that most never had any need to write telexes. Of course, since that time telexes have been replaced twice, first by the fax machine and then by e-mail.

CONTENT AND SKILL GOALS

A third general rule of thumb is that in a course it is often best to have a mix of skill goals (listening, speaking, reading, writing) and content goals (vocabulary, grammar, cultural information). As noted in chapter 1, students vary considerably in their learning styles; some students are better at memorizing, others at communication, and others at grammatical accuracy, so by including both skill and content goals you give students with different strengths an opportunity to demonstrate their ability, thereby increasing the chances that they can shine in some aspect of your course.

On the whole, VTs tend to emphasize language practice in their courses, and this is generally good in that the skill focus it provides often serves as a useful corrective in programs that tend to emphasize mastery of content. However, it is probably wise to include some content goals in your courses. Students who are accustomed to studying grammar rules and memorizing vocabulary may find your course frustrating or demoralizing if you suddenly change the rules of the game by focusing only on language skills. It thus makes good sense—both educationally and politically—to have a content mastery aspect to your course in order to increase the chances that students will feel comfortable in some portion of it.

ATTENTION TO AFFECTIVE FACTORS

The most important reason for having explicitly stated goals may be that they help students feel better about their language study, thereby improving the chances that they will learn willingly and be able to sustain that willingness over the long haul. Goals give direction to language study and serve as milestones that help learners see their progress. Without goals, language learning is a bit like rowing a boat in the middle of the ocean—even if you are moving forward, it is hard to tell if you are getting anywhere because there are no readily visible markers by which you can measure your progress. Likewise, unless learners have some way to mark their progress in English study, they may invest quite a bit of effort and still have little sense of progress. One way you can help learners sustain a sense of forward motion is by breaking the massive task of learning English into smaller and more readily measurable units—stated as goals—that help them mark and feel their progress. To this end, it is helpful to have both general long-term goals and specific short-term goals.

Broad, long-term goals enhance student morale by giving a sense of direction and vision; goals such as improved listening comprehension or increased reading speed offer the promise of a reward worth striving for. Without a sense of long-term goals, class exercises may seem to be an unrelated series of activities that are ends in themselves or that only serve to prepare students for the final test. Of course, for long-term goals to have a beneficial effect on student morale, students must be made aware of the goals—not only once at the beginning of the term but on a regular basis. It is easy for teachers to overestimate the sense of vision and purpose that students have in language learning, particularly if they are taking a required language course, and it is also easy to overestimate how well students will remember a lecture on goals given on the first day of class. To many students, that lecture is a blur of half-understood language that they listened to while wishing class would end soon. You might therefore remind students why they are doing what they are doing in almost every class. (My rule of thumb is that once students start chanting my little "We are doing this because . . ." speech along with me, they have probably internalized it.)

However, as Stevick (1988) suggests, long-term goals are not enough. They "are the hoped-for banquet at the end of a long hike. Your hikers also need snacks and water to sustain them along the path" (p. 128). Underneath the broad goals, you need to set goals that are specific and short term, goals toward which students can make observable progress during your course. For example, if the broad goal of a course is improvement of listening comprehension, more specific goals might include learning to understand the most common reduced forms of English words (e.g., *want to = wanna, don't you = dontcha*) or memorizing the names of the world's major countries and cities as an aid to understanding radio news in English. The latter goals are more finite than the broad goal of improving listening comprehension, and it is entirely possible for students to achieve them within a semester course, giving students the satisfaction of pointing to a task successfully completed.

Finally, enhancing students' interest in English study should in itself be a primary goal. English teachers naturally tend to assume that students should be motivated to study English, so you may need to remind yourself that students often have no personal reason for being in English classes; they may be there purely because the course is a required part of a curriculum. In these cases students are naturally only interested in what will get them past the test, and you cannot assume that their interest will go beyond such pragmatic concerns. If you want them to become genuinely interested in English study—as they must if they are to eventually master the language—you will need to make this a goal to work toward rather than an assumption to work from.

Materials: The Book

Unlike goals, the problem with materials is usually not one of overly abundant choice. You may be fortunate enough to find a well-stocked library in your host school, but more often the issue of materials boils down to how you deal with the assigned course text. In an ideal world, this text would be a new book with a bright, catchy cover; sturdy glossy pages; and loads of exciting readings, activities, and other goodies. However, you are less likely to be disappointed if you expect a book that is well used and possibly decorated with notes from previous users (though maybe in a language you can't read). The book may either be one written and produced in the host country or an old book from the United States or Britain—perhaps a poorly done reproduction. The cover may be done in two tones instead of color, and the pages may be slightly yellowed. On first glance the contents may not seem particularly inspiring, and this impression may not change for the better even when you study the textbook more carefully. In short, your instinctive response may well be, "I can't work with this!" The question you then face is what to do with the book.

Again, if you have done your investigative homework well, you should have a clear idea of how much freedom you have to stray from the material presented in the book. If the book is part of a prescribed curriculum—especially one leading to standardized tests—you are under an obligation to teach the course material as best you can whether you like the materials or not. Even if there is no such examination, you may still be more or less forced to stick closely to the textbook if the students or your host institution feels strongly about the issue.

What should you do if you have the freedom to retain or abandon the book? Clearly, there is no single right answer to this question: a great deal depends on how bad the book is or how much you dislike it. However, I would argue that, on the whole, it is best to try to use the course textbook rather than abandon it (though perhaps to supplement where necessary). My reasons are as follows:

1. Having a course text saves lesson preparation time. The freedom to throw away the book and make up your own lessons is exhilarating at first, when you are fresh and have a lot of good ideas. However, as the semester wears on, you may find your creativity wearing out, and cooking up each day's lesson from scratch can become a real burden.

2. The book provides continuity to the course and helps prevent it from degenerating into a series of entertaining but unrelated activities.

3. Having a book makes it easier for students to review. The alternatives are for you to invest considerable time in producing handouts or for students to spend class time copying material from the board.

4. Using the textbook can help students feel better about their English study. Lewis (1993) notes, "Teachers who like to teach without a coursebook sometimes forget that students may need the reassurance of a programme, and the feeling of 'getting somewhere.' Working through a coursebook—perhaps omitting bits, and almost certainly supplementing it—is almost always better than working entirely without a coursebook" (p. 182).

One final issue to consider is the age-old problem of finding a better textbook. Many teachers fully agree that having a text brings significant advantages—they simply don't like the one that is offered and want to find a better one to replace it. When this is possible, it is obviously the best solution to the problem of a bad textbook. However, this alternative is often less realistic than VTs think. Textbooks brought in from outside the host country are often prohibitively expensive and involve considerable administrative hassle. They may also not be well designed for your teaching situation; for example, most English books produced in the United States are designed for students studying English there and often make assumptions about students' background and needs that would be inappropriate in an EFL setting.

Textbooks found in the host country are generally a more realistic option, but VTs are often unpleasantly surprised to discover that their administration is not very enthusiastic about helping procure a new textbook for a course. The problem is frequently one of perspective. The VT is virtually always a short-term person in the department, and for the year or so that the VT spends in the host country, the advantages of having a somewhat better textbook—or a textbook that is better suited to his or her personal tastes—are significant. To long-term administrative staff, getting a new textbook every time a new VT arrives at the school is simply a headache and often produces no improvement in teaching that is visible from the school office. (I am reminded of a campaign I was once involved in at the Taipei YMCA to get our textbooks changed. The supervisor listened patiently to our complaints, then pointed to a shelf loaded with new copies of the text in question and told us that the book we wanted to get rid of was the one last year's VTs had made them buy.)

Methods

Given the extensive attention that specific teaching methods receive in chapters 7–13, here I make short shrift of the issue with two brief observations.

The first is a basic rule of thumb: the best way to develop a skill is to practice it, and the more the practice method resembles the actual application of the skill, the better. Simply put, the best way to learn to speak is to practice speaking; the best way to learn to read is to practice reading, and so on.[3] This might seem obvious, but in many cases students (and even teachers)

---

[3] Obviously, I am overstating the case a bit. As Nunan (1989, 40–45) points out, both real-world tasks (practice activities that resemble actual use) and pedagogic tasks (activities like grammar drills that isolate one specific aspect of a skill) can be useful. I emphasize real-world tasks in part because the skills and inclinations of VTs are generally more suited to realistic communicative tasks than to pedagogic ones.

simply use methods passed on to them from an earlier generation. The result is that the methods do not always fit the goals. In China, for example, one practice method commonly used by students to develop their speaking skills is getting up early in the morning to spend half an hour or so reading lessons from their textbook aloud. This practice method is not bad per se—it provides useful review of material previously studied—but reading aloud from a book is very different from organizing one's own ideas into sentences, so it is at best an incomplete form of speaking practice. Students can avoid problems created by inappropriate practice strategies by learning to think carefully about what is involved in the skill they wish to develop and then practicing in ways that faithfully replicate that skill.

A second observation is that while you should choose methods based on pedagogical soundness, you also need to consider what methods will be acceptable to the students. Some educationally sound methods may not work in your class because students find them too uncomfortable, too unfamiliar, too dubious, or simply too weird. In EFL settings, you need to pay particular attention to this problem because the students in a class share a great number of common beliefs and customs concerning language study, and you may run into united resistance if your proposed methods conflict with the students' ideas too much. The question you need to ask yourself is, to what extent am I willing to invest time and effort persuading students to reconfigure their approaches to language learning? You cannot predict how strongly a group of students will resist new and different methods for language learning—they may even be delighted to try a new approach. However, in general the more your methods differ from those students are used to, the more time you will need to spend explaining and selling the methods. Failure to do adequate public relations work may result in increasing resistance and decreased cooperation from the class. So when you are planning your course, it is best to take a good look at your reserves of patience and take a radically innovative approach only if you are also willing—if necessary—to invest time and effort in selling your program.

Language Learning Projects: Working toward Breakthrough

As indicated at the beginning of the chapter, your ultimate goal is not only to plan a good course for the students; it is also to help them learn how to effectively plan their own language learning. Students who only obediently do what the teacher tells them to will not be very well prepared for the day when they are on their own. While they are in formal language courses, they need to begin developing the habit of designing and carrying out their own language learning plans because this is what they will need to be able to do when they leave those courses.

Here I suggest an approach I call *language learning projects* (LLPs). I use this term to refer to limited, independent language study projects that students carry out as one part of their language courses in order to prepare them for autonomy—for the day when the apron strings are cut and they need to continue studying on their own without the benefit of a teacher and a ready-made course. (The discussion of LLPs below is also relevant to part-time language study outside formal language courses.)

GETTING READY FOR AN LLP

In the long run, the most important factor in determining whether students succeed in learning English or not is persistence; students who keep studying and practicing have a good chance at ultimate success while those who give up do not. The key to language study—especially when time is limited and learners may opt out—is therefore to study in a way that is sustainable—in other words, that minimizes unnecessary discouragement and provides learners with enough sense of progress and reward that they will keep at it. Before setting out to plan their own LLP, students can increase the likelihood that their project will be sustainable and ultimately successful by seriously thinking about the following questions.

How Much Time Do I Have Available for the LLP?

Time is a limited commodity, and students need to keep this reality firmly in mind when planning their LLPs. (Here I assume that the learners are doing an LLP as an independent study project, in addition to whatever other homework you expect of them. Of course, the same problem would exist if students were trying to continue their study after they graduated and got a job.) When first asked to plan LLPs, many students make big plans that would take massive investments of time to sustain. ("First, I will review English grammar and memorize new vocabulary. Then I will listen to the BBC news on the radio each day. Then I will read Dickens for an hour . . . .") Obviously, a plan of this magnitude is unrealistic for anyone who cannot devote hours a day to English study, and the danger of such unrealistic plans is that they result in failure and discouragement, feelings that do not bode well for the plan's survival.

What Opportunities Do I Have to Practice English?

EFL settings vary both in the amount of opportunity to use English skills and in the skills that students might have an opportunity to use. For example, one place may have relatively few printed materials in English but a constant flow of foreign backpackers coming through town. In contrast, in another setting, there may be few chances to speak or listen to English but a reliable supply of books, newspapers, or magazines in English. In the first setting, it would probably be easier for students to find or create opportunities to speak English, so an LLP geared toward that goal would be more exciting and easier to sustain; in the second setting, an LLP focused on reading skills would have a better chance of survival. When students have little chance to use what they learn, a study project tends to seem more pointless. In contrast, if students have a chance to use whatever knowledge and skills they gain through their LLPs, the effort is more interesting and exciting, so it is easier for students to stay motivated and keep studying.

What Do I Like Doing in English?

Students vary considerably in terms of what they enjoy and do not enjoy about using English. One student may hate the embarrassment of trying to speak English but find it reasonably comfortable and even enjoyable to make sense out of something written in English. Another student may be bored to tears by books but get a kick out of trying to talk in an alien tongue. A third may dislike English study in general but find listening to radio news in English somewhat tolerable because, even though it is hard work, the student may find out something new and interesting about what is going on the world. And so forth. The point here is that an LLP is more likely to be sustainable if the skill the student has chosen to work on is one that he or she finds reasonably interesting and even enjoyable. While this point is fairly obvious, it is worth emphasizing because students all too often ignore it, choosing goals and making plans based more on what they feel they ought to do than on what they want to do (perhaps because in their experience with English to date, enjoyment and interest have never been suggested as part of the equation). While such a spirit of self-denial is commendable, it is also dangerous when trying to keep an LLP alive; when faced with an unpleasant task, students may find it too easy to decide, "I'll do this tomorrow," and tomorrow, and tomorrow. Such self-denial is also somewhat sad in that it ignores the real possibility that English study can be rewarding. Students should be told that it is perfectly legitimate—in fact, desirable—for them to consider their own desires and interests when deciding what they want to pursue in an LLP.

As students prepare to design their own LLP, the bottom line is that their plan will have a greater chance of success if it is realistic in its time demands, if it takes advantage of whatever opportunities naturally exist or can be created for using the skills learned, and if it plays to the students' interests as much as possible.

DESIGNING THE LLP

Designing the LLP involves four main steps: choosing a goal, choosing study and practice methods, making a concrete plan, and setting criteria for assessing progress.

Choosing a (Narrow) Goal

As I have suggested, in choosing a goal it is best for learners to play to their interests and opportunities as much as possible. However, for the purposes of most LLPs, it is equally important that a learner's goal be quite specific and narrow. Goals should be specific and clear enough that they not only set the direction for the LLP but also serve as goal markers that allow learners to see how much progress they have made toward the goal. The problem with vague, broad goals such as *improve my reading* or *improve my speaking* (not to mention the classic *improve my English*) is that it is hard to tell whether or not one has actually achieved them or is even making progress toward them. Furthermore, with only limited time available to invest in the LLP, progress on a broad front is likely to be painfully slow. In contrast, given the same amount of time, progress toward a more specific goal like *improve my ability to read the news articles in an English language newspaper* or *get better at talking about my local community in English* is likely to be more evident as well as faster. Just as the flow of water in a river picks up speed when the riverbed becomes narrower, a student's progress toward a narrow, specific goal is faster than that toward a broader goal. The primary virtue of this speed is that when students can see and feel their progress, they are more likely to remain encouraged and motivated to continue the project.

Choosing Study and Practice Methods

Keep in mind that study and practice methods should be as similar as possible to the skill that a student wants to master. Students who spend a great deal of time reading English newspaper articles tend to get better at reading English newspaper articles, and so forth. Of course, as noted, things are not quite this simple. For example, students who are trying to improve their ability to read news items in the newspaper would also benefit from memorizing news-related vocabulary, such as names of places and people. However, overall this principle is a helpful one to follow.

Planning Where, When, and How Long to Study

Some students can make impressive progress in language study without having a very clear plan, just studying where and when the spirit strikes them. However, for most students, the successful maintenance of an LLP involves planning for a place where they can study and practice effectively and finding reasonably regular times when they can study. On the whole, regular, sustained effort is more likely to produce noticeable progress toward the goal than more erratic efforts are, so it is more likely to generate adequate momentum to encourage the learner to continue. Keep in mind here that the total amount of time per week a learner can give to an LLP may be quite limited, perhaps not much more than two or three hours. While this amount of time is hardly ideal—and a more significant time investment is more likely to generate encouraging results—it is often the reality for learners who are engaged in other full-time study or work. However, if the goal toward which a learner is working is narrow and specific enough, and the LLP is sustained over time, even this modest time investment can produce adequate progress to sustain motivation (whereas this amount of time would result in little apparent progress toward more broadly defined goals).

Setting Criteria for Measuring Progress

Students will tend to have a stronger and clearer sense of achievement if they can see progress in their LLPs in quantifiable ways. To some degree, the goals of LLPs serve as indicators telling students whether or not they have made progress. However, goals are intended to set direction more than to measure progress, and even specific, narrow goals are often not concrete and quantifiable enough to show students their progress. Therefore, it is generally helpful if students include criteria in their LLPs by which they can assess whether or not they have achieved their goals, indicators that tell them how much progress they have made.

While these criteria do not all need to be scientifically precise, at least some of them should be concrete and quantifiable. For example, if the goal is "to improve my ability to read the news articles in an English-language newspaper," achievement criteria should include some criteria based directly on the goals, for example, "can read and understand the gist of English newspaper articles without using a dictionary." However, it is best if there are also some very quantifiable criteria such as "have read fifty English newspaper articles and learned the vocabulary in them."

THE BREAKTHROUGH CONCEPT

One obvious limitation of LLPs as defined here is that they have learners working only toward relatively limited language improvement goals rather than toward the enhancement of all their English skills. However, on the whole I feel this trade-off is worthwhile because of all that is gained in terms of sustainability. Furthermore, I assume that eventually, for any given skill a learner is working on, there is what I call a *breakthrough point*, that is, a point at which the learner can actually begin to use the skill for a useful or rewarding purpose. For example, in the development of conversation skills, the breakthrough point might be where one learner can strike up and sustain conversations with Western tourists without being so embarrassed that she beats a quick retreat. For a second learner, the breakthrough might occur when she can understand English novels well enough to find reading more fun than work. For a third, it could be the point at which his oral skills are good enough that his monolingual boss begins asking him to translate when foreign guests come to the office.

Of course, the breakthrough point in all of these cases may not be a particular instant; it may be a longer process. Notice also that the breakthrough involves feelings as much as skill per se; it is often a point where the learner becomes willing to apply the skill because rewards (e.g., access to new people and information, a sense of achievement) have begun to outweigh the costs (e.g., hard work, potential embarrassment). But, however it is defined, a distinct and important change happens to language learners once they can begin to use their language skills, either for personal reward or practical benefit, and once learners reach this point, their continued language learning takes on more momentum because they can use the language in contexts other than language study. To return to the examples above, the conversation skills of the first learner will continue to improve as she enjoys chatting with tourists, the reading skills of the second will get better as she reads for pleasure, and the third's listening skills will be further honed as he continues to translate. From this point on, the continued use and improvement of the skill take on a life of their own.

In my experience as a language learner and teacher, once learners have reached a breakthrough point in one area, such success is likely to motivate them to continue working toward other successes in English—and perhaps even toward study of other languages. The time and effort you spend working with students on this is very well invested because you are making a contribution that goes far beyond what you might teach them about English in a few hours: you are giving them a fighting chance to find a path of language study that might continue to work for them long after your class ends.

LLPs IN LANGUAGE COURSES

While I recommend the use of LLPs with an eye to how they prepare students for life after your course ends, students need to begin engaging in them well before that if they are to develop autonomous study habits and skills they can carry with them past graduation day. As Nunan (1997, 193) argues, autonomy is a relative concept rather than an all-or-nothing proposition, and determining how much independence students are ready for and how much guidance they need at any given point is an art more than a science. My own approach is as follows.

If my sense is that students are not yet accustomed to the idea of working on their own, I ask them to carry out limited-choice LLPs, in which I first set a menu of goals, materials, and methods (usually closely related to the course I am teaching) from which they then have some freedom to make choices. For example, if the course involves a reading component, I might ask them to choose their own books, or perhaps choose whether to focus on building vocabulary or reading speed. In this situation I would probably want a fairly high degree of accountability from students for their LLPs.

If students seem to be ready for more autonomy, you can then ask them to design and carry out full-choice LLPs in which they have great latitude in choosing their own goals, materials, and methods, and demands for accountability would also be lighter.

For both limited-choice and full-choice LLPs, you would presumably ask students to make up an LLP plan that you would then give feedback on. However, how much accountability you expect after that point depends on your sense of how willing students are to take responsibility for their own progress.

It is very important to keep in mind that students will not necessarily be able to design good LLPs on their first try. Common problems are too many goals, vague goals, unrealistically high expectations, and mismatch between the goals and the methods. So, when you assign the LLPs, be sure to talk with students about how to design a good plan, and provide them with models to illustrate the concept. You will probably also need to help students during the first few weeks as they begin trying to carry out their plans, discover problems, and need to adjust or modify their plans. Of course, all of this requires an investment of time and energy from you as well as from the students. However, keep in mind that the ultimate goal—building students' ability and willingness to engage in effective language learning on their own—is worth quite a bit of effort.

A good way to increase the chances that students will follow through with their own study program after leaving your course is to talk with them toward the end of the course about how to set up and carry out their own future study plans. Again, you might even have them write down a plan and go over it with you. Of course, there is no guarantee that students will follow through with the plans they write, but this is one last chance to encourage them and get them thinking about the issue. If your course has let students take the responsibility for at least some of their own language learning efforts, there is a good chance that their English study life will continue even after their formal English study program ends. (See the end of this chapter for sample LLPs.)

For Thought, Discussion, and Action

1. **setting goals:** Choose a course you expect to teach, and do the following:
   • Describe the situation, following the models of the three case studies in the Goals section of this chapter.
   • List goals you could set for the course.
   • Discuss your course and goals with a friend or classmate. Explain the situation and the reasons you set the goals you did.

2. **matching goals and methods:**
   - Decide which of the following kinds of courses to plan for: speaking, listening, reading, or writing.
   - Decide whether you will plan for a beginning-, intermediate-, or advanced-level course.
   - Turn to the Goals Menu (appendix A), and find suggested goals for your course and level.
   - Based on the suggested goals, decide what kinds of practice activities (methods) would help students achieve those goals. Keep in mind the rule of thumb that a practice activity should be as much like the skill it is intended to build as possible.

3. **analyzing a textbook:** Choose a textbook that you have taught or may have to teach in the future, analyze it, and list its strengths and weaknesses. Then consider these questions:
   - What is the best way to use this textbook in a course?
   - What parts of it would you emphasize and use the most?
   - What parts would you deemphasize or skip entirely?

   After you analyze the textbook, discuss the strengths and weaknesses of the textbook with an English teacher from your host country.

4. **writing LLPs for students:** Using the model below, write one or more possible LLPs that students could do as part of the course you designed in step 1, setting goals.

5. **LLP for you:** Design an LLP for improving some aspect of your foreign language skills, particularly your skills in the host-country language (for more on learning the language of your host country, see chapter 15).
   - Start by considering yourself and your context:
     — How much time will you have? (Be realistic.)
     — What access to the target language and opportunities to use it do you have?
     — What do you like—and not like—about language study? How can you make your LLP as appealing as possible?
   - Make a plan for your LLP:
     — Set a narrow, specific, and appropriate goal in the target language, such as learning survival speaking and listening skills, learning to read signs, building your vocabulary for reading novels, or improving your ability to listen to films.
     — Decide what breakthrough point you might work toward.
     — Decide what study and practice methods you will use.
     — Make a study plan, including when and where you will study.

6. **doing an LLP journal study:** One way to learn more from an LLP about what works and doesn't work for you as a language learner—and about language learning in general—is to do a *journal study* as you conduct the LLP. An informal journal study would involve the following steps.
   - Before you begin the study, reflect on your previous language learning experiences and how they may affect your current LLP. You might also make a preliminary list of questions you hope to answer—things that you hope to learn about language learning through your LLP experience. Examples might include
     — Can I improve my reading speed enough that I won't become discouraged and give up on my LLP?

Sample LLPs

VOCABULARY LLP

Goal: Build my vocabulary for reading.

Method:

1. Read articles from a magazine in English, marking unfamiliar vocabulary.

2. Look up new vocabulary in a dictionary, record it in a notebook, and study/review until I can recognize and understand the new words readily.

Plan: Read and study three times a week, one hour each session, in the morning before class.

Criteria for measuring progress: I will have succeeded if I (1) create a thirty-page notebook of new vocabulary and (2) can understand all the vocabulary in it when I see it either in the notebook or in a magazine article.

FILM-LISTENING LLP

Goal: Build my listening comprehension of natural English conversation.

Method:

1. Select films with reasonably clear (modern) English.

2. The first time, watch the film all the way through with the subtitles turned off, then write a summary of the story and any questions about parts I don't understand.

3. Watch the whole film again—still without subtitles—and try to figure out the parts I didn't get the first time.

4. Go back to any unclear parts and watch them again with the subtitles (in English or my language) turned on.

Plan: Watch one film each week in the library, in two or three evening sessions.

Criteria for measuring progress: I will have succeeded if I (1) watch eight films using this approach and (2) feel more comfortable watching films in English without subtitles.

— Can I work out an effective and efficient method for building my reading vocabulary?
— Can I find an effective way to improve my listening by working with films?
- Then, as you carry out your LLP, keep a log in which you record (1) what you do in the LLP, (2) your thoughts about it, and (3) your feelings as you go through the experience.
- Eventually, look back over the journal to see what patterns and discoveries await you (for a more formal journal study procedure, see Bailey, Curtis, and Nunan 2001, 50).

Chapter 4

Evaluation, Backwash, and Grading

- Evaluation is valuable not only for determining students' skill levels but also as a way of holding students accountable and encouraging them to keep working.

- *Backwash,* the impact that your evaluation methods have on what and how students study, is a very important factor in deciding how to evaluate.

- You will need to learn the language and culture of grading in your host country; otherwise, your grades may not communicate what they are intended to.

- When grading a group of students, you will need to try to strike a balance between improvement-based grading (measuring student progress against an objective scale) and class-curve-based grading (comparing students' performances with those of their peers). The former is fairer but can be more difficult to do well. The latter is more convenient and often more readily understood, but is less fair.

Discussion of evaluation and grading may seem somewhat premature at this point; after all, you are probably still thinking primarily about what will happen during the first few weeks of your course. However, your evaluation methods have tremendous power to positively or negatively affect the ways in which students will study, and you need to make good use of this impact in order to encourage students to study and practice productively. So, you should at least begin thinking about evaluation when you are planning your course rather than waiting until the middle or end of the semester and then wondering how to put together a midterm or final exam. Failure to carefully consider your evaluation methods means running the risk of having the intentions of your course completely subverted.

First, a note on terminology. *Evaluation* may seem to be an overly technical euphemism for *testing*. However, they are not quite the same. What I consider here is broader than testing alone and consists of graded homework assignments, notes on classroom participation, and compositions written for a portfolio as well as final examinations. In short, evaluation consists of any way in which you measure and judge students' knowledge or skills.

Tests and other evaluative measures come in a variety of colors; tests alone can be broken down into four or more main categories (for further discussion, see Bailey 1998, 37–39; Harmer 2001, 321; Hughes 1989, 9; Madsen 1983, 8–9). However, the underlying purposes of almost all classroom evaluation fall into two main categories:

1. **diagnostic:** One reason to evaluate is to determine how well students are doing in their studies. This information helps students assess how much progress they are making and where they are weak and strong. It also helps you determine how effectively a course facilitates student learning. Note that the scores and grades that result from testing are often intended as much for others—school authorities, for example—as for students.

2. **motivational:** The most obvious motivational effect of evaluation on students is the incentive it gives them to study harder, but this is not the only reason evaluation can have a positive impact on student motivation. Madsen (1983, 4) points out that evaluation can also give students a sense of accomplishment by helping them see what they have learned, which can translate into more positive attitudes toward study.

I discuss specific methods for evaluating English skills in the chapters devoted to those skills. The purpose of this chapter is to raise general issues involved in evaluation and grading so that you can begin thinking about how you will deal with this aspect of your courses.

Backwash

WHAT IS BACKWASH?

A critically important issue to consider when planning evaluation methods for a course is something called *backwash* (also known as *washback*), that is, the effect of your evaluation methods on students' study and practice methods. Put simply, students tend to do what they are rewarded for and not to do what they are not rewarded for. Thus, for example, if your tests and quizzes frequently include a listening comprehension section, students are likely to work on their listening. In contrast, if you evaluate a course only with written tests, students are not likely to invest much time in developing speaking skills, no matter how important you say oral practice is. Backwash is strongest when grades are very important to students, but even when grades aren't important, backwash can still occur because students, quite understandably, assume that the evaluation system reflects the teacher's sense of priorities.

Backwash can have either a positive or a negative impact on learning, depending on how closely the evaluation methods reflect the skill that students are supposed to develop. For example, if the goal is for students to develop the ability to express their ideas in English but their exercises are graded primarily on grammatical accuracy, the backwash will pull them away from the goal; in contrast, grading on effectiveness of communication will push them toward the goal. Well-designed evaluation methods ensure that the best scores go to students who have studied and practiced in the desired manner, and will encourage students to use good study methods. Backwash becomes a problem mainly when students are forced to choose between study approaches that develop usable language skills and those which prepare them for a test.

Perhaps surprisingly, teachers sometimes don't give adequate attention to backwash because of a failure to appreciate how important grades are to students. Teachers hand out grades almost daily and can't possibly treat the assigning of every individual grade as a momentous event; students, of course, tend to feel the consequences of grades more keenly. It may be good from time to time to remind yourself that the power grades often have over students is not a product of their imaginations. In many nations, opportunity for academic advancement is limited, and examination scores and grades frequently determine who goes on and who does not. Scores and grades may also determine job placement, scholarship allotments, and less tangible rewards such as respect and pride. Students cannot be expected to ignore these realities and can thus hardly be faulted for gearing their study to result in the best grades possible.

ENSURING POSITIVE BACKWASH

Here are a number of suggestions for ensuring that the backwash from your evaluation measures is positive (see also Hughes 1989, 44–47):

1. Test the skills you want students to develop, even if it is not always easy. This advice might seem self-evident, but in practice this rule is often violated. As Hughes (1989) notes, "Too often the content of tests is determined by what is *easy* to test rather than what is *important* to test" (p. 23). For example, the difficulty of interviewing large numbers of students means that interviews are not included in standardized tests such as the Test of English as a Foreign Language (TOEFL), and the result is that oral proficiency receives minimal attention from students preparing for such exams. The bottom line is that if you want students to practice a skill, you need to include it somehow in evaluation.

2. Use direct testing measures as much as possible. A *direct measure* is one that requires students to do more or less what they would need to do in real life. For example, an interview is a direct measure because it requires students to engage in real conversation. An *indirect measure,* in contrast, assesses only one discrete portion of a skill. A test in which students only pronounce words in isolation would be an indirect measure.[1] This distinction is important because the more direct an evaluation measure is, the more likely it is to have positive backwash on students. Direct measures require students to practice skills in a way that is similar to the way in which the skills would actually be used; indirect measures inevitably push students toward practicing discrete-point skills that in real life are virtually never used in isolation. (How often do people need to fill in blanks with correct verb tenses?) This is not to say that all indirect testing is bad. Properly used, it provides a rapid way to check on and encourage important aspects of

---

[1] This distinction is similar to that between *integrative* and *discrete-point* testing. See Bailey (1998, 75–77) for discussion.

language learning, such as pronunciation and vocabulary acquisition. However, evaluation for a course should not rely on indirect measures alone, and direct measures generally should carry more weight in determining grades. (For this reason, most of the evaluation measures suggested in this book are direct measures.)

3. Ensure that students know in advance how they will be evaluated. Students who are surprised by the way a midterm or final examination is designed not only are likely to do less well but also have more good reason to be resentful. In contrast, using in-class practice, homework, and quizzes to prepare students for an examination is fairer and more likely to ensure that they study in productive and appropriate ways.

Methods of Evaluation

TESTS

The backbone of evaluation in many educational systems consists of tests, especially the familiar midterm and final examinations. In fact, testing is so often the primary form of evaluation that some people tend to assume that testing and evaluation are virtually synonymous. Thus, I begin this discussion of testing by pointing out the many disadvantages of primary reliance on tests.

Many problems with tests derive from the fact that they judge the work of several weeks or months based on a single, brief performance. One undesirable result is considerable pressure and anxiety for students, often more than is productive. Because of the unusual amount of pressure that tests generate, they are especially likely to produce negative backwash, including encouraging students to engage in short, intense periods of cramming rather than regular study and practice.

Another common problem with testing derives from the types of tests commonly used in classrooms. Indirect testing with heavy reliance on true/false, fill-in-the-blank, and multiple-choice items is common. The prevalence of this kind of testing is not surprising because there is a long tradition of testing language skills in this way, and these kinds of items are used heavily in standardized tests like the TOEFL. However, backwash from this kind of testing is generally negative—students are forced to become experts at guessing how to fill in blanks rather than learning how to really use language. Hughes (1989) also notes that "good multiple-choice items are notoriously difficult to write" and that most multiple-choice tests used by schools are "shot through with faults" (pp. 3, 61).

Despite the problems, total abandonment of testing may be neither possible nor desirable. Midterm and final examinations are deeply embedded in educational systems of many countries, and you may have no choice in the matter. Another reality is that students may be confronted with other tests after leaving your course, and lack of experience in test taking would put them at a disadvantage. Finally, well-designed testing can motivate students to study and review productively. In short, the question is often not whether or not you should give tests but how to make sure that tests have the best possible backwash.

Test design and administration are topics normally addressed by a chapter or an entire book; here I suggest a few of the most basic points to which you should attend.

1. Again, use direct testing as much as possible. Direct testing tends to have better back-wash than indirect testing, and a serviceable direct test is generally easier to design than a good indirect test because fewer tricks are involved.[2]

2. If you must use multiple-choice questions, true/false items, or the like, be sure to use an adequate number. When tests only have a few items, each counts for a large percentage of the final score, and luck plays too large a role.

3. Check a test before administering it. It is not unusual for even a carefully crafted examination to have serious flaws that escape the eye of the test designer. One good way to minimize the possibility of problems is to have another teacher look over your test beforehand.

4. Use quizzes and practice tests to introduce students to your testing methods well before the midterm. This familiarizes students with the test format, gives you an opportunity to find and correct flaws in your approach, and maximizes the possibility of positive backwash by giving students a clear idea of how they should prepare.

5. Make your tests cumulative. There is little sense in requiring students to learn the material in unit 8 for the midterm only to rule it out of bounds for the final. By promising not to test students on material covered earlier in the term, you reduce language learning to a game and increase the chances that students will lose sight of the ultimate goal.

6. Investigate local testing expectations and practices before designing your examination. It may be that nobody else cares how you test your classes, but this is not always the case, and it is better to find out before running seriously afoul of local custom. Also remember that if your class is part of a larger system that includes other school- or nationwide tests, one of your testing duties may be to prepare students for those examinations.

While you may not be able to get away from testing entirely, "it is advisable to evaluate students in a number of different ways rather than to rely almost exclusively on formal exams" (Bowen, Madsen, and Hilferty 1985, 356). Concentrating evaluation in a few major examinations increases pressure, test anxiety, and the temptation to cheat or cram rather than really learn material. It also maximizes the role of chance—one bad headache can seriously affect a student's grade if the grade is based mostly on one test. Tests are best used in conjunction with other evaluation methods.

QUIZZES

Your view of quizzes may be jaded by nasty memories of pop quizzes that teachers seemed to give more for their punitive value than for any educational purpose. It may therefore come as a minor surprise that I advocate quizzes as a large part of any package of evaluation measures. However, I have my reasons. First, because quizzes are shorter than tests, you can give them frequently, thus spreading the evaluation process out over time rather than packing it into a few exams. This tends to lower test anxiety and to minimize the role of chance in determining grades. Frequent quizzes also help students get into the habit of studying regularly and discourage reliance on infrequent bouts of cramming as a learning strategy. Finally, quizzes "have even been known to

---

[2] If you need further caution on the use of multiple-choice items, see Bailey (1998, 130) for an in-depth discussion of why good multiple-test items are so hard to design. Also see Harmer (2001, 323).

help improve attendance, punctuality of arrival, and discipline at the outset of the class period" (Bowen, Madsen, and Hilferty 1985, 357). Here are a few suggestions on using quizzes (see also the suggestions given in the section on tests):

1. For maximum positive impact, give quizzes reasonably regularly, and make sure students have some idea in advance of what you expect of them. Pop quizzes—those that are unexpected and unannounced—may do more to alienate the class than to motivate study. Predictable, regular quizzes are fairer and more likely to promote study.

2. Make quiz-item formats as much like the formats of your exam items as possible. Otherwise, they may mislead students as to how to prepare for tests.

3. Keep quizzes short. It is only because of their brevity that you can find time to give and correct them regularly, and a short quiz is often all it takes to give students the extra push to do an assignment.

HOMEWORK AND IN-CLASS WORK

An obvious and important alternative to testing is evaluation based on homework assignments or in-class work. For example, writing can and should be evaluated based on many compositions rather than on one supreme in-class effort at the end of the semester. Likewise, speaking can be judged in part based on performance in many small exercises over the course of the semester rather than on one intense interview alone. Such an approach reduces fixation on examinations and shifts student attention to the daily work of study and practice.

PORTFOLIOS

Another alternative to a final exam is a portfolio, that is, a selection of students' best work that is presented for a final grade. This approach works most naturally in writing courses, where students can be evaluated on revised versions of their best compositions. However, with a little creativity, you can adapt the basic principle underlying this approach—the idea that students get to choose their best work for evaluation—to other kinds of work as well. For example, you could include reading by having students read books, write reviews, and then turn in their best ones. In a speaking course, you might ask students to write dialogues or do role plays, tape their best work, and submit the tape. The main advantages of portfolios are that they draw on all the work a student does during the semester rather than reducing judgment to one all-important test, and they also encourage students to assess, revise, and improve their own work.

SELF-ASSESSMENT

You may not want to go to the extreme of letting students determine their own final grades, but involving them in assessing their own work, at least to some degree, can be beneficial. It helps remove you from the role of sole judge and jury; more important, it forces students to take more responsibility for their own work.

Consider this self-assessment method for an oral English class. Students fill out the following three-item form at the end of each class period.[3] Such a form encourages students to assess their own effort and serves as a regular reminder that their English progress depends largely on how hard they work, not on how well the teacher performs. It also allows students an opportunity to

---

[3] This form was generously provided by Jay Lundelius from his courses in Kinjo Women's College in Nagoya, Japan.

Self-Evaluation Form

1. I tried _____ % to use English in class today.

   90–100% I tried my best to use English today. (I prepared well for this lesson before class, and I used only English with my partners.)

   80–89% I tried hard to use English today. (I prepared for this lesson before class, and I used English with my partners almost the whole time.)

   70–79% I tried to use English today. (I prepared a little for this lesson before class, and I used English with my partners most of the time.)

   60–69% I tried a little to use English today. (I didn't prepare for this lesson before class, but I used English with my partners over half the time.)

   0–59% I didn't really try to use English today. (I didn't prepare for this lesson, and I used English with my partners less than half the time.)

2. Today I think I learned:

   ❏ a lot of English

   ❏ some English

   ❏ a little English

   ❏ almost no English

3. Comments:

give the teacher feedback on a range of issues and helps the teacher stay in touch with students' responses to and feelings about the course.

Other forms of self-assessment might entail

1. **having students check their own work:** For example, after a listening exercise, you might give a copy of the text to students and have them check their own answers or summaries.

2. **requiring students to present a short critique of their work:** For example, at the end of a composition, they might be asked to state one or two of the strong and weak points of their composition. (This, incidentally, can make it easier for you to give feedback.)

3. **having students submit a tentative grade for their work, along with a rationale:** The necessity of stating a rationale should help prevent students from taking this as a joke and provides a point from which you can give students a useful reality check. It may also be instructive for you to see what students think about the quality of their work.

Grading

The first problem with grading is that many volunteer teachers (VTs) would prefer not to do it at all. It not only goes against Western egalitarian ideals, but also seems to be a nuisance that doesn't do much to further education. Most teachers will grudgingly admit that grades can help motivate students to study harder and will accept the reality that grading is a deeply rooted part of most educational systems (including their own), so they are willing to do it when they have to. However, dislike can tempt teachers to treat grading with less respect than it deserves.

Grading is not an inherent part of evaluation. In fact, if the only purpose of grades were to help students diagnose their strengths and weaknesses, grades could easily be dispensed with; comments and suggestions would generally be much more helpful to students. Grades themselves are only number or letter codes—essentially a language—indicating the degree to which a student's performance is good or bad. The purpose of grading is in part to motivate students to work harder, but grades are also used to determine which students will be given priority in selection for good jobs, further educational opportunities, and the like. When in a system that uses grades in this way, students will take the grades you give very seriously, and these grades will be a potential point of conflict.

If a grade is essentially a message indicating your assessment of a student's performance, it is important to ask yourself what message grades send to students and school authorities. As you consider this question, you need to pay attention to two special issues:

1. Working in a foreign culture, you need to make sure that your grades communicate the message you want them to. This may be more problematic than it seems because a particular grade or score may not mean the same thing in your host country that it does at home.

2. You need to consider the standard you use for determining grades and the message that your choice of standard sends to the students. Institutions or teachers often feel the need for a nice-looking grade curve, even though it means students' scores are determined as much by the scores of other students in the class as by their own performance. This approach to grading tends to focus students' attention on their class standing rather than on personal improvement. This, in turn, may have a negative effect on the motivation of weaker students in the class. These issues will be examined in more detail in the section on class-curve grading.

THE LANGUAGE OF GRADING

One problem with grading in a new country is that the grading system may appear disarmingly familiar, only to turn out to be quite different from what you expect. For example, the A–F grading system familiar to Americans is also used in other countries, but apparent similarities in the system do not necessarily mean that grades mean what they would in the United States. Different patterns of grade distribution may mean that an A– or a 73 has quite a different significance in one country than in another.[4]

Consider the contrast between the normal grade curve in China and in the United States. In China, most university English students get scores in the seventies and eighties, a distribution similar to that in the United States. The story, however, is different at the upper and lower ends of the scale. Scores in the ninetieth percentile or higher are rarer in China than in the United States and consequently indicate greater achievement than the same scores do in the United States. In contrast, scores in the sixtieth percentile are somewhat more common in China than in the United States. It might seem that U.S. VTs could easily master the grade distribution in

---

[4]Even within the United States, the same grade does not mean the same thing in all contexts. For example, for U.S. undergraduate students, a C means average—or a little below. For graduate students, who are required to maintain a B average, the same grade is essentially a failing mark.

China merely by using the one they are familiar with and lowering everything a few points. Unfortunately, it is not quite this simple. Failing grades—those below sixty—are much rarer in Chinese universities than U.S. universities (because very few Chinese university students, having made it through a rigorous set of tests to enter university, are allowed to fail and waste the training that has been invested in them), so at the lower end of the scale, U.S. VTs need to grade higher than they would in the United States.

The point is that, in a new country, you need to learn both the code used for grading and the normal pattern of grades. Questions you should ask in trying to determine how the host-country grading system works include the following:

1. What marking system is used? Grades? Scores? Something else?

2. What does a normal grade curve look like? What is the most common grade?

3. How do students view any given grade? What grade causes rejoicing? What is considered to be failure?

4. What grades indicate truly outstanding performance, and how often are they given out?

5. What grades are officially considered failing? How does the system handle failing grades? What are the consequences of failing grades?

6. How much latitude do individual teachers have in determining their own grade curves? How do students and other teachers view a teacher whose grade curve is unusually high or low?

Unfortunately, getting a clear picture of a community's grading customs is not always easy. Often there is at least some difference between the official picture and what most teachers actually do. For understandable reasons, it is not at all unusual for teachers and administrators to describe their grading practices as being stricter than they really are. This disparity causes few problems for members of the host community; from experience, they know how things really work. In fact, they may not even be aware that there are two distinct systems. However, for you as a newcomer, the disparity presents difficulties because directing a few questions to a school official may not get you all the information you need, and if you take an idealized description of strict grading policies at face value and begin giving grades that are markedly lower than those being given by your colleagues, you could rapidly become unpopular. Alternatively, if you err consistently and dramatically in the direction of high grades, you may become popular with students but something of a pariah to your colleagues.

Consequently, be persistent in trying to get as accurate a picture of the system as possible. You may need to ask a variety of people, including students (preferably from someone else's class), and to ask indirect as well as direct questions. To the extent possible, you need to find out what people actually do rather than what they say they do.

CHOOSING A STANDARD FOR GRADING

It is probably not too much of an oversimplification to say that there are two basic approaches to grading. The first and more common is to see a grade as indicating a student's ability level at a given point in time, and this is generally determined by comparing the student with his or her classmates. The other approach is to see the grade as indicating how much improvement a student has made over a period of time, in which case the student is measured against himself or herself. Here I briefly examine the advantages and disadvantages of these two approaches to grading.

Class-Curve Grading[5]

Many teachers and school systems grade using a class curve—that is, comparing the performance of the student being graded with the performance of other students in the class. As natural as grading on the curve may seem, it is inherently unfair because a students' grades are determined as much by the other students in the class as they are by the students' own ability. A young woman unfortunate enough to have unusually bright classmates—or classmates who have had more previous exposure to English—will probably be permanently consigned to lower grades than she would have had in a duller group (unless she can manage to wrest a higher class standing from some other member of the class and knock him or her down the ladder). The sting of curve grading is sharpened if used by a teacher who always reminds students to focus on improvement and constantly urges them not to compare themselves with their classmates.

I don't want to exaggerate the potential of curve grading to create bad feelings in your classes. Despite the potential unfairness of such an approach, it is used so widely that most students accept it as an inevitable part of life, rather like colds or myopia. Grading on the curve also benefits many students—there are as many winners as losers—so grading in this fashion won't alienate an entire class. But you should not underestimate the potential of this approach to alienate some of the students in a class and to undermine their incentive to learn. When grades are based on comparison with other students, students who learn more slowly—or those whose only sin was less English training before the course began—have to struggle simply to retain their current humble class ranking, and they may choose to give up rather than invest the extra effort needed to improve their class standing. They may also resent the overseer of such a system.[6]

Despite the disadvantages of curve grading, I am not suggesting that it should be done away with completely. First, eliminating class-curve grading simply isn't possible. Many if not most educational systems have it built into them, and you cannot change that fact single-handedly. Additionally, because curve grading is the norm in many school systems, students not only expect it but may even be confused by or uncomfortable with other approaches to grading.

Another reason that curve grading will not likely disappear soon is that it is too convenient. Grading on the curve is easy, especially for a beginning teacher who is still figuring out the goals of a course. Comparing the performance of a group of students on a given task takes no preparation or planning because you can use a ready-made standard for each situation—the average performance of the students in that class. As you will see, other forms of grading require more preparation. Thus, what I suggest here is that, in addition to grading on the curve, you also make a clear, genuine effort to award grades partly based on progress. This will go a long way toward restoring the motivation of weaker members of the class to keep plugging away.

Improvement-Based Grading

If the goal of a course is to help students improve their English skills, it seems only reasonable to grade students based on how much they improve rather than on their level at any particular point in time. The motivational advantage of this approach for students who start out at a lower skill level is that they still have a relatively equal chance to get good grades; higher level students also see that, in order to get a good grade, they have to improve further rather than simply coasting.

To measure improvement, you need to test students at the beginning of a course and determine their starting skill level, final grades then being awarded based on how much progress is made during the course. One common way to measure this progress is through the use of a cri-

---

[5] The technical term for this is *norm-referenced* grading. See Bailey (1998, 35–37) for further discussion.

[6] In programs that allow students to choose the course level at which they study, another problem with curve grading is that it gives students a vested interest in being placed in classes that are at too low a level for them.

Beginning (1–2): For all topics, can express self only haltingly and with difficulty; is frequently unable to express ideas at all. Often fails to understand slow, clear, simple sentences, even after repetition or clarification. Mistakes (inaccurate pronunciation, intonation, or grammar) or limited vocabulary causes communication breakdowns.

Functional (3–4): Can discuss limited range of topics (self, immediate environment) with patient interviewer. However, on other topics communication is difficult and often breaks down; interviewer's patience is tried on almost all topics. Often misunderstands or fails to understand interviewer unless ideas are clarified or repeated. Mistakes sometimes interfere with communication, and lack of vocabulary seriously hinders communication.

Intermediate (5–6): Can discuss familiar topics easily and deeper or professional topics with difficulty. Can discuss own field much better than other topics of similar complexity. On unfamiliar topics, circumlocutions and breakdowns occur; patience of interviewer may be tried. Has trouble understanding rapid or informal speech but little trouble with clear, moderately slow speech. Range of vocabulary is adequate for familiar topics but still limits communication in some areas. Mistakes are still common but don't often interfere with communication.

Advanced (7–8): Can discuss wide range of topics; discusses own field with ease. Is occasionally forced to resort to circumlocutions or explanations by lack of vocabulary, but problem is generally resolved quickly; patience of interviewer is almost never tried. Communication virtually never breaks down on any but the most obscure topics. Can understand normal speech without difficulty and can follow some informal or rapid speech; interviewer doesn't need to pay any special attention to speech. Mistakes occur but rarely interfere with communication.

Nativelike (9–10): Easily discusses a broad range of topics and can understand even informal and rapid speech. Still has foreign accent, but this causes interviewer no difficulty. Mistakes are rare and almost never affect communication.

teria system. Consider the sample scale in the box, designed for an oral skills course that stresses communicative effectiveness.[7] The idea, then, is to determine where on the scale students are at the beginning of a course and how far along the scale they progress during the course.

Given the advantages of improvement-based grading, why is it not used more often? One reason is that it requires more preparation than curve grading, especially because of the need for pretesting and a criteria system (note that designing an effective criteria system involves a clear sense of goals and a lot of work). This demands additional work from you at the early stages of the course, when you may still be focused more on getting through the next class period than on long-range plans.

Another problem with improvement-based grading is that it is difficult to see skill improvement over short periods of time, especially in broadly defined skill areas. Improvement in general skills such as reading and speaking takes place relatively slowly, and one or two months of study may not make enough difference for improvement to be noticeable. As Underhill (1987, 56) points out, this is particularly true at the advanced stages of English study, when progress becomes increasingly hard to detect. Considering the sample criteria system above, within a three-month course, students who started at level one might reach two or even three, but a student who started at four would probably still be in the four range at the end of the course.

---

[7] For a more sophisticated speaking proficiency scale, see the American Council on the Teaching of Foreign Language's (1999) *ACTFL Proficiency Guidelines—Speaking.*

RECOMMENDATIONS FOR COURSE GRADING

1. Base your grades on improvement as well as ability level. Despite the problems involved in initially setting up an improvement-based grading system, in the long run the effort involved in setting goals and designing a criteria system works to your advantage because it forces you to prepare more carefully and ultimately makes your grading process simpler and fairer. Improvement-based grading also leads to more positive backwash than curve-based grading because the former focuses attention on skills rather than classmates.

   However, as I have suggested, grading solely on improvement may be neither wise nor possible. It is difficult and problematic because the picture of student ability that such grades communicate may well be inaccurate. School authorities and others often take grades to indicate how good a student's English is, and your grades therefore need to represent ability as well as progress. It is therefore often wise to make the final grade a compromise between progress and ability. As for balancing ability and improvement (or effort) in grading, a good rule of thumb in borderline situations is to put a little extra weight on the side on which a student is stronger. One could argue that this is the fairest approach, and it is certainly the most politic.

2. Let students know how they will be graded. The most important way to ensure a sense of fairness in grading is to communicate clearly and regularly with students about what your goals and evaluation methods are, and how you will grade. You can do this by explaining your grading system to students and by being consistent in the way you evaluate. Many students will not fully understand explanations in English and will rely heavily on their experience in early tests and homework assignments to help them figure out what you are really after. Students who know what is expected of them are far less likely to become hostile over a bad grade than students who feel that they have been misled or caught by surprise.

For Thought, Discussion, and Action

1. **backwash:** Find a test paper used in your host country, and analyze it to see what kind of backwash you think it would have on students. Then, if possible, discuss your analysis with an English teacher from the host country to see if his or her analysis agrees with yours.

2. **direct test measures:** Imagine a course that you might need to teach, or choose a course you know you will teach, and then do the following:
   • Describe the course.
   • List evaluation measures you could use for the course. For any testing, use direct measures as much as possible.
   • Optional: Afterward, look at the evaluation measures suggested for the sample courses in chapter 6 as a point of reference.

3. **opinion poll:** Survey several friends (classmates, etc.) to find out the following: (1) What evaluation measures did they like least and most when they were students, and why? (2) What advice would they give for making the less palatable measures more palatable?

4. **portfolios:** For one course you will teach in your host country (or a sample course described in chapter 6), think of one or more ways you could incorporate some kind of portfolio as an evaluation measure. If possible, discuss this question with one or more teachers from your host country to see what they think about the idea of portfolios; also ask whether they have ever tried portfolios or heard of a teacher using them.

5. **self-assessment:** The chapter suggests that it may be good to include at least some student self-assessment in your courses and even to consider allowing it to influence the final grade. List ways you might adapt this idea to a course you will teach in the host country, and consider the advantages and disadvantages of using this approach. Then, if possible, discuss this question with one or more teachers from your host country to see what they think; also ask whether they have ever tried using self-assessment or heard of a teacher trying it in their country.

6. **grade curves:** From several teachers or students from your host country, get as clear a picture as possible of what local grading practices are and what the local grade curve usually looks like. Use the questions suggested in the section The Language of Grading.

7. **fair evaluation:** Discuss how to evaluate and grade in a way that motivates and encourages the weaker students in a course (those who tend to get low grades) as much as possible yet is still fair and motivating for students who tend to get good grades.

8. **improvement-based grading:** The chapter suggests that it is desirable to determine students' grades at least partially based on how much improvement they make in English (not just how they rank in comparison with their classmates). Design one or more ways to incorporate some improvement-based grading in a course you will teach. Then, if possible, show your ideas to someone who has taught in your host country, and see what he or she thinks of them.

9. **proficiency criteria:** Using the proficiency scale presented in this chapter as a model, design your own scale (e.g., for listening, reading, writing) for a course you will teach. As you design your scale, keep two things in mind:
    *   The scale will be more useful if the top and bottom ends correspond fairly well to the highest and lowest skill levels of students in the course. To be more specific, you should set the low end by the lowest skill level you think a student entering the course might have, and your top end, by the highest level you think any student might achieve by the end of the course.
    *   While the scale is partly an overall picture of students' proficiency at different levels, it should also clearly reflect the goals you set for the course so that you can assess how much progress students make toward those goals.

    For a point of reference, you could compare your proficiency scale to those established by ACTFL (http://www.actfl.org/). At the time of writing, the Web site included proficiency scales for speaking and writing. Versions of the ACTFL proficiency guidelines for listening and reading can be found on a number of Web sites and in Rubin and Thompson (1994, 15–21), Omaggio Hadley (2001, 469–76), and Marshall (1989, 41–47).

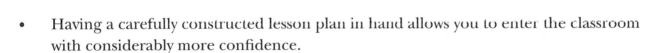

Chapter 5

Lesson Planning and Classroom Survival

- Having a carefully constructed lesson plan in hand allows you to enter the classroom with considerably more confidence.

- Effective lesson planning, especially during your early days of teaching, rests heavily in good habits such as setting aside quality time for planning and putting the plan in writing.

- One key strategy for establishing rapport with students is expressing interest in them, their country, and their nation.

- Creating a warm, friendly class atmosphere makes teaching and learning easier for all concerned. Fun is a legitimate part of the language classroom.

One of my strongest memories from my early years of teaching has to do with the never-ending search for lessons (e.g., activities, games) that "worked." For all but the most self-confident volunteer teachers (VTs), the overwhelming priority during the first few months of teaching is getting through as many class periods as possible without disasters such as exercises that take twice as long as planned, instructions that students completely misunderstand, and activities that students respond to with overwhelming apathy.

Another form of catastrophe—possibly the worst—is running out of activities when the class period is only half over. During my first year of teaching, my response when caught short was to have the class play Hangman, a harmless little spelling game that could easily dispatch half an hour of class time before everyone began to get restless. It didn't teach much English, but it allowed me to survive a class period without running out of material. In many ways, Hangman serves as a symbol of my early teaching days because the primary object of my class planning was to prevent myself from winding up like the hanging man himself, dangling in front of a class to which my inexperience had been suddenly revealed. As long as my focus was primarily on my own lack of confidence and need to avoid embarrassing myself, it was difficult to see past my needs to those of the students.

Ultimately, of course, your goal in each day's English lesson should be to provide a good learning experience for the students. However, until you have the confidence that you can get through a lesson with your dignity intact, it is difficult to focus on higher level issues such as how to use the class hour as effectively as possible. This chapter addresses the issue of planning for the class hour, with an eye to getting you past the survival stage as quickly as possible.

Basic Lesson-Planning Habits

Ideally, much of a teacher's planning should already be done even before he or she sits down to make up tomorrow's lesson plan. First, the overall course goals help determine what kinds of activities are needed and why, so that teachers don't need to start from scratch each day with the question *What will I do tomorrow?* Furthermore, having a clear sense of overall goals often helps teachers focus on a relatively limited and stable set of activities that they draw on more or less regularly for lessons, thus decreasing the amount of time that needs to be devoted to generating new ideas for the next day's class. Of course, teachers will want to build in some variety and variation from day to day lest the course become overly monotonous, but they will not need to rely too much on novelty and variety to keep the course interesting because the overall sense of purpose and direction will provide much of the drive necessary to engage students' interest and participation. In fact, as Stevick (1988, 7–8) notes, this very regularity even helps students relax in class because it gives them a sense that the teacher knows what he or she is doing. This sense of overall structure and direction also helps give teachers confidence that helps them weather days when students aren't very responsive or when an activity doesn't quite go as planned.

This description, of course, is the ideal, and it is worth working toward. However, the problem for beginning teachers is often precisely that the big picture is not yet entirely clear. While you have probably chosen tentative goals for your courses, and perhaps even a set of methods you plan to use regularly, you are also no doubt all too aware that quite a bit of trial and error lies ahead before you will be fully confident that your choices of goals and methods are good ones. At this point in your teaching life, overall course goals may be as much of a source of concern as they are of security, so for the moment your course goals have only limited value as a rock on which to anchor your sense of direction and confidence. Furthermore, your ability to predict how things will go in class—how students will respond to a given activity or how long it will take—is also probably still somewhat shaky. During the early phases of your teaching life, the confidence with which you enter the classroom is often based less in your sense of long-term goals than in the efficacy of your day's lesson plan. So it seems appropriate to begin this chapter on lesson planning and classroom survival with a discussion of the most basic—and important—lesson-planning habits that can maximize the chances of a good day in class.

The most important of these habits is also the most obvious: you need to make a plan for each lesson. A few gifted individuals can regularly wing it in the classroom and get by reasonably well, but such people are the exception rather than the rule (and many members of this select minority are more skilled at entertaining than educating). Teaching well and establishing a good classroom atmosphere are hard enough even if you prepare properly; to skimp on preparation is to beg for a lousy day in class.

The second important habit is to block out quality time in your weekly schedule for making lesson plans. Preparation can seem a rather ephemeral and undefined activity, at least when compared with classroom teaching or composition correcting, and it is therefore sometimes relegated to scraps of time left over from other activities. However, during your early days as a teacher, effective lesson planning probably places more demands on your concentration and creativity than paper grading or other activities do, so you should plan when your mind is freshest. Reserving prime time specifically for preparation ensures better lesson plans.

A third basic habit consists of writing down your lesson plans—in some detail—rather than keeping them in your head. A written lesson plan gives you something to which you can refer in class when you need to jog your memory and leaves you a written record to draw on if you want to use that particular lesson again. However, the most important advantage is that writing a plan down forces you to think it through more carefully. Class plans you dream up but do not write down have a tendency to seem more thorough than they in fact are, much in the way that a polluted river seen in dim moonlight may appear a lot nicer than it really is. Letting plans first see the light of day on paper is generally very helpful in ensuring that you have worked out the details.

The final habit is that of writing flexibility into your lesson plans. One of the hardest things for beginning teachers (and even more experienced ones) is to accurately predict how long any particular activity will take. Sometimes an activity you thought would only take a few minutes engages students for a whole class period; other times, an activity you thought would generate discussion for at least thirty minutes dies after only three. For this reason, it is wise to have contingency plans, and as you plan lessons, you should decide what parts of the lesson you can jettison if things start running overtime and what additional material you can throw into the breach if the original plan doesn't last as long as you thought. As you gain teaching experience, your ability to estimate how long activities will run (and the closely related issue of how enthusiastically students will respond to them) will gradually improve. However, the more important difference between the novice and the veteran is that the veteran has learned from hard experience that the unexpected will happen and that things rarely go entirely as planned, so it is wise to be prepared to make quick changes to the plan.

Aspects of a Lesson Plan

A BASIC LESSON PLAN FORMULA

There are as many ways to structure a lesson plan as there are different teaching situations, and no single plan can serve as a model for all situations. However, for planning many English classes, a basic initial formula would consist of the following parts:

1. **preview:** Giving students an overview of the day's lesson conveys a sense that there is a definite purpose and plan behind the day's activities. (This step may be done either before or after any warm-up activities.)

2. **warm-up:** Just as a concert often starts with a short lively piece to warm the audience up, a lesson often starts with a brief activity that is relatively lively. Its main function is to generate a good class atmosphere, but it can also be used for reviewing material from previous lessons or introducing new material in the day's lesson. Incidentally, the warm-up tends to set the tone for the lesson, and if it involves real communication, it will tend to reinforce the importance of genuine communication right from the beginning of the class period.

3. **main activities:** These are the main course of the day's menu, the more demanding activities to which most of the lesson will be devoted.

4. **optional activity:** This is an activity that you hope to use but are ready to omit if you are running out of time. (Normally, I simply designate one of my main activities as optional by marking it *If time allows* in my lesson plan.)

5. **reserve (or *spare-tire*) activity:** This is an activity that is not a key part of your lesson plan, but you have it available in case the other parts of the lesson go more quickly than planned, leaving you with unexpected time at the end of the class.

How might this formula be applied to a specific lesson? The following sample lesson plan is designed for a fifty-minute class period in an oral skills class for secondary school students.

Sample Lesson Plan

(PREVIEW) INTRODUCTION (5 MINUTES)

1. (Put the words *healthy, exercise, diet* on the board.)
2. "Today's lesson is about how to stay healthy." (Explain healthy if necessary.)
3. "One way to stay healthy is to get lots of exercise." (Explain . . . .)
4. "Another way is to have a good diet." (Explain . . . .)
5. "Today we will learn vocabulary for talking about health. We will also practice using the right part of speech (gerunds) for talking about kinds of exercise."
6. "Let's start with a warm-up exercise."

(WARM-UP) SURVEY: WHAT'S YOUR FAVORITE KIND OF EXERCISE? (10 MINUTES)

1. (Ask everyone) "What is one kind of exercise?" (As they answer me, I list two or three kinds on the board in gerund form—walking, playing basketball, swimming.)
2. Assign survey. "In a minute, please survey three or four classmates." (Explain/demonstrate survey if necessary.) Instructions:
   - Ask three or four classmates, "What is your favorite kind of exercise?" (Put the question on the board.)
   - Write down their answers—in the right form.
   - This is to practice speaking, so speak in English! If you don't know a word in English, ask me.

- You only have five minutes!
- Get up and start!

3. Debrief.
   - Have students volunteer answers—put them on the board—use gerund form.
   - Go over the words on the board (especially any new ones)—using sentence My favorite exercise is . . . .
   - Encourage students to write new words in their notebooks.

(MAIN ACTIVITY) SMALL-GROUP TASK: A HEALTHY MENU (20–30 MINUTES)

1. Tell students I am new in China and want to have a healthy diet here.

2. In groups, have students make up the best possible menu for me for breakfast, lunch, and dinner, and be ready to explain their choices to me.

3. Remind students that the purpose is to practice speaking English.

4. Debrief. Have first group give me the breakfast menu, and explain why they chose the foods they did. Then have one or two other groups report on breakfast. Then repeat for lunch, dinner.

5. Follow up by describing a healthy daily diet in the United States.

6. Close by reviewing any new words.

(MAIN ACTIVITY—IF TIME ALLOWS) DICTATION (10–15 MINUTES)

1. Dictate the following short passage to students for listening/writing practice. (Use procedure for Dictation from chapter 7.)

   (1) My favorite kind of exercise is walking. (2) Running makes my knees hurt, and it makes me too hot in the summer. (3) Swimming is nice, but I can't find a swimming pool. (4) I like walking because I can always find a place to walk, (5) and because it doesn't make me too hot.

2. Have students compare their dictations in pairs and help each other.

3. Debrief by having the students say each sentence aloud (in chorus) while I write it on the board.

4. Afterward, they check, and I walk around to see how they did.

5. Close with brief comments on their writing (e.g., capitalization, punctuation).

(RESERVE ACTIVITY) HEALTH PROVERBS

1. Put the following health-related proverbs on the board:
   An apple a day keeps the doctor away.
   An ounce of prevention is better than a pound of cure.
   Early to bed, early to rise, makes one healthy, wealthy, and wise.

2. Then have students guess what they think the proverb's meaning is and whether they agree with the wisdom contained in the proverb.

3. In pairs or groups, have students think of similar health sayings in their language and translate these into English.

4. Have groups report. Different groups will probably have translated the same sayings, so compare the translations.

5. Close by choosing the translation that seems closest to idiomatic English.

The emphasis in this course is mainly on practicing speaking and listening skills, but secondary goals include helping students build their vocabulary knowledge and their ability to use grammar structures in conversation. (The activities for this lesson are drawn from appendix B, Culture Topic Activity Ideas for Oral Skills Classes.)

OTHER NOTES ON LESSON PLANS

1. **timing:** Note that the lesson plan includes an estimated time for each activity. Initially, you may have trouble accurately estimating how much time any given activity will take. However, planning an approximate time for activities, and even writing the time into your lesson plan, is still a good idea. Doing so allows you to see how your actual chronological progress through the lesson period is matching up with what you had planned, so that you are more quickly alerted to the need to begin taking remedial measures, such as speeding the activity up, slowing things down, or preparing plan B.

2. **closure:** Note that a specifically designated closing step is written into most of the activities in the Sample Lesson Plan. Students generally feel better about ending an activity if it is somehow wrapped up and concluded rather than simply stopped, so the closing should be part of the plan. The closure step need not be very long; for example, having students quickly report what happened during their practice is a quick, light way to give a sense of closure to the activities in the plan. A teacher comment or suggestion could also provide closure.

3. **variety:** Note that while the lesson plan emphasizes oral skills practice, a dictation activity is also included to provide a break from the heavy diet of speaking practice. Students generally stay more alert if activities vary during a class period.

Managing the Classroom

All teachers have to find a classroom style that they are comfortable with, and experience is the only tried-and-true way to do this. Meanwhile, here are a few practical pointers that may make managing a classroom a little easier.

SEATING

There are two primary considerations in seating. First, you want students sitting fairly close to each other when they are engaged in pair or small-group work. Physical proximity tends to make students more willing to talk to each other because it helps create a sense of group affinity and closeness; having students relatively close to each other also has the practical advantage of helping keep the general noise level down. The second main consideration is that you want to be able to get as close as you can to as many groups as possible so that you can see and hear what they are doing and interact with them easily and naturally.

In classes where desks are easily movable and space is ample, achieving the two goals above is not particularly difficult. For pair or small-group activities, students can simply move their seats closer together, and for all-class activities, you can have students move into a row or semicircle arrangement. (Many Western teachers take it virtually for granted that the best seating pattern is a circle. For example, it allows students to have more eye contact with each other and quite literally moves the focus of the class away from the teacher, at least to some degree. However, in classes with many students, circles often become so large that students are only close to the classmates sitting to their immediate right and left, and the empty space in the middle becomes a forbidding no man's land that tends to dampen the conversational atmosphere. In contrast, traditional row seating arrangements have the advantage of placing more students close to each other. My personal solution to this dilemma is to use a semicircle or forum arrangement that allows for multiple rows, hence placing more students closer together.)

The greater challenge occurs in classrooms where the desks or chairs are lined up in rows and bolted to the floor, and problems are exacerbated if students scatter themselves as widely as possible throughout the classroom (though they often tend to avoid the front row). Such a situation, while challenging, is by no means the end of the world. For lectures or other teacher-focused activities, this seating situation does not pose serious problems, although you may want to gently but firmly require that students not all bunch toward the back of the room as far away as possible from you. (Suggestion: Officially designate a few rows toward the back of the classroom as off-limits.) For group work, the trick is to get students into groups of three or four, bunched in a square or triangle rather than spread out in a long line. (When you ask students to form their own groups, they often naturally form a group of people sitting in the same row, with the result that the group is seated in a long line and the people at the far ends often cannot hear what is going on in the center. It is better for each group to consist of students from two different rows, front and back, so that they are closer together.) Ideally, as many groups as possible should be immediately adjacent to an aisle so that you can more readily interact with them.

EYE CONTACT

Good eye contact is one of the main ways to establish and maintain a sense of student involvement in the lesson, especially when speaking to the whole class. While you do not need to catch the eye of each individual student in the classroom, you should try not to always look at a few favored students or a favored spot in the middle of the classroom. Rather, make a conscious effort to look from time to time at the students toward the sides of the classroom and at those sitting far to the back and the front.

YOUR SPEECH AND VOICE

One of the most helpful things you can do for students—and one of the most important ways to maintain a degree of control and order in the classroom—is simply to speak loudly and clearly enough for students to hear you easily. Conversely, one of the surest ways to lose students' attention and control of the classroom is to force them to strain too often and too hard to hear what you are saying. Granted, some teachers can effectively use a firm, quiet voice that motivates students to quiet down precisely so that they can hear what the teacher is saying, but this is a dangerous strategy for beginning teachers to adopt because it tends to work only when the teacher has already established a clear sense of presence and control. For most beginning teachers, the wiser strategy is speaking in a clear, reasonably loud voice that students have little trouble hearing.

A related issue is that of how quickly you should speak. When attempting to put a point across in class (e.g., giving instructions), you want to make sure that it is understood. You may therefore be tempted to make your speech as easy as possible to understand. Within bounds, this is not a bad thing, and VTs need to learn how to communicate as clearly and simply as possible. However, if your speech becomes simplified to the point that it is unnatural—for example, if all your contractions are ironed out into fully pronounced words—it loses some of its value as listening practice for students. Try to strike a balance, speaking slowly and clearly (though not unnaturally) when necessary, and a little more normally at other times in order to challenge students' ears.

Last but not least, speak with the expectation that students will listen to you. If you ask questions and do not wait for an answer, give instructions but do not insist that they be followed, or simply keep talking without seeming to care whether students are listening or not, you send the signal to students that it is OK for them to tune you out, at least much of the time. Through your manner, try to convey the message that you want students to listen and respond—and that you are willing to wait or follow up as necessary so that they do.

TEACHER TALK

There is some debate as to how much the teacher should talk in a language classroom; some practitioners feel that teacher talk should be kept to a bare minimum while others point out that teacher talk provides one of students' main opportunities for listening practice. My own feeling is that in an EFL setting, particularly one in which students have few other opportunities to hear native English, you should not be overly concerned about talking often in class. However, as noted above, listening to you may be quite demanding for students, so you need to give them opportunities to speak because they need the practice and because they may need a break from the strain of trying to follow you.

INSTRUCTIONS

One of the most common reasons discussion activities don't go well is that instructions are either too complicated or are not presented clearly. Basic tips for ensuring that instructions are understood include the following:

1. Keep instructions as short and simple as possible. Lower level students, especially those with poor listening comprehension, are easily thrown by complicated instructions.

2. Make instructions as specific and clear as possible. Vague instructions such as *Talk about . . .* don't give a clear direction. Discussion starts faster and moves with more purpose if you assign students a more specific task, such as making a list, making a decision, or designing a plan. (For more on tasks, see chapter 8.)

3. Repeat the instructions, using the same (or almost the same) wording.

4. Write down your instructions in your lesson plans, even verbatim. This permits you to repeat instructions more than once using the same words.

5. Speak more slowly and clearly than normal when giving instructions.

6. Check students' comprehension of instructions by having them repeat the instructions back to you. (Asking "Do you understand?" is generally of little use because the instinctive human response to this question is to nod your head whether or not you have any idea what the teacher is talking about.)

7. Check to see if students are actually doing the activity as you instructed. Often students appear to have understood the instructions, and they may well have thought they did, but when they begin the activity, it becomes clear that they either didn't understand all the instructions or misunderstood some of them.

MOVEMENT

One way to establish better rapport with students, as well as to maintain better control of the classroom, is to step out from behind the podium (or teacher's desk, or whatever) and move closer to the students. Physical closeness tends to create a feeling of emotional closeness, and students will tend to feel closer to you emotionally if you are near them during at least some of the lesson. I would suggest four rules of thumb for where you should be when:

1. When you need to write on the blackboard or use other things at the front of the class, stay near the front so that you don't have to constantly run back and forth.

2. When you are speaking to the whole class for extended periods, stay at the front of the classroom but as close as practicable to the front row of students. Using a semicircular seating arrangement helps in this situation because you are closer to more students.

3. When students are working on their own, or in pairs or groups, move around the classroom to check on them or simply to be nearer to them.

4. When a student is speaking to you in front of the whole class, and you want the other students to hear what is being said, move away from the student who is speaking. This may seem counterintuitive: if you are having difficulty hearing the student, your natural tendency is often to move closer. However, if you want the rest of the class to listen, move further away so that the student is forced to speak up.

QUESTION AND ANSWER

You will greatly enhance the effectiveness of a question asked to the whole class if you pause before calling on someone to answer; this ensures that everyone has the time and the motivation to think through an answer.

THE BLACKBOARD

In many classrooms around the world, the blackboard is still the teacher's primary medium for sending visual messages to students, so I conclude with a few suggestions on how to use the blackboard (or whiteboard, or other type of board).

1. Make sure your writing is large enough for people in the back to read.

2. Try not to waste a lot of time writing on the blackboard during class. If you need to write something relatively long, do so before class. (In poorer countries where students do not have access to textbooks, you may need to write the necessary material on the board so that students can copy it before or after class.)

3. Try not to talk to the blackboard. If you need to write something on the blackboard, pause for a moment and allow students a moment of respite from the sound of your voice.

4. Use the blackboard to entertain. The main attraction of many of my classes is the pathetic attempts at drawing with which I illustrate points. Students laugh at the drawings, I make my point, and the atmosphere in class is a little lighter. If you can draw well, so much the better.

5. When they are available, using devices such as overhead projectors or computers equipped with projectors has considerable advantages. However, remember that such equipment is somewhat more vulnerable to technological mishaps than blackboards are, so have a backup plan in case a bulb burns out or a virus suddenly lays your computer low.

Establishing a Good Class Atmosphere

The success or failure of an English class should not be measured primarily on its popularity—it is, after all, a class rather than a variety show—but how students respond to your lessons is a real and important question, for pedagogical as well as emotional reasons. A class that both you and the students enjoy is not only much easier to face each day but also more likely to generate positive feelings toward learning English. Of course, student response to your class is not entirely within your power to control; some students no doubt disliked school or English class long before they ever met you, and you cannot always expect to see a complete reversal in their attitudes. However, by developing a good rapport with the students and by keeping your class as interesting as possible, you can often make a significant difference in students' attitudes and response.

ESTABLISHING A GOOD RAPPORT

Perhaps the single most important step toward establishing a good rapport with the students is learning their names. In a foreign country where you have large classes and the names all seem strange to you, learning the names of all the students in a class can require a considerable investment of time and energy. However, the investment will pay significant dividends as the term goes on, and it is generally worth the effort (at least for those classes you see more often).

Gower and Walters (1983, 49) list a number of ways to learn student names, including the following:

1. At the beginning of a course, try to memorize students' names using the Name Game. Have student A say her name, have student B say his name and the name of student A, and continue until the last student has to recite the names of all the students in the class—just before you do the same. This game requires considerable concentration and tends to drag in classes with more than thirty students, but it is a good way for you to learn a lot of names quickly and to see that the students learn each other's names (if they don't know each other already). The Name Game is, incidentally, an excellent object lesson in the importance of repetition and concentration in memorizing vocabulary.

2. Have students make up name/biography cards (as suggested in chapter 2). If possible, have students attach a small photograph.

3. Keep an attendance list; this forces you to review names.

4. Especially during the first few lessons, consciously make a point of using students' names.

5. While students are doing pair or group work, spend time mentally reviewing their names.

6. Use the returning of homework assignments or papers as an opportunity to review names.

One reason learning students' names is effective in developing rapport is that it is convincing evidence of your interest in getting to know students as individuals. Another effective way to show your interest in students is simply by responding to what students say in language classes as much as—or more than—you respond to whether or not they say it correctly. This shows not only that you consider language use to be genuinely communicative but that you consider the students people whose ideas and feelings deserve to be treated with respect.

Another important approach to developing rapport with students grows out of your interest in the students' country and culture. Having students tell you about their nation and culture during class gives them valuable practice in explaining their culture in English and demonstrates your interest in learning more about them and the culture that shapes them.

KEEPING CLASS INTERESTING

I have mentioned several of the most important ways to keep class interesting, but a quick review here may be helpful.

Ensuring that students have a clear sense of direction and progress will go a long way toward maintaining morale. As suggested, setting specific, narrow course goals allows students to more readily perceive progress, and regularly reminding students of why they are doing what they are doing is also helpful.

Regular use of communicative activities helps keep class more interesting. One of the perennial favorite pastimes of the human race is chatting; most people love to talk about themselves, their activities, other people, world events, and just about everything else, and there is no reason not to take advantage of this interest in the classroom. Language practice activities that allow students to say what they want to say are inherently more interesting than noncommunicative drills.

One of the newer buzzwords in English teaching is the term *information gap*. The idea is that you structure a communicative activity so that student A knows something that student B doesn't, thus ensuring that A has something to communicate. (This is in contrast to situations in which both partners already know what the other is going to say, a situation not uncommon in dialogue practice.) One of the best things about teaching English in a foreign country is that when you communicate with students, you do not need to create an artificial information gap because the difference between your culture and theirs provides an incredibly rich fund of interesting topics to communicate about. Students will generally be quite curious about your country and its ways and willing to initiate the greenhorn (you) into the mysteries of their own culture. Some of the most memorable compositions I have ever read were stories my students wrote about life in southern China during their childhoods; likewise, one of the speaking-class activities I always look forward to is having my Chinese students pick China's top ten heroes, listening to the rationales they present for their choices, and then responding with a few U.S. heroes of my own. Taking advantage of this information gap whenever possible allows you to raise the interest level of your class while teaching and learning about something that is important in its own right.

Another way to enhance interest levels is by giving language learning activities some of the appeal of games. You can do this with many kinds of activities by introducing an element of fun and lighthearted competition. Consider a few examples:

1. Conversation activities often seem more enjoyable if some kind of choice needs to be made. For example, a mock job interview becomes more interesting if you have the employers interview more than one prospective employee and then announce which candidate they decided to hire and why.

2. Content lessons can be livened up by introducing them with a short contest. For example, instead of just launching into a lecture on U.S. holidays, divide students into groups and give them a few minutes to list as many holidays and their dates as possible. Reward the group that compiles the best list with praise or whatever else you have in adequate supply. You can do the same with vocabulary (e.g., lists of colors, animals, feelings) or even grammar (e.g., lists of mass nouns, ways to describe things in the future).

3. Even subjects as drab as spelling or vocabulary can become a bit more interesting if you turn them into contests (spelling bees being a case in point). I, for example, liven up my Chinese vocabulary memorization by competing against myself. Each day as I look at my vocabulary list, I check to see if I can quickly and accurately pronounce the Chinese characters and state their meaning. If I can't, I have to review the word but leave it on the list. When I get one right, I allow myself the satisfaction of crossing it off my list.

Finally, part of the art of being a good teacher is knowing when to lighten the pressure a little by scheduling what I call *candy:* a game, song, or film for class. All of these can have educational as well as recreational value, but teachers would be kidding themselves if they didn't admit that they often use such activities more because students like them than because they offer the most efficient road to language proficiency. However, remember that one of the most important goals of any language program is to help students become more interested in studying the language, and a song that makes up for weakness in grammar teaching efficacy by kindling a student's desire to learn may affect the student long after a grammar point would be forgotten.

For Thought, Discussion, and Action

1. **lesson plans (task A):** Imagine that the following dialogue is from a textbook you will teach, and design an outline plan for a lesson that is based on use of this dialogue. Use the Sample Lesson Plan from this chapter as a model.

   > (Han, a teacher who is applying for a job as a translator, is being interviewed by Bob. Pay special attention to verb tenses.)
   >
   > Bob: Please tell me about your education, Mr. Han.
   > Han: I graduated from Zhongshan Teachers College in 1965. I was an English major.
   > Bob: How about your work experience?
   > Han: I have been teaching in Hua Dong middle school for the past thirty years.
   > Bob: Have you ever been a translator?
   > Han: No. I have always been a teacher.
   > Bob: Why are you applying for this job?
   > Han: Because I don't like children very much.

2. **lesson plans (task B):** Choose a lesson or unit from a local English textbook (preferably one that is widely used), and make a lesson plan for a two-hour class period. If possible, discuss your plan with a teacher from your host country.

3. **information gap:** Imagine you are teaching the dialogue in number 1 above and you want students to use the dialogue as a model for practice conversations in pairs. However, you also want to ensure that there is an information gap in the exercise. List three ways you could modify the activity so that there is an information gap. Also write out the exact instructions that you would give students before the activity.

4. **tasks:** You want students to practice talking about different kinds of jobs, but you want to give them a more precise task than just saying "Talk about jobs." (1) Design one or more specific pair or small-group tasks that involve conversation about jobs. (2) Write

out the exact instructions you would give students before the activity. (After you finish, check the speaking activity tasks suggested in chapter 8 for reference.)

5. **student feedback:** In many cultures, students would be reluctant to give negative feedback to a foreign teacher. (1) List some alternative strategies for finding out how students are responding to your course, and (2) ask someone who has taught in the host country how realistic (appropriate, effective) your proposed strategies might be.

6. **What would you do?** List several classroom management problems you anticipate or are concerned about (e.g., students who persistently talk while you are talking, who never speak in class, or who repeatedly miss class without explanation). (1) List possible strategies for dealing with each. (2) Discuss your strategies with a friend, classmate, or someone with experience teaching in the host country. (Some potential problems are discussed in chapter 14.)

7. **games (task A):** Choose one or more language-based games you know (e.g., Hangman, Scrabble) and analyze their value for English teaching. List what language skills or knowledge they could be used to teach; also note the skills and knowledge that they would not teach.

8. **games (task B):** Imagine that you want students to memorize the dialogue in lesson plans (task A) in class, but you want to make this activity as much like a game as possible. (1) List several ways you could turn this activity into a game. (2) Pick the one that seems most promising (i.e., enjoyable or interesting) and write out the instructions you would give students for the activity.

9. **songs:** Pick an English song that you like, and consider how you might use it as a language teaching activity. (1) Analyze and list the language points you could use the song to teach. (2) Design a teaching activity using the song that would effectively teach useful language knowledge or skills. List the steps of the activity and the instructions you would give.

Chapter 6

Putting It All Together: Sample Course Plans

It seems only right to conclude this section of the book with a few examples of what a plan for a semester course might look like. This chapter presents several teaching situations commonly confronted by English teachers in EFL settings and general course plans and typical lesson plans for each. These should give you some idea how to integrate the material in previous chapters to produce a plan for a course; with a few alterations, perhaps you could even use one of these as a preliminary plan for one of your own courses.

Course One: Beginning General English

SITUATION

This secondary school English course is for a class of fifty students who have had little previous English study. The students have already studied a few basic grammar structures and some vocabulary and can say a few common phrases, but they understand very little of what you say in class—including most classroom directions. This required course is part of the regular curriculum, so students expect to do some homework most evenings. The textbook for the course contains simple dialogues, short readings, vocabulary, and grammar notes. Your school expects you to teach the material in the book.

GOALS

Because this course is part of a larger program, you need to teach certain material so that students are ready for the following course next year. To a large degree, then, the textbook will determine what material you teach and which skills you emphasize. You can certainly set some of your own goals, however. One should consist of building students' listening skills so that they can follow directions in class and teaching them to ask questions so they can get the information they need in class. A second should be to help students see that English is a tool for communication, not just a subject for classroom study.

METHODS

- Have students study new vocabulary and grammar structures as homework as much as possible; the short readings can also be studied at home. This leaves much class time free for practice.

- Use in-class listening exercises to review vocabulary and build listening skills, especially the ability to understand classroom directions in English.

- Read the dialogues aloud and have the class repeat after you. This may be a good way to work on intonation and pronunciation and to ease students into more challenging speaking tasks.

- Have the students practice the dialogues in pairs—first as memorized set pieces and then as freer conversations. In this way, the students will get some practice in speaking and using new grammar structures and vocabulary.

- For the readings, encourage students to practice asking information questions (e.g., *What does . . . mean?*). Also, use material from the readings to create reading exercises (e.g., write statements on the board to which students are required to respond with *true* or *false*).

- Combine listening and elementary writing by asking students to write down short sentences as you say them (dictation). You could also ask students to write short dialogues.

EVALUATION

You should try to integrate your testing and evaluation methods with those of the rest of the program, finding out what methods other teachers use and following suit. However, you also need to see that your evaluation process encourages the kinds of practice you want. If your school generally only uses midterm and final examinations, you might want to give occasional quizzes to encourage students not to put all their study off until the night before the exam. If the testing methods generally used in your school do not create positive backwash for communicative language use, you might give listening quizzes or grades for participation in pair practice.

TYPICAL LESSON PLAN

1. **warm-up:** For example, give students practice in understanding classroom directions by giving directions in English (e.g., *open your books, find a partner*) and having students do what you ask.

2. **review of homework vocabulary:** For example, embed new vocabulary in simple sentences that are factually either true or false. Then say the sentences (or write them on the board), and have students respond with *true* or *false*.

3. **review of homework reading passage:** For example, first encourage students to ask questions about the reading; your responses then serve as listening practice. Then check comprehension by dictating simple questions. Have students first write down the questions and then answer them.

4. **choral dialogue reading:** Read the dialogues chorally, then have students practice the dialogue in pairs.

5. **preview of next lesson:** Introduce one or two points (sentence structures, grammar points, words, or phrases) from the next lesson by using the material in informal question-and-answer with students; see if the students can figure the new material out for themselves by guessing from context.

Course Two: Intermediate Oral English

SITUATION

This intermediate-level conversation course is for a large class of university students (not English majors). The students have already studied English for several years (mostly vocabulary, grammar, and reading) but have weak speaking and listening skills. They come from a variety of different majors, so it is not clear how they might use English after graduation. They seem enthusiastic, but this is not a core course, so they will probably not have much time to do English homework. (The course was recently added to the curriculum to encourage students to build strong oral English skills, but it is not integrated into the rest of the program and meets only once a week for two hours.) There is no textbook or tape for the course. No photocopy machine is readily available. You have a fairly free hand with the course because you do not need to consider a standardized test or follow-up course.

GOALS

The only goal set by the school is to improve students' spoken English, but you should probably also set some goals that are narrower and at least a little more specific. Obviously, the main goal should be to give students an opportunity to practice conversation using the English they have already studied. You may also wish to teach some new vocabulary, phrases, or grammar to facilitate classroom exercises, but as a secondary priority. A content element in the course could be based on a series of common social situations (e.g., making conversation with a new acquaintance, politely refusing an invitation) and the cultural and language knowledge necessary for dealing with these situations. Another goal might be to get students in the habit of practicing English with each other outside class—two hours a week of in-class practice won't result in much improvement in their speaking skills.

MATERIALS

Because there is no textbook, you may want to create your own. Make a list of situations that you wish to cover in class. If you don't have a book with a ready-made list, look through other English textbooks for ideas (see also appendix B). For each situation, write a short model dialogue containing vocabulary, phrases, or structures relevant to the situation. The dialogue should also be a good model of appropriate cultural interaction. Pertinent cultural information (e.g., what constitutes an acceptable excuse for refusing an invitation) might be presented as a brief talk or embedded in the model dialogues.

METHODS

- In class, use dictation or dictocomp (see chapter 7) to give the students listening practice and as a way to dictate your "textbook" to them, lesson by lesson.

- Spend class time on speaking practice based on the situations (e.g., practice dialogues, role plays).

- As a focus of class practice, discuss cultural issues raised by the situation or comparison of Western culture with the host culture.

- If possible, have students practice speaking in pairs or groups outside class. Alternatively, if you can make and reproduce tapes and students have access to tape players, listening homework would be a good use of their time.

EVALUATION

For this kind of course, you will probably have to give a final grade, but it may not count for very much and hence may not be a very potent motivator for students. The best approach to such situations is often to do enough testing to show that you take the course seriously but to be rather generous with your grades. In short, this situation calls for the carrot more than the stick.

If possible, do beginning and final interviews—either with individuals or groups—to encourage students to practice communicative conversation during the course. Participation grades based on in-class pair and group practice would also reinforce the message that the main goal of the course is to practice and build skills. Quizzes or tests that require students to write dialogues dealing with the kinds of situations discussed in class would be another way to assess mastery of language and culture points.

TYPICAL LESSON PLAN

This plan is for a lesson on how to politely borrow something.

1. **warm-up:** For example, ask to borrow things from several students, using the language you want to introduce. If the class likes to joke around, ask to borrow some absurd items or offer to return things after ridiculously long periods of time. This tests their listening and introduces the idea that there are cultural rules about what can be borrowed from whom for how long.

2. **dictation of model dialogue:** Dictate a model dialogue (which you have written) that contains the language and culture points you wish to introduce (e.g., *Could I borrow . . . ? Would you lend me . . . ? I need this because . . . . Would it be all right if I gave this back tomorrow?*).

3. **pair practice:** Using the material in the model dialogue, have the students politely borrow things from each other. As they get the hang of this, you might introduce ways to politely refuse to loan something.

4. **practice activity:** Have the students try to borrow as many things as possible from as many other students as possible. Insist that in order to borrow, they need to come up with good reasons—and the same for refusing to lend.

5. **discussion/talk:** Have a discussion with students about the "rules" in the host country for borrowing money (books, notes, etc.)—who can you borrow from, how much can you borrow, and for how long? Compare the answers with those for Western culture.

6. **homework:** Have students meet in pairs or small groups to repeat the activity (above) to practice the material from the dialogue. For the next class, they should be ready to report what happened.

Course Three: Intermediate English for the Test

SITUATION

This general university English course prepares students for a standardized examination. The students are non-English majors who have studied English for several years. They can understand classroom directions and simplified talks as long as you speak slowly and clearly, and they can express themselves in basic spoken English; their reading skills are stronger, although they tend to read slowly and use their dictionaries often. The required textbook consists mainly of reading passages, vocabulary lists, and grammar notes and exercises. At the end of the year, the students have to take a standardized examination that has reading, vocabulary, grammar, and listening sections. Student interest in the course does not appear very strong, although they are willing to do some homework because they want passing scores on the standardized examination.

GOALS

Obviously, the main goal of the course should be to prepare students for the examination. However, an important secondary goal should be to get students to see English as a tool for communication—not just a test subject. If students do not become interested in English, they may cheerfully abandon it as soon as the test is over.

METHODS

• Use in-class time for relatively communicative forms of language practice. Because of the pressure of the examination, students will probably be willing to study grammar and vocabulary and to do listening and reading practice as homework.

• In class, review and practice grammar and vocabulary through speaking exercises.

• Focus in-class reading practice on skimming and reading for main ideas. (These skills are useful both for test situations and for real-life reading.)

- For listening practice, give talks based on topics from the reading texts, using vocabulary introduced in the texts.

EVALUATION

Aspects of the course not directly related to student examination performances are probably best not included in the grading process—you will need to sell these to students on their inherent interest and value. Tests modeled on the standardized examination would help students prepare for it.

TYPICAL LESSON PLAN

(This plan is for a one-hour lesson introducing conditional sentences and containing a story about a girl who finds a lot of money.)

1. **warm-up:** For example, ask the students, "What would you do if somebody gave you $100?" Follow up with pair practice.

2. **discussion of the reading text:** Have the students ask any questions they have about the homework reading text. Then check comprehension by orally asking a few questions and having students write short answers.

3. **practice activity/survey:** Have the students practice using conditional sentences by surveying each other about what they would do if somebody gave them a million dollars.

4. **talk:** Give a short talk related to the reading text and using vocabulary from it. Have students take notes. Follow up with comprehension questions.

5. **preview of next lesson:** Prepare for the next reading text by quickly skimming it in class.

Course Four: Preparation for Study Abroad

SITUATION

This special one-semester preparation course is for people who are going abroad to study for graduate degrees in an English-speaking Western country. The students can read a broad range of materials in English, although they tend to read slowly, carefully, and with much dictionary use. They can understand much of what you say on general topics as long as you speak slowly and clearly, but they have trouble with natural or quick speech, and there are many words that they can read but don't understand when they hear them. The students are well motivated, but most have jobs and sometimes cannot come to class or do homework. The course textbook consists mainly of articles about life abroad, and the articles are read aloud on an accompanying tape.

GOALS

Building reading skills should be a primary goal of this course because, for academic work in the West, these students will need to learn to cope with large reading assignments quickly. They will also need to be able to follow lectures, even those that contain unfamiliar vocabulary and are not delivered in standard English (faculty may be from a variety of countries). Students will need to be able to discuss readings, express their own opinions, and critically evaluate readings. If time permits, introducing the basics of writing an academic paper would also be desirable.

METHODS

- In class, build students' listening skills by giving talks on subjects such as culture, study skills, and university life and by having students practice note-taking. The talks should challenge students' listening skills and force them to guess.

- In class, have students practice skimming articles to get the gist as quickly as possible. Focus the discussion of readings on analysis of the author's main ideas, bias, and assumptions.

- For practice of many basic academic writing skills, have students write critiques of the readings.

- Have students work independently at home as much as possible. In particular, encourage them to read as much as possible outside class, using whatever materials are available but limiting dictionary use.

- Because the students' reading skills are stronger than their listening skills, a good approach to listening homework might be to have the students first listen to the tape, taking as many notes as possible, and then check their comprehension by reading.

EVALUATION

Students in such a class will probably already be quite motivated to improve as much as they can before departure, so formal evaluation might not even be necessary except to help students pinpoint weaknesses. To encourage students to work as much outside class as possible, you could offer to go over any work they do independently. For example, encourage students to tell you about any extra reading they do. If they want to practice writing, you might suggest that they write and submit short reviews of books they read.

TYPICAL LESSON PLAN

1. **warm-up:** For example, give anyone who independently read a book or article the chance to do a quick review and recommendation for the class.

2. **small-group discussion of readings:** Have students in groups quickly discuss the homework reading, answering questions like these: What were the main ideas of the text? Was the author objective? Was this a good article? Stress that students need to explain and back up their opinions.

3. **large-group discussion:** Have the groups report their decisions and then discuss them. During the discussion, answer questions about the reading.

4. **talk:** Give a talk on a topic related to the reading, using some of the new vocabulary introduced. Have the students practice taking notes.

5. **preview/reading practice:** Have the students skim the next article under time pressure.

Course Five: TOEFL Preparation

SITUATION

This private night school course is for advanced-level students, many of whom are preparing to take the Test of English as a Foreign Language (TOEFL) in the hope of studying abroad. The class meets two evenings a week. The school has provided a textbook that has dialogues and readings about life in the West. You have obtained a book with sample TOEFL materials, but the students don't have a copy. This course is not a TOEFL course per se, but you know that in advertisements for the course the school claims that it helps people prepare for the TOEFL, and this is the reason approximately half of the students are in your class. The others are interested in improving their English for a variety of reasons.

GOALS

In this course, helping students prepare for the TOEFL is clearly important, but you also need to provide a general English course that will benefit students who will not take the TOEFL. TOEFL items include grammar, vocabulary, listening comprehension, reading comprehension, and writing, so a good strategy would be to strengthen students' skills in these areas in ways that will enhance their test performance and improve their ability to use English for other purposes.

METHODS

- It is probably safe to assume that students who want to take the TOEFL will be willing to invest extra time doing TOEFL-related homework, so you might organize them at the beginning of the course to copy parts of your TOEFL book for their homework. This will give them a chance to practice TOEFL-specific skills without requiring the whole class to spend a lot of time doing multiple-choice grammar or vocabulary items. Other students in the class can do homework from the course text.

- Reading exercises that stress rapidly getting the gist of a text would benefit both the test takers and the non–test takers. You can add a speaking component to these exercises by having students read a passage, then try to answer comprehension questions on their own, and finally discuss their answers in small groups.

- Listening exercises modeled roughly on TOEFL items would be useful to anyone in the class.

- A useful approach to writing practice would be to find out what kind of writing is required by the current TOEFL and use it as a vehicle for teaching more general writing skills.

EVALUATION

In a private school, grades are likely to be unimportant or not given at all. Since students have presumably paid for the course, they are likely to be self-motivated. Feedback on performance would thus be more useful than emphasis on scores. For students who are interested, you might organize a practice TOEFL that simulates the general format, rules, and time pressure of the examination.

TYPICAL LESSON PLAN

1. **warm-up:** For example, start with a short listening comprehension exercise based on and using vocabulary from the homework reading. The format might be modeled on one kind of TOEFL item.

2. **question and answer:** Answer any questions the students have about language points in the homework reading.

3. **small-group discussion:** Have students in small groups discuss comprehension questions about the reading, covering both content and reading-between-the-lines issues, such as main idea and author bias. Close with a large-group discussion.

4. **writing:** Have the students write a short in-class essay following a TOEFL-type format. Follow up with class discussion of ways to organize an essay on the essay topic.

5. **preview of next lesson:** If time permits, quickly skim the next reading assignment.

Course Six: The English Club

SITUATION

This informal evening class, which is open to anyone, meets once a week for English conversation practice. The students who come have a huge range of skill levels. There is little consistency in who shows up or how large the group is. Some students are very interested in improving their English, and others are mainly interested in having fun and meeting new friends. There is no textbook, and no examination is expected. The sponsors' only stated goal is that participants improve their English, but an important implicit goal is that participants enjoy the class.

GOALS

With such a wide range of skill levels and no consistency in attendance, you should not expect to carry out an organized program of study. More realistic goals would be to give students a chance to practice their speaking and listening in a communicative setting and let them have as much fun as possible in the process.

METHODS

- Use games for warm-ups, conversation practice, and opportunities for people to meet each other.

- Use many pair and small-group activities because they allow students to work at their own level much more than large-group activities do. Interviews and opinion surveys are especially good because they are conceptually simple—and thus can be done even by beginning-level students—yet can result in in-depth conversations. (For ideas, see appendix B.)

- Give simple talks introducing Western culture so students have a chance to improve their listening and learn something interesting.

EVALUATION

Probably none.

TYPICAL LESSON PLAN

(This plan is for a lesson on occupations.)

1. **warm-up:** For example, start with a game, especially one in which students meet and chat briefly with others in the class they don't know (e.g., *Find the person in the class whose birthday is closest to yours, and be prepared to introduce him or her*). Close with introductions of anyone you haven't seen before.

2. **survey:** Briefly introduce the topic and a few key language items. Based on the topic, give students one or more questions, and ask them to conduct a quick survey of their classmates (e.g., *What are the most difficult jobs?*). Close with survey results from a few volunteers.

3. **talk:** Give a short talk on the general topic, introducing Western culture and comparing it with the local culture.

4. **small-group discussion:** Allow students to divide themselves into groups (so that they work with others they are comfortable with), and give them a discussion question (e.g., *Which occupations are more suitable for women, and which are more suitable for men?*). Close the exercise with reports from a few groups and general class discussion.

Course Seven: The Last English Course

SITUATION

This general English course is for students who will finish a three-year training program at the end of the semester and begin working as secondary school English teachers. A reading text is available for your course, but the school has given you considerable freedom to decide what you will teach and what materials you will use. The students have a fair command of basic grammar and vocabulary, can understand clear English, and can read newspaper and magazine articles—although only with difficulty and the help of a dictionary. After graduation, these students will work in areas where there are few naturally occurring opportunities to use English outside their classrooms, and when teaching they will only need to use very basic English. (Many of their English teaching colleagues will not use English in class at all.) Under these circumstances, it is not unusual for the skills of graduates to gradually deteriorate. There are few local opportunities for students to use English, but there is a locally published weekly newspaper in English, and English language radio broadcasts can be received almost everywhere in the country.

GOALS AND MATERIALS

For students in this last semester, becoming more independent and self-motivated as language learners and learning how to design and carry out language learning projects (LLPs) is probably more important than covering one more textbook. Given the availability of the English newspaper and radio broadcasts, these resources would seem to be a reasonable focus for your course in the hope that greater familiarity will increase the likelihood that students will take advantage of these after graduation.

METHODS

- Set up a program of reading the English language newspaper, especially skimming through and picking out interesting material rather than slowly working through all of each issue.

- Set up a program of listening to radio news. Have students choose the types of stories they will focus on according to their interests.

EVALUATION

Since the goal is to encourage students to be self-motivating, you should minimize evaluation in favor of encouragement. If possible, dispense with testing altogether, and instead have students do self-reporting of how much they read and listen. If they don't begin evaluating their own progress now, they will be less ready to do it after they graduate. If you need to give a grade for the course, you might either give fairly easy quizzes and tests or have students write reports on what they read and listen to.

TYPICAL LESSON PLAN

1. **warm-up—bulletins of the day:** Have students report what they heard on the previous night's news. You are available to answer questions about vocabulary, names, or whatever students ask.

2. **small-group discussion:** Have one or two students take responsibility for organizing a small-group discussion of one of the articles from this week's newspaper. The discussion leaders assign discussion questions and manage the time. You circulate among the groups to answer questions or join in the discussion until the leaders call a halt. Then, as the groups report, be available to answer questions and make comments.

3. **closure:** Close, for example, by asking for predictions related to a number of ongoing stories in the news. Students can check their guesses when listening to the news that night. (See chapter 7 for more discussion of courses based on radio news.)

PART II

Aspects of English Teaching

The first six chapters of this book have described how to construct a language course. Part II examines in more detail the basic building blocks used in constructing a language course. Chapters 7–10 address four basic language skills: listening, speaking, reading, and writing. Chapters 11 and 12 consider vocabulary and grammar, and chapter 13, the role of culture in language teaching. Chapter 14 concludes with discussion of some of the problems most often faced in EFL classrooms.

Chapter 7

Listening: Putting the Horse before the Cart

- In many settings, listening is the language skill used most often and the channel through which students get much of their language input. Developing listening skills is thus even more important than developing speaking skills.

- Students need to learn to use both bottom-up and top-down strategies when listening.

- Even in places where there are few chances to speak English, there may be relatively more opportunities to listen to it, so listening skills are a good target for breakthrough-type plans.

One of my most frustrating language experiences occurred in 1978 during a summer in Russia. I had recently completed a college minor in Russian, and even though I was under no illusion that I was fluent, I assumed that I would at least be able to cope with basic conversation. I was thus disheartened to discover that, when confronted with real Russians in conversational situations, I was virtually helpless. The problem was not my speaking skills; I could generally make myself understood, if only imperfectly. The real problem was that I could understand almost nothing that I heard—everything seemed to be a blur of sound that was less clear and much faster than the Russian my teacher had always used in class.

Consequently, my speaking skills were virtually useless because I had no idea what to say. Even as simple an act as buying books involved emotional trauma because, when I plucked up my courage and asked the price in Russian, I could never understand the response. After several futile attempts to communicate with me verbally, the clerks generally resorted to writing or holding up fingers. Naturally, this was quite humiliating for someone who had spent three years in Russian classes, and I was frequently tempted to preserve my pride by pretending I had never studied any Russian at all.

Unfortunately, my experience with Russian is typical of that of many English learners. Bowen, Madsen, and Hilferty (1985) comment, "Students with ten years of English instruction and even more find that when they arrive [in an English-speaking country] they have major difficulties trying to comprehend even simple sentences of spoken English" (p. 83). This happens in part because many language programs—intentionally or accidentally—devote more attention to speaking skills than to listening skills. Another reason is that even when provided, listening practice often consists of the teacher's slow, clear classroom speech or language tapes on which unrealistically clear and formal voices read aloud materials that students have already read in their textbook. For students whose goal is to listen to native English speakers, listen to the radio, or watch films, such a diet is inadequate.

Students with weak listening skills face several problems. The first, illustrated by my example, is that they cannot function well in most conversational settings no matter how well they can speak. In contrast, students whose listening skills are good but who do not speak well can generally at least keep a conversation going by being good listeners and occasionally responding with simple questions, short answers, or even grunts and nods. A second problem is that much of students' language input normally comes from what they hear, and if this channel is blocked, students will learn less new English. So an emphasis on speaking at the expense of listening puts the cart before the horse, resulting in a learning process that is slower and more difficult.

A third problem arises from the frequency with which listening skills are used; as noted in chapter 3, listening may well be the most often used language skill. Hedge (2000) points out that "of the time an individual is engaged in communication, approximately 9 percent is devoted to writing, 16 percent to reading, 30 percent to speaking, and 45 percent to listening. It is also undoubtedly the case that contemporary society exhibits a shift away from printed media and toward sound, and its members therefore need to develop a high degree of proficiency in listening" (pp. 228–29). Even in EFL settings where native speakers of English are few and far between, students can often listen to English radio programs, television, or films, but students who have not had much listening training will be ill-prepared to take advantage of these opportunities. This is especially unfortunate in that, given the scarcity of other opportunities to use English in many EFL settings, listening represents one of the few realistic targets for a breakthrough of the type described in chapter 3.

Listening Skills: The Problem and the Goal

For native speakers, listening is so natural and easy that they may underestimate how difficult listening in a foreign language is. However, a student trying to understand spoken English is confronted with an impressive range of obstacles and has to learn to

1. hear small differences between English sounds (e.g., the subtle differences between the vowel sounds in *fear, fair, fire, far,* and *fur*)

2. comprehend reduced forms of pronunciation, which are very common in normal spoken English (e.g., *fer* for *for; ta* for *to; wanna* for *want to*)

3. attend to intonation or emphasis cues (E.g., only intonation and emphasis distinguish "You want *him* to go?" from "You want him to *go!*")

4. adjust to regional, class, or group accents

5. understand a great deal of vocabulary when they hear it (This often presents serious problems for learners in EFL settings because they learn most vocabulary through reading.)

6. understand grammar structures

7. understand rapid speech (Even speech in which students know all the vocabulary and grammar may be impossible to understand if it comes faster than students can process it. As Ur 1981, 19, notes, this is especially true when students listen for longer times because, as fatigue from listening to an unfamiliar language sets in, comprehension drops.)

8. develop a range of cultural background knowledge (Lack of background information can deprive students of vitally important clues for comprehending a message; it also reduces their ability to predict what they might hear; see chapter 13.)

When you consider all the ways in which a spoken English sentence can trip up students, you may find it miraculous that students ever learn to understand English at all. Fortunately, students do not need to be able to cope with every aspect of every utterance in order to comprehend. As Omaggio Hadley (2001, 179) describes it, the process of comprehension is much like that of completing a puzzle. Learners don't need to have every piece of the picture in place in order to make sense of it; at some point, the puzzle pieces that learners do understand allow them to guess at the whole picture, and this hypothesis guides the process of completing the picture.

Listening comprehension involves two basic processes, one known as *bottom-up* processing and one known as *top-down*. To understand these, imagine that you are a student who sees your English teacher on a crowded sidewalk and hears her say a muffled sentence including the words "How . . . today." One way you make sense of the sentence is through bottom-up processing—using the smaller pieces of the picture to figure out the larger picture. In this case, you use the words you heard—*how* and *today*—as data to help you understand the sentence. The other way to make sense of what the teacher said is through top-down processing—using background knowledge to guess what goes in blank spots in the picture. As Ur (1984) points out, "A real-life listening situation is normally rich in environmental clues as to the content and implications of what was said" (p. 5), and in the example, the context makes it fairly likely that the teacher's murky utterance was some kind of greeting. This knowledge helps you fill in the missing words.[1]

---

[1] For a detailed and entertaining introduction to bottom-up and top-down processing, see Bailey (1998, 47–49).

The analogy of completing a puzzle, as useful as it is for understanding the comprehension process, goes astray at one point: it implies that the goal is to complete every last piece of the puzzle. However, as Hedge (2000) notes,

> Many language learners fail to realize that when they listen to their first language, they do not actually hear every word. They also fail to appreciate that we integrate linguistic knowledge with our existing experience and knowledge of such things as topic and culture, and do not need to hear every word. This means that learners often have unrealistic expectations and try to understand each word of a listening text. (p. 237)

Unfortunately, many learners set this goal for themselves because it was the one language teachers set for them in their early years of English study. Learners who have this expectation may have trouble with listening at higher levels because they tend to freeze when they come across words or phrases they don't understand.

The real goal in most listening is not to understand every word but to comprehend the information that the listener wants or needs from a message. In the previous example, the key is for the student to realize that the sentence beginning with "How . . . today" was probably a greeting; whether it was "How are you today?" or "How're ya doing today?" makes little difference. In some cases, a listener needs a high degree of comprehension (and retention); more often, getting the gist of a message is sufficient, and the rest is ignored or quickly forgotten.

These points have two important implications for learning and teaching listening skills. The first is that, in listening practice exercises, you do not need to expect 100 percent comprehension in all cases. The expectations you set for listening exercises, like the goals of listening in real life, should be appropriate to the situation, and you should often ask only that students work to understand the main points of a message.

The second implication concerns teaching methods. In real life, even native speakers do not always understand or hear every word when they are talking with someone or watching television—people mumble, cars pass by, and so forth. In most cases, however, these gaps do not cause serious communication problems because native speakers are skilled at filling them in; using situational or linguistic clues, they can guess much of what they did not hear or understand. Likewise, as students practice listening skills, they need to practice using top-down as well as bottom-up strategies—using all the clues available to help them guess.

Some obstacles to listening comprehension should probably be discussed and practiced in isolation; for example, comprehension of reduced forms deserves some special attention, especially if you are working with intermediate- or advanced-level learners. However, in general, the best approach to building listening skills is ample practice listening to the teacher, tapes, or whatever material is available.

Listening Tasks in Class

The basic listening comprehension activity consists of a few elements:

1. **text:** Here *text* simply means something to listen to—for example, a story told by the teacher, a dialogue on a tape, or a TV show.

2. **context:** As I have pointed out, in real life most listening takes place in a context that provides clues for listeners as they try to comprehend a text. (This is in contrast to many language tests, in which students are often asked to listen to language with no context at all.) For example, understanding a conversation is easier because listeners can see the expressions and gestures of the person they are talking to; understanding

a radio news broadcast is easier if the listener knows that the text is a news broadcast, which follows certain rules and patterns. So you should generally set some context for listening exercises by explaining the background, showing pictures, and so forth.

3. **purpose:** In real life, listeners often have some idea why they are listening to something, so it is entirely appropriate—and generally a good idea—to tell students what they are listening for before they hear something. While the most basic purpose of a listening task should be general comprehension, often the purpose should be more focused.

4. **task:** Most listening exercises work better if they are tasks, that is, if students are expected to respond in some way to the material instead of just listening to it. The task keeps students alert and helps focus their listening.

The types of listening practice activities suggested here are arranged roughly according to the level at which they are most likely to be appropriate, starting with those for beginning-level students. (Assigning a precise level of difficulty to these tasks is hard because you can make them easier or more difficult by adjusting the vocabulary, speed of delivery, clarity of speech, depth of content, and so forth.) While the activities here focus on listening practice, many also involve practice of other language skills.

SHOW AND TELL

This informal but engaging activity involves bringing pictures or other objects to class, showing them, and talking about them. Show and Tell provides listening practice and arouses interest in a topic; it also serves as a good informal warm-up or as a break from other types of class activities.

TOTAL PHYSICAL RESPONSE (TPR)

TPR is a Simon Says activity in which you give students instructions, and they respond by doing what you ask (rather than by speaking). Because students respond with action rather than speech, they can focus more fully on listening to what you say (rather than having to worry about generating an oral response at the same time).

This activity builds listening skills, especially for students at lower levels, and can be used to introduce or review vocabulary and even grammar structures. The physical activity makes for a good warm-up activity at the beginning of class or a break in the middle. TPR can be especially useful for teaching basic classroom instructions to students with very low-level listening skills, but it can also be used for more advanced levels; for example, I have walked students through weddings and baseball games TPR-style in lessons on Western culture.

1. Before the activity, make a list of the instructions you wish to use (e.g., *Open your books. Turn to page 6. Touch your nose with your friend's pen.*).

2. Conduct the activity in a gamelike manner, repeating instructions and building up speed for faster student responses.

3. To make the activity more like a game, add the Simon Says element; that is, tell students they should only carry out the instruction if you preface it by saying, "Simon says."

TRUE/FALSE LISTENING

For this activity, prepare a number of short statements, some true and some false, and present them to students as an informal quiz. This activity can be used for reviewing vocabulary and culture content from previous lessons while providing listening practice. The more this seems like a game, the better—try to fool your classes with absurd statements and deadpan delivery.

1. Write a set of statements, drawing material (e.g., vocabulary, cultural information) from previous lessons. Some should be obviously true, others obviously not or perhaps even ridiculous (e.g., *Today is Tuesday. Students love tests.*). The activity is more enjoyable if the statements are a little tricky without being mean.

2. Ask students to listen to each statement, decide if it is true or false, and write down T or F on a numbered sheet. After the exercise, have students check their answers as a group, or ask everyone to shout out the answer (based on Ur 1984, 77–78).

DICTATION

In dictation, you read a short passage to students, and they write it down word for word. This activity is useful for practicing basic listening skills as well as basic writing skills such as capitalization, spelling, and punctuation. Dictation is recommended mainly for lower level students.[2]

1. Choose a short passage or dialogue.

2. Before dictating the passage, introduce any words you think will be new to the students. Also, briefly set the scene by providing appropriate background information. This helps students bring top-down strategies into play and gives you a way to increase or decrease the difficulty of the exercise, depending on how much information you give.

3. Tell students just to listen. Read the entire passage aloud.

4. Read the passage again, breaking it into lines corresponding to phrases or clauses, and have students write it down word for word. Lines should be relatively short—no more than seven or eight words. (Longer lines overload students' short-term memory.) If necessary, repeat each line two or three times.

5. Read the dialogue straight through one final time so that students can check their work.

6. Have volunteers or the class as a whole read the dialogue back to you as you write it on the board. Students can then check their work by looking at the board. Alternatively, have volunteers write different lines on the board, give the students a handout with the text and have them check their own work, or collect the dictations and check them individually.

TIPS

- While dictating, wander the aisles to see how much difficulty students are having. If necessary, slow down and speak more clearly. If the dictation is too easy, speak more quickly and naturally.

- One problem with dictation is that it trains students to listen for every word more than for meaning. One way to minimize this problem and focus students' attention more on meaning is to dictate questions and then ask students to answer them.

---

[2] There are a variety of procedures for dictation. This one is based on Bailey (1998, 13).

DICTOCOMP

In dictocomp, you read a short passage to students and have them write down what you say. Unlike dictation, however, in dictocomp you read the whole passage to students several times at a fairly natural pace rather than stopping after each sentence. This forces students to listen for and remember ideas, not just words. Dictocomp is more challenging than dictation, involves more listening for ideas and speaking practice, and requires students to draw more on their grammar knowledge.[3]

1. Choose a short passage or dialogue. The passage might only be five to ten sentences long.

2. Set the scene of the passage for the students.

3. Instruct students to listen and try to remember. Then read the passage twice at fairly normal speed, not pausing between sentences.

4. Tell students they may jot down key words and phrases (not every word) as you read. Then read the passage a third time, slightly more slowly.

5. Either individually or in groups, have students try to reconstruct and write down the passage as they remember it. (Having students work individually takes less time; working in groups provides an opportunity for speaking practice and mutual assistance.) Tell students they need not use exactly the same words as the original passage, but that the meaning should not be changed and the English should be grammatically correct.

6. Write the original passage on the board (or give it to the students as a handout), and have students check their work. As they check, circulate and answer questions, particularly on the grammatical accuracy of what they wrote. If it seems helpful, hold a general question-and-answer time. Alternatively, have groups write their passages on the board (but this can be slow).

TIPS

*   To make a dictocomp activity more or less difficult, alter the length and difficulty of the passage, read the passage fewer or more times, read more quickly or slowly, or add or eliminate pauses between sentences. The right level of difficulty is the one at which most students can write down the gist of the passage after the third hearing. If they get most of it after the first reading, the dictocomp is too easy.

*   If the passage is a dialogue, let students know who is speaking when—otherwise, they will be confused as to who is saying which sentence. One way to do this is to act out each character by changing your voice and body position. Another is to put a minimal outline on the board (e.g., *Jim:* _____. *Judy:* _____. _____. *Jim:* _____.)

DICTATION FOR REDUCED FORMS

One listening problem you might want to focus on in class involves the reduced forms that are very commonly used in most dialects of natural spoken English, such as *doncha* (*don't you*), *gonna* (*going to*), and *wanna* (*want to*). Students will be hard put to follow conversation between native speakers, movie dialogues, and the like if they cannot understand reduced forms.

---

[3] I have drawn my approach to dictocomp (also called *dictogloss*) from Bowen, Madsen, and Hilferty (1985, 272–73). See Bailey (1998, 47–49) for a slightly different approach.

1. Design a dialogue for dictation that includes a number of reduced forms like those mentioned above. (Reduced forms occur mainly in informal spoken English, so for this kind of dictation, it is better to use dialogues than to use passages of written English.)

2. Conduct the dictation following the procedure suggested above, but be sure to read the lines naturally and fairly quickly and to use the reduced forms of the target items.

3. To check students' work, have students listen to your reduced sentences again and repeat them in their complete form.

STORIES

Stories are a relatively enjoyable way to give students practice listening to extended discourse, albeit of a fairly easy and interesting kind. In my experience, students especially like informal personal stories about you and your country, but you might also tell stories widely known in your home country or throughout the West, such as children's stories, stories from film or literature, or true historical accounts.

1. Choose a story you want to tell, and prepare as necessary.

2. Tell the story. My assumption is that this is best done as informally and naturally as possible; ideally, you want students to perceive this as a break from class rather than another exercise. However, you might at least ask students to try to remember as much of the story as possible, thereby hinting that this is not entirely free time in which they can doze off.

3. As for checking comprehension, the inherent appeal of stories makes them one kind of listening practice for which accountability may not be necessary; many students will strive to understand just because they are interested. If, however, you wish to treat a story as a listening task, you can have students respond in the following ways:
   - Have students take notes and then write a summary or retell the story to a classmate.
   - Require students to be ready to ask a question or two—a comprehension question or one that pursues issues raised by the content of the story—after you finish.
   - Have students discuss what they liked and did not like about the story, or what they found interesting or surprising.
   - Have students revise the story to improve it or make it fit into their cultural norms better.
   - Leave off the end of the story, and have students devise an ending of their own.

FOCUSED LISTENING

In focused listening activities, you help students anticipate what they will hear by giving them clues in the form of questions to answer or outlines, forms, or graphs to fill in. These clues help students focus their listening and make listening practice easier, especially for lower level students. They also encourage students to listen for important information rather than for every word.

1. Prepare a short talk of some kind—for example, a story or a lecture.

2. Decide what clues you will provide. They can consist of anything that gives some signal as to what you will say and that gives direction to students' listening, such as a set of questions to answer, a form to fill out, a graph to fill in, or a partial outline to fill in.

3. Write the clues on the board, or give students a handout. Ask students to look the clues over so that they know what they should listen for. To enhance motivation and encourage active listening, you might ask students to predict what your talk will be about.

4. Tell students to listen to your talk and take notes, writing down information that will help them complete the task. (If you want them to write full answers to your questions, tell them you will give them time to write after the talk.)

5. Give your talk.

6. Check comprehension (see Talks and Lectures below).

An additional—and potentially lighthearted—form of focused listening involves altering a passage or dialogue, introducing contradictions or absurdities. Students then either shout out or take notes when they hear something suspicious (for more ideas along these lines, see Ur 1984, especially 75, 81, 116–17).

PROBLEM-SOLVING SITUATIONS

In problem-solving activities, you orally describe a problem situation to students, have them take note of relevant information, and then ask them to deal with the issue. A classic in this genre is Sophie's Choice, an exercise in which students hear about a young woman who has to choose one of three appealing-but-flawed men as a marriage partner or ignore them all in favor of a career opportunity (Byrd and Clemente-Cabetas 2001). In another well-known activity, Spaceship, the world is about to be destroyed by a meteor, and a spaceship can take a limited number of people off to a new planet to restart the human race. Students are presented with candidates and their qualifications, and have to choose who should be on the spaceship.

Problem-solving activities obviously involve speaking as well as listening practice, but I list them here because the amount of information students need to take in through their ears weights the activity significantly toward listening. (See chapter 8 for further discussion of small-group discussion activities.)

1. Locate or design a situation that gives students a problem to solve. For example, if you were doing Sophie's Choice, you would prepare to explain Sophie's situation and the qualifications of each of her suitors. If the main focus of the activity is on listening practice, make sure the situation involves a fair amount of information that students have to listen to.

2. Present the situation and relevant information to students orally, having them take notes. You might also want to allow them to ask questions.

3. Have the students discuss the problem situation in English in small groups, and prepare to offer a solution and their rationale.

4. Have each group present its solution and rationale.

5. Close the exercise in one of these ways:
   - Have the class debate the merit of the solutions offered, perhaps following up with a vote.
   - Comment on the solutions offered, pointing out their weak and strong points.
   - Offer your own solution (preferably one that is ingenious and entertaining).
   - Review new vocabulary (or sentence structures) that emerged during the discussion.

- Either look for problem situations in commercially available texts (see, e.g., Ur 1981, 74–79), or custom design them to fit the students' needs and interests.

- Make a problem-solving activity into a focused listening task by giving students a graph or form to fill out. For example, for an activity like Sophie's Choice, you could give students a simple table like the following before you give information about each of the eager suitors:

	Age	Occupation	Income	Interests	Bad Habits
Tom					
Dick					
Harry					

TALKS AND LECTURES

Talks and lectures help students improve their listening and note-taking skills, especially their ability to guess when listening to longer stretches of discourse in which they cannot catch every word.

1. Locate information and prepare a talk.

2. Tell students what you are going to talk about, and ask them to take notes. (Taking notes forces the students to listen more carefully.)

3. Give the talk. If students' listening skills are not strong, you may lose your audience, so keep an eye out for the glazed-over look that says your audience has been left behind.

4. After the talk, check comprehension by
   - asking questions
   - having students write a summary of your talk
   - giving a short quiz
   - having students write (and ask) follow-up questions based on what you talked about

TIPS

- A natural place to begin looking for topics is in your own experiences and areas of expertise. However, it is also good to consider students' needs, and if you can give a talk on a subject that is pertinent or useful to the students, so much the better. Talks on language learning and related areas, study skills, and so forth obviously help students in two ways at once. (You might use some of the information in this book as materials for talks on language study and learning.) Talks on cultural topics are also especially useful.

- You can make your talk easier to follow by first giving students a list of questions to listen for the answers to or by writing a simple outline of the talk on the blackboard. Also write down key new vocabulary words that you use. Visual aids of any kind are very helpful.

- For maximum benefit, you should choose the level of difficulty at which students can follow much of what you are saying but still have to guess some of the time. (Also remember that students may need some instruction on how to take notes.)

- When checking comprehension for talks on culture topics, you could have students talk or write about corresponding aspects of their own culture, or have students work in groups to list similarities and differences between their culture and the one you talked about.

Listening outside Class: Recorded Material

Developing listening skills to a high level takes a long time and considerable practice, and generally the practice that a student gets listening to the teacher in class is not sufficient. An important part of a good listening program therefore involves giving students listening comprehension homework and getting them accustomed to making good use of other listening practice opportunities available in many EFL settings.

Even in many developing nations, recordings of English on tape and CD are widely enough available that you can assign listening homework—and begin breaking the unfortunate tradition of trying to learn speaking and listening skills primarily from books. Recordings include material that spans the spectrum from simple dialogues to academic lectures, and the methods for using these materials for listening tasks are essentially the same as discussed in the previous sections. Here, therefore, I focus primarily on the advantages and disadvantages of the tape or CD format itself and suggestions for its use.

As a vehicle for listening practice, sound recordings offer three main advantages. The first and most obvious is that they allow students to practice listening to spoken English even outside class. The second is that, when listening to recorded materials on their own machines (as opposed to in a group in a language laboratory), students have a high degree of control: they can stop the tape or CD and review when they need to. The third is that a recording will not slow itself down the way a softhearted teacher will, so students must to try to follow along at the speaker's rate of speed. This fact, combined with students' ability to control the number of times they listen, makes recordings a good way to expose students to more rapid, natural speech (assuming the English in the recording is in fact fairly natural).

The great drawback of this format is that listening to tapes and CDs can be very boring. Students have no visual stimulus other than a slowly rotating tape or rapidly spinning CD, and from personal experience I can assure you that both tapes and CDs keep right on rotating without protest if a student nods off to sleep. The problem is often exacerbated by the content of the recording, which does not often have entertainment as a primary consideration. Unfortunately, finding new, more stimulating material is not always an option, so if students are to use recorded material effectively, they need to learn to stay alert.

STUDYING WITH RECORDINGS

Staying alert while listening to a recorded dialogue, story, or lecture is easier if students treat it as a puzzle to be unraveled. I suggest teaching students to use an approach something like the following:

1. Students should first listen to the whole recorded passage once, trying to get the general outline of the picture. If a script is available, students should not use it at this time—if they do, they will probably read more than listen. Taking notes or making an outline helps students stay on task; this also gives visible form to the puzzle.

2. Students should listen again and try to fill in the blanks in their outline. They should stop the tape and go back over sections as necessary.

3. Once the students can squeeze nothing more from the recording, they should look for clues. A glossary of new vocabulary items would be especially helpful because it provides helpful clues without giving away the whole puzzle. Armed with new hints, students can return to the tape or CD for a third assault.

4. Finally, if a script is available, students should use it as the answer key to check their comprehension and solve any remaining mysteries. Afterward, it doesn't hurt to review the recording one or two more times for new vocabulary items. (Incidentally, students who listen again after a good night's sleep will often be surprised to discover that they can understand things that fatigue caused them to miss the night before.)

If you assign recorded listening homework, you should cover it in class to give a sense of closure to the activity and to ensure that students actually did the work. If students do not have a script of the recording, you should go over the main points so that students can determine how well they solved the puzzle. If they have a script, you might provide closure by discussing the content of the tape or CD or simply by asking students what parts they found difficult and why.

CHOOSING APPROPRIATE RECORDED MATERIAL

In choosing recorded material for homework assignments, the material's level of difficulty deserves careful attention. In my experience, teachers and students frequently err on the side of choosing listening material that is too difficult. I have alluded to the belief that a good, stiff dose of hard work, even if painful, will do wonders for language progress. The listening skills version of this hypothesis is that if you listen to an unintelligible, opaque news broadcast long enough, it will eventually become clear. While this theory may appeal to ascetic tendencies, it is not a very effective way to develop listening skills. Listening to overly difficult material is very frustrating, and repeated listenings can improve students' comprehension only to a certain point. If material is too hard, students are frequently forced to give up on their ears and find another way to decipher the message (often by reading scripts, if available). Material that is too difficult also forces students and teachers to invest large amounts of time in working with small amounts of material, reducing the amount of both listening practice and vocabulary reviewed.

If you cannot find material at the right level of difficulty for the students, I feel that it is generally better to err on the side of using material that is rather easy. Relatively easy recordings tend to reduce learner anxiety, and you can assign larger amounts of material. Such material also allows students to guess the meaning of new words from context more easily and increases the chance that they will be able to understand words and phrases that they have previously learned by reading. Students thus get practice in rapidly recalling the meanings of semifamiliar words and improving the speed at which they process and comprehend what they hear.

In the beginning, you may find it quite difficult to predict how easy or difficult the students will find a given listening passage. Experience as a language learner will help sensitize you to the difficulties students face, but the best way to check the difficulty of material is usually the traditional trial-and-error approach: try some material in class, and see how much of it students can comprehend. My rule of thumb is that if most of the students can understand some of the material the first time through and get the highlights on a second try, the material is suitable.

When you are choosing recorded material, another question to ask is whether or not the material provides genuine listening comprehension practice. While this question might seem obvious, the point is still worth making because many commercially produced listening materials involve little comprehension practice. For example, some tapes and CDs that accompany textbooks consist entirely of a voice reading aloud the material found in the text. Of course, if the student has read the text before listening to the recording or reads it while listening to the recording, little actual listening comprehension practice occurs. Many tapes and CDs consist of pattern drills that require students to manipulate sentences or fill in blanks; these also require little comprehension once the student has figured out the pattern of the drill. In order to develop listening comprehension skills, students must listen to material that is new to them and that demands comprehension rather than a mechanical response.

PRODUCING YOUR OWN RECORDED MATERIAL

While making your own material requires an extra investment of time, producing materials tailored to the needs of your classes is often well worth the effort. It allows you to control the level of difficulty, choose content that you think students will find interesting, and personalize recordings by bringing in local topics or people. It also allows you to give students listening material for which they have no script.

There are several kinds of material you might consider recording:

1. **stories, either from a book or—even better—from your own personal experiences:** When teaching in China, for example, I taped several stories about my adventures exploring in Taiwan and placed them in the language laboratory for anyone who was interested. When references to my adventures began cropping up in conversations later in the semester, I knew that quite a few students had listened to the stories. If you can get other English speakers to record stories based on their experiences, so much the better—students will be exposed to different voices and accents.

2. **lectures, formal or informal, on topics of interest:** Recording talks of your own gives you a chance to share ideas from fields you are interested in, and you can also record talks given in English by visiting speakers.

3. **recorded interviews:** One of the best kinds of listening material consists of recorded interviews you conduct in English with other teachers, friends, visitors to your school, or even any experts you can locate. For example, I often choose a topic or issue based on students' reading material and record an interview with another English speaker about the topic. Because these interviews are relatively unplanned and informal, they have the features of natural language (e.g., false starts, fillers, reduced forms) that are too often absent in commercial recordings. The fact that they are based on material that students have read means that students already have some background knowledge and vocabulary for the topic, so students can employ top-down strategies, but the spontaneity of the interview means that students cannot fully predict its contents.

Recordings need not be professional; in fact, it may be better if they are not. Normal speech is not flawless, and there is no reason why recordings should be. The main result of insisting that recordings have no mistakes in them is that they become more burdensome for you to produce. If you make a mistake while recording, just say "whoops" and go on.

SOUND QUALITY

Obviously, when making your own recordings, working with CDs or MP3 files instead of tapes has many advantages, including clearer sound (no tape hiss) and greater durability. However, tapes and tape recorders are still widely used and no doubt will be for some time to come.

When making tapes—and in working with recordings in general—you should pay attention to sound quality. Students already face many obstacles in efforts to understand recorded material, and there is no reason to exacerbate the problem with poor sound quality. Here are several words of advice:

1. Always check tapes for sound quality. The sound quality on tapes deteriorates as they are used, so do not assume that a tape that was good last semester is still good. Also, each time a tape is copied, there is some loss in sound quality, so copies of a tape made for students won't sound quite as clear as the original.

2. If you plan to use a tape repeatedly over more than one semester, make a copy of the master right away, and use the second-generation copy to make further copies for students. The sound on the copies will not be as good as that of the master, but the master will deteriorate if it is often used for making copies, and eventually you will have to make the tape all over again.

3. Learn a little about tape and tape recorder maintenance, and pass that knowledge on to students. Poorly made tapes will quickly foul the tape recorder heads as they rub against the tape during recording and playback, so use the best tapes possible, and clean the heads on tape recorders frequently. Dirty tape recorder heads result in poor sound quality and damage tapes. A bit of cleaning will often make the difference between a tape that is almost unintelligible and one that is reasonably clear.

LANGUAGE LABORATORIES

Language laboratories can be divided into two basic categories. The more useful ones consist of individual machines that students can use for doing homework. Such labs provide a place where students can work at their own pace on recordings of their own (or the teacher's) choosing. The more problematic (but thankfully increasingly rare) kind of language laboratory is essentially a master console hooked up to sets of headphones that allows a teacher to play a tape or CD for a class. Such a setup allows a teacher to let an entire class hear the same recording under favorable listening conditions but also forces students to all listen to the same material at the same pace in an environment that is often stultifying.

On the whole, a volunteer teacher (VT) can provide clearer and more lively listening practice for a class by speaking in person than playing a tape can, so teaching in a language lab tends to be more of a hindrance than a help to a VT. However, it is not unusual for VTs to be placed in language labs because the school looks at the lab as a status symbol and wants to give the guest teacher the best. If you find yourself in such a situation, the problem is often more cultural than educational. You will need to gently persuade your school to let you teach in a classroom that does not hinder communication by blocking space into little cubicles. It may help to point out to your school that the real value of a language lab is that it replaces a native speaker, allowing any teacher to present students with native-quality speech. You might also plead unfamiliarity with the equipment and suggest that someone more skilled in its use could do a better job, pointing out that your expertise is in direct conversational interaction.

If you have to teach a language lab course using taped material, the main battle is generally against boredom, so remember to turn off the master tape or CD from time to time and wake students up with interaction or variety. TPR activities are helpful in labs; having students raise hands in response to questions helps keep them awake and lets you check on whether or not they are paying attention. Language labs are also good settings for letting students listen to songs; music breaks the boredom, and students are much more likely to be able to hear the words to a song over headphones than through a small speaker in a big classroom.

Radio Programs

In many parts of the world, radio broadcasts provide one of the few opportunities to hear English regularly—and hence one of the best opportunities for the kind of breakthrough described in chapter 3. Voice of America and BBC World Service broadcasts are audible in many countries, and even many non-English-speaking nations (including China, Japan, and Russia) have English language broadcasts, usually news programs.[4] Because of their fresh, timely content, radio news programs tend to be inherently interesting, and the absence of a script forces students to rely on their listening skills. A course of study that involves radio news also has an unusually high degree of validity for students because the ability to understand radio news is a useful skill in and of itself. Recently, the number of news programs in English—and other kinds of English language programming as well—found on television has been increasing in a number of host countries.

The problem with most radio news is that, for a number of reasons, it is quite difficult for learners to follow. First, while the speech of radio announcers is usually clear and relatively standard, it may be somewhat rapid (especially when compared with that of the average English teacher). A second and larger problem is that news contains much low-frequency vocabulary and many names of places and people. Third, frequent and sudden jumps between topics make news programs difficult to follow; often just as the listener has figured out what the announcer is talking about, the announcer switches to a new topic. Finally, news items are usually short, so they often include little background explanation or redundancy.

Because the availability of English news broadcasts makes radio news one of the best chances for students to develop an English skill that they can continue to use over the years, a particularly valuable course for advanced-level students is one designed to prepare them for radio news. Elements of such a course would include

1. studying names of places and prominent people in current affairs. Place names are especially important because they often occur at the beginning of an item to establish the context.

2. practicing by listening to lots of news items, using both bottom-up and top-down comprehension strategies. Students will need to be able to rapidly decode words as they hear them as well as guess effectively to fill in the many holes left by words or points of information they lack.

3. regularly keeping up with the news using any means possible—including newspapers and news reports in the students' native language. The more students know about current news, the more vitally important background information they will bring with them to the task of understanding an English news broadcast.

At the early stages of a course, it is helpful to record news broadcasts so that students can listen to them more than once. This also allows you to provide students with a vocabulary list, and perhaps even a script if you are feeling magnanimous. In the beginning of such a course, you might focus on a few ongoing news stories (e.g., the Middle Eastern peace process, AIDS research) rather than exposing students to a broad range. Choosing a focus not only simplifies students' task but also demonstrates an effective strategy—building up background knowledge of a story—for making radio news broadcasts easier to follow.

---

[4]Government-sponsored English language news broadcasts may well have underlying propaganda purposes, so listening to them may be a sensitive issue. Be aware not only of what English broadcasts can be heard in your host country but also of which are politically acceptable for you to use or recommend in class.

As students improve to the point where they can get the gist of a story even by listening to it only once, you can assign them to listen to radio or television broadcasts as homework and to come to class with notes or summaries for class discussion. Alternatively, you can give each student a "beat," having him or her be responsible for stories on a given topic or news from a particular part of the world. Using this approach, students still need to listen to the whole news broadcast to find out if there is any news about the country they were assigned to, but they will have a stronger sense that some part of that broadcast is their responsibility.

The goal of a radio or television news course is that ultimately students will become comfortable enough listening to news broadcasts that they will continue to listen long after your class ends. For students who have limited opportunities to use English once they leave school, news broadcasts might be one of the few channels through which they maintain and develop their English skills.

Films and Videotapes

English language films are viewed widely throughout the world, either in theaters or on videotape or DVD. English language television programs—both imported and locally produced—are also shown in some countries. Of these listening opportunities, films are probably the most widely available and the most challenging, so I focus on films here.

Films have a number of important virtues as an opportunity for English practice. The picture helps students maintain interest, transmits cultural information, and gives students a valuable set of clues to work with as they try to decipher what they are hearing. Films are also designed to be entertaining, so the content is more compelling than that of textbook dialogues. A final benefit for advanced-level students is that films often have very natural English and provide a good opportunity to practice listening to material that has a range of accents and styles.

The great curse of movies flows from the final advantage: the natural conversational language in many films tends to make them difficult to understand. A student watching most modern films will encounter rapid, fragmented, or unclear speech; unfamiliar vocabulary (especially very informal vocabulary); regional or class accents; and problems arising from gaps in background knowledge. Additionally, the sound in many films is less than crystal clear; some actors talk over the sound of screeching brakes or gunshots; others habitually mumble. As a result, it is not unusual for unprepared students to get lost somewhere early in a film and sit in bewilderment through the next hour and a half.

In recent years, the increased availability of first videotape machines and then DVD players has made teaching film courses a much more realistic option, even in many developing nations. As with radio programs, one of the best arguments for offering film courses for advanced-level students is that such courses can pave the way for students to feel comfortable watching English language films after they graduate. Students who learn to sit back and enjoy a film, satisfied with comprehending as much of the language as possible and guessing the rest from the picture, can often tolerate enormous quantities of film watching.

In one common approach to teaching English with films, you show a film in small segments, allowing students to see each segment several times and supplying all the necessary vocabulary. Chopping the film up in this way lessens its appeal but has the virtue of making the film easier to understand, and this approach may be viable for classes that are not yet ready to watch films in their entirety. In a second approach, you provide students with an introduction (often a plot summary), a vocabulary list, and a list of comprehension questions, and then show the film in its entirety (preferably twice). (Films on DVD generally have English language captions that can help students follow the dialogue—not to mention giving them a little extra speed-reading practice.) This approach maintains the integrity of the film but is generally not very effective in helping students understand unfamiliar language in it; a written list of words does little to prepare students to recognize these words aurally when they come darting out of a cloud of barely understood dialogue. This approach is most suitable for students who are already very advanced in their listening skills.

If you have the opportunity to teach a course to advanced-level students using films, I recommend an alternative method that prepares students for a film by giving them an overview (which enhances their ability to employ top-down strategies), exposes their ears to some of the voices and vocabulary (which enhances their ability to employ bottom-up strategies), yet leaves the film—and its appeal—intact. This method requires quite a bit of preparation on your part, but if you use it in a sustained way in a film course, the results are worth the effort.

1. Choose an interesting film that has as much clear dialogue as possible. Finding such a film is easier said than done; in my experience, you will often need to sample several films to find one that is suitable.

2. Watch the film, and take notes on each segment of dialogue, noting where the dialogue occurs so that you can locate it later.

3. Select five to ten key segments of dialogue (hereafter called *scenes*). Include some but not all of the main turning points of the plot, scenes that contain key vocabulary, and scenes that are important to the plot but especially hard to follow. For a normal feature film, the total time of the selected scenes should be about ten minutes.

4. Record these scenes onto an audiocassette, CD, or digital sound file, leaving a few seconds of silence between each scene. If you want to be really professional, use a microphone to record numbers at the beginning of each scene, or even vocabulary items and explanations.

5. Prepare written material based on the scenes on the recording. I generally include a list of the film's characters, a brief introduction to the setting for each scene, and a list of vocabulary items for each scene.

6. Prepare a list of comprehension questions that students will answer when they view the film. These may be based on the scenes selected for the tape or CD and on other portions of the film.

When using this approach, I normally spend some time going over the tape or CD recording with students before they see the film—studying the recording is usually very hard work because the scenes appear without much context, so students may need help and encouragement. Then I show the film at least twice. In my experience as a learner and a teacher, the second showing of a film is very valuable because students hear many things that they miss the first time.

Here are a few general comments about the use of films. First, it is important to let students hear the sound as clearly as possible. The speakers on many TV sets are small, and many classrooms echo, conditions that make the soundtrack of a film even harder to understand. If you can run the soundtrack of a film through a listening lab and have students listen on headphones, students will understand much more of the film. Another approach is to run the sound through a public address system or stereo.

Second, be sure to preview films before showing them because your remembered impressions of how hard a film is to follow may not be very accurate. Ideally, you should preview films along with someone who isn't a native speaker of English and can help you determine how difficult the film will be for students.

Although the discussion here focuses on videotaped films, documentaries and TV shows make equally good—if not better—classroom material. Documentaries are usually narrated in nice, clear English, so they are easier to understand than many films. TV shows are more manageable than films because they are shorter, and the sound recording of studio-taped programs also tends to be clearer. Commercially produced videotape series designed for English teaching, if available, can also provide an excellent initiation into film and TV viewing.

Evaluation

Many of the tasks listed in the section Listening Tasks in Class can readily be adapted for quizzes and tests. Below I suggest a few relatively easy evaluation methods that have positive backwash. As in that section, the tasks are ordered more or less by level of difficulty.

TRUE/FALSE STATEMENTS

Make a number of statements, some true, some false, and have the students simply write down T or F. This type of quiz is good for checking vocabulary as well as listening and can be used even at beginning levels. Two cautions: unless you intend to test knowledge as well as listening skills, be sure your statements test listening comprehension, not mastery of trivia. Also note that this kind of quiz makes it relatively easy for students to cheat, so keep an eye out.

DICTATION OR DICTOCOMP

Dictations or dictocomps are easy to give and can be used to check basic writing skills as well as listening. (The main problem with dictation is that its backwash may focus students too much on listening for words instead of meaning. As noted in the section on listening tasks, one way to ensure that students do not totally ignore meaning is to use questions as the dictation items and ask the students to answer the questions.)

LISTENING COMPREHENSION PASSAGES

Listening comprehension passages can consist of stories, dialogues, readings, or lectures presented one or more times. Comprehension can be checked in several ways:

1. Have students take notes and turn them in.

2. Ask students to write an outline or summary.

3. Ask a series of true/false questions based on the passage.

4. Give students short-answer questions.

5. Have students fill in a grid, form, or outline.

For the last three methods, decide whether or not to give students the task or questions before they hear the passage. If you do, you will help focus their listening and make the task easier. If not, you are testing memory or note-taking as well as listening comprehension.

For Thought, Discussion, and Action

1. **listening opportunities:** Talk to one or more people from your host country (or people who have lived there) and find out what opportunities students there might have to listen to English. Are there many English speakers? TV programs? Radio news broadcasts? Films? Other opportunities?

2. **top-down and bottom-up listening practice:** Consider a language learning experience (or course) you have had, and analyze the listening practice it provided. Did it mainly provide practice using top-down listening strategies, bottom-up listening strategies, or both? How effective overall was the course's approach in building your listening skills?

3. **listening activities:** Imagine a course you will teach, or choose one of the sample courses in chapter 6. With that course in mind, go through the list of listening activities in this chapter and select several that you think would be suitable for regular use in that course. Be ready to explain the rationale for your choices.

4. **dictocomp:** If you are already teaching an English course that involves listening skills, prepare and conduct a dictocomp according to the instructions given in the chapter. Alternatively, try another kind of activity that you have not used before.

5. **problem-solving situations:** This chapter mentions Sophie's Choice and Spaceship as problem-solving situations that can be used for both listening and speaking practice. Design a problem-solving situation of your own for use in a speaking/listening skills class. Share your situation with other teachers, and ask for their suggestions.

6. **recorded interviews:** Practice making your own listening material by recording an interview with an English speaker.
   - Choose a topic (ideally one related to a lesson you will teach in an English course), and prepare a list of interview questions related to the topic.
   - Locate an English speaker, and record an interview with that person.
   - Turn the recording into material for focused listening by preparing a list of comprehension questions for students that cover the main points of the interview. (Your original interview questions already provide a good outline to work from.)
   - Prepare step-by-step instructions for students outlining how they should study using the tape. (Try to make the process as much like a game or a puzzle as possible.)

7. **radio news:** Design one or more sample language learning projects (LLPs) students could do that involve using English radio news broadcasts to build listening skills.

8. **films to improve listening:** Survey several people about their experiences with trying to build their foreign language listening comprehension by watching movies. Questions include these: (1) Did they have some kind of plan or method? If so, what was it? (2) How successful was the effort? (3) What problems did they encounter? (4) What did they like about using films? (5) What would they do differently if they were to try it again?

9. **subtitles:** When using English language films to study English, students often need to choose whether and how to use subtitles (especially true if they are watching a film on DVD). Analyze and list the relative advantages and disadvantages of each of the following approaches to using the film for English study, and decide what knowledge

and skills each approach would build—and not build. (Assume the film will be viewed twice.)

- Host-language subtitles are visible for both viewings.
- English subtitles are visible for both viewings.
- No subtitles are visible for the first viewing; English subtitles are visible for the second viewing.
- No subtitles are visible for either viewing.

Sample LLP for Advanced-Level Listening Skills

Goal: Build listening comprehension, especially top-down skills and ability to listen to natural conversation between native speakers of English.

Material: Western TV situation comedy series (DVD format).

Plan: Study one episode a week, two hours of study divided into two sessions.

Method:

Session 1

1. Watch the episode straight through one or two times with no subtitles showing. Note which parts of the episode I didn't understand; guess what might have been said.

2. Turn on the subtitles, and re-view the parts in question. Check my guesses to see if I was right. Note any new expressions I want to remember.

Session 2

1. Review new material I made note of.

2. Watch the episode again with the subtitles off.

3. Watch the episode again with the subtitles on to check my comprehension.

Criteria for measuring progress: I will have succeeded if I

- watch a whole season of the series (approximately ten to fifteen episodes)

- can now generally follow the dialogue in each of the episodes I watched, even if the subtitles are not turned on

- feel more comfortable watching the series without the subtitles turned on

- can understand more of a new episode the first time I watch it, even without subtitles, than I could before starting the LLP

Chapter 8

Speaking: A Linguistic Juggling Act

- Speaking in a foreign language involves a variety of operations, and learning to perform all of them quickly requires extensive practice.

- During speaking practice in class, the more students who can talk at any given time, the better. Pair or small-group work allows more students to practice speaking than large-group discussions or teacher-centered activities do.

- Most adult learners will not achieve native pronunciation in a second language. Clear but accented pronunciation is a more realistic goal and possibly a more desirable one.

- Some correction of students' errors may be helpful, but there is little evidence that correction improves students' accuracy much. Overcorrection can make students self-conscious and discourage them from speaking.

Having spent two years in a Japanese program that focused almost exclusively on speaking, I should have at least a fair command of spoken Japanese. However, I don't. Part of the fault is no doubt mine—I certainly could have been more persistent in seeking out the many Japanese on campus for practice. But part of the problem also lay within the program, which consisted mainly of memorizing dialogues and learning to perform them as fluently as possible in class. This approach was successful in teaching me quite a bit of Japanese vocabulary and even some grammar, but it gave me precious little practice in expressing my own ideas in Japanese. Thus, when I could rope a Japanese friend into speaking with me, I was generally trying to construct my own sentences for the first time, much like a piano student who shows up for a recital having practiced only scales. The results were uneven at best—whenever I wanted to say something that fortuitously coincided with a sentence I had memorized, I could rattle it off fluently and flawlessly, but whenever I tried to say anything else, I had to hem and haw for an agonizingly long time as I tried to put even basic sentences together. Unsurprisingly, I found these forays into real conversation frustrating and eventually gave them up to go back to memorizing the dialogues and getting a passing grade.

Unfortunately, this kind of problem is not uncommon in EFL settings. In class, genuine speaking practice may be neglected in favor of choral drills or memorization, and other practice opportunities are hard to come by, so students' ability to speak lags far behind their knowledge of grammar and vocabulary. Often, your school has invited you, the native speaker, for exactly this reason, hoping that your presence will improve students' spoken English. In fact, sometimes you may get the feeling that everyone expects your appearance in the classroom to have a miraculous impact on students' speaking skills, even in classes of thirty or more, where you can hardly speak to each student once a day. (Some students may get around this problem by visiting you and practicing at all hours of the day and night.)

Even if you can't personally provide each student with extensive practice opportunities, one of your greatest contributions—and most important roles—is to create an environment where students speak in English for communicative purposes, often for the first time. Your presence forces students to use English and does much to enhance their motivation by making English come alive as a vehicle for communication. However, much of your success as a teacher of spoken skills will also ride on how effectively you create vitally important practice opportunities for the students. In the discussion of teaching spoken skills here, the emphasis is on ways to provide students with the kinds of practice they need in order to develop oral skills.

The Process of Speaking: The Problem and the Goal

When you consider the parts of the speaking process individually, no single part presents overwhelming difficulties. For example, neither pronouncing a word correctly nor deciding what verb tense to use is impossibly difficult if you focus all of your attention on that single problem. The difficulty arises from the fact that, like a juggler who is trying to keep ten balls in the air at the same time while tap-dancing and playing the harmonica, a speaker has to perform a rather long list of operations simultaneously. Consider, for example, the case of Kim, a student who has overslept and arrived late for English class for the third time this week. He is now standing in front of a stern-looking foreign English teacher who wants an explanation. A peek inside his head will give a good illustration of all the things he needs to consider in producing a sentence:

1. **goals:** "Should I try to win mercy or sympathy?"

2. **strategy:** "How would this foreigner react if I lied and she found out? Should I be honest and play the contrite sinner, or lie and play the misunderstood victim?"

3. **listener's background knowledge:** "Does she know the local traffic situation? Maybe I can get away with an excuse about the traffic."

4. **word choice:** "Do I say *crowded traffic* or *busy traffic?*"

5. **grammar:** "Is it *Excuse me to be late, excuse me being late,* or *excuse my being late?*"

6. **pronunciation:** "Pay attention to that consonant cluster at the beginning of *Excuse . . . .*"

7. **intonation:** "Does *Excuse me for being late, but there are always many cars in the morning* end with falling or rising intonation?"

8. **gestures and facial expressions:** "Do I look her in the eye or avoid her eyes? Do I smile or look unhappy?"

Finally, poor Kim's problem is compounded by the fact that he doesn't have very much time to make all of these decisions—it won't be long before the patience of an annoyed teacher wears dangerously thin.

Of course, not all communication situations involve the immediate pressure Kim faces, but the steps involved in speaking and the need to perform them quickly are normal parts of the speaking process. The time element deserves special attention. Some people—mostly English teachers—will wait indefinitely as a learner of English struggles to construct an utterance, but most people are not so saintly and will sooner or later give up on speakers who cannot communicate at a reasonable pace. A student who can communicate an idea even faultily without slowing the conversation down too much is more likely to be able to sustain conversation when the opportunity arises than is a more accurate but slower comrade. Quicker students, then, are likely to have more conversation and practice opportunities and therefore continue to improve. These students will almost certainly also find conversation easier and more enjoyable, so they are more likely to seek out any opportunities that exist.

Hence, if students are to reach a breakthrough point in spoken English, their primary goal is to learn to express their ideas in English with a fair degree of fluency. Accuracy is also desirable, and issues such as correct grammar and proper use of vocabulary should not be neglected. In fact, communicative effectiveness and accuracy cannot be entirely separated; if a student's grammar or vocabulary is too far wide of the mark, the listener may get the wrong message or no message at all. However, it is safe to say that the goal of most speaking situations is communication more than formal accuracy, and a course intended to teach speaking skills should emphasize the former.

Clearly, then, one of your most important roles in a speaking class is seeing that students get the maximum possible amount of practice speaking English, particularly kinds of practice that allow students to express their own ideas. This is especially true for students at intermediate and advanced levels of speaking skills, but even at beginning levels it is desirable to give students choice in what to say so that they have to communicate ideas as well as words.

A second important role is seeing that students get new language input. Actually, in most EFL settings, students will get much of their new language input (new vocabulary, phrases, and grammar structures) from textbooks. Your role is thus to ensure that they learn material in ways conducive to improving their speaking skills. That is, you need to stress that students should learn how to productively use new vocabulary and grammar structures to express their own ideas in English, not just use vocabulary and grammar knowledge receptively to comprehend other people's English.

Your final role is helping students learn for themselves what kinds of practice are effective for developing spoken skills. Students in many countries often practice their speaking at home by reading texts aloud or memorizing dialogues. While these forms of practice can be useful, the skills they develop are not entirely the same as those necessary for expressing one's own ideas, and students need to learn how to choose forms of practice that fit the goals they are trying to reach.

Pairs, Small Groups, and Large Groups

If I asked you to describe a good conversation lesson, the first picture to pop into your head might be of a teacher briskly fielding questions from an enraptured student audience or of a lively class debate. On a little reflection, the problem with the first option is fairly evident—in this kind of exchange, the teacher does most of the talking. The second activity might initially seem to be an improvement because it is more student centered; presumably the teacher need not say very much. However, the large-group focus of the activity means that at any given time only one student has a chance to speak, so in a fifty-minute class with twenty-five students, even if the teacher never says a word, each student would only get two minutes of speaking practice. Students would spend most of the period listening to their classmates, an activity that is probably less useful than listening to the teacher speak.

So, how should in-class speaking practice be set up? In general, students should work in pairs or small groups as often as possible because this arrangement allows more students to practice at the same time. Pairs are the most efficient grouping in that they allow the most students to talk at once, but as Harmer (2001, 117) notes, the effectiveness of any pair work is affected quite a bit by how the two students get along. Small groups (of three or four students) still give many students an opportunity to speak but provide a little more space for personality differences. For example, in a small group, the presence of at least two other people means that a shy student can sit back and listen most of the time but still feel like a participant. As Ur (1981, 7) points out, the physical closeness in small groups also helps improve motivation, so they provide a good environment for encouraging reluctant students to make their first attempts at speaking.

However, breaking students into pairs and small groups is not without problems, the main one being that some students won't practice spoken English with their classmates unless you are watching. Sometimes they are being lazy; in other cases, the problem is that they feel the only useful speaking practice is conversation with an English speaker who has native mastery of the language and will correct all their errors—in short, they expect to do their practicing with you! These students are often reluctant to practice with their peers because they doubt the usefulness of such practice or because they fear making uncorrected errors, building bad habits, and incurring a vague host of other evil consequences.

Faced with students who resist practicing spoken English with each other, you probably need to resort to a combination of persuasion and persistent pressure. For your campaign of persuasion, you might begin by suggesting that the main problem in speaking is one of quickly forming thoughts into English sentences and that this kind of practice does not require a native speaker as listener. (In fact, it doesn't require any listener at all, and I quite heartily advocate that students talk to themselves in English if they don't mind occasional quizzical looks from passers-by.) A culturally relevant analogy may also help; for example, you might have students ask themselves who will learn kung fu (or violin, or basketball) more rapidly—a student who practices two hours every day or one who only practices during the weekly half-hour lesson with the teacher?

You might also point out that students should not worry that their errors will be reinforced if they spend too much time talking to classmates. As Brown (2001) notes, "There is now enough research on errors and error correction to tell us that 1) levels of accuracy maintained in unsupervised groups are as high as those in teacher-monitored whole-class work, and that 2) as much as you would like not to believe it, teachers' overt attempts to correct speech errors in the classroom have a negligible effect on students' subsequent performance" (p. 181).

To encourage students to speak English in class, I personally prefer a prescription of light-toned nagging ("Kim, that doesn't sound like English") and occasional pep talks on the importance of practice.[1] It is also important to be realistic about how far from supervision you can reasonably expect the students to practice English. A good rule of thumb is this: break students into the smallest groups in which most of them will speak English a significant percentage of the time.

In-Class Methods and Tasks

This section briefly discusses activities often used in speaking classes. As in chapter 7, the activities are presented roughly according to difficulty level. (See also appendix B.)

MEMORIZING MATERIAL

Having read my rather negative depiction of dialogue memorization, you may be surprised to see it suggested here. However, for beginning-level students, a good case can be made for some memorization of sentences or short dialogues that contain a large percentage of high-frequency phrases and sentences like *How are you?*, *What is that?*, *My name is . . .* and so forth. Memorizing typical sentences may also help students learn sentence patterns and grammar. Furthermore, Stevick (1988, 51) argues that the conceptual simplicity of memorization and the strong sense that they have mastered the content makes memorization an emotionally reassuring task for beginning-level students. Finally, it may provide a good way to ease reluctant classes into speaking.

When requiring students to memorize passages or dialogues, encourage them to keep as focused on communication as possible. While fluent delivery is nice, it is also important for students to know what they are saying. Here are the steps for guiding students to memorize a short dialogue in class (from Stevick 1988, 70–76).

1. Choose a short dialogue or passage that contains a high percentage of material that is valuable in exactly the form in which it is memorized; in other words, commonly used phrases and expressions such as *How are you?* and *What time is it?*

2. Have students listen to you say the whole dialogue once or twice.

3. Teach the pronunciation of any new words.

4. Begin the process of memorization. A good trick for helping students memorize is to build each sentence up from the end, an approach that preserves natural sentence intonation. For example, you would say,
   Today. (Students repeat.)
   A nice day today. (Students repeat.)
   It's a nice day today. (Students repeat.)

---

[1] Some teachers have students monitor each other, levying a minimal fine on students who speak something other than English in class (the proceeds eventually to go to a class party). I am personally uncomfortable demanding money from students and even less comfortable making the speaking of their native tongue a misdemeanor, but it seems to work for some. Ur (1981, 20) suggests that placing a tape recorder near an offending group may increase the members' English practice.

5. If you are working with dialogues, have students role-play the dialogue in pairs, perhaps even acting it out. To close, have a few pairs recite their dialogues in front of the class, accompanying the language with appropriate actions.

CHORAL DRILL

Choral drill is essentially the all-class, repeat-after-me exercise in which you say something and students repeat it. While choral drill is of limited value in building communicative language skills, it can be useful for practicing pronunciation and intonation, for reviewing material, and for getting beginning-level students more accustomed to opening their mouths and speaking.

1. Choose a dialogue from a textbook, read it aloud line by line, and have the students repeat after each line. So as not to overload their short-term memory, break long sentences into shorter parts. Students will pay more attention to pronunciation and intonation if they repeat after listening to you rather than reading aloud from a dialogue in their textbook, so if the dialogue is from one of their textbooks, have them close the book.

2. Have students try to replicate your pronunciation and intonation.

3. As with memorized dialogues above, have students role-play the dialogue in pairs, and close with a few short performances.

TIPS

- If the goal is to build students' mastery of normal speech intonation, use dialogues and other texts that approximate spoken (rather than written) language. (Learning to read literary texts aloud is also of some value, but probably more for students at higher levels.)

- As with memorization, when repeating longer sentences preserve normal intonation by building them up from the end. For example, you would say,
  "had ever eaten?" (Students repeat.)
  "the best she had ever eaten?" (Students repeat.)
  "my cooking is the best she had ever eaten?" (Students repeat.)
  "Did she really say my cooking is the best she had ever eaten?" (Students repeat.)

CLASSROOM CHAT

Classroom chat is my term for informal conversation between you and students in the classroom. In some ways, classroom chat is actually more valuable as listening practice than speaking practice because of the limited amount of time each student spends speaking. However, teacher-student interaction can be a good model of genuine communication if you are really interested in what you ask students about, and the motivational impact of conversation with a native speaker may improve students' attitudes toward speaking English in ways that go beyond the practice it provides, especially if the interaction is enjoyable and nonthreatening. Classroom chat is a good way to begin or end a lesson or to provide a break in the middle; it is also a good way to introduce a topic and warm up before moving into a more organized activity related to the topic.

1. From whatever texts the class has been working with, come up with questions that will generate real communication. For example, if today's lesson in the book is on travel and the present perfect verb tense, a natural way to start class is by asking students, "Have you ever been to . . . ?"

2. Chat with students, keeping the interaction communicative by responding to what students say rather than just passing judgment ("Good!") or making grammar corrections.

TIPS

- Try to avoid asking questions whose answers you aren't really interested in. If you are really interested in the students' answers, your enthusiasm will spread to the students. If you ask real questions and expect real answers, this activity is a good way to establish the idea that English use should be communicative.

- When you ask a question, first address it to the class as a whole, and give everyone a moment to think before calling on someone. This pause allows all the students in the class to practice formulating a response even if they don't always have a chance to verbalize it. Talking with students in a random order also helps; students who don't know whether they will be called on next are more likely to try to think of a response to every question.

- To minimize teacher talk, start a line of questioning or a chain of dialogue, and have the students continue it. For example, after asking student A "What did you do yesterday?" (for practice in past tense verbs), have student A ask student B the same question rather than doing it yourself.

- Remember that students called on to respond in public may get nervous and freeze. One way to help students who panic is to ask a question that involves limited choices (e.g., "Do you like reading or watching TV?"), which helps students toward a response. *Yes/no* questions are easier to answer than open-ended ones but generate less speech.

- To reduce tension in class, rely mostly on volunteers to answer questions, only occasionally calling on students who rarely volunteer.

- As useful new words or structures emerge in the course of conversation, write them on the board.

MODEL-BASED DIALOGUES

Model dialogues are a staple item in textbooks used for oral skills courses, so the question is how to use these dialogues.[2] As I have suggested, beginning-level students sometimes benefit from simply memorizing short, basic dialogues, but as learners move on and the dialogues get longer, this approach is less and less useful. If the dialogues are at all realistic—culturally and linguistically—a more productive approach is to use them as models of interaction involving both language and behavior. What is important here is not the dialogue as a whole but the *moves* that it illustrates—the things people do with language. (These are often called *functions*.) Consider the following sample dialogue:

Kim: *Let's* go get some food.
Jan: I *would* really like to, *but* I have a test tomorrow.
Kim: *Can't you* study later?
Jan: Not *really*. This is a *pretty* important test and I haven't prepared much yet.

---

[2] Even the idea of learning speaking skills from a book is rather odd; the very nature of the format pulls students toward reading and away from conversation. Arguably, a set of tapes might be a better "textbook" for a speaking course.

Moves (functions) in the dialogue include the following:

- **suggestions:** *Let's + simple present tense verb* is one of the most common ways to suggest doing something. *Can't you . . .* introduces another suggestion but a rather pushy one. Apparently, Kim and Jan are close enough that Jan doesn't feel the need to be overly polite.

- **polite refusal:** Jan uses the pattern *I would like to, but + (specific reason)* to refuse Kim's invitation; note also that she uses the words *really* and *pretty* to make the refusal less abrupt. Here, students should learn both the language and the idea that, to be polite in a Western context, an excuse should be believable and specific.

Treating a dialogue as a model of both language and culture moves will teach students to pay attention to patterns of behavior as well as language, and practicing the moves allows students to rehearse and learn specific material. This kind of practice is good for classes of mixed levels because students who are unsure of themselves can stay close to the model, while those who are more comfortable have the freedom to improvise.

1. Choose a dialogue that is a reasonably realistic model of how people interact as well as a good model of English.

2. Analyze the dialogue, and note the moves in it.

3. Present the dialogue to students, and have them analyze it. First, have them tell you what the participants in the dialogue do with language (the moves); then have them tell you what language is used to carry out the move.

4. After the points have been introduced and explained, have the students practice a dialogue that has the same kinds of moves but not necessarily the same content as the model dialogue. For example, after studying the dialogue above, you might give student pairs the following instructions: (1) "Student A, make a suggestion to student B, and be persistent." (2) "Student B, keep finding polite excuses for refusing." This kind of practice allows students to improvise but also helps make sure that they will practice new material learned from the text.

5. To quickly give closure to the practice, select a few pairs (either at random or by asking for volunteers) to perform their dialogues. (The most obvious option for closing is to have all the pairs perform their dialogues, but this consumes a lot of class time and is often boring.) A more enjoyable way to achieve the same end is to ask pairs what happened in their little encounters (e.g., "What excuse did Kim give you for refusing your invitation?"). Closing the activity in this way draws attention to the content of the conversations and helps keep the focus on communication.

TIPS

- Encourage students to personalize dialogues, using their real names and backgrounds or creating new identities and playing new roles.

- To make pair practice livelier, have students move from partner to partner cocktail-party-style (see below) rather than practicing only in seated pairs; rotating also allows them to practice the moves in the dialogue several times instead of just once.

- Being stuck with an uncooperative partner can make pair practice burdensome, so either let students change partners often or choose their own partners. In my experience, partners who choose each other eventually learn to work with each other reasonably well.

ROLE PLAYS

Role plays are a form of pair practice that allows students the freedom to play, improvise, and create. As Ur (1981,10) points out, many students feel freer behind the mask of a role, and the element of creative play involved in role plays can do much to make a lesson livelier. Role plays are useful as a way to practice language as well as culturally appropriate behavior.

1. Create situations and roles for students. You may want to base these on a dialogue or something else you have studied in class (see Model-Based Dialogues). When the situations are based on material from the textbook, role plays give students a chance to practice using previously studied material in a less controlled activity.

2. Pair students, and give them their roles. Often you will want to write each role on a separate piece of paper so that each member of the pair knows something about the situation that the other doesn't—as often happens in real life. Consider the following example:

   A: There is a very good movie in town tonight, and you want a friend to go see it with you. B often goes to films with you, so you have decided to persuade her to go.

   B: You plan to go to a party tonight with some classmates. These classmates don't want to invite A, so they have asked you not to tell her about the party.

   After giving the members of each pair their roles, you might want to give them a moment to think about how to handle their situation.

3. Have students carry out the role play. While students should practice material they have studied, also encourage them to be creative and improvise.

4. To close, one alternative is to have one or two pairs do their role play for the whole class. This serves primarily to give a sense of closure and need not go on long. (Having each pair perform takes too much time, and other students spend too long sitting and waiting. Listening to classmates stumble through dialogues is not very good listening practice.) Another way to close is to ask a few students what the outcome of their role play was (e.g., was the invitation accepted?). This is much quicker than having students perform but still provides a sense of closure.

TIPS

- Encourage creativity. If students make an effort to entertain, role plays are more enjoyable to do and watch. Be realistic, however, about the fact that not all students are hams, and not all will be great public performers.

- While public performances may run too long if you are not careful, they have the advantage of allowing you a chance to comment on language or the cultural appropriateness of how students handle the situation.

SURVEYS

Surveys, which involve asking the same few questions several times to different people, are a good way for students to repeatedly practice questions and answers in a format that encourages genuine communication. (For lower level students, the survey is one of the easiest formats for relatively free communicative interaction.) Also, coming up with survey questions that involve a real information gap and are of genuine personal interest to a class is relatively easy.

1. Decide on a topic or list of questions. This activity works better when you and the students are genuinely curious about the results of the survey.

2. Tell students what the purpose or topic of the survey is. Either list the questions you want them to ask, or give students a general topic and allow time for them to write their own questions individually or in groups.

3. Tell students how many classmates they are expected to survey and approximately how long they have to do it. Alternatively, assign a time limit for each short interview.

4. Have students survey each other. You may need to occasionally encourage them to move on to a new partner. You can either join in or wander and eavesdrop.

5. Close the activity by having a few students report their findings.

TIPS

- Have students move around the class as they conduct their interviews to make things more lively and keep everyone awake.

- Variation: Before the survey, have students work in groups to prepare questions, and have each group member ask the same questions. Later, the group members can get back together to compare notes and report results.

INTERVIEWS

Interviews allow pairs of students to converse in greater depth. They are a good activity for intermediate- or advanced-level oral skills classes because they allow in-depth exploration of a topic and provide students with practice in explaining opinions.

1. Decide the topic(s) on which students will interview each other.

2. Give directions for the interviews. Tell the students the suggested topic and approximately how much time they have. If you want students to write their own list of questions, allow a few minutes to do this.

3. Pair the students. Often it is good to find a way to pair students with someone other than the person sitting next to them (who they probably already know fairly well).

4. Have students carry out the interviews. Once student A finishes interviewing student B, you can ask them to switch roles or even partners. You may want to set a time limit and call out when partners should switch roles.

5. To close, ask a few students to report some of the more interesting things they learned from their partner during the interview.

TIPS

- Topics that involve opinions or information not shared by everyone in the class are best because they make interviews more genuinely communicative.

- Role plays and interviews mix nicely; for example, one person might be a reporter, and the other, a famous person.

COCKTAIL PARTIES

Cocktail parties are a free form of speaking practice in which students get out of their seats and converse with different partners in a style similar to that of a cocktail party. The basic rules of a cocktail party are that (1) you should talk to more than one person rather than talking to the same person the whole time, (2) you should generally stand as you chat rather than sitting, and (3) after talking with someone for a while, you must close your conversation and move on to someone else.

For this activity, you can either specify a topic (presumably related to other material the students have been studying) or give them greater freedom by providing a list of suggested (but optional) topics. Note that the activity is relatively noisy, so consider the impact the chaos will have on nearby classes.

1. Explain the basic rules of a cocktail party to students. Also teach them a few lines for striking up conversations (e.g., *It sure is hot today*) and for closing them (e.g., *Well, it's been nice talking to you, but it's getting late and I need to get going*).

2. Let the students know whether or not you want them to practice specific material (e.g., from a model dialogue), how long they have to talk, and how many people you expect them to talk to.

3. Turn students loose, and join in. When time is up or enthusiasm runs thin, call the students back to their seats.

4. Close by asking a few students about their conversations. This is generally more enjoyable—and other students will pay more attention—if you ask a specific question appropriate to the activity (e.g., *Tell me a little about the most interesting conversation you had* or *What new things did you learn?*) rather than have students summarize all their conversations.

PRESS CONFERENCES

One good speaking activity involves having the students prepare questions on a given topic and then interview you press-conference style. This activity is good for speaking and listening practice, and for encouraging student initiative; it also helps students to get to know you and your culture better.

1. Choose a topic for the activity, and be sure you are prepared for any questions students might ask about the topic.

2. Tell students that they are reporters interviewing you so that they can write a story for the local paper. Give them the topic and some time to prepare questions related to it. Students can write questions individually, but it is often better for speaking practice to have them work in groups.

3. Have students conduct the interview like a press conference. To ensure that a few zealous students don't dominate the process, you might allow each group to ask one question in turn. That way, shyer students get their questions asked by the group representative. If there is less need to protect shy students, simply require that everyone ask at least one question.

4. If you plan to require a written report, have students take notes. You may also want to put new vocabulary on the board.

5. To close, ask comprehension questions, or ask a few volunteers to tell you what they found most interesting or surprising in what they learned from the interview. Alternatively, ask each student to write a short report based on the interview.

PAIR OR SMALL-GROUP TASKS

These activities require students to work together in pairs or groups to deal with a task that will generate a visible result. Merely telling students to discuss something is generally not enough; a well-defined task gives students a clear sense of direction and lets them know exactly what they are expected to produce. Here are some examples of tasks:

- Make a list (e.g., *List the most beautiful places in your country.*).

- List reasons (e.g., *List ten reasons why middle school children should—or shouldn't—study a foreign language.*).

- List advantages and disadvantages (e.g., *List the advantages and disadvantages of using standardized examinations to determine who should have the opportunity to enter university.*).

- Prepare directions (e.g., *Prepare a list of directions for how your foreign teacher should bargain at the market,* or *Make a list of suggestions for choosing a good bicycle.*).

- Decide whether or not (e.g., *Decide whether or not middle school students should be allowed to date.*).

- Make a choice (e.g., *Your foreign teacher has been offered two jobs on returning home: a stable but boring job in a bank and a riskier but more rewarding job putting out oil-well fires. Which should the teacher take?*).

- Decide whether you agree or disagree with (a statement) (e.g., *Not wearing seatbelts when riding in a car should be against the law.*).

- Rank or prioritize (e.g., *In order of importance, rank your country's ten greatest heroes.*).

- Make a plan (e.g., *Plan the ideal three-day local vacation trip for your English teacher.*).

- Solve a problem (e.g., *Your foreign teacher is interested in world news but can't understand TV news programs in your country. What suggestions do you have for how the teacher can find out about world news while in your country?*).

1. Place students in pairs or groups of three or four.

2. Give groups a task (not just a topic—see above), and tell them how long they have to complete it.

3. Have each group appoint one recorder to write down what the group decides.

4. While groups discuss, wander from group to group, listening in and looking at what they have written. As you look at their lists, help with language difficulties, or just comment on their ideas.

5. To close, have each group briefly report their conclusions as you take notes on the board, and then discuss them.

TIPS

- Have groups consist of three or four students. Such groups are small enough that each student feels a sense of ownership, so even students who say little tend to remain engaged by listening and mentally formulating language.

- Small groups often work best if there is a discussion leader, so have the students in each group appoint one.

- Make sure one person in each group is entrusted with taking notes for the group. This tends to bring the group together, as everyone tends to look at the same piece of paper. It also makes it easier for you to see how groups are doing—for example, whether they are on task—and makes it easier for you to join in by commenting on a good point they have made, making a suggestion, or offering a correction. (In a noisy room, looking at the notes is often the only way you can know what is going on in each small group.)

- When the time comes for groups to report, ask each group to report just one comment or idea at a time rather than having one group give a long report while others sit and wait. (If one group reports everything first, the others are often left with not much to say.) Make several rounds of the class if necessary.[3]

- Remember that intercultural situations and topics can provide a rich fund of material for small-group discussion. (See chapter 13 and appendix B.)

DEBATES

Debates are good for generating excitement and interest in a topic, but a serious drawback is that during the debate phase of the activity, only one person can speak at a time. The debate format suggested below therefore includes substantial small-group activity.

1. Introduce the issue to be debated either as a statement (e.g., *Adolescents should be encouraged to take jobs.*) or a question (e.g., *Should adolescents be encouraged to take jobs?*). You may wish to supply some background to the issue and some relevant vocabulary.

2. Put students into small groups (teams), and either assign or allow them to choose an affirmative or negative position on the topic.

3. Have each team prepare a case consisting of one or more reasons why they hold the opinion they do and an explanation and examples or other evidence that support their view. (This phase of the activity provides most of the speaking practice, so allow ample time.)

4. For the debate phase, I recommend a "Ping-Pong" format that follows lines of argument one at a time. The procedure for each line of argument is as follows:
   - One affirmative team states one of its arguments (with explanation and support).
   - One negative team responds to the affirmative team's argument with either questions or a counterargument. The students must respond directly to the argument raised by the affirmative team—they cannot begin a new line of argument.

---

[3] The primary value of small-group discussion lies in the practice rather than in the final reports, so keep the time devoted to reports to a minimum. However, as Ur (1981) so nicely puts it, "It is not fair to students to ask them to put a lot of effort into something, and then to disregard the result . . . . What groups have done must then be displayed and then related to in some way the teacher and class; assessed, criticized, admired, argued with, or even simply listened to with interest" (pp. 22–23).

- Either the original affirmative team or another affirmative team responds to the negative team, and so on, following the line of argument until development ceases and repetition sets in.
- One negative team begins a new line of argument, and so on.

5. As the teams develop a line of argument, roughly keep track of the flow of the arguments in a flow chart on the board.

6. At the end, close the debate by praising especially good points made by various teams.

TIPS

- A good topic for debate and discussion has the following characteristics:
  — Students have some knowledge about the topic and some interest in it. It is hard to start a discussion when students have little idea what they are talking about.
  — Opinion is divided. No matter how good a topic is, if the students all agree, there won't be much debate.
  — The topic is not too politically or culturally sensitive.

- One way to locate good topics is to keep an eye on what issues are being debated in the local press and other media. You might also ask the students to suggest topics.

LARGE-GROUP DISCUSSIONS

The idea of uninhibited and freewheeling discussion is quite appealing in theory, and many volunteer teachers (VTs) consciously or unconsciously take this as the ideal for a good speaking class; in fact, some VTs become quite critical of classes that do not respond well to this method. However, the limited practice that the large-group discussion format allows each student severely diminishes its value as a form of speaking practice. The primary virtue of large-group discussions may therefore be as an occasional treat to break the monotony of class or as a way for you to arouse class interest in a topic you wish to lecture about or have students write about. As a regular item on the class menu, large-group discussion is best limited to small classes of advanced-level students, and in order to ensure adequate conversation practice, it is generally good to have students first prepare in small groups.

1. Introduce the topic and any necessary vocabulary. (See Debates for suggestions on the characteristics of good discussion topics.)

2. Have students prepare in small groups. (This is where the students get most of their speaking practice, so allow ample time.) Require each group to come to consensus on a position that they can present to the rest of the class.

Speaking Practice outside Class

Getting students to practice speaking English outside class as homework is not always easy. They may be too busy with other homework, find it too awkward to talk to their peers in a foreign language, or simply not have enough interest in English to practice when the teacher isn't around to make them do it. However, the limited amount of class time available for speaking practice means that some practice outside of class is virtually essential if students are ever to develop their spoken English very far, so one of the goals of your courses should be to teach students to take responsibility for their own practice. To reach this goal, over time you should try to move students toward less structured, more voluntary activities. The menu of homework activities here is arranged from those that provide the most accountability to those which provide the least. (Most of these activities are very similar to those discussed as in-class activities, so I confine my comments to their use as out-of-class assignments.)

MEMORIZATION AND RECITATION

The use of memorization assignments for homework has one great advantage: students can readily be held accountable because you can easily tell who did the homework and who didn't. These assignments can therefore be useful in getting students into the habit of doing spoken work outside of class, and assigning them is better than assigning no speaking homework at all. However, memorizing a text for recitation in class is quite different from expressing one's own ideas in English, which limits the value of this kind of practice. Memorizing texts also tends to be hard, boring work. So, while memorization assignments are well worth considering as an option, they certainly shouldn't be the only kind of oral practice you assign students.

DIALOGUES AND ROLE PLAYS PREPARED OUTSIDE CLASS

Having students create their own dialogues or role plays outside class is provides a fair degree of accountability yet allows students to practice expressing their own ideas in English. The main problem is that, once students have invested time in preparing a dialogue or role play, you need to give them a chance to perform, but watching such performances—especially if they are not very interesting—may not be the best use of class time. One way around this problem is to spot-check by selecting a few pairs or groups to perform and then allowing other groups to volunteer. If you have each group perform, put a time limit on the performances, and do everything possible to encourage performances that are creative and interesting for other students to watch.

SMALL-GROUP DISCUSSIONS OUTSIDE CLASS

Out-of-class small-group discussions can be handled in the same way as in-class small-group discussions and have the same benefits. The absence of direct supervision makes accountability more of a problem, but you can hold students somewhat accountable by having them turn in notes, tell you what the conclusions of their discussion were, or even just report how long they talked. Another way to provide accountability is to use the out-of-class discussion as preparation for an in-class activity, such as a debate. Some students may still take advantage of your absence to avoid speaking English, but as long as some groups are speaking English a significant amount of the time, the activity is probably worth continuing.

For advanced-level students, a useful variation of this activity is an ongoing discussion group focused on a particular kind of topic or material. Examples include a group that gathers to listen to and discuss the news or a reader's club that meets to discuss books. Another possibility is a group in which members take turns preparing presentations that the group then discusses. For example, I once participated in a Chinese language study group in which the three members each regularly made a presentation in their academic area. We thus rotated among discussions of Chinese history, literature, and linguistics.

Appointing group leaders—or having groups choose their own leaders—ensures that someone in each group is responsible for getting things started and simplifies the process of holding the group accountable. Also, as with in-class small-group discussions, groups will find it much easier to start their discussion and keep it moving if you provide a specific question (task) and clear instructions for how the group should report on their discussion.

FREE CONVERSATION ACTIVITIES

For motivated students at any level, the ideal way to practice is to begin bringing English into their daily lives and using it for real communicative purposes. Students can do this in a variety of ways:

1. gathering at English tables in a cafeteria or English corners on campus where students socialize and discuss issues in English (or at least partially in English)

2. chatting in English in the dormitory or while taking a walk

3. talking aloud to themselves or thinking in English

By breaking away from the idea that English is only used when they are in class or doing homework, students greatly increase their opportunities for practice. Combining English practice with social activity, as the first two methods above do, can also make English practice more enjoyable.

Heavy-handed attempts to hold students accountable tend to destroy the spontaneity and fun of such activities, turning them into another form of homework. Indirect approaches, such as casually asking students what they talked about at the English table, are often sufficient to show that you consider such activities important.

FISHING FOR ENGLISH SPEAKERS

If you are in an area where there are other English speakers, an assignment to consider is sending intermediate- or advanced-level students out to find and speak with them. Because of the enormous range of situations possible, generalizations are difficult; sending students off to make friends with GIs is not quite the same as having them waylay tourists. However, no matter what kind of English speakers the students talk to, even a small dose of such practice helps reinforce the idea that learning to speak English is mastering a skill that involves more than grammar and vocabulary. Also, if some students are lucky enough to establish relationships with English speakers, they may have the opportunity for a lot of excellent practice.

If you require students to try to make contact with English speakers outside class, it is important to teach them culturally appropriate ways of approaching and interacting with their quarry. What little practice they might have in an aborted conversation with an annoyed Westerner could be outweighed by negative feelings, so students need to know how to start out on the right foot. For example, they need to be warned of the dangers of seeming too pushy or giving the impression that their desire to practice resembles the interest of a cat in a scratching pole more than that of one human interested in communicating with another.

It also helps if students being sent out to start conversations with strangers have a clear and culturally appropriate mission. For example, you might have students interview foreign English speakers on their reasons for coming to the host country or on their impressions of it. Having a clear rationale for the activity will help students know how to start the conversation and will make it more likely that the interviewees will cooperate.

Pronunciation

No matter how good the English of your host-country English teaching colleagues is, unless they learned native pronunciation at an early age, they will probably still have a marked foreign accent. One of the most valuable contributions you could make to your program would therefore seem to be your native pronunciation. Unfortunately, this theory does not always work out well in practice. First, many VTs teach students who have already studied English for years and whose pronunciation habits are not easy to change. A second problem is that native speakers of English produce sounds so naturally that they are often not aware of how they do it, so even when you know that the students' pronunciation is wrong, you may not know what the problem is or how to correct it. Finally, many VTs work in countries where the standard English pronunciation taught is different from their own. This is particularly a problem for non-British teachers working in countries that were once British colonies. Most VTs are American, but in many countries school systems and materials still follow a British pronunciation standard. (Despite my impeccable Minnesota English, a school in China once decided that I should be replaced by a Chinese teacher during the pronunciation segment of my English course lest students pick up bad U.S. pronunciation habits from me.)

The upshot of all this is that teaching pronunciation may not be as easy as it looks. However, by giving students reasonable expectations, drawing their attention to the various aspects of the problem, and being a model of native pronunciation, you can make a valuable contribution to your program.

GOALS AND EXPECTATIONS

Many students, even those whose pronunciation is quite clear, are dissatisfied with their pronunciation and see the chance to study with a native speaker as the long-awaited opportunity to finally achieve native pronunciation. However, in practice this goal is very rarely achieved no matter how good the teacher or student is because changing pronunciation habits is inherently very difficult, especially for adult learners. Furthermore, it may even be unwise to try. A foreign accent signals the fact that a speaker should not be held to the same level of linguistic and cultural expertise as a native and serves to protect the speaker from misunderstandings. Also, the effort that is necessary to lift a student's pronunciation from the level of good to native could generally better be invested elsewhere. Thus, a wiser and more realistic pronunciation goal for most students is clear but accented pronunciation, not native accuracy (Brown 2001, 284; Carruthers 1987, 192; Scarcella and Oxford 1992, 165).

I do not mean to say, however, that improvement in pronunciation is undesirable or impossible. When pronunciation problems affect intelligibility, it is vitally important for students to try to improve their pronunciation. Moreover, most students can improve their pronunciation to some extent. Some pronunciation problems occur because students have an incorrect idea of how a word should be pronounced. For example, accenting the wrong syllable in an English word often hinders communication, and this problem is relatively easy to correct with instruction. Most students can also make limited improvements in their ability to pronounce sounds. For example, while they may always say *dis* instead of *this,* they may be able to learn to distinguish long and short vowels (e.g., the difference between *hear* and *her*) in such a way that listeners can hear a difference. Most students can achieve a level of accuracy that makes them easily intelligible, and many can do much better.

ASPECTS OF PRONUNCIATION

Many students tend to think of pronunciation primarily as accurate production of the sounds of English words, but this aspect of the problem is neither the only one nor the only important one. Consequently, one way to help students improve is by ensuring that they are aware of all of the important issues.

1. **accurate pronunciation of sounds:** As I have suggested, accurate pronunciation really has two aspects, ability and knowledge. Students first need to learn to pronounce as many of the sounds of English as possible accurately. The particular sounds with which students will have difficulty depend to a large extent on what students' first language is, but some sounds in English, such as the *th* sounds in *think* and *this,* or the short vowels in *head, hit,* and *put,* are difficult for students from many language backgrounds. The second aspect is making sure that students know what sounds they should pronounce in a given word. Common pronunciation problems include omitting sounds, adding extra ones, or simply pronouncing the wrong sound.

2. **syllable stress:** Unlike many other languages, English requires that one syllable in each word be stressed more than others. The importance of putting the stress on the right syllable in English cannot be underestimated; as Bowen, Madsen, and Hilferty (1985, 85) point out, putting the stress on the wrong syllable is more likely to make a word unintelligible than is mispronouncing one of its sounds. For many students who are especially hard to understand, misplaced syllable stress is the main problem.

3. **sentence word stress:** In English sentences, not all words are given equal emphasis. Key words (usually the words that contain new or important information) are stressed and pronounced more slowly and clearly than other words. Take, for example, the question *Are you going to go to Boston?* If the focus of the question is on where the listener will go, the sentence will sound something like *Ya gonna go ta Boston;* the word *Boston* will be pronounced clearly and with more emphasis. If, in contrast, the emphasis is on who is going, the sentence will sound like *Are you gonna go ta Boston?* While students don't necessarily need to learn to use reduced forms of the unimportant words in sentence, they should learn to stress key ones.

4. **sentence intonation:** Intonation patterns in English sentences primarily indicate the degree of certainty of an utterance, that is, whether it is a statement, question, or suggestion. Statements rise to a plateau and end with falling intonation. Most questions and suggestions end in rising intonation; however, *wh-* questions (*who, what, where, when, why,* and *how*) end with falling intonation. It is important for students to learn these patterns in order to communicate meaning as well as to avoid unwittingly sounding rude or indecisive.

5. **enunciation:** Some students lack confidence in speaking or are unsure of their pronunciation, and therefore speak either very quietly or not very clearly. Obviously, this makes them more difficult to understand, and students should therefore be reminded that speaking audibly and clearly is an important aspect of pronunciation.

TEACHING PRONUNCIATION

The ideal approach to student pronunciation problems is for you to work individually with each student, listening for problems, explaining the proper pronunciation (or intonation, etc.), modeling correct pronunciation, and listening to the student practice. However, this is usually not possible because of time limitations and class size, so the discussion here focuses on approaches you can use with a class. These approaches fall into two categories: teaching students what sounds they should produce and practicing pronunciation.

Listening and Pronunciation

Unless you are fortunate enough to have very small classes, it will be difficult to give much individual attention to students' pronunciation. Students must therefore learn to rely on their ears to tell them how closely their pronunciation approximates that of the models they are trying to imitate. However, many students are not in the habit of listening carefully before attempting to repeat. In fact, they have often been trained for years to immediately repeat whatever the teacher says, no matter how vague their impression of the jumble of sounds they are trying to reproduce. Another problem is that while students are listening to the teacher's spoken model, their attention is often focused more on preparing to repeat than on listening. The teacher's sentence consequently serves less as a model for pronunciation than as a starting shot announcing that students should try to speak.

The first approach to pronunciation is thus helping students develop the habit of listening carefully before they speak. To do this, the first time you say a word or sentence, ask students to listen—just listen. They should not murmur the utterance quietly after you; instead, they should concentrate on fixing the sound in their memories. Repeating the model utterance several times before asking students to repeat allows them more chances to listen and helps break their habit of blurting out a response as soon as you finish.

Exercises that require listening but no oral response may also help sharpen students' listening skills. Minimal-pair drills are particularly good for helping students learn to hear the difference between similar sounds. *Minimal pairs* are words that are pronounced exactly the same with the exception of one sound (e.g., *pin-pen, bid-bit*). To help students learn to hear the difference between the short *i* and *e* sounds, for example, ask students to raise their pen when you say the word *pen* and a pin when you say *pin*.

Training students' ability to hear sound distinctions will not necessarily result in good pronunciation. However, students who have not clearly heard a sound obviously have less chance of producing it correctly than those who listen carefully.

Modeling Pronunciation

Most native speakers of English have not formally studied the mechanics of English pronunciation, so it would be helpful to do some homework in this area so that you are prepared to explain how sounds are made if necessary.[4] However, you will almost certainly be expected to serve as a model for pronunciation, and a limited amount of choral drill can be useful for this purpose. Steps for such a drill would be as follows:

1. Choose a text that represents normal spoken English (as opposed to more bookish language). A dialogue from a textbook would be a good choice.

2. Read sentences aloud, clearly but at a fairly normal speed. Have students listen to each sentence once or twice before attempting to repeat it. Remind them that they should be listening to and trying to mimic the rhythm, stress, and intonation patterns of your speech as well as your pronunciation.

3. As suggested previously, build longer sentences up from the end.

---

[4]A detailed introduction to the sounds of English can be found in many ESL and introductory linguistics texts (e.g., Ur 1996, 48, for standard British English, and Brown 2001, 297, or Goodwin 2001, 134–37, for North American) as well as on many Web sites. Also look at English textbooks in your host country so that you know what standard students have been taught and what phonetic system they use.

- If you want students to prepare a choral drill of a dialogue before class, it is best if they have a taped model to work with. Without having heard a dialogue before they repeat it, they may wind up polishing an incorrect performance.

- Choral drill is best in small doses. It generally only takes a short period of drill for students to get the point you wish to make, and drill beyond that point rapidly turns into mindless parroting.

- One enjoyable way to practice the rhythm of English sentences is by turning a dialogue from a book, preferably one with short sentences, into a jazz chant. In essence, you find the natural rhythm of each sentence and then chant it with emphasis on the key words, something like a group cheer at a football game or a chant at a protest rally (e.g., *Hell no, we won't go.*). Clapping or pounding desks adds to the festive nature of the activity. This exercise is particularly good for driving home the point that not all words in English sentences get equal stress.

Performance of a Text

Once students can repeat accurately after a spoken model, the next step is to have them practice speaking from a written text. Keeping pronunciation accurate while reading a text aloud is more difficult than repeating after a teacher, but it is still easier than maintaining correct pronunciation in free conversation because students can focus their attention on pronunciation rather than grammar or word choice.

1. Choose a text, and copy it for the students. If the goal is to teach daily conversational English, choose a text that represents normal spoken English, though an argument can be made for sometimes including texts of literary and cultural merit (e.g., famous speeches, poems) that were also intended to be read aloud or recited.

2. Go over the text with the students in class, and have them take whatever notes they need on pronunciation, syllable stress, sentence intonation, and stressed words.

3. Have the students practice reading the text aloud (either in class or at home). Students should become very familiar with the text, though I suggest that you not normally require them to memorize it because the time and effort devoted to memorizing the exact words distracts attention from the primary point of the exercise.

4. Either have students perform the text in class or—if the equipment is available—have them tape a reading of the text. The advantages of the latter approach are that students don't all have to listen to each other read the same text and that you can listen at your leisure, but the disadvantage is that it takes more of your time.

Accuracy in Free Conversation

Students cannot depend on always having someone around who is willing and able to correct their errors in pronunciation and intonation, so the final task—learning to maintain accuracy in pronunciation and intonation as they engage in conversation—is largely up to students. Ultimately, students need to learn to hear serious discrepancies between their own pronunciation and that of the models to which they are exposed, and then correct their own speech.

ADAPTING TO THE LOCAL STANDARD

As suggested in the introduction, you may have some difficulty if the pronunciation standard used in your host institution is different from your own. My first suggestion in such situations is that you generally use your normal accent in class, whether it is the proper one or not. Rather than forcing yourself to unnaturally mimic another accent, remind students that there are a variety of different English accents and that students should become comfortable listening to as many as possible. On the other hand, when teaching pronunciation, try to minimize any markedly regional features of your accent and conform as much as possible to that standard of English being taught (usually North American or British).

A second suggestion is that you familiarize yourself with the local standard. Look at a copy of a local textbook that teaches pronunciation to find out (1) how students are told to pronounce, (2) what notation system (if any) is used to transcribe sounds, and (3) what students are and are not taught about pronunciation. Having this information will make it much easier for you to decide how to approach your pronunciation lessons and will help you harmonize your lessons with the local system. Students may be held accountable for pronunciation or phonetics on general tests outside your class, and if what you teach does not conform to the local standard, the students' exam scores may suffer for it. Knowing the local system also enables you to point out ways in which your pronunciation differs from the local standard so that students who choose to model their speech on yours are aware of potential trouble spots.

Correction

As mentioned previously, research has shown that correcting students' grammar errors when they speak often does not result in any improvement in their grammatical accuracy, so you should not assume that correcting students frequently when they speak English is necessarily useful. Also, correction can disrupt communication and discourage learners. However, error correction probably helps learners at least a little, and, summarizing the research, Hendrickson (1987, 358) suggests that teachers should correct errors at least some of the time—not least because many learners want and expect it. The question thus becomes when and how to correct.

Correction is most called for when errors interfere with communication—when you can't understand what a student is trying to say. The disadvantages of interrupting here are minimal because communication has already broken down, and the student needs to know that the message is not getting through. According to Hendrickson (1987, 358–61) and Omaggio Hadley (2001, 268), other kinds of errors that are good candidates for correction include

1. errors that are highly stigmatized, that is, errors that might result in a student seeming rude, offensive, or ignorant. (I am reminded of a young official at a bicycle registration station in Guangzhou who led me into his office, filled out a form for me, then turned around and, with a smile, said "Get out!" Sensing miscommunication, I suggested gently in Chinese that *get out* was not entirely polite. He took this news in, pondered a minute, brightened up, and said, "Get out, please!")

2. frequent or patterned errors. For example, correcting occasional confusion between countable and uncountable nouns is less important than correcting a consistent, patterned failure to use plural forms.

3. errors that reflect misunderstanding of a point that you have recently taught. For example, the *-s* added to verbs used in conjunction with the third-person singular

pronoun (*I go/you go/she goes*) deserves more attention if you taught the point this week than it might at other times.

Some students are put off less by correction and learn more from it than other students, so part of the art of knowing when to correct is being sensitive to how much intrusion the students can bear.

One form of correction you can use in class is the one used most often by native speakers in natural conversation: a corrected repetition of the learner's faulty utterance (e.g., Student: "I like to listen radio." Teacher: "Ah, you like to listen to *the* radio."). This kind of subtle correction disrupts communication less than directly pointing out errors does, and students will eventually learn to listen for it; however, unless you explicitly point out this habit to students as a form of correction, many may miss these repetitions. A more direct approach to correction is to pinpoint the error by interrupting and repeating the few words right before the mistake (e.g., Student: "And then I eated the food." Teacher: "And then I . . ."), giving the student a chance to self-correct. This approach is appropriate for errors that are easy to correct quickly.

For either of the approaches mentioned above to work, your feedback needs to come as soon as possible after the erroneous statement. If you restate an utterance or call attention to an error immediately after it has been made, students are more likely to be able to find the problem. Delayed correction is often more obtrusive because you first need to remind students of what they said wrong, which students often mistake for the correction itself, thus creating confusion and necessitating further explanation. Here's an example:

Teacher: A minute ago you said "I like to listen radio."
Student: I like to listen radio.
Teacher: No, no, you said "I like to listen to radio," but you should say "I like to listen to the radio."
Student: Pardon?

All too often in such cases, you can begin correcting the error only after the student has been publicly convicted of committing it, so it is usually better to let the error go or make a note of it for later.

A final note on error correction: Many students have the mistaken impression that all native speakers of English should and will correct mistakes; in fact, I have heard students complain quite bitterly about native speakers who fail to live up to this assumed obligation. You should let students know that this is an unreasonable expectation for native speakers of any language. Most people are not language teachers and do not engage in conversation for the purpose of teaching language. Additionally, in most Western cultures, correcting other people's mistakes is considered rude. As I have noted, native speakers sometimes repeat corrected versions of flawed utterances, but they generally correct or teach overtly only when asked or when communication breaks down completely.

Students need to understand this because many believe that the only real road to success in English lies in being surrounded by native speakers who will overtly correct mistakes, a view that subtly suggests that any other approach is hopeless. Of course, being immersed in an English language environment is very helpful to a learner, but not because of correction. The main advantage of having such an environment is that it provides more opportunities for practice and extensive English language input. However, whether students are in an English-speaking environment or not, they will only benefit from English input if they learn to attend to it and then correct their own mistakes.

Evaluation

When considering evaluation of spoken skills, you should keep two goals in mind. Obviously, one goal is to find out how well the students can speak. However, I would argue that in many situations an even more important goal is the backwash that oral testing creates: students are most likely to practice speaking if you test oral skills. Backwash is especially important to consider with regard to spoken skills because they are more difficult to test than other language skills, with the result that such testing is often neglected.

Interviewing is generally the best way to evaluate spoken skills, so I focus on interviews here. However, complete reliance on interviewing may be impractical in many situations, so other approaches to evaluation are also briefly discussed.

INTERVIEWS

Interviewing is the form of evaluation closest to actual conversation and therefore has excellent backwash on students. It also allows you a rare opportunity to focus on individual students' speaking skills in a situation where you can determine their level of speaking skill relatively accurately. The main drawback of interviewing is that it is very time-consuming, sometimes prohibitively so for large classes. Interviews are often used as a pretest (and a chance to get to know the students at the beginning of a course) and as a final examination.

Preparing for the Interview

The first step in preparation is deciding what exactly you are looking for. Grammatical accuracy? Use of material taught in your course? Pronunciation? Overall communicative skill? Something else? Your choices should flow naturally from the goals you set for your course and the kinds of practice activities you have asked students to engage in. The backwash will be stronger if you let students know well before the final examination how they will be evaluated and how they should prepare.

Secondly, draw up a list of topics or questions, giving yourself an adequate supply so that you need not use exactly the same ones with each student. Questions should reflect a range of difficulty so that you have easier questions for students at lower levels and more challenging ones for those with more advanced-level skills. Open-ended questions are best (e.g., *What do you think about . . . ? Tell me about . . . ?*) because they don't result in dead-end, yes/no answers; they also allow you to see how much students can elaborate on a point, which is one indication of their level of speaking ability. Natural questions for a pretest interview with students you don't know would be questions about their backgrounds, families, interests, and professions. For a final interview, you might discuss issues raised during the course, other courses the student is taking, or future plans.

Many teachers draw up a marking chart to help them grade during the interview. A simple chart consists of a list of the items you are looking for with a point scale for each. Consider the following simple example for a course in which communicative effectiveness was stressed:

Ability to express ideas	1	2	3	4	5
Range of topics	1	2	3	4	5
Listening comprehension	1	2	3	4	5
Intelligibility	1	2	3	4	5

In designing such a scale, make sure it clearly reflects the goals of the course so that students are rewarded for doing what you have asked them to do. While this point may seem obvious, it is worth emphasizing because sometimes the skills you have emphasized in your course are difficult to assess—and you may be tempted to place more emphasis on other aspects of spoken skills that are easier to assess.[5]

Conducting the Interview

Normally, you should allow at least five minutes on average for an interview, plus a little time between interviews so that you can take notes and give scores. For advanced-level students, you will need longer interviews to give you an idea of their range of competence. Interviewing students is a demanding task, and your ability to make good judgments will drop quickly as you become tired. It is therefore best not to plan to do several hours of interviews in one fell swoop.

Generally, a one-on-one interview should have three basic phases: warm-up, body, and wind-down. The following is one typical approach:

1. **warm-up:** Open with a few easy pleasantries to relax the students. During this phase, you may also try to determine approximately how good their spoken skills are so you can choose appropriately challenging questions for the body of the interview.

2. **body:** Try to challenge the students' speaking (and usually listening) skills by asking more challenging questions and maybe asking the students to perform tasks such as describing a picture, explaining how to do something, or entering into a role play with you. Hughes (1989, 105) suggests that you not dwell on a question if an interviewee gets into trouble; rather, switch to another topic to give the interviewee a fresh start. Be careful not to turn a pleasant chat into an overwhelming ordeal, but be sure to raise topics and ask questions that give students a chance to show what they can do.

3. **wind-down:** End with a few easy questions so that the students don't leave the interview feeling devastated.

Taping interviews allows you to focus on the conversation during the interview and to listen again after the interview—but makes the process even more time-consuming. Taking notes during the interview and assigning a grade immediately is much more efficient but can distract both you and the student during the interview. Getting a second opinion from a colleague who either participates in the interviews or listens to them on tape does much to increase the reliability of your grading.

PAIR OR SMALL-GROUP ASSESSMENT

If you have large classes, one-on-one interviews may be impossible even once during a semester. In such cases, a good alternative consists of assessing students as they talk to each other in pairs or small groups. This approach is less time-consuming than one-on-one interviews as well as closer in nature to the pair and small-group activities often used in oral skills classes, so it tends to have very beneficial backwash on the seriousness with which students engage in those activities.

1. Design one or more testing tasks for pairs or small groups. These should be as similar as possible to the kinds of activities that you normally use in class. For example, if you often have students do pair work based on model dialogues, this would be a good test

---

[5] In designing a scoring chart for interviews, you might want to look at a proficiency scale such as the one in chapter 4. However, remember to adapt the ideas on such charts so that your assessment chart reflects the goals of your course.

task. Or, if you have students do a lot of small-group tasks, base your test activity on one of these. Normally you will choose one basic test format but have a list of different topics or questions from which the pairs or groups will draw.

2. Design a scoring system to use as you listen to the pair or group. As with scoring systems for interviews, the system should be designed to reinforce whatever you have emphasized in your course.

3. Let students know what the test format will be, preferably as early as possible. In fact, you might do a dry run in class so that students are very clear about what you expect from them (and so that you don't need to waste a lot of time during the test explaining the format to students).

4. Organize students into pairs or small groups, and schedule a time for their test.

5. When they arrive for the test, have them draw one or more test tasks from a hat. (You may want to have each group arrive a few minutes before their test, draw their topic, and prepare a bit while the previous group is having their test.)

6. During the test, take notes, and assign a tentative grade. (You may want to wait until you have heard all the groups before assigning a final grade.)

LISTENING AND WRITING QUIZZES

For extremely large classes, you may find that any evaluation of oral skills is difficult and can only be done once or twice, resulting in fewer grades and less reinforcement than you would like. In these cases, you may supplement oral skills evaluation with quizzes that require students to listen to something and respond in writing. Obviously, written quizzes are not an ideal way to assess speaking skills, as no actual speaking is involved. However, listening is a vital part of oral communication, so testing listening tends to have the positive backwash of forcing students not to rely on text study alone. Writing does not involve as much time pressure as speaking, but, like speaking, it is a productive skill that requires students to learn to express their ideas in English. So, in situations where other oral assessment is impossible, this method provides at least some incentive for students to practice oral skills and build their productive command of English.

A simple form of this quiz involves orally asking students questions and having them write answers. A more complicated approach is to orally present students with a situation and require them to write dialogues based on your instructions. (Dialogues are more appropriate than essays because the language in dialogues is closer to the language of daily communication.)

1. Design a conversation framework that involves moves and functions you have taught in class, for example, *First A and B meet on the bus and greet each other. A then asks why B didn't come to dinner last night. B apologizes and offers an excuse. A then invites B to dinner another time.*

2. Present the framework to the students orally while they listen and take notes.

3. Ask the students to write a conversation consisting of six turns (A—B—A—B—A—B) that follows the framework and accomplishes the moves it requires. Encourage students to write the shortest dialogue that fulfills the instructions.

4. Grade the dialogues for linguistic accuracy and for cultural accuracy and appropriateness.

133

This type of quiz is not without problems. Students often need some time to get used to this format, so you should practice with the class a few times before the first real quiz. The format also puts students whose speaking skills exceed their listening skills at a real disadvantage; I have seen some flawless dialogues that had nothing to do with the instructions given. However, the stress on listening is also the greatest advantage of the quiz; the backwash will encourage students to focus on oral English rather than just studying the book.

For Thought, Discussion, and Action

1. **speaking practice:** Locate a textbook used to teach English oral skills classes in your host country. List the types of speaking activities it includes. For each activity, carefully analyze the kinds of skills and knowledge that the activity would help students build and the kinds it would not help them build.

2. **small-group speaking practice:** This chapter suggests that in order to build speaking skills, you should give students as much practice in pairs or small groups as possible, but also points out that students may not always cooperate with this approach. Find one or more people who have taught English in your host country, and ask them how students there respond to pair and small-group activities. Also ask for suggestions on how to ensure that students use English as much as possible in such activities.

3. **speaking activities and course plans:** Imagine a course you will teach, or choose one of the sample courses in chapter 6. Then, with that course in mind, go through the list of speaking activities in this chapter and select several that you think would be suitable for use in that course. Be ready to explain the rationale for your choices.

4. **model-based dialogues:** Using either a dialogue from a host-country English book or the sample dialogue below, analyze the dialogue for the moves (functions) it contains. Then write a plan for an oral skills lesson making use of this dialogue.

   Sample dialogue: Anne and Mick are arguing—politely—over whether cats or dogs make better pets. (Listen especially for how they indicate disagreement.)

Anne:	I think that cats usually make better pets than dogs. For one thing, they are quieter.
Mick:	That may be true, but sometimes they make a lot of noise crying at night.
Anne:	For another thing, cats are more affectionate.
Mick:	Really? I don't think so.
Anne:	Of course they are. They always love to sit on your lap.
Mick:	That's just because they want something from you.
Anne:	Yes, but they are so sweet about it.

5. **cocktail parties:** If you are already teaching an English course that involves speaking skills, prepare and conduct a cocktail-party activity (or another activity that you haven't used before) according to the instructions given in the chapter.

6. **small-group tasks:** Choose one or more of the following topics, and turn it into a well-defined task for oral skills practice: *food, weather, pollution, local history, cultural values.*

7. **speaking practice outside class:** Find one or more people who have taught in your host country, and talk with them about how realistic it is to assign speaking homework outside class. What problems might be encountered? What out-of-class speaking assignments might work best?

8. **the local pronunciation standard:** Find out what pronunciation standard is used for English in your host country (British? American? Other?). Also find out what phonetic notation system is taught in textbooks in your host country, and learn to read it. (Many, but not all, countries use the International Phonetic Alphabet.)

9. **learning pronunciation:** Reflect on an experience you had learning the pronunciation of a foreign language (preferably one quite different from English). How hard or easy was it? What kinds of instruction and practice were most helpful to you?

10. **correction:** Reflect on your previous language learning experience. Did any of your teachers correct you as you spoke the target language? If so, how did they correct you? How did you react to the corrections? What approaches to correction did you find most helpful?

11. **interviews:** This chapter suggests that interviews are the best way to assess students' speaking skills but notes that interviews may be too time-consuming for use in some teaching situations. Locate one or more people who have taught in your host country, and find out whether individual or group interviews are normally possible in the classes you will be asked to teach. If these assessment measures would not be realistic, ask about other measures used to ensure that students are encouraged to build their speaking skills.

12. **language learning project (LLP) for speaking skills:** Design an LLP you could suggest to students to build their speaking skills as part of an English course.

Sample LLP for Advanced-Level Speaking Skills

Goal: Build spoken fluency, that is, my ability to express ideas in English reasonably quickly and smoothly; practice incorporating material (new words, phrases, grammar structures) learned from texts into my productive spoken skills

Material: For example, texts in English from a textbook, magazine, or storybook

Plan: Read and retell two texts a week, one text per study session, about one hour per session

Method:

1. Read the story or passage, and make a rough outline of the content.

2. In the outline, include new words, phrases, and grammar structures I want to learn and incorporate into my spoken English.

3. Using my outline—but not the original text—retell the story or passage aloud in English to myself. Try to look at my outline as little as possible.

4. After I retell the story, look back at the original text, and check to see if I correctly incorporated the new material I wanted to learn.

5. If possible, retell the passage a second time without looking at my outline.

6. At the beginning of my next study session, quickly retell the old passage for review before I look at the new one.

Criteria for measuring progress: I will have succeeded if I

- study twenty stories or passages using this method

- can now more fluently and confidently go back and retell these stories or passages, incorporating some of the new words, phrases, and grammar structures

- can apply some of the new material I learned in other speaking situations

Chapter 9

Reading
and Decoding

- Effective reading involves both bottom-up and top-down strategies.

- Many students of English learn to read in a slow, careful manner that relies almost exclusively on bottom-up strategies (intensive reading). Overreliance on this reading approach makes reading slow and often painful, and tends to discourage students from doing any more reading than necessary.

- Students who also learn to read in a more rapid, active way (extensive reading) are more likely to reach a breakthrough point where reading becomes a useful and even enjoyable skill.

Like many students of Chinese (and other languages), I learned to read by slowly carving my way through short but difficult texts with a dictionary, trying to memorize every word and figure out the grammar of every sentence. Not surprisingly, this was not an activity I enjoyed. However, fate intervened in the person of a Chinese history professor who suggested that, since I had three years of Chinese under my belt, it was time for me to start using it in his class. He presented me with a collection of short stories—Chen Ruoxi's *Lao Ren* (Old People)—and told me I had a week to finish the book and write a critique. I was horrified. I had never tried to read anything longer than a short story before, at least not within one week, and knew that there was no way I could apply my look-up-every-unfamiliar-word strategy to a whole book and still finish on time. So I resigned myself to disaster, calculated how much material I had to cover per day, and scraped through it as best I could.

To my great surprise, two things happened. First, despite the large number of words I didn't recognize, I could catch the general drift of the story and, in the end, could write a critique of which I was even moderately proud. Equally important, for the first time in my foreign language reading life, I actually became interested in what I was reading.

Admittedly, this challenge came to me in the right form at the right time. Chen Ruoxi's clear, straightforward style made her work relatively easy to read, and I found the Cultural Revolution setting of the stories fascinating. I had also been studying Chinese long enough that my reading vocabulary was adequate for making some sense of what I was reading. But I still feel lucky that my history professor intervened when he did because I was well on the way to entrenching the habit of a painfully slow, careful approach to reading Chinese and had already started to believe that this was the only way an American could ever read Chinese—or any foreign language.

The intensive reading approach with which my study of Chinese reading began is natural for beginning-level students. When almost every word and structure is new, this slow approach makes sense as a way for students to learn new words and grammar. What often happens, however, is that heavy use of intensive reading as a strategy for learning vocabulary and grammar becomes confused with reading itself. For many students, the single greatest problem in learning to read a foreign language is that habits and skills intended for language learning become their only approach to reading, resulting in both poor reading strategies and a miserable experience. My discussion of reading skills in this chapter thus gives much attention to intensive reading and extensive reading, and to the importance of teaching students to read extensively as well as intensively.

Reading: The Problem and the Goal

Even when people learn to read their first language in elementary school, their attention is often focused primarily on the problem of decoding words, so it is not surprising that they often instinctively tend to think of reading as looking at words, one after another, and then adding them up to see what they mean. However, studies show that reading is in fact a combination of bottom-up and top-down processes. In reading, bottom-up strategies consist primarily of combining vocabulary and grammar clues to build toward meaning. Top-down strategies, however, are equally important. When good readers begin reading a text, they generally have some knowledge of the topic. This knowledge, combined with clues provided by the genre of the text, will enable readers to guess much of what they will read before they read it. For example, even before beginning a newspaper article with the headline "Plane Crashes in Alaska," good readers have a rough idea what kind of material the article will contain and even the order in which it will appear. As they read, they do not devote equal attention to every word or sentence.

Material they already know receives less attention than new material, and material they expect is skimmed over more quickly than material they don't expect. The best way to understand reading is therefore to see it as a process of active guessing in which readers use a variety of clues to understand a text and to take what they need or want from it, generally as quickly as possible (for further discussion, see Carrell and Eisterhold 1987, 220–23; Hedge 2000, chapter 6; Scarcella and Oxford 1992, 95).

This reading process is quite different from the way most students of English—or any other language—are first trained to read. Instead of being encouraged to use extralinguistic knowledge, students are expected to carefully decode a text, slowly studying every sentence and word and constructing meaning almost entirely from the aggregate meaning of the words on the page. To ensure that they understand every word and every detail of the text, students are encouraged to make heavy use of reference works and devote large amounts of time to relatively short texts.

Intensive reading is not necessarily bad. It is necessary when material is very difficult or when a high degree of detail comprehension is necessary, and the slow, careful approach to each text allows students to study vocabulary and grammar. However, if this approach to reading is the only one students learn, the following problems arise:

1. Readers who rely on bottom-up processes to the exclusion of top-down processes often have comprehension problems. Habitual focus on detail means that intensive readers often get the details but miss the general picture. As Bowen, Madsen, and Hilferty (1985, 230–31, 244) note, the time spent decoding also causes readers to lose the drift—hence the meaning—of a text, and may even result in more mistakes in comprehension.

2. Intensive readers are slow and are consequently unable to read very much material. This reduced input from reading, in turn, slows other important parts of the language learning process. For example, the limited amount of text that is read means that readers review and consolidate less vocabulary (see chapter 11). The intake of cultural knowledge through reading is also limited. For students who go abroad to study, slow reading can even limit opportunity for social interaction; for example, on U.S. college campuses, international students who are intensive readers are often noted for their absence from any activity other than classes and meals—they need to spend most of their time at home or in the library struggling to cope with reading assignments.

3. The general unpleasantness of intensive reading—as both a language learning and a reading process—tends to discourage students from reading English. This unpleasantness is too often exacerbated when teachers assign short but very difficult texts packed with new words, a practice that further diminishes any interest students might have had in English reading.

It may be argued that intensive reading is necessary at the early stages of learning English, when learning vocabulary and grammar is more important than learning reading skills per se. However, if students come to believe that this slow, word-by-word process is the only way to read in a foreign language, they have little chance of ever reaching a breakthrough point where reading in English becomes so rewarding and interesting that it is self-sustaining. Students who eventually learn to read well enough to understand English novels, magazines, or newspapers without intolerable investments of time and effort will tend to maintain or even improve their skills after leaving formal English language programs; in contrast, those who only read slowly and painfully are more likely to regress. For this reason, students should be introduced to and encouraged to use extensive reading approaches as early as possible.

Methods for Teaching Intensive Reading

Intensive reading is the core of English programs in many countries, and the methods and assumptions used in intensive reading classes may have a significant impact on the ideas and learning strategies that students bring into your class. Traditional approaches to intensive reading tend to focus more on building students' knowledge of English grammar and vocabulary than on teaching reading skills per se, and such approaches also implicitly teach students to rely mainly on bottom-up reading strategies. A typical unit is often taught as follows. First students are expected to carefully read a passage at home, looking up all the new words and making sure they understand the grammar in each sentence. They may even be asked to memorize the passage or translate it. Then, in class, the teacher lectures on the text (often in the host language rather than in English), explaining most of the grammar and words or questioning students on these points. Students are not encouraged to guess but are expected to work hard and make sure they know all the right answers.[1]

You may be called on to teach intensive reading lessons at some point in your career, and when you are, it is important to use these lessons to build students' vocabulary and grammar knowledge. However, you should also modify the approach described above to place more emphasis on building reading skills and to balance bottom-up and top-down strategies.

IN-CLASS METHODS FOR BEGINNERS

Most volunteer teachers (VTs) do not teach students who are at the very beginning stages of learning to read; however, if you are asked to teach true beginners, the first task is to help them see the correspondence between written symbols and spoken words and sentences. Here are a few basic methods:

1. **teaching the alphabet:** English spelling is rich with irregularities, but there is enough correspondence between letters and sounds that knowing what sounds the letters of the alphabet commonly represent will benefit students.

2. **reading aloud as students follow along:** This will focus students' attention on words rather than letters and will help them begin learning to pronounce words as units instead of as collections of discrete sounds. Bowen, Madsen, and Hilferty (1985, 224) also note that following along as someone reads is a good way for students to learn what punctuation is for.

3. **having students read aloud:** You can have the class read a text aloud as a group (resulting in a fair amount of cacophony) or have them read semiaudibly to themselves. Sometimes you might ask individual volunteers to read a passage aloud, but be sensitive to the fact that what is almost effortless for you is very difficult for students who are just learning to read. Practice should provide maximum support and expose students to minimum public embarrassment. At very low reading levels for English learners, texts should consist primarily of words that students already know in spoken form. This allows a little thrill of discovery when a new word is successfully decoded and helps reinforce the link between written and oral language.

---

[1] You may have colleagues who regularly teach in this fashion, so before judging them too harshly, remember that many English teachers have had only limited opportunity to use English and are thus in the difficult position of trying to teach a language they cannot speak fluently. The advantage of the small amount of material covered with an intensive reading approach is that, with limited preparation, teachers can present a credible English lesson. And despite the flaws of intensive reading, nations that make heavy use of it often still produce many students who eventually become quite proficient in English.

IN-CLASS METHODS FOR INTERMEDIATE AND ADVANCED LEVELS

For students who can read simple texts (e.g., dialogues, stories, articles) in English, a good basic approach to intensive reading lessons consists of three parts:

1. a prereading activity (in class) for building use of top-down skills

2. reading and study of text (outside class) for building vocabulary and grammar knowledge and bottom-up reading skills

3. questions and comprehension check (in class) to focus on meaning

Here I focus on each of these in turn.

Prereading Activities and Skimming

One way to encourage students to use top-down strategies is by using prereading activities that require students to actively make predictions about what they are about to read. Some basic prereading activities are described below.

PREDICTING

Even before starting to read a text, skilled readers can often make at least some educated guesses about its content based on the title of the text and other available clues (e.g., author, source, general kind of text). Even if the predictions are incorrect, getting students to guess will make them more alert when reading than if they are simply moving their eyes purposelessly over a string of words.

1. Give students a text. (If the text is from some source other than the course textbook, you might try to preserve its original setting. For example, photocopy an article from a magazine directly from its original location so that students can see that it is from a magazine.)

2. Have them look at the text's title and setting, and ask them to make one guess as to what the text is about. (If the text is by an author the students might know, the name is another clue they might be directed to.)

3. Encourage all guesses, right or wrong, but especially those which seem to make good use of the evidence available.

4. Have students check their guesses when they reread the text more carefully later.

SKIMMING

This common prereading activity involves quickly looking over a text and reading a few select parts to get an idea of what it contains. Many students resist the idea of skimming in a foreign language (largely because of well-developed intensive reading habits), so in-class skimming exercises play an important role in familiarizing students with this skill as well as convincing them of its legitimacy and value.

1. Give students a reading text. (Skimming practice works best with texts that are more than one page in length.)

2. Tell students to skim through the text quickly, reading only the following parts:
   • titles and subheadings
   • a few sentences from the introduction
   • the first lines of some paragraphs

- proper nouns (names) and numbers (These are easy to spot and generally helpful in quickly determining what is being discussed.)
- a few sentences from the conclusion

3. Give students a time limit (one that makes slow, careful reading of the text impossible), and turn them loose.

4. When the time is up, ask students what they have discovered about the text and what guesses they have about the remainder of its contents. You might even list their guesses on the board and have the students check them out after they have read the passage more carefully.

While students are skimming, it may help if you call out the time, creating an atmosphere somewhat akin to that of a horse race. Hearing how much time they have not only reminds students to keep moving but adds a degree of fun and freedom that may help convince them that it is really okay not to be reading carefully. The ultimate goal is for students to develop the habit of skimming a text on their own, so over time you should encourage students to first skim whenever they read an English text, especially a long or difficult one.

Focused Reading

In this activity, which is similar to focused listening (described in chapter 7), you first give students several questions, then have them quickly read through the text to find the answers. The questions help give focus and purpose to the students' reading and make the task easier by providing valuable hints as to what is coming in the text ahead. This activity can be used to preview a text that you have assigned as homework or as an independent in-class activity.

1. Look over the text you will assign, and write several comprehension questions that cover the main points of the content.

2. Write the questions on the board, and give students a time limit that is adequate for reading the text but tight enough that they are pushed to read quickly.

3. Have students quickly read through the text to find the answers.

4. Check by asking students for the answers to the questions.

For lower level students, use simple comprehension questions. For advanced-level students reading more sophisticated texts, open-ended opinion questions are generally better (e.g., *Was the author of this story biased?*).

In a variation on this activity, you have students skim a text, write their own focused reading questions, and finally read the text to answer their own questions. Having students generate their own questions is one way to encourage them to think more actively about what they should be looking for as they read.

Reading and Studying the Text outside Class

There is nothing inherently wrong with having students read and study intensive reading passages in class, and it may be a good idea from time to time so that you can see how students read a passage. However, class time limitations will mean that you often ask students to read and study passages at home. Intensive reading textbooks usually come equipped with a supply of reading passages, vocabulary lists, notes on grammar, and comprehension questions, so the question is what the students should do with all these resources as they study at home. One possibility is to require students to study using a procedure like the following:

1. Students read the entire passage straight through. During this first reading, they mark unfamiliar vocabulary and structures, but they do not stop to look these up in the glossary or a dictionary. (This first reading helps students build extensive reading skills.)

2. Students study unfamiliar grammar structures and vocabulary. Tell them to learn the meaning of new words and structures as well as note how they are used in the passage.

3. Students read the passage again, more carefully. During this second reading, they stop to study any problematic points of the text.

4. Students prepare questions to ask you about any section of the passage they do not understand. While the emphasis is primarily on comprehension of the passage, they should also note questions on grammar and vocabulary.

In-Class Intensive Reading

The traditional in-class intensive reading lesson consists largely of lecture on the passage. One problem with this approach is that, too often, the lecture is unnecessary and boring for students who did their homework well and over the heads of those who didn't prepare or whose listening skills are weak. Another problem is that a lecture approach encourages students to passively wait for the teacher to solve problems. Here are some alternative uses for class time.[2]

QUESTION AND ANSWER ABOUT THE TEXT

The goal of an intensive reading lesson is not just to explain what a particular text means but to teach students how to unravel the mystery of a text for themselves. Students should therefore play as active a role as possible in figuring out each reading passage and should be encouraged to take the initiative by asking you for whatever explanation they need. Consider the following typical paragraph from an intensive reading passage:

> Scientists at Sussex University appear to be on the way to discovering how the mosquito, carrier of diseases such as malaria and yellow fever, finds its target. They have found that the best way to avoid being bitten is: stop breathing, stop sweating, and keep down the temperature of your immediate surroundings. Unfortunately the first suggestion is impossible and the others very difficult. (Guangdong Bureau of Higher Education 1991, 17)

A procedure for dealing with this passage through question and answer in class is as follows:

1. Have students ask you questions about whatever they don't understand. (If they have prepared the passage as homework in the manner suggested above, they should come to class with some written questions ready.)

2. When possible, respond to questions by giving clues so students figure out the answers to their own questions. Consider a few examples:
   - The word *target* (line 3) might cause some confusion, particularly if students' dictionaries only list a basic meaning such as *something to shoot at*. You might respond by asking whose target is being discussed and then asking students to consider what a reasonable mosquito might be interested in. You could also encourage them to look at the following sentence (where the implication is that the target is *you*).
   - Students preoccupied with knowing the exact meanings of words might ask about *Sussex University* (line 1). This question probably isn't worth the investment of much

---

[2] Intensive reading lessons are often used for teaching grammar and vocabulary. To keep the focus here on reading, I have rather artificially segregated these aspects of teaching into their own chapters (see chapters 11 and 12, respectively).

time, so you might just reassure the class that it is only important to know that this is the name of a university.

- The insertion of the long clause "carrier of diseases such as malaria and yellow fever" in the first sentence (lines 1 and 2) might trip up some students, especially those who read slowly. A good tactic for dealing with complex sentences is to have students break them down into smaller, simpler sentences. Here the result would be two sentences: (1) *Scientists at Sussex University appear to be on their way to discovering how the mosquito finds its target.* (2) *The mosquito is a carrier of diseases such as malaria and yellow fever.*

- The phrase "keep down the temperature of your immediate surroundings" (line 5) might cause confusion, especially because it seems to be an absurd suggestion. To respond to this, you probably first need to ask the class whether these suggestions are intended to be serious or not and have them note lines 6 and 7. Having established that the suggestions are not serious—indeed, they may be intended as a joke—go back to the phrase in question, and piece the meaning together using the meanings of the words.

One problem with relying on student questions is that students in some cultures are too shy to ask or may be accustomed to listening to the teacher lecture, so you may need to invest some time and nurturing before you can be reasonably sure that students will ask when they don't understand. You can minimize this problem by isolating some potential trouble spots in the text and asking whether or not students understand them; it is easier to get students to nod yes or no than to get them to ask questions. Another alternative is to require students to each write one question about the reading passage and give it to you before class. A more punitive strategy is to give a comprehension quiz after your class explanation, perhaps even focusing on those points you suspect students should have asked about but didn't.

For classes that go to the opposite extreme by asking about everything, set limits on the kinds of questions that you will answer. One suggestion is to make a rule that you will only answer questions relevant to comprehending the passage being discussed. For example, you might tell students that you are willing to explain what *target* means in this passage but refuse to be drawn into an exhaustive explanation of all of its other possible uses. Such a rule will make life easier for you because contextualized questions about vocabulary, grammar, and meaning are easier to deal with, and it will keep students focused on the primary goal: comprehension of the text.

STUDY OF WORD USAGE

One advantage of intensive reading is that its slow pace allows students to note how words are used in a text, so that they learn usage along with meaning. However, students often study only the meaning of words unless you remind them to attend to usage as well, so devoting some class time to examining word usage is often a good idea.

1. Choose several words or word groups from the text that are new to students.

2. Call students' attention to the first word, and have them note the words around it necessary for proper usage. For example, in the passage above, if students underline *on the way* as a new item, they should note that it is followed by *to* + a gerund ("to discovering"). This is in contrast to *the best way* in the following sentence, which is followed by an infinitive ("to avoid").

3. After students note the usage of a new lexical item, a time-honored practice method is to have them make a sentence using the new item—either right after you point out the usage of an item in class or as a homework assignment. Making sentences is a good way

to help students remember the usage of a new item as well as explore variations. While this exercise can easily degenerate into copying if you ask students to create sentences for a long list of words, I would recommend it in limited doses for items that pose usage problems.

LISTING OF MAIN POINTS/OUTLINING

For intermediate- or advanced-level students who are reading expository passages, a useful exercise is to have them outline the flow of ideas in the passage. This can be done either as an individual reading/writing activity or in class as a small-group project. For an in-class activity,

1. Divide the students into groups, and have each group list the main ideas of the reading passage. Ask them to write out each main idea in a brief, clear sentence; encourage them to state ideas in their own words rather than copy directly from the text. For students at a more advanced level, require a proper formal outline that both summarizes the main ideas and makes clear the relationship between them.

2. As the groups report, list the main ideas on the board.

3. To close, ask the class to decide which of the ideas in the text is most important.

INTERPRETIVE DISCUSSION OF A PASSAGE

To fully comprehend a passage, students, especially those in advanced-level classes, often need to understand more than the surface meaning of the text. The opportunity for careful scrutiny of a passage created by intensive reading can be profitably used to deal with deeper questions related to bias, tone, and purpose. Such questions are challenging—after all, even native speakers of English might debate an author's objectivity or purpose—so this activity is best used only with relatively advanced-level students. Such questions, however, are critical to comprehension of a text, and students who are thinking of them as they read are more likely to notice clues that throw light on the answers.

1. Have students work in groups to answer the following questions about the passage:
   - **main idea:** What is the author most concerned about communicating?
   - **bias and stance:** Is the author objective or biased? Does the author portray a character in a sympathetic or unfavorable light?
   - **tone:** Is the author serious or joking?
   - **purpose:** Why was this written? Is the author trying to entertain? Persuade? Explain? Some combination of these?

   Also tell students to be ready to support their answers by pointing out evidence in the passage that supports their hypotheses.

2. Close by having each group present its theory and evidence for class discussion.

In-Class Methods for Teaching Extensive Reading

To a much greater extent than intensive reading skills, the development of extensive reading skills may mean that reading in English becomes rewarding and enjoyable enough to become an end in itself. If such a breakthrough occurs and students begin to regularly read English books, newspapers, and magazines, they will naturally continue to develop their reading skills, vocabulary, and cultural knowledge. Unfortunately, students reach this breakthrough point only after considerable study and practice. Two important preconditions for a reading breakthrough, the acquisition of a large recognition vocabulary and a fund of cultural background knowledge, are discussed in chapters 11 and 13. This section focuses on two aspects of building extensive reading skills: increasing reading speed and enhancing ability to guess unfamiliar vocabulary.

READING SPEED PRACTICE

One important aspect of helping students develop extensive reading skills involves training them to read more quickly. This can be emotionally difficult for students accustomed to intensive reading because they are more comfortable reading at a slower pace. However, as I have noted, increased reading speed enables students to cover more material and enhances their comprehension. Reading specialists suggest that the minimum effective reading speed is 200 words per minute, the average is 250, and the optimum is 400–500 (Bowen, Madsen, and Hilferty 1985, 244). For many students, reaching these speeds will require breaking some deep-rooted habits, and speed-reading practice in class is one good way to start.

Improvement in reading speeds tends to be very gradual, so students should not expect their speed to improve dramatically during a semester course. However, doing exercises like this in class helps students see the importance of working to increase their reading speed. The primary value of this type of the exercise lies not in the actual practice in rapid reading that it provides but in its power to break the habit of reading slowly and intensively. The fact that this activity goes on in class with the teacher's approval also helps convince students that it is really acceptable to read in this way.

1. Find passages that are short enough to read within a class period and easy enough that students don't often need to resort to dictionaries. (Ideally, you should use readings that are somewhat longer than those often used for intensive reading. However, you may have to make do with whatever reading passages are in students' textbook by doing a quick, extensive-style reading of a passage in class and having students read it more intensively for homework.)

2. Estimate the number of words in the selected passage.

3. Have students quickly read the text as you keep time. To remind them that they are working against the clock, mark the time elapsed on the blackboard, or simply call out the time. When students finish reading, have them note how long it took them to read the text, and then divide the number of words read by the time taken, arriving at a words-per-minute figure.

4. Have students record their scores and try to increase them over time.

5. After the exercise, do a quick comprehension check to remind students that speed is not the only goal. Ask general questions on main points so that the focus stays on getting the gist of the text quickly rather than on comprehension of details.

GUESSING VOCABULARY

In extensive reading, students should keep dictionary use to a minimum because frequent dictionary stops slow reading speed and tend to break the train of thought, thus hampering comprehension of the broader flow of ideas and making reading less enjoyable. If students are to learn to read extensively, they need to develop the habit of guessing the meanings of unfamiliar words or skipping over them and forging ahead. The following useful exercise for helping students become more comfortable guessing could be combined with the exercises described above for building reading speed.

1. Have students quickly read a passage in class, underlining unfamiliar words but not stopping.

2. Have students report some of the words they underlined, and choose a few for class discussion. (Here you might remind students that they are to practice guessing; many at this point will naturally tend to start thumbing through their dictionaries.)

3. For each word, have students ask the question: *Can I quickly guess enough about the word to keep going?* In many cases, they need only a general idea of the meaning of an unfamiliar word, which they can often guess from context. For example, in the sentence *She picked the chrysanthemum and smelled it,* knowing that a chrysanthemum is some kind of flower is probably sufficient, and a student who guesses this can continue reading without any serious loss of comprehension.

4. If the students cannot guess much about an unfamiliar word, have them next ask themselves: *Do I need to understand this word?* Readers can often skip over unfamiliar words without serious loss of comprehension, and this is preferable to repeated stops. Of course, when skipping over a word results in complete loss of the train of thought, students should stop and look the word up, but for extensive reading they also need to learn to become comfortable not knowing the exact meaning of every word they run across.

Extensive Reading outside Class

For students to achieve a breakthrough in reading, they will almost certainly need more extensive reading practice than is possible in class, so an important part of a reading program is having students read outside class. While English language reading material may not be easy to come by in some countries, often at least some books, newspapers, or magazines will be available in English. When such reading material is available, extensive reading skills are often worth special attention because of the potential for breakthrough.

CHOOSING MATERIAL

In some situations, not much reading material in English of any kind is available, but often the problem is finding material of an appropriate difficulty level for the students rather than simply finding material. In China, for example, a wealth of textbooks are available, as are English newspapers and novels in English. The hard part is finding longer texts—interesting fiction, in particular—for students who are not quite ready for classic English novels.

One option is to develop your own lending library. While this may take time and ingenuity, it allows you to establish a collection of books that you select to fit your own purposes. If you have a generous expense account, you can make trips to a well-stocked bookstore in a provincial capital or order books from home, but if you are working within more limited means, you might try some of the following approaches:

1. If friends and relatives at home owe you favors, tell them what kinds and levels of material you need, and ask them to haunt rummage sales for inexpensive or free books. As noted earlier, many countries have reduced postal rates for printed material, so mailing books is often not outrageously expensive (though it may take a long time).

2. Write your embassy or consulate to see what free materials are available.

3. Subscribe to a magazine or newspaper so you can stay in touch with world events and build a collection of current events reading material.

4. Other foreigners who are leaving your host country may be willing to leave old books, magazines, and other reading material behind, so let people know about your library-building dreams.

Assuming that some choice is available, the best materials for extensive reading are interesting and not overly difficult. To the extent that students can choose whether to read or not, you might think of the decision as a form of cost-benefit analysis: students will be willing to read when the benefits gained from reading outweigh the investment of time and effort. The break-even point will differ from student to student and will depend greatly on the material available, but it is safe to assume that students are more likely to voluntarily read interesting and easy materials than those which are neither.

Different rules of thumb have been suggested for determining what level of difficulty is appropriate for an extensive reading text. Scarcella and Oxford (1992, 108) believe that a text is too difficult if a student has to resort to the dictionary more than once or twice per page to look up unfamiliar words that can't be guessed and are important for comprehension. Bowen, Madsen, and Hilferty (1985, 231) suggest that if a student gets 85 percent of the words right when reading a text aloud, the text is not too hard. My more rough-hewn approach is to have students open a text they are considering and read a paragraph or so from the middle. If they can more or less follow what is going on, the text is probably easy enough for extensive reading.

ALL-CLASS READING ASSIGNMENTS

Sometimes you have enough copies of a book to have all the students in your class do extensive reading practice with it. A suggested basic cycle of activities would go as follows:

1. For in-class prereading activities, see In-Class Prereading Activities and Skimming above.

2. Whether the reading material is a short story, an article, or part of a novel, assign a certain amount of out-of-class reading, and suggest approximately how much time students should spend reading. This will remind students to work toward increasing their speed. As with intensive reading, giving the students comprehension questions or broader interpretive questions will help focus their reading.

3. To provide accountability and closure, combine extensive reading assignments with writing or discussion activities. Perhaps the best activity is an oral or written evaluation, recommendation, or review of the book. For lower level students, this might simply be a brief statement as to why they did or did not like what they read; you might ask students at a more advanced level for a review or critique. (See chapter 10 for a discussion of review writing.)

INDIVIDUAL READING ASSIGNMENTS

When possible, it is good for a course to incorporate limited-choice language learning projects (LLPs) (see chapter 3) in which students choose some of their own reading material. While LLPs may be somewhat more difficult to manage than having all the students read the same thing, they are preferable for students at higher levels because individualized LLPs accustom students to choosing their own material. LLPs are also often a practical necessity when you can't find enough copies of any single book for everyone in the class. The extra trouble of setting up and managing such a system is generally well worth the effort because, when students can choose their own material, they are likely to consider reading in English as an activity that might become an ongoing part of their lives. For such situations, the following is a suggested cycle of activities:

1. Tell students roughly how much material you expect them to read, and then have them choose their own reading material. (I generally specify the general number of pages I expect students to read and have them choose books with approximately that number of pages.) To make the system more flexible and enhance accountability, you might use contracts that specify how much reading students will do, in what books, and by what date. For example, if you ask everyone to read at least 300 pages during the semester, one student might read one 70-page and one 230-page book; another student might read two 150-page books. Quantifying assignments by number of pages tends to push students toward books with small pages and big print, a problem you may wish to account for in your calculating system.

2. Encourage prereading activities. For example, ask for a very brief preliminary report on the kind of book and possibly some guesses as to what it contains.

3. As discussed above, encourage students to time themselves as they read and try to build their speed over time.

4. To provide accountability in a natural way, have students write reviews or present recommendations orally in class. Students could also be asked to write summaries, responses, or cultural comparisons. Cheating is obviously easier if the students are reading books you haven't read, but your knowledge of what a text is likely to contain and the student's report usually give you a sufficiently clear idea of how well the student has done the reading.

Hedge (2000) suggests a "reading syndicate" variation of this procedure "in which members of a group read different books and share their experiences. The outcome is often a peer conference in which students can take on the roles of asking questions as well as answering them" (p. 219).

Evaluation

Evaluating reading through written reviews, oral book reports, and other such measures has the significant advantage of having better backwash than examinations, placing more emphasis on daily work and avoiding the unhealthy emphasis on one heroic study effort that often accompanies examinations. However, for situations in which you need to give quizzes or tests, here are some suggested methods.

BEGINNING-LEVEL READING TESTS

For students at very low levels, testing their ability to comprehend sentences is appropriate. You can construct one such test by writing a series of statements and asking students to mark them true or false. A variation involves making up a list of questions to which students have to answer yes or no. The statements and questions can be based either on general knowledge or on a picture drawn on the board.

SKIMMING-SKILL QUIZZES

To construct a simple skimming-skill quiz, give the students a passage, and ask them to skim and find out as much as they can in a very limited amount of time. When the time is up, have them write down the main ideas of the passage. When grading such quizzes, be careful to give higher scores to students who provide a sketchy overview of the whole passage than to those who do a thorough job on the beginning of the passage but ignore the rest.

PASSAGE AND COMPREHENSION QUESTIONS

The traditional reading comprehension test consists of several short reading passages (of no more than a few paragraphs each) and comprehension questions for each. The kinds of questions you ask will depend in part on what you have emphasized in your course. If you have stressed guessing vocabulary from context, you should include some items that test this skill. If your focus has been on content comprehension, questions should emphasize this aspect of the passage. If you have had students work with issues of author bias, tone, and other deeper aspects of comprehension, these are fair game as well. Intensive reading tests normally evaluate students' comprehension of both main points and details, so give students ample time to read the passage carefully. You may even allow students to use dictionaries.[3] Passages for extensive reading tests should be longer, time constraints should be tighter, less emphasis should be placed on detail comprehension, and dictionary use should almost certainly not be permitted.

Here are some test items you might consider:

1. **true/false:** True/false (or yes/no, good/bad) items are easy to grade, but you need a great many to have a reasonable level of test validity.

2. **multiple choice:** Like true/false items, the various forms of multiple-choice items (including matching) are easy to grade. However, as noted in chapter 4, they are difficult to construct well. Their backwash is also questionable as they encourage students to hone skills in guessing between alternatives. My personal feeling is that you should avoid using multiple-choice items unless they are widely used in your host country and students need to be prepared for them. In that case, try to learn locally how items are normally constructed.

3. **short answers:** These items take various forms. The most obvious would be a simple question such as *What are the writer's two main arguments?* However, completing sentences (*The writer feels that smoking . . .*) and filling in a form or grid are other useful forms of short-answer items. Short-answer items can be more difficult to grade than true/false or multiple-choice items; some answers will be partly correct, others may not be wrong but appear off topic, and others may simply be hard to decipher. However, short-answer items can more easily go straight to the heart of a passage than can multiple-choice or true/false items (which tend to force you into testing details), are easier to construct, and tend to have better backwash.

---

[3] In real-life intensive reading, students use dictionaries, and their effective use is an important part of the skill being tested. However, if part of your goal is to prepare students for other reading tests, make sure that the rules of your test conform to those of tests students will take outside your class.

PASSAGE AND OUTLINE

Another way to check reading comprehension is to ask students to read a passage and then write an outline. (Outlines work best for expository passages.) This task is more difficult than answering questions and should probably only be used with classes that have had practice with outlining. However, it is a good task when you want students to extract the most important elements from a passage.

You can make passage-and-outline tests somewhat easier by using short-answer questions that are organized around an outline of a passage. In other words, your questions might look something like this:

1. What is the main thing the author is trying to persuade us to believe?

2. What is the first reason?

3. What evidence does the author mention to support this first reason?

4. What is the author's second reason?

5. [etc.]

Hughes (1989, 126–28) suggests an interesting variation in which students are given an article (in his example, one on migraine headaches) and several randomly ordered statements describing the contents of the passage. For example,

- She gives some of the history of migraine.

- She recommends specific drugs.

- She recommends an herbal cure.

- [etc.]

Students then read the article and place the statements in the order used in the article.

PASSAGE AND SUMMARY

A simple form of reading test that is especially appropriate for testing extensive reading skills involves giving students a passage to read within a time limit, then taking the passage away and having students write a summary of its contents. This kind of test is easy to administer (though in large classes you may need help collecting the reading passages from students promptly) and has good backwash, but it also places fairly heavy demands on students' writing skills. This type of test is best used with students who have practiced writing summaries of passages in class.

CRITIQUE

A very challenging intensive reading examination consists of giving students a passage that presents an argument and having them write a critique or rebuttal of the argument. This tests critical thinking skills and writing skills as well as reading comprehension, and is only appropriate for classes in which this kind of critical reviewing has been practiced.

TRANSLATION

For VTs who can speak the language of the host country, the ultimate detail test is having students translate a passage in English into their own language. This test, again, is only recommended for classes that have had practice in translation.

CLOZE TESTS

Cloze tests are sometimes used to evaluate reading skills, so I discuss them briefly here. Cloze tests contain a passage from which words have been deleted (every tenth word or so); students read the passage and fill in the blanks with appropriate words. Open-ended cloze tests allow students to fill in the blanks with any words they think would be appropriate; multiple-choice cloze tests give students options from which to pick. My rather lukewarm attitude toward cloze tests is due in part to the fact that it is not clear that they measure reading skill (Hughes 1989, 129). However, my main objection is that their backwash may be to encourage students to practice cloze exercises rather than to read.[4]

For Thought, Discussion, and Action

1. **learning to read a foreign language:** Ask one or more classmates (friends, etc.) about their experiences learning to read in a foreign language. What language was it, and how different was it from English? Did they learn through intensive reading methods, extensive reading methods, or both? What were the challenges and rewards? Based on their experience, what advice would they give about teaching students to read in a foreign language?

2. **doing intensive reading:** First, locate a typical English textbook from your host country that includes reading passages. Then prepare a lesson plan in which you teach the text intensive-reading style. Finally, ask a teacher from your host country to give you feedback about your proposed lesson plan.

3. **doing speed reading:** If you already teach a course that involves reading skills, try preparing and conducting a speed-reading exercise (or another activity of a kind that you have not used previously) according to the instructions in the chapter.

4. **getting students to ask questions:** In many countries, getting students to ask questions about a text is not always easy. List several strategies you think might help prime the question-asking pump, and discuss the strategies with someone who has taught in your host country.

5. **finding reading materials in English:** Using any available sources of information, try to find out what kinds of reading materials in English are available in your host country. Questions to consider about each kind of material include
    *   How widely available is it?
    *   How much does it cost? Can students afford it?
    *   What is its level of reading difficulty?
    *   Would it be interesting to students?
    *   Would it be more appropriate for students to use for intensive reading or extensive reading?

6. **doing extensive reading (task A):** The chapter suggests that it may be a good idea to assign students extensive reading as part of their homework. Talk to one or more people from your host country, and find out how realistic such assignments would be in your setting.

---

[4] See Bailey (1998, 60–63) for discussion of potential pitfalls in the use of cloze tests and how to avoid them.

7. **doing extensive reading (task B):** Imagine you have been assigned to teach one of the sample courses described in chapter 6 (probably course three, four, or seven). Design a sample extensive reading LLP you could suggest to students as part of one of these courses.

Sample LLP for Advanced-Level Reading Skills

Goal: Build reading speed for novels in English.

Material: A novel that is interesting and not overly difficult.

Plan: Read for one hour a night, three nights a week.

Method:

1. At the beginning of each session, mark the time and the page number I start from.

2. Read as quickly as possible without completely losing the train of the story. As long as I have a rough idea of what is going on, keep reading.

3. Do not stop to look words up in a dictionary unless I become completely lost. (If this happens often, find an easier novel.)

4. At the end of the hour, mark how many pages I have read.

5. Over time, try to increase the number of pages I can read in an hour. (Reading speed only improves gradually, so do not expect sudden leaps in my reading speed.)

Criteria for measuring progress: I will have succeeded if I

- finish reading two or three novels using this approach

- reduce my average reading time by several minutes per chapter (as measured by my page-per-minute score)

Chapter 10

Writing: Keeping Your Head above Water

- By making writing a communicative activity, you increase students' interest in writing and your interest in what they write.

- Students need to learn to find and correct their own errors, so it is not necessary or even desirable for you to find and correct every error on each paper.

- The ability to write well entails learning to plan and edit as well as write.

- Large classes in EFL settings make it important for you to learn to respond to student writing quickly and efficiently, and to find ways to reduce the paper-marking load.

I was teaching at Fu Jen University in Taiwan the first time I was offered a chance to teach writing, and I was delighted to accept—writing courses paid time and a half! However, before long I discovered that I had not driven a particularly sharp bargain. The sheer weight of the paper correction load more than justified any extra money I was getting; week after week I slogged through stacks of papers, finding and correcting the same grammar errors each week in papers students had obviously written just to get through the assignment. As the course went on and my energy dwindled, I began resorting to tactics such as letting papers pile up on my desk or giving students long assignments so that I could rest for a week or two while they wrote. Of course, the problem with these tactics was that when I finally did get around to grading the accumulated compositions, it was all I could do to get through the papers, let alone make the experience educationally productive.

I no longer find writing courses such a nightmare to teach; in fact, now I rather enjoy them. But some of the headaches mentioned above—students' lack of interest in what they write, slow improvement in grammatical accuracy, and the burden of correcting papers—never vanish entirely. This chapter discusses traditional concerns related to the teaching of writing, such as various tasks that can be assigned, the steps in the writing process, and the mechanics of paper marking. However, this chapter would not be complete—or even very helpful—if it ignored the practical problems that confront a teacher in the large writing classes that are typical of EFL settings: the grandest writing theories seem irrelevant when you are confronted with a pile of compositions you don't want to read. I offer no magic solution to these problems, but I discuss ways to minimize them, not the least of which is seeing that both you and the students have some interest in what is being written.

Message and Form in Writing

Many ESL textbooks approach writing by teaching students the proper forms of written English (how to write a sentence, a paragraph, and so on) and then coming up with topics to give students an opportunity to practice using these forms. Other approaches begin with the message, encouraging students to find something they want to say and moving to the question of what form will best help them communicate their message. There is no conclusive evidence that either of these approaches to teaching writing is the right one. However, I would suggest that a writing course that stresses the message is generally more interesting than one that stresses form and that, by stressing the message, you can use the inherent human desire to communicate as an engine to draw students into writing. Also, as pointed out previously, the tradition in many countries is to overstress the formal aspects of language learning, so the volunteer teacher (VT) would do well to be a corrective to this tendency whenever possible.

Be forewarned that even if you intend to focus on writing as a communicative activity, it is very easy to become overly concerned with formal accuracy. One reason is that written language is generally expected to be more formally correct than spoken language, so flaws seem to cry out for correction. The relative permanence of written language also means that teachers can scrutinize compositions slowly and carefully, devoting far more time to ferreting out grammar errors than they can with ephemeral spoken language. Finally, obsession with grammar and form is sometimes fueled by a cult of martyrdom among writing teachers, who compete with each other to see who slaves for more hours over each batch of papers. In this competition, well-marked papers are concrete evidence of the teacher's merit.

The thrust of my argument here is not that you should ignore grammar and form; training in grammatical accuracy and the forms of composition should be an important part of any writing course. However, overemphasis on form can lead to neglect of the message itself. In turn, students may fabricate messages in order to practice grammar or expository form. Students' tendency to ignore communication is compounded when compositions have no audience other than the teacher, and as Raimes (1983) notes, "Traditionally, the teacher has been not so much the reader as the judge of students' writing" (p. 17). Compositions that come back to students covered with grammar corrections and comments on form serve to confirm the students' belief that writing is a formal exercise. Unfortunately, most students aren't very interested in writing formal exercises, and most teachers aren't very interested in reading them.

We would be kidding ourselves if we thought that students wrote compositions primarily because they wanted to tell us something; students in writing courses are generally all too aware that the primary reason they are writing any given paper is that the teacher requires it. This, however, does not mean that students cannot become interested in conveying a message if they are given the chance. Below are several general principles that will help you ensure that a writing class is as communicative—and interesting—as possible:

1. Make an effort to generate interest in topics before asking students to write. One way to do this—and get in some good speaking practice—is to discuss a topic before writing about it. If students have not considered or discussed an idea, they are less likely to become deeply interested in it. An equally important reason for talking over ideas is to demonstrate that you are genuinely interested in the ideas themselves as well as the composition that they lead to.

2. Use naturally existing information gaps and opportunities for communication. There is a great deal you don't know about your host country, about its history and culture, and about the students, so compositions are a natural opportunity for the students to educate you. What the students don't know about each other (e.g., stories from childhood) is a second natural information gap. Take advantage of these.

3. Ask students to write their own ideas in their own words as much as possible. Many writing texts are filled with exercises that require students to rearrange sentences or correct flawed compositions. Such exercises can be useful for teaching specific writing skills, but they certainly do not provide students with an opportunity to communicate in writing. A steady diet of such exercises will drill home the impression that writing is simply making sure that words appear in the proper formal patterns.

4. See that writers have a real audience for their ideas. If you have asked students to write about their culture, respond to what they say as well as to how they say it. If you are having them write about themselves, have them share what they write with other members of the class. Students need to experience the interest of others in what they have to say if they are to make an effort to communicate.

In-Class Writing Activities

Normally, a writing course includes a mix of writing activities, including shorter, one-off writing activities done in class and longer assignments that involve writing at home. This section introduces a number of in-class writing activities. (Many of these involve other language skills in addition to writing, and are introduced elsewhere in the book, so they receive only brief treatment here.)

COPYING

Students at very beginning stages of writing need practice that allows them to focus on basic formal features of written English—spelling, capitalization, and punctuation—as well as on grammar and vocabulary. For students who are completely unfamiliar with the roman alphabet, copying sentences or even short texts from the textbook or blackboard is a way to learn English handwriting.

DICTATION

Dictations provide an opportunity for students to focus on capitalization, punctuation, and spelling without needing to worry about grammar at the same time, and they can be used even at very elementary levels. (For procedure, see chapter 7.)

DICTOCOMP

As a writing exercise, dictocomp is somewhat more challenging than dictation and is a better way to practice basic grammar points. (For procedure, see chapter 7.)

NOTE-TAKING

Note-taking is a valuable skill to develop in and of itself, and it is a good way to develop listening and writing skills. The writing component can be strengthened if you ask students to use their notes as a basis for writing a summary or response to what they heard. (For procedure, see Talks in chapter 7.)

SPEED WRITING

Helping students develop smoothness in their writing can be quite difficult if they see grammar and spelling errors as unforgivable crimes and always break their train of thought to look up words in a dictionary or check a grammar rule. Such students tend to write slowly and painfully, and the progression of their ideas often seems choppy. One solution to this problem is an activity called speed writing, in which students put their ideas down on paper in as uninterrupted a manner as possible, leaving correction for later.

One goal of speed writing is for students to increase the amount of text they generate over time, so to be effective, this activity needs to be repeated, and students need to keep track of their scores so that they can see their progress. Students may be concerned that they will make many more mistakes when writing so rapidly, but students are often almost as accurate when writing quickly as when writing slowly and carefully.

1. Give students a topic, and tell them to write as much about it as they can within a limited amount of time, perhaps five to ten minutes.

2. Have the students count and record the number of words they have produced.

3. Award praise based on how much text is produced.

IN-CLASS ESSAYS

Even if you prefer to have students do most of their writing at home, having students write in class occasionally is generally a good idea. One advantage is that you can actually see how quickly or slowly students produce text, how much they use reference tools, and so forth. This will help you determine what problems students face in their writing and what kinds of practice they need.

1. Give students a topic or question on which to write, and set a time limit. (One common practice is to give students thirty minutes—five for planning and twenty-five for writing.)

2. As students write, observe their writing process, and see what you can discover. In most real-world writing tasks, people normally use reference tools such as dictionaries, so you might consider allowing dictionary use.

3. When the time is up, collect the papers, and respond to them as you would other papers.

FILLING OUT FORMS

One of the world's great preoccupations is the producing of forms, so a special kind of writing you might address in class is filling out forms. The formal language of most forms (e.g., *marital status, occupation, length of intended stay*) is worthy of special attention.

Out-of-Class Writing Activities

Reaching a breakthrough point at which students can write in English well enough to deal with education or work-related tasks—or even social correspondence—involves more than the ability to produce text in English. Generally, people expect a higher degree of organization, clarity, accuracy, and polish in written than in spoken language, so in addition to generating texts, students need to learn to plan and edit them. To this end, much of the work in most writing courses involves students' producing multiple drafts—working mainly outside class—that help them learn to write texts that are relatively well planned and carefully polished.

The writing process is often described as having three parts: planning, writing, and revising. You need not always insist that students strictly follow this three-step process in their writing because it is not entirely natural; normally some planning and editing occurs during the writing phase, and new plans often emerge during the editing phase (for further discussion, see Omaggio Hadley 2001, 312; Richards 1990, 108). However, especially as students move toward more advanced levels of writing skill, they should begin learning that good writing starts before the first sentence is written and doesn't end with the last word of the first draft. An important part of teaching writing is thus introducing all three steps, stressing their importance, and providing students with practice in each.

PREWRITING AND PLANNING

The planning of a composition can be broken down into three parts: generating ideas, organizing them, and noting them down for later reference.

Generating Ideas

Essentially, generating ideas means finding something to say. Sometimes ideas come naturally, but students are often faced with the problem of being required to write about something they have never thought about or have no opinions on, and if they do not generate ideas before starting to generate text, their papers will be harder both to write and to read.

Many of the speaking skills activities discussed in chapter 8 (such as pair and small-group tasks, debates, and large-group discussion) are effective ways to help students generate ideas before starting a paper. Brainstorming, another useful prewriting activity, involves giving students a topic or question and having them think of as many ideas as they can as quickly as they can; all ideas, no matter how absurd or farfetched, are written down. After a large number of ideas are generated, students go back and choose those which seem worthy of further thought.

I also find it useful to talk with students in writing classes about when and how they think best. For example, I tend to think best when walking alone and talking to myself, jotting ideas down in a little notebook as they occur to me. Others may find that they think best sitting in a quiet room or talking ideas over with friends. Many students' natural tendency is not to think about what they will write at all until they start writing, so talking with students about where and how they do their best thinking will help underscore the importance of thinking as a part of the composition process.

Selecting and Organizing Ideas

This step is probably the most difficult one to isolate from the others; writers continue to add, subtract, or move ideas throughout the writing process. However, making an initial effort to select and organize material will give students a good head start.

The first—and sometimes most difficult—decision students have to make is exactly what aspects of a topic to focus on. Most topics are broad enough to allow more than a single approach, so students need to decide what points to emphasize. The second step is determined by the first. Having decided what to focus on, students need to look at their material and decide what ideas and details suit the focus. The problem most often encountered here is that students are reluctant to omit any of the precious material that they so painfully generated, and they often try to find ways to shoehorn almost all of it in. You will need to stress that part of becoming a good writer is learning to eliminate irrelevant material. Finally, students need to arrange the points in the most effective order and decide what to say about each.

Noting Ideas Down

Perhaps the most important aspect of teaching students to plan what they write is ensuring that they actually do it. Students are often tempted to cut corners in their work, and preparation for writing is one of the corners most often cut. Many students don't see it as important, or simply don't do it because they are busy and it is easier to get away with not preparing a composition than with not writing it. If you require students to produce a written plan before they write—anything from a scribbled list to a neat outline—it is not only easier to hold students accountable for the planning phase of writing but also more likely that they will produce a good paper.

Before starting to write, students should at the very least list the main points of their paper. Students at a more advanced level can often benefit from learning how to write formal outlines because they require students to decide what points they will make in what order and to consider how points relate to each other (e.g., which are main points and which are supporting points). The ability to write a good outline is a skill that may take students some time to master, but it is very helpful in more advanced writing.

TYPES OF WRITING ASSIGNMENTS

Often, the types of writing you have students do will be determined in part by the materials you work with, by a school curriculum, or by the students' specific needs. However, usually you will have some leeway in determining what kinds of compositions you ask students to write. This section discusses various types of out-of-class (homework) writing that could be included in a program.

Dialogue Writing

For beginning-level students, dialogue writing is a good way to allow some creative freedom in writing while still keeping the task conceptually simple. Dialogues can be based on models in student textbooks. (See Model-Based Dialogues in chapter 8.) The dialogues can be performed in class as well as handed in.

Stories

Narrative writing is conceptually easy because chronological order provides a natural and simple organizational pattern, and most students have ready-made material in the form of their own experiences. A final bonus is that many people enjoy telling stories about themselves, and these stories are often fun to read. (Students can also practice narrative writing by retelling or summarizing a story that they have heard or read, though this tends to be less interesting for both the writer and the reader.) Story-writing assignments are a good opportunity to encourage writers to think about how to structure what they write for maximum effectiveness with a given audience. A story-writing activity can be conducted as follows:

1. Introduce a topic by sharing an experience you had (e.g., a remarkable coincidence, dangerous incident, or particularly stupid mistake). Either write the story out for the class, or present it orally.

2. Ask the students to respond with a similar story from their own experience.

3. Once the stories are written, have the students share them with other class members either by reading them aloud (in small classes) or by passing them around to be read by other students. Public sharing is probably best when stories have already been edited and polished, thus allowing students more confidence and pride in the quality of their work, but sharing rough drafts for peer response can also be useful.

Personal Letters

Letters are an easy genre but one in which students can write about a broad range of topics ranging from the very simple to the profound. As Raimes (1983) points out, "If a language student will ever need to write anything in the second language, it will probably be a letter" (p. 85). Letters thus have the advantage of high surface validity; students who assume they will never write an academic paper in English might well consider the possibility of writing a letter in English much more realistic and hence have more motivation to learn this skill. Many students also have experience writing letters in their own language, so it is not as abstract and foreign a genre as some other forms of writing.

1. Introduce basic conventions of personal letters, such as the following:
   • typical ways to start a letter (e.g., *Dear . . .*)
   • formatting of letters (e.g., where to place the opening, closing, and date)
   • typical closings for a letter (e.g., *Sincerely, . . .*)

2. Assign a topic about which you want students to write to you, preferably one appropriate to the personal letter genre. Here are some possibilities:
   • Assign a topic that is generated by a situation—either serious or light: a letter of apology for some misdeed or a love letter to a famous movie star.
   • As Ur (1981) suggests, present students with a "provocative" letter that is "insulting, appealing, complaining, threatening" (pp. 98–105) and ask them to produce a response. (Ur suggests combining the letter writing with class discussion.)

- Have students write an advice letter based on a problem (e.g., where to go for winter vacation, how to get the best price for a product you are interested in) that you have encountered in your host country (though it is best if this issue is not too personal or sensitive).

Now many people write e-mail messages instead of personal letters, so a variation on personal letter assignments involves teaching students to write e-mail messages. One of the advantages of e-mail is that, with the growing access to computers around the world, in many settings the students can get real writing practice through e-mail pen pals, chat rooms, and other online opportunities.

Business Letters

Another writing skill that may be personally useful to students is the ability to write business letters. In many ways, business letters are short expository compositions, so the basic organizational patterns of expository writing can be taught in the context of business letters. Like any other form of expository writing, the business letter is composed primarily of paragraphs with the following components: point(s), explanation, and specific details or evidence. The importance of accuracy in business letter writing also provides a natural context for the introduction of proofreading and editing skills. Students may see the importance of making a good impression in an application letter—hence not making too many grammar mistakes—more readily than in other writing assignments, so business letters may be an opportunity to motivate them to invest the time and effort necessary for developing editing skills.

Application Letters and Résumés

In many countries, the business letter students are most likely to write is a letter of application, accompanied by a résumé, so this assignment has high face validity. Application letters also provide a good opportunity to discuss cultural aspects of how one presents oneself. For example, a student writing a business letter needs to learn to get to the point quickly without indulging in a long flowery prelude that a Western reader might find superfluous and annoying. Also, students writing application letters need to learn the fine art of presenting their strong points in an objective, quantifiable way so that they do not seem subjective and overly boastful to a Western reader. It isn't as good to say, "I was the best student in my school" (subjective judgment) as it is to say, "I had the highest grade point average" (objectively demonstrable fact).

1. Teach students the format you want them to use for their letter and résumé.

2. Introduce basic conventions for writing an application letter, such as those above.

3. Create one or more job advertisements to which students will respond with their application letters and résumés.

4. Have students outline their letter and résumé, carefully choosing points they wish to make and supporting the points with explanation and detail. You may want to go over these and provide feedback before students write.

5. Have students write the letters and résumés and turn them in. Alternatively, combine this activity with a simulated job fair in class in which some students take on employer roles and others take on job-seeker roles. The letters and résumé could then be read by the employers and serve as the basis for a job interview.

Opinion Papers (Basic Expository Writing)

Perhaps the most basic expository writing assignment is a paragraph or short composition that presents an opinion and reasons for it. While writing an academic paper or a business report is obviously more complex than expressing an opinion in a paragraph, the basic point-explanation-detail organizational pattern is the same for all of these.

1. Start with an opinion question, such as "What is the best place to visit in your country?" or "What do you find most difficult about learning English?"

2. In response to your question, have students write a paragraph or short paper that
   - first states their opinion
   - then explains anything in the opinion that needs to be explained (For example, if students suggest that the national capital is the best place to visit, they should develop the answer by explaining why.)
   - concludes with specific details and examples

Explanatory Papers (Expository Writing)

Expository writing can be divided roughly into two kinds: writing that explains and writing that persuades. However, the distinction is somewhat artificial; argument virtually always requires explanation, and most expository writing has at least some element of persuasion. Both types have the same basic point-explanation-detail organizational pattern: an idea is usually presented at the beginning of a section of discourse (which may range in length from part of a paragraph to several pages), developed through explanation, and supported with examples, concrete details, and evidence that make the ideas clearer, more memorable, and more convincing. Explanatory papers are generally more interesting to read if you point out to students that good explanation takes the background knowledge of the audience into account. Therefore, they should try to make an educated guess as to what you already know and don't know so they avoid wasting a lot of time and ink explaining things you already know. For VTs working outside their home countries, one of the most natural and interesting writing assignments involves asking students to introduce some aspect of their culture to an outsider (the teacher).

1. Decide on one or more aspects of the host culture that you would like to learn more about (see appendix B for possible topics).

2. Present students with your question(s) about their culture, and ask them to write a paper introducing that aspect of their culture to you.

3. After you have gone over students' papers, you might spend some class time asking follow-up questions, in part to emphasize the idea that you were interested in what they had to say in their papers as well as how good their English was.

Research Papers

Research paper assignments not only help students build useful research and writing skills, but are also an opportunity to learn more about the topic they research. In English language classes, one particularly appropriate research paper involves having students research and write a report on some aspect of your culture (or another culture that is foreign to them).

1. Either assign topics, or have students pick their own. Topics that are fairly narrow and specific tend to result in better papers.

2. Have students research their topic using whatever library resources are available, particularly material available on the Internet.

3. To give the project a stronger communicative aspect, have the students share what they learn—or at least the most interesting highlights—with their classmates. Brief classroom presentations are one option but tend to consume a large amount of class time. (If you choose to have students do presentations, you might have students work and present in groups.) Or have the students generate a one-page highlights handout for their classmates, or hold a poster session during which the students display their work.

4. Suggest that, when writing up their results, students compare and contrast their findings with their own culture.

Argument Papers

One of the best ways to hone expository skills is by writing argument papers. This activity can be integrated with reading and speaking skills if it is based on an article that students read, discuss in class, and finally write about.

1. Locate an article that presents a controversial viewpoint or raises a controversial question. (See Debates in chapter 8 for ideas on choosing topics.)

2. Have students read the article in class or at home and make notes on their response to it.

3. To help students generate and clarify ideas, you might have students discuss the article in class, either as a pair or small-group task or debate activity.

4. Have students write the paper.

Critiques

A critique or review is a special kind of opinion paper that evaluates a book, film, article, or even an idea. Most critiques contain the following parts: (1) a summary, (2) a discussion of the strong and weak points of the subject, and (3) a final judgment and recommendation to the potential audience. The main difference between a critique and an argument is that the former purports to examine two sides of an issue fairly. The appearance of fairness is critical to the success of the critique, so it is particularly important to discuss both good and bad points. Critique writing thus provides good practice in examining an issue from a variety of different viewpoints.

Critical reviews are among the most demanding forms of writing to teach, particularly if the text (or book, movie, or article) being reviewed is from another culture. Critique writing requires a high level of comprehension of the text being reviewed and places heavy demands on students' critical thinking skills. This is especially true if the text being reviewed has been produced by a competent professional; flaws are often not immediately obvious, and the student is thus at a loss to do anything more than humbly praise. However, the greatest problem is often deciding on a standard by which to judge the book. A reviewer can certainly start with the question, *Did I like it?*, but ultimately needs to answer the more difficult question, *Was it a good book?* The former question is one of personal taste; the latter implies a standard that is more universal, and finding such a standard can be a real problem.[1]

However, critique writing also offers significant benefits. First, it can be a good way to get students interested in writing because it draws on one of the most natural of human instincts—the

---

[1] When having students write critiques, I ask that they first try to determine the purpose(s) of a work and then judge it on whether or not it achieves its purpose. The problem is that it can be very difficult for students from non-Western backgrounds to decide what the purpose of a Western text might be, and I thus need to devote considerable time to discussing the genres of Western writing and media and what range of purposes is normally found within each genre.

desire to evaluate. (After seeing a film or reading a book, the first topic of discussion is inevitably *Was it good?*) Critique writing also helps students learn to think critically about what they read or see rather than taking the printed or recorded word as sacred. Finally, critique writing is a good way to respond to books, articles, tapes, or audiovisual material, and is thus an effective way to combine writing with reading or listening.

1. Choose an article (or book, film, or other work) that you want students to critique. Articles that are somewhat controversial, unusual, extreme, or risky often work best; those which are highly polished and play very safe tend to be hard to critique. (Rule of thumb: If you can't find much interesting to say about a text, students will probably also have a hard time.)

2. Have students read the article and note its strong and weak points.

3. To help students generate ideas, have the students discuss the article in small groups in class. However, for this kind of writing assignment—in which there are often only a limited number of good points a review might reasonably make—it is important that you not reveal too much of your own viewpoint.

4. Have students write the review.

A Brief Detour

Whether or not students in a given host country really need training in expository or academic writing genres is a question that should be raised more often than it is. The common assumption that expository writing should be the focus of EFL writing courses may arise more from the fact that many English teachers are trained in academic environments where expository writing is stressed than from the actual needs of students. However, for a number of reasons, training in expository writing may benefit even students who will not function in an academic world:

1. Familiarity with norms of Western expository and argument writing will help students in their English reading. Many texts—including journal articles, editorials, and even some magazine articles, newspaper articles, and books—follow these norms, so familiarity with how this kind of writing is put together will give students a clearer idea of what to expect as they read.

2. Knowledge of the norms of expository writing is also a window on the culture of the West. For example, the preference of most English-speaking Westerners for a simple, direct form of business communication rather than a more ornate or flowery style reflects the way business is done in the West; Westerners' impatience with communication that is indirect, unexplained, or unsupported by specific factual information carries over into spoken as well as written communication.

3. Expository writing skills require the ability to analyze issues and problems as well as to write about them, so teaching expository writing almost inevitably moves from the realm of language into the Western approach to critical thinking skills. In learning expository writing, students have intense, sustained exposure to different modes of organizing and presenting ideas, and this provides a rare and precious opportunity to wrestle with an important aspect of another culture.

EDITING AND REWRITING

In foreign language study, it is generally recognized that the hardest skill to master is writing, and no matter how good students are, they are unlikely to reach a level where they can turn out a polished, flawless first draft of a composition in English. (In fact, this is a trick that even most native speakers of English can't pull off with any regularity.) An essential part of learning to write is therefore learning how to edit and revise one's own work.

Editing can be divided into two processes: revising to improve its content and proofreading to catch and correct errors.

Revising

In theory, most students would accept the notion that it is good to revise their papers. However, for a number of understandable reasons, in practice students' enthusiasm for actually doing such revision tends to be weak. One problem is that students may see little reason to invest further time polishing a presentation of ideas they never had any real interest in. A second problem is that even when students do try to revise, they often do so the same night as they write, when they simply have neither the energy nor the freshness of perspective to see flaws of organization and logic that they might notice the next morning. The upshot is that many students never actually do any revision or make only limp efforts that don't produce any markedly noticeable improvements. Granted, as Harmer (2001, 146–50) points out, with the growing availability of computers and word-processing software, it is now considerably easier for students to revise their work because they do not need to copy papers in their entirety. However, human nature being what it is, getting student writers to revise will probably always be a challenge.

One of the best ways to convince students that revising really is worth the effort is to ensure that they actually revise papers, and seriously enough that the effort generates results and allows them to see for themselves how much better a revised paper can be. One way to ensure that real revision happens is to use class time for revising, not least so that students attempt revising some time other than the same night the paper was written. Another approach is to occasionally have students hand in drafts that you then hold for a period of time before handing them back—unedited—for revision. This approach allows students a rare opportunity to look back on their own work with fresher minds and higher energy levels than they normally bring to the task. A final way to ensure that students actually write a second draft of a paper is to have them turn in both the old and the new draft to you. You then grade the new draft based partially on improvement.

Another approach, called *peer editing*, involves having students exchange papers in order to give each other feedback on content. Initially this may not work very well because students often go to the extremes of either being too polite to their classmates or too zealous in the role of critic. You may need to remind students that the reader's role is to offer helpful suggestions rather than final judgments and that the writer's role is to listen to and take note of the suggestions rather than defending himself or herself from them. Of course, the writer may ultimately choose to reject suggestions, but it is best to listen carefully first; even an unwise suggestion may alert the writer to a point that needs improvement.

Peer editing can be enhanced by giving students a checklist to guide their revision efforts. A simple list of such questions might include

- Is there anything that I don't understand?

- Is there anyplace where I want to know more?

- Is there anyplace where I wanted an example?

- Is there anything that seems out of place?

- Is there anything that seems unnecessary?

Ultimately, the most important thing you can do to help students develop editing skills is to make writing a communicative activity in which they take a genuine interest. The more interested students are in their message and the response of their audience, the more likely they are to master revision skills. Without that interest, no amount of theory will help.

Proofreading

Proofreading is a difficult skill for most students to master, not so much because they cannot correct mistakes as because they cannot find them. Sometimes both teachers and students assume that proofreading means mechanically applying grammar rules to every sentence in a composition, thereby ferreting out the bits that are wrong. However, it is more realistic—and helpful—to view proofreading as looking through a text to find things that students are not sure about, which they can then check in a reference book if they have the time and inclination. In short, students are not looking for mistakes; they are looking for places where they are not sure. If students can write on computer word-processing software, the grammar-checking function can help students locate many probable errors and provides feedback as they attempt to correct the offending sentence. However, ultimately it is best for students to build their own ability to see potential trouble spots, and this ability depends heavily on language sense, an instinctive knowledge of what is definitely correct and what is dubious. Students who have been exposed to a great deal of correct English can often tell that something looks funny, whereas students who don't have this sense generally can't proofread very well. (This is one reason it is important for students to read and listen to as much English as possible.)

One exercise that helps students improve their proofreading skills involves handing out a composition into which errors have intentionally been inserted by an evil-hearted teacher and then asking students to find and correct the errors. The advantage of this approach is that students can all work together on the same composition in groups. As students become more skilled in spotting errors, the next level is to have students exchange compositions with each other for proofreading. While students' ability to spot errors in their classmates' compositions is often not dramatically better than their ability to see their own mistakes, generally they can call their partner's attention to at least a few points that need to be checked. Finally, it is worthwhile occasionally to have students proofread their own papers in class. (This last exercise should be used sparingly; once students get the idea that they can proofread in class, they aren't likely to do it at home. However, limited doses of in-class proofreading may drive home the point that if students proofread when their minds are fresh—instead of at midnight—they may find mistakes they would otherwise miss.)

Ultimately, students' ability to catch and correct their own errors depends in part on their becoming aware of their personal problem areas—patterns in the mistakes each student tends to make. By paying attention to the compositions you edit and keeping a record of the errors that appear most often, students can learn what they personally need to pay special attention to so that they can narrow the field of their proofreading efforts.

Teaching students how to use reference tools is another important aspect of helping them develop proofreading skills. Bilingual or monolingual dictionaries that have plenty of examples are especially valuable tools for writing because the examples provide students with models of grammar and usage as well as word meaning.

THE WRITING AND FEEDBACK CYCLE

Going through all the steps suggested above for a paper results in a process that involves several rounds of drafts, feedback, and revision. A typical cycle might look something like this:

1. Students do prewriting activities in class, followed by planning of the composition (making notes or an outline) at home.

2. You give students feedback on their plan, either orally or in writing.

3. Students write the first draft.

4. You read the first draft and give feedback.

5. Students revise and make a second draft.

6. You do final marking and grading.

This is obviously a lot of work to put into one paper, and you do not need to have students go through all of the steps above for every writing assignment; at times you may wish to have them do an exercise that only involves planning a paper, or you may practice the editing stage alone by having students edit a composition written by someone else. However, going through all of the steps for at least some of the writing tasks you assign is worth the effort so that students become used to the idea that all of these steps are an important part of writing.

Responding to Student Writing

RESPONDING TO CONTENT

You should not be the only audience students write for, but you will often be the audience they are most influenced by. Thus, if you want students to take writing seriously as communication, you must respond to a paper's message as well as to its grammar. You may agree, disagree, ask questions, add information, or comment on what you find interesting or confusing; sometimes you need to tell students that you suspect they were just filling paper. The point is that your response should convince students that you are paying attention to what they have to say.

Comments in the margin are the best way to give feedback about specific aspects of a composition because the proximity of the comments to the portion of the text you are talking about makes them easier to understand. Questions in the margin are an especially effective way to help students know how to revise and improve their papers while encouraging them to think for themselves. Unlike comments like *awkward* or *confusing*, questions don't seem like a slap on the wrist, and they establish a sense of conversation rather than judgment. (Students are generally more willing to look over and learn from your feedback if you write an occasional *good* or at least *OK* amidst your margin comments.)

Comments at the end of the composition can provide a general summing-up of the strengths and weaknesses of a composition, and perhaps a few personal responses to the ideas. Here are a few suggestions:

1. The longer comments are, the less likely they are to be absorbed and digested, so it is better to make one or two points clearly than to discuss every flaw in the paper. (Remember that deciphering your handwritten comments may take some effort, especially if they are scrunched in at the bottom with lines leading all over the page.)

2. Students are more likely to read the comments if you include some good news with the bad. Generally you can find at least one nice thing to say about a paper, and this takes some of the sting out of other comments. It also helps if you phrase bad news as suggestions for improvement rather than criticisms.

There is no reason to confine your responses to written comments. Assuming that you have students write about something you are genuinely interested in, there is no better way to convince students of your interest than to talk with them about the papers. If, for example, you had students write about the best place to go for a holiday, you might spend a bit of class time asking follow-up questions, such as how to get there, where to stay, and what to see—you might even try the place out and come back to report. (When teaching in Guangzhou, my colleague and I had students report on the merits and problems of various brands of bicycles. Part of our response was then to use the advice to guide us as we bought bikes.)

RESPONDING TO FORM

There is no single sure-fire approach to composition marking that will ensure rapid student progress in formal accuracy (Bowen, Madsen, and Hilferty 1985, 263; Omaggio Hadley 2001, 317). In fact, one of the most frustrating aspects of teaching writing is that no matter how carefully you mark papers, students' formal accuracy often improves only slowly. This is especially true in EFL settings where students can only devote a limited amount of time to English study and an even smaller portion of that time to writing. However, marking grammar, spelling, vocabulary, and cultural errors is still an important part of responding to student compositions. Feedback can help students improve accuracy, particularly if you ensure that students pay adequate attention to the feedback; they will not be able to correct every error pointed out to them, nor will they learn from every correction, but they will learn some of the time. Another important reason to provide feedback is that students expect it, and if you don't provide it, students may assume that you are derelict in your duty. The question is thus not whether to mark errors but how to mark effectively.

Raimes (1983, 149) points out that the goal of your marking strategy is to help students improve their own editing skills. This suggests that marking a paper well usually does not mean finding and correcting every mistake in it; it means giving students the fewest clues that will enable them to locate and correct a substantial number of their errors. If all goes well in your class, over time you should be able to give fewer and vaguer clues, thus forcing students to rely more on their own skills.

For students who have little ability to find and correct their own errors, the best marking system is one that helps students locate errors and gives them clues as to what is wrong. This is normally done by underlining errors and marking them with proofreading symbols that indicate what kind of error was made. A basic system might include the following symbols:

S   spelling mistake
T   verb tense error
WW   wrong word
N   problem with a countable noun (which should either be plural or preceded by a determiner like *the, a, this,* and so forth)
Awk   awkward
F   wrong form of word (e.g., verb form instead of noun)
∧   insert word(s) here
Ø   omit

Using such a system takes a little additional effort in the beginning because you need to design it and teach it to students. However, the advantage of such a system is that dramatically simplifies the editing process but still requires students to correct their own mistakes, hence increasing the likelihood that students will learn from them.[2]

For problems that students should be able to diagnose and cure by themselves, you may choose to simply point out the problem by underlining it. Another method, appropriate for students with more advanced editing skills, is to mark lines or paragraphs that have errors, indicating only the number of mistakes, and having students both find and correct the problems on their own. This approach has the advantage of training students to locate errors by themselves, albeit with some help. As students become even more skilled proofreaders, you may choose not to mark errors in student compositions at all, instead making a comment at the end of the paper as to the problems students should look for as they edit. These last approaches assume considerable editing skills on the part of students and may initially prove impractical for many classes. However, the goal should be to move in this direction because these approaches reinforce the idea that students ultimately need to be able to find and correct their own errors.

When you notice problems that students probably can't correct on their own, you might occasionally just correct the error for them. However, such corrections often deal with points far enough above students' current skill level that they won't learn much from the correction and are easily ignored by students, so they should be kept to a minimum.

Having invested effort in marking a paper, you should ensure that students pay attention to the feedback. This may sound obvious, but often, after several hours correcting and grading, you will be tired of a batch of papers and more than happy just to hand it back to students and move onto something else. Likewise, students often look at the grade, glance at the errors, and file the paper away. Even with the best intentions in the world, busy students will generally not pore over their mistakes unless there is a good reason to do so. The tragedy of this situation is that maximum pain results in minimum learning.

One way to ensure that students learn from your feedback is to avoid letting overwork consistently drive you into omitting the editing stage of the composition process. Even if you do not feel that you have time to have students write a completely new draft of a paper you have marked, ask them to correct the errors you have marked and turn the original draft back in so that you can check the corrections. (If you mark the corrections in a color of ink that differs from that of your original marks, the new corrections will be easier for students to find.) Another way to encourage students to learn from their mistakes is to have them keep a personal grammar notebook in which they make note of their errors and corrections. Keeping such a notebook is one of those good intentions that students honor more in theory than in practice, so you might want to collect the notebook occasionally to show students that you are serious.

GRADING COMPOSITIONS

Skilled professionals can often grade compositions reliably and consistently by relying on overall impressions. However, the ability to grade reliably in this way takes considerable experience to develop and is often difficult to maintain as the grader becomes tired. Thus, I would not recommend this approach to VTs who are grading large numbers of compositions.

A more consistently reliable approach involves establishing a set of criteria before beginning to grade compositions. You can draw on a ready-made scale like the American Council on the

---

[2] Many ESL, grammar, and writing books contain examples of marking systems, but you can easily design a system for yourself, and it may be best if your system reflects the grammar points you have emphasized in class.

Teaching of Foreign Languages' (1999) *ACTFL Proficiency Guidelines* (see the note in chapter 4), but often it is best to design your own system based on the points that you have emphasized in your course. Designing a criteria scale forces you to carefully think through what you are looking for as you grade and will both speed grading and help you remain more consistent and fair, even as your eyelids droop and your mind begins to cloud. In order to avoid writing a new scale for each assignment, you may want to design a basic system based on the course goals and then modify it to handle the special features and emphases of specific assignments. The Goals Menu in appendix A may help you decide what to look for when setting up a the system.

One way to make grading a little more precise—and to give students clearer feedback—is to give two grades to a composition, one for form and one for content. Perhaps the greatest advantage of this is that you are reminded to respond to the content of papers as well as to their formal accuracy. It is easy for grammar errors to loom disproportionately large in the mind of a tired grader, and this can create problems if you tell students in class that content is most important but wind up letting grammar determine most of your grade.

Managing the Load

One of the unpleasant realities of teaching a writing course is that it often turns into a slugging match between you and piles of student compositions, a match that turns especially frustrating when you spend long hours trying to salvage poorly written papers only to find that the next round is little better. To a certain extent this reality is inevitable. As Raimes (1983, 4–5) points out, even many adult native speakers of a language find writing difficult, and the consensus is that writing is the most difficult language skill for nonnative speakers to master (Bowen, Madsen, and Hilferty 1985, 253; Nunan 1989, 35). Also, no matter how well a writing teacher manages homework assignments, teaching writing generally requires more out-of-class effort per hour of class time than teaching other English skills, especially to the large classes that are not uncommon in EFL settings.

The analogy I use for writing classes is that they are like going hiking with a heavy backpack—no matter how you arrange the pack, carrying it will take some effort. However, the hike offers rewards as well as work, and by arranging the pack well, you can make the trip much more pleasant. As promised in the introduction to this chapter, I offer no ultimate remedy for the paper correction problem, but I suggest a few ways you can minimize your burden and maximize your effectiveness through your choice of writing assignments and through editing and marking strategies.

ASSIGNMENTS

The bane of the writing teacher's existence is the raw-sewage paper—the unplanned, unedited paper written by a student who believes it will get a decent grade if only it is long enough. There may well be a place for free writing in a program, but no teacher should be forced to read all of it any more than a piano teacher should be required to listen to hours of a student playing scales. Careful structuring of assignments can do much to prevent this situation.

1. Guarantee that students plan and edit a paper before you have to read it. As suggested in this chapter, you can ensure planning by giving students time in class to plan—under your watchful eye—and by asking to see written evidence of planning. Likewise, to increase the chances of a serious attempt at revision, have students write a draft of a paper and bring it to class. Once you check to see that a draft was written, either give

students time in class to revise, or make revision a homework assignment. Alternatively, collect the papers and hold on to them for several days before giving them back for revision.

2. Make the goals of a writing assignment very clear and specific. This helps students know what they are supposed to focus on and makes your work easier by giving a clearer focus to your response. Consequently, when you sit down to read student papers, you will already know what limited set of points you are looking for. A variation on this is to have students submit a list of points on which they want feedback, thus requiring students to focus your editing. This method has the added advantage of involving students more actively in feedback.

3. Put upper (not just lower) limits on the length of compositions. As long as students believe that long compositions will get higher grades than short ones, they will be tempted to skimp on planning and editing in order to save as much time as possible for generating text. Even students who have good intentions about editing their massive creations are often so exhausted by giving birth that in the end they just cut the umbilical cord and go to bed. Putting upper limits on length helps students take seriously your pleading assertions that long is not necessarily good and can help ensure that students reserve some time for planning and editing.

4. Choose topics you are genuinely interested in. Like most writing teachers, I am guilty of having asked students to write on topics of dubious appeal such as *Describe a room* or *My summer vacation* because these are examples of a particular form of writing (description and narration, respectively), but after years of suffering through stale piles of essays, I have finally learned not to ask students to write about things I don't want to read about. Having students write about things you want to read about helps student motivation by making writing more genuinely communicative and makes reading the papers much less draining for you.

RESPONSE AND CORRECTION

For responding to the ideas in a paper, short comments or questions in the margins of a paper often take less time to write than comments at the end, and—as noted above—may be more effective.

When dealing with error marking, the keys to efficiency are focus and selectivity; marking a paper is much easier if you know exactly what you are looking for and if you are not looking for everything. This approach to marking is also generally better for students than marking every error in a paper because they are most likely to benefit from correction if there are a only limited number of lessons to be learned from it; a paper covered with corrections tends to overwhelm more than teach. Selective marking is also less likely to drive weaker writers into a state of despair every time they get a paper back.

One way to focus your marking is to look primarily for errors related to points you have taught in class and let most other errors go. A second approach is to look for patterns in a student's mistakes. This tends to be more time-consuming, but such tailoring of feedback can be very helpful to students. Other criteria for deciding what errors to mark include the seriousness of the error (those which interfere with communication being most important) or the difficulty that students will have correcting the problem.

LOW-TEACHER-INVESTMENT WRITING ASSIGNMENTS

Generally, to get enough writing practice, students will need to write more than you can reasonably expect to read and respond to, so you will need to give some writing assignments that you can either process very quickly or not read at all. When giving any of these assignments, you should spend some time selling students on the idea that writing practice is still valuable even when no teacher is available to carefully mark every error. As in the development of any other language skill, writing practice is useful in and of itself, especially if students are using it actively as an opportunity to rehearse the application of points learned in class or through reference materials. Assignments that do not necessitate lengthy teacher response include the following:

1. **journals:** Journals give students an opportunity to write about daily events, past experiences, thoughts, or almost anything else. You only need to read over entries occasionally and comment briefly, generally responding to the ideas more than the language.

2. **material to be shared with other students:** As suggested above, you might have students write for each other instead of for you. Material written to be read by other students can include personal stories, position papers on issues (as a prelude to discussion or debate), or newsletters on personal or local events.

3. **pen-pal writing:** For this type of writing, you find people, presumably from your home area, who are willing to correspond with the students by letter or by e-mail. Retirees or students might be good potential correspondents. The advantage of writing in pen-pal programs, in Internet chat rooms, and so forth is that it provides a form of writing practice that you do not need to edit while reinforcing the idea that writing is a real communication skill rather than a lifeless class exercise.

Evaluation

I will say little about tests for writing because writing is a skill area where it is especially important to deemphasize testing in favor of grades on other writing assignments. Timed writing under testlike conditions is rare in real life, and it has the undesirable effect of discouraging planning, editing, and use of reference tools. In-class testing does, however, ensure that you see student compositions that you know were not copied or written by someone else, and for which you have a reliable idea of how much time was invested. Therefore, while the majority of a writing course grade should generally be based on the regular assignments, it may also be wise to include in-class writing tests.

An in-class writing test is essentially the same as an in-class composition. Give students a topic and a time limit within which to complete an essay. The topic(s) should be within students' range of knowledge and should include an indication of the type of writing expected (e.g., letter, argument). It is best if the topic presents a clearly defined task rather than only a general topic. *Explain why you do/don't . . .* is much better than *Write about . . .* because the former gives students a better idea of what is expected of them. If the topic is clear, thirty minutes is generally more than adequate to produce a writing sample. Students should be encouraged, perhaps even required, to spend some time taking notes and organizing before they begin to write; in fact, you may want to ask students to hand in their preparation notes along with the paper (though students may find it faster to write their notes in their native language than in English). Students should also be encouraged to save a few minutes at the end to check for mistakes, though they will probably only catch a few of the more obvious errors at best. There is no good reason not to allow students to use dictionaries unless your test is intended to prepare them for a standardized test in which dictionaries are not allowed.

Plagiarism

Over years of teaching writing to students from non-Western cultures, I have been struck by the extent to which their problems in the content aspects of writing (e.g., organization, use of detail, placement of main idea) are similar to those faced by Western students. I have seen problems such as rambling paragraphs, unsupported assertions, new arguments in conclusions, or misplaced main idea statements in compositions written by U.S. students in Indiana as well as Chinese students in Guangzhou. In one problem area, however—plagiarism—cultural differences regularly cause non-Western students special problems in English writing classes. Different cultures have rather different notions of what is and is not fair use of the work of others, and Western culture tends to be stricter in this area than many others. This is not to say that plagiarism is not found in the West (it is) or that a knowledge of what is and is not plagiarism is inherent in Western students (it is not). However, teachers coming out of a Western system may have rather different assumptions about what is considered plagiarism than students in a host country do, so the issue deserves special attention.

Teachers from Western cultures need to start by recognizing the high degree of stigma Western culture attaches to plagiarism and reminding themselves that rules that govern borrowing the work of others are cultural norms rather than moral imperatives. The West tends to see unmarked use of others' work as stealing—*plagiarism* is, after all, the name of a crime. But this is not the only possible interpretation of copying. For example, borrowing the words of others could also be seen as a sign of respect (imitation is the sincerest form of flattery?); absence of citation could also indicate that any literate person would be expected to know what was being quoted. Thus, Western teachers should not expect that those from all other cultures will look at copying exactly the same way they have learned to.

A second problem concerns what exactly plagiarism is. Westerners, particularly Americans, have been brought up in an educational system that places a high value on individual creativity and expression and not much faith in imitation of the work of others as a legitimate or helpful way to learn. The exact opposite is true in many other cultures, particularly Asian ones, where imitation of models is a common mode of learning. In such a context, the difference between original and borrowed work is not as clear as it would be in the U.S. system, and the stigma attached to copying is not nearly as comprehensible. In a writing class in China, for example, the admonition "Don't copy!" does not necessarily convey the same message that the same words would convey in Michigan. My Chinese students understand that they should not copy other students' compositions lock, stock, and barrel, and would expect a reduced grade if they did so. However, they are sometimes genuinely surprised to be accused of plagiarism because they modeled a composition on something from a textbook and included sentences and phrases (perhaps slightly rewritten) from that text. An unexplained command not to copy does not necessarily communicate the message that Westerners consider using a model in such a way inappropriate.

My point is not that you should turn a tolerant eye to student copying, but rather that one of the cultural lessons students need to learn as a part of their English education is what exactly does and does not constitute plagiarism in your culture. Learning this lesson means not only learning how to use quotation marks or citations but also learning to discern the boundary between appropriate and inappropriate use of a model. In most cases, a single lecture will not dispose of the problem; it will have to be worked out gradually over time. During this process, there are three important points to remember:

1. Find out what the local norms are for using the work of others—not only what is and is not acceptable according to the stated rules but also what the unwritten norms are. Remember that teachers and staff who teach English in your school are presumably more influenced by Western norms than most people in the host country, and they may present a Westernized picture of the situation to you in order to meet your perceived expectations. You may need to do a little digging among other people as well to find out how seriously the rules are taken. It may also be enlightening to find out how borrowing is handled traditionally in the host culture.

2. Spell out your expectations very specifically for the students. For example, with regard to using vocabulary and sentence structures from other books, I generally tell my students that any time they use the same three words in the same order as another text, they must use quotation marks and citations. (I often find that before students hear this guideline, they assume that it is acceptable to use long phrases or even sentences.)

3. Students may have a rather different idea than you have of what is and is not a crime, so in dealing with violations of Western fair-use norms, try to keep moral indignation under control, at least until you are sure the student was cognizant of the seriousness of the offense. Some students cheat and should be dealt with accordingly. However, not all students who run afoul of Western plagiarism norms do so with malice aforethought, and you need to remind yourself that genuine misunderstanding may be part of the problem.

For Thought, Discussion, and Action

1. **learning to write:** Think back on your own experience of learning to write in a foreign language. What were the most significant challenges? What kinds of activities and practice helped you the most?

2. **enhancing your interest in student writing:** This chapter suggests that, as often as possible, you should ask students to write about topics you are interested in reading about, especially if you are the main or only audience for the composition. (1) Think about and list interesting topics students could write to you about (especially with regard to their culture). (2) If possible, run this list past someone with experience teaching in the host country to see which topics are likely to also appeal to students (and weed out any that are overly sensitive or inappropriate).

3. **doing speed writing:** If you teach an English course that involves writing, try having students do a speed-writing exercise according to the instructions given in the chapter. (Teachers who have not had much experience with this activity may have be concerned that students will make too many mistakes when writing quickly, so to set your heart at rest, it is probably a good idea to check over students' work at first to see whether or not the number of errors goes up dramatically. It probably won't, but seeing is believing.)

4. **choosing writing activities:** Choose one of the sample courses from chapter 6. With that course in mind, go through the list of writing activities in this chapter and select several that you think would be suitable, both in class and out of class. Be ready to explain the rationale for your choices.

5. **generating ideas:** Ask several classmates or friends how they generate ideas when trying to write a paper and how they organize the ideas before writing. Make note of useful strategies that you could suggest to students.

6. **telling stories:** List good personal-experience stories that might effectively prime the pump for a story-writing assignment for the students. If possible, share these with someone who has taught or lived in your host country in order to get an idea how students might respond to the stories and which ones might work best in a writing class.

7. **investigating e-mail access:** Find out how much access students in your host country have to e-mail and whether giving them writing assignments using e-mail or the Internet would be practical.

8. **designing marking systems:** Devise a marking symbol system you could use when editing papers in a writing class (perhaps a modified version of the system suggested in this chapter).

9. **responding to (large numbers of) papers:** Find one or more people who have taught writing in your host country and ask them (1) how large writing classes usually are, (2) how much time they have to spend responding to papers, and (3) what strategies they use for coping with the demands of paper editing.

Sample Language Learning Project for Advanced-Level Writing Skills

Goal: Build note-taking skills; build listening skills; build ability to accurately write simple compositions (based on DVD documentaries).

Material: Television documentaries or feature programs in DVD format (e.g., National Geographic features).

Plan: Listen to one or two features a week, and write one or two compositions a week.

Method:

1. Watch the documentary (with the captions turned off) and take notes on the content. (Repeat if necessary or helpful.)

2. Write a composition that tells the story in the documentary.

3. Watch the documentary again with the English captions on. Check my composition against the text of the documentary. Make note of new vocabulary and phrases I want to learn.

Criteria for measuring progress: I will have succeeded if

- I study ten documentaries using this approach

- I create a notebook that is at least thirty pages long

- the compositions toward the end of the notebook are longer and more detailed than those at the beginnin.

- I feel more skilled and confident in note-taking

Chapter 11

Vocabulary: Students in Charge

- Mastery of a foreign language involves learning thousands of words, and teaching more than a fraction of them in class would be difficult. In vocabulary study, it is therefore especially important for students to learn to rely primarily on their own efforts.

- Students do not need to learn to use every new word to the same degree. For reading and listening, students need a large receptive vocabulary of words that they can understand but not necessarily use productively.

- The teacher's main role in vocabulary teaching is facilitating student study and providing accountability.

The very idea of teaching vocabulary strikes me as somewhat problematic. Not that vocabulary can't be taught—it can be, and teaching it is not terribly difficult. But looking back on my own language learning experience, I note that not very much of my foreign language vocabulary was taught to me in a language class by a teacher, or by anyone at all. I learned most words by studying textbooks, using vocabulary lists and flash cards, guessing from context while reading or listening, or looking them up in my trusty old dictionary. In short, I did most of my vocabulary learning on my own. More to the point, I don't see how I could have developed an adequately large vocabulary had I learned only new words taught in class.

On a moment's reflection, it is not hard to see why students must be self-reliant in vocabulary acquisition. First, they need to learn thousands of words, more than even the most zealous teacher is likely to be able to explain in class. Second, learning any single word often involves much more than memorizing its basic meaning; it also involves learning how it is used, what other meanings it has, what connotations it has, what other words it is used with, how formal it is, and even how frequently it is used. Obviously, such a thorough introduction to a few words, let alone the huge number of words students eventually need to master, would take far too much class time.

This chapter examines what students need to achieve in vocabulary study and how they can pursue these goals. Throughout, I argue that vocabulary study provides an especially clear case for why it is so important for learners to take command of their own language learning.

Vocabulary Acquisition: The Goal

It is helpful to think of command of vocabulary as falling into two categories: productive and receptive. *Productive* command of a word involves being able to use it appropriately in speech or writing. As suggested above, productive command can require knowing quite a lot about a word. Take the everyday word *dog* as an example:

1. **basic meaning:** A *dog* is a four legged creature that can be trained to chase sticks.

2. **other meanings:** *To dog* = to follow persistently; *dog-tired* = very tired; *a dog* = something worthless or useless; *dogs* = slang for *feet; You dog!* = *You scoundrel!*

3. **parts of speech:** *Dog* is usually a noun but can also be a verb (*The scouts dogged his trail for hours.*). It can also modify nouns like an adjective (as in *dog tag* or *doghouse*).

4. **usage:** When it is a countable noun (*a dog, dogs*), it usually refers to an animal. When used as a mass noun (*I like dog*), it refers to a controversial dinner option.

5. **connotation:** Even though people think of the *dog* as man's best friend, the word generally has bad or insulting connotations. However, *dogs* (feet) has a rural flavor (or is associated with old Hush Puppies shoe commercials). *You (swarthy) dog!* has a slightly antique sound to it, conjuring up visions of a swashbuckler in an old pirate movie.

6. **collocation:**[1] *Dog* is often paired with *cat* (*It's raining cats and dogs.*).

7. **level of formality:** When referring to the animal, *dog* is not markedly formal or informal. *Dog-tired* is somewhat informal, and *dogs* (feet) is very informal.

8. **frequency of appearance:** The word *dog* is much more common than the synonym *canine.*

---

[1] *Collocation* refers to the degree to which words tend to appear together—to be good friends, so to speak.

Students do not need all of this information about the word *dog* to begin using it in speech or writing, but they need to know that these other aspects of vocabulary exist and that learning them is an important part of learning how to use words properly. A word needs to fit in its sentence and context in terms of meaning, usage, connotation, collocation, formality, and frequency, and may be amusing, unintelligible, or even offensive if it does not.

Receptive command of a word involves being able to comprehend it, generally in context. The good news is that receptive command does not involve as thorough a knowledge of usage, collocation, and the other issues mentioned above as productive command does. In fact, even with only a weak grasp of a word's meaning, a student can often still understand it when it appears in context (as most words do). The bad news is that students need receptive command of a very large number of words if they are ever to be able to read or listen to native English. A productive vocabulary of 1,000–2,000 words is generally adequate to allow people to express themselves in daily English interaction (DeCarrico 2001, 287; Fox 1987, 308–09). However, a vocabulary of 7,000–10,000 words is necessary to make most average texts accessible; in fact, an educated native speaker of English may have a receptive vocabulary of 45,000–60,000 words (Gairns and Redman 1986, 65).

These figures suggest that a good working vocabulary has a particular shape. To be functional, students need a relatively small fund of words that they know well and can use productively in speech and writing, and a much larger receptive vocabulary of words that they understand in context. This point is worth emphasizing because some courses of English study do not make much of a distinction between productive and receptive vocabulary; from the beginning, students are expected to be able to use all the words they learn. The problem is that teachers or curriculum designers, realizing that it is impossible for students to gain full productive control over many words very quickly, may cut down on the amount of vocabulary.[2] This, quite predictably, lengthens the amount of time it takes students to reach a breakthrough point in reading or listening.

Learning and Teaching Vocabulary

Some English teachers feel that an important part of their job is to carefully select the words students should learn and then devote class time to teaching those words. However, this approach can be problematic because you aren't always in a position to carefully select what words students will learn. You may not know what words a student should and shouldn't learn, and even if you do, choices are often determined primarily by what words appear in textbooks. The larger problem, however, is practicality. Time in class devoted to vocabulary explanation is too often time taken away from other class activities, and as Lewis (1993, 122) notes, it would take literally hundreds of hours for a teacher to teach students an adequately large vocabulary. You should also ask yourself why students can't be expected to study vocabulary on their own. In my experience, I have made far more progress when I have structured and carried out my own vocabulary-learning programs than when I have relied more on a language class to determine my rate and method of vocabulary acquisition.

Given the importance of students' taking charge of their own vocabulary acquisition, the discussion in this chapter centers more on how students learn vocabulary than on how you teach it. You most certainly should teach vocabulary in class as the need and opportunity arises, but equally important in vocabulary teaching are

---

[2] Lewis (1993, 9) points out that for many years an influential view in the language teaching field was that the vocabulary load should be minimized for students while grammar was stressed. In contrast, he argues persuasively that "the first thing students need to do is to learn to understand quite a lot of words" (p. 115).

- helping students set appropriate goals for their vocabulary learning efforts

- integrating vocabulary teaching into the practice of other language skills

- encouraging students' efforts and fortifying their resolve by checking up on them

How these roles work themselves out in the classroom will vary somewhat according to the students' level.

BEGINNING LEVEL

At this level, you may not need to devote as much attention to helping students set vocabulary acquisition goals because the words they learn are determined largely by their textbooks, and much of the vocabulary presented is high-frequency vocabulary over which students need productive as well as receptive command. The smaller amounts of vocabulary introduced—and the relatively greater importance of each item—mean that you can and should find ways to introduce and practice new words in class. On quizzes and tests, you should hold students accountable for receptive and productive command of all or most of the vocabulary introduced in the materials.

INTERMEDIATE LEVEL

At this level, students' reading and listening skills should begin to move ahead of their writing and speaking, so your first task is to talk with students about the difference between receptive and productive vocabulary; furthermore, you should encourage them—as they learn new words—to make a distinction between vocabulary they need for productive and receptive use (Bowen, Madsen, and Hilferty 1985, 325–26).

Secondly, you need to devote attention to teaching students to become better independent vocabulary learners. Text materials at the intermediate level will probably be introducing larger amounts of new vocabulary, so you will not have time to introduce and practice every new word in class; your focus should thus turn toward helping students understand what they need to learn about new words. As new vocabulary appears during various kinds of English lessons, you should raise questions of formality, connotation, and so forth (see below) in order to increase students' attention to these issues.

Finally, you need to motivate students to devote more attention to vocabulary acquisition, stressing it as part of your evaluation program. Regular, short quizzes are an especially effective way to get students in the habit of studying vocabulary daily rather than relying on pretest cramming. (On quizzes and tests, you should begin making a distinction between vocabulary you expect students to have productive command over and vocabulary that you only expect them to understand in context.)

ADVANCED LEVEL

At this level, students need to move toward the ability to read and understand English as it is used outside the foreign language classroom, so the need for a large receptive vocabulary is pressing. They should also be doing more work with real English materials and less with textbooks, so they will naturally encounter a wide range of new words, many of them relatively low frequency. Students need to make most of their own decisions about which words to add to their vocabularies, and while you might still hold students accountable for limited sets of new words encountered in your class materials, much vocabulary testing should occur indirectly through reading and listening comprehension tests.

Your task, then, especially when teaching intermediate- and advanced-level students, is less to teach vocabulary than to help students learn how to go about the task themselves. To this end, the following sections consider what students are up against as they build their vocabularies. I find it helpful to think of the problem of learning a new word as having three parts:

1. discovering what the word means

2. memorizing the meaning(s) of the word

3. learning other features of the word (e.g., usage, connotation)

The discussion of these three problems assumes that learners in EFL settings acquire most of their new vocabulary from books. Of course, it is good if students can also learn new words through listening, and students should have a chance to hear new words in class, on tape or CD, or in any other way possible. However, in EFL settings, books are usually more widely available and generally easier to use than any aural source of new vocabulary, so for the foreseeable future this is likely to be how EFL students learn most new words.

Strategies for Learning Vocabulary: The Discovery Phase

The first step in learning a new word is discovering what it means. As noted previously, this would not be a problem if a student needed to learn only a few words. However, to build a large receptive vocabulary, students need to discover the meanings of literally thousands of words, so efficiency becomes a primary concern in considering strategies for finding out the meanings of unfamiliar words.

DICTIONARIES

When a student encounters an unfamiliar word, the most obvious strategy for finding out what it means is to look it up in a dictionary. This strategy obviously has a number of significant advantages. Good dictionaries provide a wide range of information on connotation, usage, and other issues as well as on meaning, so they are very useful for students who want to gain productive control of a word. However, an equally great advantage of dictionary use is that dictionaries make students self-sufficient in their ability to discover meanings of new words. It is thus worthwhile to invest class time in teaching students what kinds of dictionaries to use and how to use them.

In some countries students rely heavily on small, inexpensive, glossary-type dictionaries—in either print or electronic form—that do little more than list words in English along with a translation into the host language. Such dictionaries often only list one or two possible translations of each English word, promoting the false belief that there is a neat one-to-one correspondence between all English and host-language words. The absence of examples or information on usage also subtly encourages students to ignore usage when memorizing words. On the other hand, these dictionaries are usually adequate for helping students discover the meanings of new words they encounter while reading. Moreover, the availability and convenience of these dictionaries are advantages that should not be overlooked.

Dictionaries (printed or electronic) that have more information are better, especially if they have an ample supply of examples so that students can learn usage as well as meaning. Examples reinforce the notion that ideas are expressed differently in different languages and that a host-language word that would be translated one way in one English sentence will often have to be translated differently in another context. There is nothing wrong with bilingual dictionaries (despite the prejudice of many English teachers against them) if they include adequate examples in English.[3]

As students begin to use English-English dictionaries, one initial problem may be learning how to efficiently locate the desired word. This involves learning and practicing alphabetical order so that looking up a word does not take too long. The greater problem is teaching students what to look for in an entry. Many students view learning vocabulary as a simply finding out what the host-language equivalent is, so they may be satisfied as soon as they locate it. You may need to explicitly teach students to pay attention to other important information. Of course, students cannot stop and engage in a serious learning effort every time they look up a word, but once they have invested the time in locating the word, they can certainly invest a few extra seconds in glancing at the entry to learn a little more than the word's basic meaning. Questions you should teach students to ask themselves include

- **Does this word have a host-language equivalent or not?** Some English words have close host-language equivalents; others don't. In a good dictionary this should be obvious from the entry; if a lot of explanation and examples are necessary for the word, it probably has no single equivalent, and the student should remember to pay special attention to this word.

- **How is this word used?** Encourage students to examine at least one example of how the word is used and to remember the example as a model for usage.

- **Does the word have a strong connotation?** Are strong negative or positive feelings associated with it? Is it associated strongly with a certain context? The pattern of examples will provide important clues.

- **Is this word markedly formal or informal?** Again, students should look at the examples.

- **How is it spelled?** Unfortunately, English spelling is not as logical as that of many other languages, so this requires special attention.

- **How is it pronounced?** Saying the new word aloud a few times not only allows pronunciation to be learned but is also an aid to remembering the word.

The main disadvantage of relying heavily on looking up unfamiliar words in dictionaries is that it is slow. When students are first learning how to use dictionaries, time spent looking up words is time well spent in developing a useful skill. However, once students know how to use dictionaries, each minute spent looking for a word is essentially a minute wasted. When there are only a few words to look up, this is not a serious problem, but if you ask students to read a passage that is loaded with unfamiliar words, they may spend the lion's share of their study time simply thumbing through pages (a fact that you should consider before giving students assignments that will involve extensive dictionary use).

GUESSING WORDS FROM CONTEXT

Guessing from context, discussed in chapter 9 as a reading strategy, is also a strategy for learning the meanings of new words. For example, in the sentence *Harry paused in the garden to smell a petunia,* students should have a fighting chance to guess that a petunia is a flower, so they may not

---

[3] Many companies publish learners' or advanced-level learners' dictionaries that are especially designed for students of English and include many examples.

need to look up *petunia* in a dictionary. One advantage of this approach is that students do not need to stop reading and break their train of thought to look a word up. Another is that students learn the word in a context, which helps them learn more about the word than its basic meaning.

The main problem with guessing as a strategy for discovering the meaning of new words is that it doesn't work very well unless the context is very clear or the student knows a lot about the topic; in other words, this strategy works best when students are reading very easy texts. (Even a few new words or unfamiliar cultural assumptions on a page may muddy the context enough that effective guessing becomes very difficult.) Unfortunately, many students spend little time reading easy texts. Beginning- and intermediate-level students often have to study textbook passages that are intentionally packed with new vocabulary, and the inherent difficulty of English books, articles, and so forth can make guessing hard even for advanced-level students. Therefore, guessing new words often becomes most efficient as a strategy for learners at very advanced stages of English study who already have much lexical and cultural knowledge.

One way to make guessing vocabulary words a more effective strategy is by having students memorize common English word roots and affixes. Many English words are constructed out of a finite stock of prefixes (e.g., *bi-, sub-, de-*), suffixes (e.g., *-ation, -ed, -er*), and word roots (e.g., *-scrib-, -graph-, -vis-*), and students who memorize the more common ones have a much better chance of correctly guessing the meanings of new words constructed from these elements. Knowledge of these roots and affixes is particularly helpful in dealing with many of the low-frequency technical words of English—words that are otherwise hard to learn because they appear infrequently and are easily confused with each other.

TEXTS WITH GLOSSARIES

Glossaries are vocabulary lists with host-language translations or explanations in English, and they are often found in textbooks after reading passages or dialogues. When such text-glossary combinations are available, there are considerable advantages to relying heavily on them to discover meanings of new words:

1. Learning a word from a glossary is faster than looking it up in a dictionary. The time saved on each word may seem insignificant, but when multiplied by hundreds, the time saved is substantial.

2. Getting the meaning of a word from a glossary is easier and often more accurate than guessing. This advantage is especially important for students at lower or intermediate levels, for whom guessing is often not an option.

3. When the glossary accompanies a text, each new word appears in a context that provides an example of its use.

In many cases, the textbooks you use in class will already have glossaries. However, in most countries more than one series of English textbooks is available, so as a strategy for building receptive vocabulary, you might also encourage students to seek out and study other materials with glossaries.

Of course, the best glossaries are often those students make for themselves. Once students have taken the time to look a word up in a dictionary, it takes only a little additional investment of time to write down the new word, a gloss, and a brief example of usage in a notebook. Keeping a vocabulary notebook and studying and reviewing it is a particularly useful study method not only because it increases the chance that students will actually learn the words they look up (words looked up but not reviewed are generally soon forgotten), but also because over time the vocabulary notebook becomes a glossary tailor-made to the student's interests and needs.

VOCABULARY LISTS

Many English textbooks, especially those published in England and the United States, contain lists of the vocabulary to be learned in each lesson. Such lists facilitate assigning vocabulary homework, but they are totally useless to a student who is trying to figure out what a word means. If you are using a text with such lists, it will be a great help to the students if you write easy English explanations of the words or appropriate host-language translations on the board or a printed page. This is extra work for you, but it will save students hours of paging through dictionaries.

Strategies for Learning Vocabulary: The Memorization Phase

Having located an explanation of what a new word means, the learners' next task is to get that meaning into their memories. Unfortunately, word meanings can be slippery little creatures. Often even after several attempts to learn a word, the only thing you can remember about it when you run into it again is that you have looked it up before.

Research suggests that people have at least two kinds of memory: short term and long term. Short-term memory holds a limited amount of information (about seven items) for brief periods of time. After that, the information is quickly forgotten. Long-term memory can hold an apparently unlimited amount of information, but it takes more work to get information into long-term memory (for further discussion, see Gairns and Redman 1993, 87; Stevick 1988, 29–31; Stevick 1996, 27).

On TV shows, you may have seen experts who can memorize pages from telephone books within minutes using powerful memory techniques such as associating words with mental images. (I still remember how to say the words *fried* and *elephant* in Russian because of a particularly vivid mental image I created associating these two words.) One elaborate scheme, popular in Europe in the 1600s, involved mentally placing words of one category (e.g., fruits) all in different positions in an imaginary room and then constructing an entire memory house or palace as a system for vocabulary recall.[4] The principles suggested in the following section do not promise anything quite so dramatic. However, students can do much to improve their vocabulary memorization approaches by paying attention to three basic factors: concentration, repetition, and meaningful manipulation.

CONCENTRATION

The most basic principle is that learners need to remain alert and pay attention as they try to memorize, and it helps if they seriously intend to remember what they are studying. This is certainly not a novel idea, but neither is it a point that should be neglected. Anyone who has spent much time studying a foreign language knows how easy it is for the eyes to keep moving over a glossary or text long after the brain has ceased to function.

One way for students to stay alert as they work is to use memorization methods that involve physical activity. The combination of mental and physical activity appears to enhance memory, and as long as students are moving, their minds are less likely to switch off. Some methods include shuffling flash cards, walking around while memorizing, mouthing words out loud, copying words, and moving pen and cover over a glossary.

Another way to improve concentration is by using memorization methods that involve performance or response; for example, constructing a sentence using the new word. Vocabulary memorization strategies that call for response from learners tend to keep them focused on the

---

[4]For a fascinating discussion of this process as used by Matteo Ricci, missionary and language learner in Ming Dynasty China, see Spence (1984). For a less exotic discussion of mnemonic techniques, see Rubin and Thompson (1994, 80–82).

activity and help prevent their minds from wandering. For example, when I study words on a vocabulary list, I find it more effective to test myself on each word rather than simply looking at it. Usually I cover the gloss and then check to see if I can get the word right. If so, I allow myself the gratification of slashing the conquered word with a highlighter; if not, I have to try again the next day. The point of this self-testing is not just that it helps check progress; equally important, it helps me stay alert and keeps me moving.

REPETITION

Repetition does not guarantee that a word will find its way into long-term memory, but it certainly helps; a word that you see ten times is more likely to stick in your memory than a word you see only once, much in the same way that you are likely to more quickly learn the name of someone you see every day than someone you meet only rarely.

Sometimes a combination of sheer concentration and repetition is enough to allow a student to memorize words. The Name Game, described in chapter 5, is a case in point. Through concentration and frequent repetition, you can learn dozens of names in one class period—albeit at the price of some hard work—and I often use this exercise with classes to show what is possible.

However, research indicates that a more efficient route to memorization lies in introducing a word in a meaningful context or relatively memorable way and reviewing it later. (A good strategy is to review new words soon after initial contact—within the next day or so—and to review again some days or even weeks later.) In a well-structured curriculum, this kind of delayed vocabulary review can be built into the program. However, it can also happen more naturally through extensive reading. Students who read frequently and widely review huge amounts of vocabulary naturally—and are much more likely to come across low-frequency vocabulary soon enough after learning it that they have not forgotten it. This is one reason extensive reading should be a part of vocabulary acquisition programs. The same beneficial effects for memorization can derive from repeatedly hearing, speaking, and writing words.

MEANINGFUL MANIPULATION

Apparently, something about using a word in a meaningful way helps it sink into long-term memory and stay there. Many language learners have found that a word really sticks in their memories for the first time once they have found an opportunity to use it. As Gairns and Redman (1986) note, "More meaningful tasks require learners to analyse and process language more deeply, which helps them to commit information to long-term memory" (p. 90). Using words in communicative ways is therefore one of the best ways to memorize them.

The implication for language study is again that communicative language practice of all kinds is a necessary part of a good vocabulary-learning strategy. Using words productively in meaningful speaking and writing may have a special power to aid memory, but seeing or hearing words as part of meaningful communication is also an effective way to facilitate memorization. Thus, vocabulary acquisition is best not undertaken as a program unto itself (hence the problems students have when they attempt to memorize dictionaries—as some students actually do!) but rather as part of programs of reading, listening, speaking, and writing.

Strategies for Learning Vocabulary: The Familiarization Phase

As I have mentioned, for productive command of a word students need to know much more than just a word's meaning—knowledge of its usage, connotation, collocation, level of formality, and level of frequency is also important. Even for receptive use, knowing the denotation of a word may not be enough; understanding the impact of a sentence may hang on knowing the connotation of a word or even its level of formality. How, then, are students to become familiar with all of these aspects of a word?

While introducing each new word fully in class is not practical, it is generally a good idea to point out some of these features of words in order to sensitize students to the issues they need to consider in their own vocabulary acquisition. While you can do this in any lesson as the occasion arises, intensive reading lessons provide a natural opportunity for examining selected words in more depth. Consider, for example, the following reading passages:

> The world's coldest continent, and the most difficult to reach, is Antarctica. For centuries, people have wondered what this continent is really like, since it is covered with solid thick ice and deep snow. (People's Publishing House 1984, 267)

You might call students' attention to collocation by pointing out the phrases *thick ice* and *deep snow*. From a purely semantic level, it isn't at all obvious why you couldn't use the word *deep* for both *ice* and *snow* (particularly for the Chinese students who read this book; in Chinese, the same word is used to describe depth in both snow and ice). The fastest—and probably most accurate—explanation for why *thick* goes with *ice* and *deep* goes with *snow* is that in English this collocation is habitual.

> A TV reporter wanted to find out what people thought of a new film, so she decided to interview people as they came out of the theatre. She asked one woman what she thought of the film. "It was excellent," the woman replied. "I thought it was the best film I've seen in years." Then she stopped a young man and asked him the same question. "It was dynamite!" he said. (People's Publishing House 1984, 264)

This passage provides a good opportunity to make a point about formality. Note the switch between the proper woman respondent ("It was excellent") and the colloquial young man ("It was dynamite!"). Usage points could also be made about the words *think* (What did you think *of* the film?), and the phrase *came out* ("came out *of* the theatre").

Ultimately, however, you cannot treat every new word in this way, so students must learn to seek this information out for themselves. Another reason students need an adequate diet of extensive reading and listening is that patterns of usage, formality, and connotation emerge only if students see new words repeatedly in a variety of contexts. I remember learning a Chinese term (*jiao xun*) that my textbook translated as *teaching*. In an effort to be diligent, I tried my new word out on my teacher at the end of class with what I thought was the Chinese equivalent of *Thank you for your teaching* (*Laoshi, xiexie nide jiaoxun.*), but her response was to chuckle and head off to the lounge to announce what I had just said. It was only some years later when reading a novel that I finally figured out what had gone wrong: I noticed that every time this particular word appeared, it was in the context of an elder admonishing a penitent youth. The pattern of use revealed by extensive reading showed me what the textbook had not told me.

Evaluation

Vocabulary can and should be tested as an integral part of the evaluation of all language skills. To some extent this happens naturally; when you test reading comprehension or ability to discuss an issue, you are also indirectly testing vocabulary. However, some evaluation of vocabulary acquisition per se is often desirable, the main justification being the positive backwash it has on students' interest in learning words (Hughes 1989, 146–47).

Learning vocabulary requires steady work over a long period of time. Students who cram words into their memories before a final examination often lose much of what they learn soon after the examination. According to Gairns and Redman (1986, 90), about 80 percent of what is learned is lost within the first twenty-four hours in the absence of review, so short periods of intense study followed by long slack periods do not do much for vocabulary building. A testing pattern that helps build better habits in students would consist of frequent cumulative quizzes. This would both require students to work regularly and to review what they learn rather than forgetting it once the pressure is off.

The simple type of vocabulary quiz items suggested here are not ideal in terms of their backwash—better backwash results from testing of listening, speaking, reading, and writing skills. Many of these items only require students to memorize a translation or explanation of the target word. However, this low-level command of new words is a good start toward receptive control, and what these quiz items lack in depth they make up for in ease, thus making it possible for you to give short but frequent quizzes.

1. **English word—definition:** Give students the words you wish to check, and have them provide definitions, synonyms, or even translations into the host language. This kind of item is very straightforward conceptually and easy to explain to students, but it is problematic in that students may know the meaning of the test word but not know a synonym or a good way to explain it. Translation is simplest for students but may be hard for you. Since many words have more than one meaning, it is a good idea to provide a sample sentence with each test word.

2. **host-country equivalent—target word:** For this simple quiz, write the host-language equivalents of the words you wish to test. Then present these to the class and ask students to produce the English words. This kind of item checks spelling as well as meaning.

3. **fill-in-the-blank:** Find a reading passage that contains words you wish to test for, then delete the target words from the passage and list them at the bottom of the page. Students then choose the proper word to fill in each blank. In order to make this kind of quiz or test at least somewhat communicative, you need to make sure that in most cases the context makes one of the deleted words a particularly good choice; otherwise completing the test turns into a language puzzle.

4. **sentence with target word—response:** Write questions that contain the words you want to test, underlining them. Make sure comprehension of the words is important to understanding the question. Then have students write appropriate answers that demonstrate that they understand the test words. An alternative to this is to write true/false statements using the test words and have students respond appropriately.

5. **matching:** Present two groups of words, and have students match them based on some kind of relationship (e.g., antonyms, synonyms, same kind of thing, same part of speech).

6. **sentence writing:** To test productive command of vocabulary items, have students use the test word in a sentence that demonstrates that they know the meaning of the word. (Sentences like *Pragmatic is an English word* don't count.) This kind of item encourages students to memorize sample sentences along with new words and is most appropriate for high-frequency words that students need in their productive vocabulary.

For Thought, Discussion, and Action

1. **your vocabulary learning experiences:** Reflect on your previous foreign language study, and ask yourself how you learned most of your vocabulary. (Was it taught in class? Did you memorize lists? Did you simply use the language a lot?) In order of importance, list the ways through which you learned vocabulary, and compare notes with a classmate or friend.

2. **all about** *contact:* Review the different aspects of mastering a word by analyzing the word *contact* the same way the word *dog* is analyzed at the beginning of this chapter.

3. **textbooks with glossaries:** If you are already in the host country, visit a local bookstore, and look for English textbooks that have good vocabulary lists with glosses. Make a list of books you could recommend to students who want to build their vocabularies.

4. **memorizing words:** Survey several classmates or friends on what methods they have used for memorizing new words in foreign language study and how they feel these methods worked.

5. **word memorization strategies:** Experiment with different strategies for memorizing words as follows:
    *   List two or three different memorization strategies you want to try out (e.g., word association, review from a list).
    *   Locate several lists of vocabulary words that are unfamiliar to you (either words from a foreign language or even obscure English words, perhaps from a Graduate Record Examination study list).
    *   Use the first strategy for list one, the second strategy for list two, and so forth. Compare the results.

6. **vocabulary teaching:** Using one of the sample courses in chapter 6, design a strategy for encouraging students to build their vocabulary as part of the course. Be sure to consider the probable level of the students as well as what phase (discovery, memorization, familiarization) of the process you want to assist them with. Be ready to explain the rationale for your strategies.

Sample Language Learning Project (LLP) for Advanced-Level Vocabulary Building (A)

Goal: Build receptive vocabulary for reading comprehension.

Material: English textbook that contains both reading passages and glossaries.

Plan: Study three times a week, an hour or so per session.

Method: For each session,

1. Review vocabulary from previous lessons that I have not yet learned.
    *   Cover the gloss (definition, translation, explanation) for each word I will review. Then look at the word and see if I can remember the meaning.

- If I can quickly and accurately recall the meaning, highlight or cross out the word, and move on to the next.
- If not, keep it on the list and try again during my next session.

2. Study the vocabulary from today's passage or glossary.
   - Covering the gloss, test myself on each new word. If I already know it, highlight it or cross it off the list.
   - If I don't know it, pause and try to memorize it.

3. Read the passage. As I encounter new words from today's glossary, pause briefly to review them and notice how they are used.

4. End with a quick review of the new vocabulary from today's lesson.

Criteria for measuring progress: I will have succeeded if I

- study all the texts in the book

- can correctly remember the meanings of most of the new words after I finish studying the book

Sample LLP for Advanced-Level Vocabulary Building (B)

Goal: Build receptive vocabulary for reading comprehension.

Material: Any book in English that I find interesting and not overly difficult; a notebook in which I list new vocabulary.

Plan: Study three times a week, an hour or so per session.

Method: For each session,

1. Review vocabulary in my notebook that I have not yet learned (see above).

2. Read today's chapter (or passage). As I read, mark unfamiliar words that I want to learn. Don't mark and learn every unfamiliar word. Keep the number reasonable, and give priority to words that appear to be more common or useful.

3. After I finish reading, look up the new words in a dictionary, write them into my notebook, and try to memorize them.

4. Reread the chapter. As I encounter the new words I studied, pause briefly to review them and notice how they are used.

5. End with a quick review of the new vocabulary from today's session.

Criteria for measuring progress: I will have succeeded if I

- finish studying an entire book using this approach

- create a notebook that is at least thirty pages long

- can understand all the vocabulary items in the notebook when I review the notebook and if I see the words when reading texts

Chapter 12

Grammar: Finding a Balance

- In many countries, grammar study is emphasized to the point that it almost becomes synonymous with language study—and this is one reason many students dislike studying English. One of your tasks is to help students gain a balanced view of grammar study, recognizing the importance of accuracy in language use but restoring a focus on communication that makes language study more meaningful and enjoyable.

- Mastery of grammar involves knowledge of grammatical forms and skill in using those forms. For building the latter, adequate practice is necessary.

- Students' grammar systems normally develop through gradual elaboration from simple to complex. As with vocabulary, there are different levels of control. Students may first gain receptive control of a structure and only later learn to produce it. In the case of low-frequency structures, they may never need to gain productive command.

One thing that most students of English would agree on is that they don't particularly like studying grammar. As Stevick (1988) notes, "Difficulties with grammar cause more discouragement and drive away more students than anything else in our profession" (p. 82). What makes this worse is that many EFL classes place special emphasis on grammar, analyzing sentences and drilling structures to the almost complete exclusion of other activities, so by the time students reach your class, many of them are thoroughly fed up with both grammar and English.[1] Others will have become firmly convinced that the road to English success lies through the grammar book and will lie in wait for you with questions that would confound any grammarian.

On the whole, volunteer teachers (VTs) are not a population known for love of grammar. Many native speakers of English have unpleasant memories of grammar drills in Spanish, French, or German classes and have no inherent affection for the subject. Matters are worsened by the fact that the average native speaker of English has little explicit knowledge of English grammar rules, so grammar is not a particularly easy subject to teach. The instinctive response of many VTs is to try and avoid grammar teaching as much as possible.

I am not going to try to convince you that grammar is really enjoyable to teach and learn (though it need not be as bad as it is often made out to be). Grammar, however, cannot and should not be ignored, so in this chapter I examine what role is appropriate for grammar in language teaching and how it should be taught.

Grammar: Some Basic Points

WHAT IS GRAMMAR?

One source of problems in the EFL grammar classroom lies in misunderstandings about what grammar is. Some students view grammar rules as an unimportant set of conventions useful for passing tests but of dubious value in actual English conversation. However, the more common tendency is to go overboard in the other direction, viewing grammar rules as something close to the language learner's version of the Ten Commandments.[2] In this view, grammar rules prescribe correct and unequivocal answers to all language problems, and each rule is an indispensable imperative that learners must obey at all costs.

A better understanding of grammar would fall somewhere between these two extremes. Like most human behavior, language use tends to be patterned, and one way to remove some of students' excessive awe of grammar is to point out that grammar rules are actually less regulations than they are descriptions of patterns in the way English speakers construct sentences. Some of these patterns are stronger than others. For example, a great many English nouns form their plural by adding an -s at the end, so knowing this basic rule enables students to both comprehend and accurately produce many utterances.[3] Knowledge of such common patterns is very helpful to students as they attempt to construct sentences. Other patterns are weaker, and the rules that describe them cover fewer situations. For example, no single, easy rule can enable students to predict whether they should use an infinitive (to + *verb*) or a gerund (verb + *-ing*) following a verb, so

---

[1] See Faber (1991) for a vivid account of how grammar-obsessed teachers in Latin courses almost destroyed his love of language learning. As he comments, "They're right in insisting on the importance of grammar, but who says you've got to have it first, as some kind of brutal initiation?" (p. 43).

[2] This analogy is only partly meant in fun. Remember that many of the cultures in which VTs teach give the written word a much higher level of respect than is common now in the West, and the grammar book often inherits some of this almost sacred authority.

[3] This rule is actually a little more complex than it seems, especially in speech. The -s ending is sometimes pronounced /-s/, sometimes /-z/, and sometimes /-ez/.

mastery of this problem requires a lot of memorization of individual words and situations. For the student who wants a rule for everything, you could find or create rules to explain even the most idiomatic expressions, but the more complex the set of rules becomes and the fewer situations it covers, the more it hinders attempts to learn language rather than facilitating them.

If the students are still too awestruck by grammar, you might further point out that since a grammar is simply a description of language patterns, there is no single definitive grammar of English. Instead, descriptions of English use a variety of grammar systems and terminology. (The commonly used systems tend to be quite similar, but there are some differences, and it is therefore important for you to learn the system and terms used in the country where you will be teaching.[4]) In other words, to argue over whether the word *eating* in the sentence *I like eating hamburgers* is a verb or a noun misses the point—once students understand what the sentence means and how it works, the proper categorization of each word is of marginal usefulness (unless students will face a test that demands such analysis).

Another point you could make about grammar is that, like languages, grammar rules change over time. Examples of changes in English over the past few centuries can be seen in even a casual perusal of Shakespeare or the King James Bible. For example, many English speakers are familiar with the Bible's Ten Commandments in the old King James wording (*Thou shalt not kill.*), which uses vocabulary and grammar that has long since disappeared in normal English usage. Changes are still occurring, and students may hear or read English that does not conform to the rules they have memorized. For example, one change now taking place in American English involves the growing tendency to use *their* rather than *he* or *she* in sentences such as *I hope no one forgot their book.* (In this case, the change is due to a growing unwillingness to use *his* or *her* to refer to a group that includes both men and women.) Thus, occasionally when answering questions about what is grammatically right, you will have to answer that two alternatives are correct, although for different settings.

The point is that students will have a better perspective on language learning if they take a more descriptive and utilitarian view of grammar. Their purpose in studying grammar should be to find out how speakers of English construct sentences, not to master a divine canon of grammar rules per se. A rule that enables a student to construct many correct sentences is worth learning; a rule that is impossible to understand or covers only one or two situations is a hindrance rather than a help. Grammar rules are helpful to students if and only if they make the mastery of English easier.

HOW IS GRAMMAR LEARNED?

It may be instructive to briefly consider how children learn a language. A baby learning English usually begins speaking with single-word sentences like "Cookie!", often accompanied by much waving of arms and feet. Later, she progresses to "Sally cookie!", an utterance that is generally perfectly intelligible in context as a request rather than a statement of identity. She then moves on to "Sally cookies now!" and then, over time, slowly but surely continues experimenting and elaborating on her sentence constructions. No matter how diligently parents teach or correct, Sally is not likely to jump in a week from "Sally cookie!" to "Mother, may I please have a cookie?"

Adults may not learn language exactly the same way children do, but current wisdom in the field suggests that there are similarities. Adults also tend to start by learning simple basic rules and gradually elaborating their system through experimentation. To use the analogy of drawing

---

[4] One system you may run into that is quite different from traditional grammars is transformational grammar (TG). TG is intended more for linguists than language teachers, so before you buy a grammar reference book, you might make sure that it uses more widely used, traditional grammar systems.

a picture, adults naturally tend to sketch an outline first and go back to fill in ever-finer levels of detail later rather than completing one corner of the picture in full detail before moving on to another. In other words, adults are not likely to master all of the verb system before going on to adverbs; they are more likely to gain a rudimentary control of both and then—through trial and error, aided by whatever input is available—to elaborate that control (Hedge 2000, 11). As Bowen, Madsen, and Hilferty (1985) describe the process, "Students usually learn their grammar one small piece at a time; they do not need (and indeed could not immediately assimilate) an entire system" (p. 166).

The first implication of this for teaching is that it is normal for students to go through an interlanguage period during which they have incomplete control of structures they are trying to learn—a "Give Sally cookie" stage. It is not normal for them to rapidly master the verb system of English down to a fine level of control, no matter how clearly you explain it to them. A second implication is that students need an opportunity to digest grammar input by trying out modifications in their interlanguage grammar system through language practice. Again, to improve their control of grammar, listening to you explain grammar is not enough—they need to practice using it.

HOW WELL SHOULD GRAMMAR BE LEARNED?

One way in which grammar is similar to vocabulary is that it can be used in two basic ways: receptively for comprehension in reading or listening, and productively in speech and writing. This suggests that, as in the case of vocabulary, it is normal for a student to have complete productive control over some grammar rules and only receptive control of others. Of course, this is what normally happens whether you want it to or not; usually students gain receptive control over a structure before they learn to use it productively. However, you need not assume that students must ultimately master all grammar rules for productive control. Some grammatical structures in English are not used very much, and by no means do students have to be able to produce every one. Even basic verb tenses, such as the past perfect (e.g., *By 8:00 he had slept for ten hours.*) or the past perfect progressive (e.g., *By 8:00 he had been sleeping for ten hours.*), are not often used and can usually be replaced with a rough equivalent that is more straightforward (e.g., *He slept ten hours before 8:00.*).

One implication is that some grammar points are more important than others and that students do not need to gain total productive control over every structure they encounter—certainly not right away. The goal is rather for students to first learn rules that are relatively useful and easy to grasp and to fill in the details as time and need dictate (Scarcella and Oxford 1992, 174). The teacher who insists on complete productive control of every fine detail runs the risk of overloading students' circuits and burning them out. Again, students and teachers need to remember that the goal is not mastery of an abstract system of theory; it is practical mastery of a communication skill, and the goal in learning grammar is to learn that which is useful in communicating.

Teaching Grammar

Usually when you are teaching grammar, you will be working with a textbook that determines what grammar structures are to be introduced and provides exercises intended to teach these structures.[5] As you prepare for your class, the issue is thus usually not deciding what to teach but rather how to approach the material in your text.

---

[5] If there is no text for your course, you can probably find a locally produced text that has grammar lessons—of all the kinds of English teaching materials, texts that center on grammar are the most widely produced. Also see appendix C for grammar books that could serve as the outline of a grammar course.

The steps I suggest below for a grammar lesson follow more or less those described in Ur (1988, 7–10): (1) presenting a structure, (2) explaining it, and (3) practicing it (Cross 1991, 17–19, and Eisenstein 1987, 287, suggest a very similar approach). The approach is basically inductive; that is, it allows students a chance to figure out the structure before you explain it to them. In general I favor this approach because problem solving makes students more active participants in the learning process; I also suggest it for VTs because you may not yet have a clear sense of what students need to have explained to them and what they don't need or can't handle, and a deductive approach (explanation first, examples and practice later) may lead you into overly long and elaborate grammar lectures. An inductive approach allows students to try a structure out before you explain it, thus giving you a chance to assess what problems they have with it and what needs to be explained. However, for reasons of culture or learning styles, some students are more comfortable with a deductive approach, so you should experiment with the ordering of steps below to find out what works best with your students.[6]

PRESENTATION

For students, the first step in mastering a new grammar structure is simply noticing it. This point is easy to overlook when you are teaching students from a textbook that explicitly highlights grammar points in a way that forces students to attend to them whether or not the students are ready and willing to do so. However, the natural development of students' emerging grammar systems doesn't always follow the neat plan laid out in a textbook, and for their command of grammar to continue developing, students need to get into the habit of noticing new grammar structures when they read or listen to English. The idea is that "once a student becomes aware of a particular grammar point or language feature in input—whether through formal instruction, some type of focus-on-form activity, or repeated exposure to communicative use of the structure—he or she often continues to notice the structure in subsequent input, particularly if the structure is used frequently" (Fotos 2001, 272).[7]

The most basic way to present a structure in class is to use it communicatively in a classroom chat activity (see chapter 8) with students. For example, if the structure for the lesson is the future verb tense, you might begin the day's lesson by asking a few students, "What are you doing this weekend?" At this first stage, the goal is to let students hear or see multiple examples of the new structure and give them an opportunity to figure out for themselves first what it means and then how it works, so you need not demand that students immediately use the structure when responding to your questions. They may well have already studied the structure in their books and have some idea how it works, but reading about a structure in a book and using it in conversation are two very different things, so it is still nice to give them a breathing space before requiring production. (Given that students may already have had some contact with the new structure, another goal of this part of the in-class lesson is to find out how much they already know about it.)

You might also focus the presentation of a new structure through games or drills specifically chosen to illustrate it. For example, when introducing a new structure such as the plural ending, you might first hold up one book and say, "One book," then hold up two and say, "Two books." Here, once students seem to understand, you could encourage them to start experimenting with production, responding to what you hold up. However, as above, your main goal is receptive comprehension, so you should only involve production as students seem willing and ready.[8]

---

[6] Eisenstein (1987, 286–88) suggests that an inductive approach may work less well with older students, with students who are used to grammar explanations, or in cultures where guessing—especially in public—isn't favored.

[7] This idea is known as Schmidt's noticing hypothesis. See also Larsen-Freeman (2001, 37).

[8] Larsen-Freeman (2001, 257) suggests that if you introduce grammar using texts generated from your computer, one trick for calling students' attention to new grammar structures is to highlight them in boldface.

EXPLANATION

There are good reasons not to expect that lectures will make a dramatic impact on students' progress toward grammatical accuracy. One problem is that, even in the same class, students often have different levels of grammar knowledge, so when you lecture on a grammar point, some of the students will already understand it, others will lack the foundation to comprehend your explanation, and others will probably be bored and not pay attention; only a percentage—all too often a small one—will actually learn much from your lecture. A greater problem is that conscious knowledge of grammar rules does not guarantee the ability to produce accurate English. In fact, conscious knowledge of grammar rules is not a necessary precondition to the ability to produce English accurately, a fact demonstrated daily by most native speakers (who have little explicit knowledge of grammar rules) and by many students who do well on grammar tests but still make frequent errors in communication situations. Understanding a grammar point may be the first step toward mastering it, but it is only the first step.

Then why explain grammar structures at all? At a very practical level, one reason is that in many countries lectures on grammar are an expected staple of the language classroom diet, and if this familiar part of the routine suddenly vanishes, students may be disoriented or dissatisfied. (Another argument for explaining grammar is that it is by explaining grammar that many language teachers learn it themselves!) However, going beyond such practical concerns, explicit teaching of grammar points can also be genuinely useful to students, particularly if—as Brown (2001) argues—it calls new grammar structures to students' attention in ways that

- are embedded in meaningful communicative contexts

- contribute positively to communicative goals

- promote accuracy within fluent, communicative language

- do not overwhelm students with linguistic terminology

- are as lively and intrinsically motivating as possible (p. 363)

Often text materials will provide explanations of new structures and examples of their use, so by the time students reach your class, they will presumably have already encountered some explanation of new structures. Also, if you have allowed students to play with the structure during the presentation stage, you should have some idea how well students already understand the structure. The goal of the explanation phase is thus generally to clarify main problem areas, advancing students' understanding of the structure by one or two steps. Here are a few pointers on explanations:

1. Try to start explaining at the right level so that you do not waste time telling students what they already know or talking over their heads. It is more important to be to the point than to be comprehensive.

2. Keep explanations as short and simple as possible, with a limited number of variations and details that will tend to confuse and overload students. Avoid the temptation to prepare overly thorough explanations of grammar points in order to impress your class.

3. Remember that some points are better memorized than explained. For example, little needs to be said about irregular past tense verb forms (e.g., *eat/ate, write/wrote, read/read*)—students just need to learn them.

4. Examples are often much easier to understand than explanations, so be sure to include several. Given the tendency of students in many countries to read better than they listen, it is also a good idea to write examples on the board.

5. Use pictures, diagrams, and graphs in communicating a point. For example, many grammar teachers explain English verb tenses with time-line drawings.

PRACTICE

Obviously, understanding a grammar rule is not the same thing as being able to apply it to communication problems, so a third important step in the study of grammar is practice. Grammar practice ranges on a continuum from highly controlled practice, in which learners need to make very few choices, to free communicative practice in which learners need to apply grammar rules to real language use situations. The challenge is greatest in productive use of grammar—speaking and writing—so I focus on this here.

Highly Controlled Practice

One problem usually not faced by VTs is having to design controlled grammar exercises (e.g., fill in the blank, find and correct the error in the sentence, restate the passive sentence in the active voice)—many English textbooks have an adequate supply. Such exercises can be a useful first step in mastering a grammar structure because they allow the learner to concentrate on applying a structure in a controlled situation in which other problems are eliminated. These exercises are also useful for checking to see if students have a basic understanding of the grammar point.

The simplicity of these exercises is, however, also their most serious drawback. Exercises such as choosing the right verb tense to fill in a blank or restating a passive sentence in the active voice are unlike actual language production precisely because the learner can focus on one problem to the exclusion of all others. They are very unlike real-world grammar application problems and should not constitute the major part of a student's grammar practice diet. You certainly should not feel that your duty consists primarily of seeing that students do every exercise in the book.

Moderately Controlled Practice

An intermediate step between highly controlled exercises like those mentioned above and natural practice activities would be controlled communicative activities in which students must construct their own sentences and express their own ideas, but with their attention still clearly focused on the target structure you want them to learn. For example, consider the following activity for practicing relative clauses in which students are divided into pairs and asked to practice a short conversation as follows:

A: (pointing into a crowd) Who is that woman?
B: Which one?
A: The one . . . (e.g., who is wearing a hat, who looks like an angel).
B: Oh, that's . . . (e.g., Angie, Kim).

This exercise is communicative in that it can involve real conversation about real people (e.g., other students in the class or people in a picture), and students have some freedom to express their own ideas. However, students still know exactly what grammar structure they need to produce and can focus their attention on it. Many textbooks contain such exercises, and they can also generally be readily adapted from dialogues in the textbook.

Free Practice

For grammar practice to be realistic, it ultimately needs to involve solving multiple language problems at the same time. To this end, free practice is best if it takes place in a communicative context, where the students need to pay attention to what they are saying as well as getting their grammar right. You can often find topics of conversation that naturally require the target structure to appear frequently, thus providing good practice in using that structure. Here are some examples:

1. For the present continuous tense, have students talk about something while they watch it happen—perhaps a classmate's actions or action on a videotape. This will elicit many sentences, such as *Sally is smiling* or *The man is eating dinner.*

2. For relative clauses, have students discuss what kind of friends (or movies, food, weather, etc.) they like. Of course, the different kinds can be distinguished with adjectives as well as relative clauses (e.g., *I like rich friends.*), but many other ideas virtually demand relative clauses (e.g., *I like friends who do my homework for me.*).

3. To practice use of plural nouns as topics, have students discuss what animals they like or don't like and why (e.g., *I don't like dogs because they are stupid.*).

Writing is an especially good skill to combine with grammar lessons because it serves as an intermediate step between applying a grammar rule in discrete-point exercises and quickly applying it in speaking. Like speaking, writing requires students to apply grammar rules while in the midst of a host of other decisions, but unlike speaking, writing allows students time to think about how to apply a grammar structure and even time to consult reference tools. Writing also makes it possible for students to go back and check the language they have produced in order to learn from their mistakes.

Evaluating Grammar

There are two issues to address in evaluating students' grammar competence. One is whether or not students know the target structure, in other words, whether or not they can manipulate it under ideal circumstances. The second question is whether or not they can apply their knowledge under the conditions of normal language use.

EVALUATING BASIC GRAMMAR KNOWLEDGE

The classic grammar test involves use of discrete-point grammar items that focus students' attention on a particular grammar problem. The main value of such items is that they allow you to determine whether or not students have a basic understanding of the target structure. Basic types include

1. multiple choice—for example, *Tommy _____ the apple.*
   A. eat
   B. eaten
   C. eated
   D. ate

2. fill in the blank—for example, *Tommy _____ (eat) the apple.*

3. correct the error—for example, *The apple fell on Newton's head.*

4. rewrite—for example, *Rewrite the following in passive voice: Tommy ate the apple.*

As pointed out in chapter 4, creating good discrete-point test items is a complicated science, but two rules of thumb will help you ensure that a discrete-point test is reasonably good:

1. Always have someone else check your test items to ensure that you haven't overlooked any ambiguities during test construction.

2. Use a large number of test items. If your test has only a few items, a few poorly designed questions or lucky guesses by students can make a big difference in the final grade.

Discrete-point grammar tests have a number of advantages: they are easy to grade, they let you check whether or not students have studied specific grammar points, and they prepare students for other discrete-point tests (e.g., the Test of English as a Foreign Language [TOEFL]) that they may face in the future. On the other hand, they also have very serious disadvantages. While such tests tell you whether or not students have grasped the basic concept of a grammar structure, they do not tell you how well students can apply this knowledge. Worse, the backwash from heavy use of such test items is generally negative because they reinforce the belief that knowledge of grammar theory is more important than the ability to apply it to real-life situations. So, as much as possible, it is best to test grammar knowledge in conjunction with other skills such as speaking and writing, where grammar knowledge is actually applied to language use.

EVALUATING THE ABILITY TO APPLY GRAMMAR KNOWLEDGE

Evaluating grammar in the context of language use rather than through discrete-point tests has two primary advantages. The first is that evaluating grammar in use (usually speaking or writing) allows you to assess not only how well students know grammar rules but also whether or not students can apply them. The second is that the backwash from this kind of testing encourages students to learn how to apply their knowledge rather than being satisfied with an understanding of grammar theory. The simplest way to assess grammar as a part of speaking tests is to add a grammatical accuracy component to whatever scoring system you use for interviews or other kinds of speaking tests. (See chapter 8 for a discussion of assessing speaking skills.) Of course, if you want to test whether or not students have learned particular grammar structures, you will need to use speaking tasks that ensure that students produce the target structures. In other words, in your interviews, pair work, or whatever format you use for evaluation, you will need to include some tasks that are at least somewhat controlled. These might be exercises like the moderately controlled exercises mentioned above or topics that naturally elicit certain structures. (Note that in the latter case, you also need to let students know that you are looking for certain target structures.)

When you attempt to assess grammar during interviews or other kinds of speaking tests, one problem is how to note (1) whether students used the target structures and (2) how successful students were in doing so. Imagine that you want to check how well students have mastered use of the past tense, and you are using a small-group assessment approach like the one described in chapter 8. The task you have given students is to ask each other what their very first day at their university was like (e.g., were there problems? surprises?), and you have also told them you will be paying attention to how well they use past tense verbs. For such a test, scoring may be easier if you make up a simple criteria system like the one below:

> 4: Produced the target structure frequently and was usually correct
>
> 3: Produced the target structure a number of times; may have hesitated or self-corrected but was ultimately correct at least half the time
>
> 2: Tried to produce the target structure several times but was generally slow or inaccurate
>
> 1: Rarely produced the target structure; was slow and inaccurate
>
> 0: Never produced the target structure

Admittedly, such a simple system is rather impressionistic and does not allow you to achieve a high degree of precision in your scoring. However, it is simple enough to use quickly. More importantly, such an approach has good backwash in that it encourages students to use the target structure in a relatively natural conversational setting. (For a higher degree of precision, you can record the students' conversation and score it more carefully at your leisure. This, however, involves a lot more work.)

Written work is the other natural context within which to assess grammar because grammatical accuracy is especially important in writing and because it allows you to assess grammar at your leisure. In the same way that you can design practice activities to call for certain grammatical constructions, you can plan a writing task so that it naturally elicits target structures. For example, a written dialogue about favorite fruits should elicit the use of plural nouns as general subjects (e.g., *I like pears but I hate grapes.*); a composition about childhood experiences should elicit past tense verbs (e.g., *I wore diapers for several years.*). If you wish to ensure that students produce certain target structures, list those structures and tell students to be sure to use them. Writing tasks that are explicitly designed to test grammar are, of course, less natural than normal writing tasks because they focus students' attention on grammar rather than communication, but the loss in naturalness may be made up for by the certainty that you will get the material you need for your evaluation.

Answering Grammar Questions

It seems fitting to conclude this discussion of grammar with a few comments on the art of coping with knotty grammar questions in class. It seems that almost every English class has at least one student who is obsessed with grammar and loves to ask questions like "Should I use an infinitive or a gerund after a verb?" The problem VTs often face is not only that they may not know the answer to a question like this (at least not when couched in these terms), but also that they don't really understand the question itself.

The first and most important rule for survival is never to attempt to answer a grammar question—particularly one presented in theoretical terms—unless the student gives you an example. By demanding an example, you move the issue onto more familiar ground; even if you don't understand the grammar terminology, you will generally be able to determine whether a specific example is correct or not, and the example will help you understand the question. Another reason to insist on examples is that they serve as a check on the accuracy of the question. Over the years, I have found that a great many impressive-sounding grammar questions, once understood, turn out to be essentially gibberish. Student grammar questions often begin as specific examples that the student recasts (often incorrectly) in half-understood theoretical language. Once you make the student present the original example, it is much easier to get to the heart of the matter.

A final reason to require examples is that this reminds students that grammar study is intended to lead to application and that application of grammar rules is often highly situational, a fact that tends to get lost when discussion of a rule remains theoretical.

A second tactic you can use when you aren't sure how to answer a question is to take the students' example, think of several more, and try to work out the rule along with the students. The pedagogical advantage of this approach is that it encourages the development of inductive skills and active learning; the practical advantage is that it gives you time to think.

If you have looked at a few examples and are still puzzled, you may be tempted to try to bluff your way through the situation with a long answer containing lots of obscure, grammarlike terms. However, a better choice is probably to confess your ignorance and promise to find out the answer. This may be somewhat embarrassing at first (though most language teachers get used to it rather quickly), but if you actually carry through, you will demonstrate diligence and learn something at the same time.

For Thought, Discussion, and Action

1. **learning about students' attitudes toward grammar:** Ask one or more people who have taught in your host country how students there typically view grammar and grammar study.

2. **reflecting on your own grammar study (task A):** Reflect on your experience studying the grammar of a foreign language. Did you enjoy learning the grammar or not? What did and didn't you like about it? How do you feel about teaching grammar? Share your thoughts and experiences with a classmate:

3. **reflecting on your own grammar study (task B):** Reflecting on your experience studying the grammar of a foreign language, list lessons you might pass on to others about learning it. What did and didn't seem to work for you? What would you try if you could start over?

4. **observing changes in grammar:** In this chapter, two examples are given of how English grammar has changed over the centuries. List other examples.

5. **using grammar terms:** See if you know the following English grammar terms and concepts and can explain what they are:
   - verbs (regular and irregular, transitive and intransitive)
   - nouns (singular and plural, countable and uncountable)
   - adjectives
   - adverbs
   - pronouns
   - articles (definite and indefinite)
   - determiners
   - prepositions
   - modal auxiliaries
   - verb tenses (e.g., simple present, simple past, simple future, present progressive, present perfect)
   - voice (active and passive)
   - gerunds and infinitives
   - clauses (dependent and independent)

6. **presenting grammar points:** Think of activities you could use to present the grammar points listed in number 5 to students, especially activities that give students a chance to figure out what the structure you are introducing is used for before you explain it explicitly.

7. **explaining grammar points:** For one or more of the grammar points in number 5, prepare a clear simple explanation. Use examples, visual aids, or anything else that will help you explain clearly and effectively.

8. **practicing grammar points:** For one or more of the grammar points in number 5, prepare a moderately controlled practice activity that will help students learn to use the structure accurately and appropriately.

9. **making grammar fun:** For one or more points in number 5, create a game that will help students learn the point in a way that is effective and at least relatively entertaining.

Chapter 13

Teaching Culture

- Culture should be included in language courses because studying culture enhances students' ability to understand and interact effectively with people from other cultures and more effectively express themselves to foreign audiences. Study of culture can also make language courses more interesting.

- The culture of a group consists of members' shared ideas, particularly their shared knowledge, views, and patterns.

- Western culture, U.S. culture, British culture, and other cultures are not monolithic entities; considerable cultural variety exists even within any nation.

- In many countries, students may have mixed feelings about Western culture. It is therefore important to present your culture in a way that is as objective and sensitive as possible.

English has become a world language, used far beyond the confines of U.S. and British soil, so it can no longer be assumed that all English speakers come from Western cultural backgrounds. Many nations in which English is not indigenous, especially ex-British colonies, recognize English as one of their national languages, and English has taken on a life of its own in countries such as India, Nigeria, and Singapore, which have cultural backgrounds decidedly different from those of the United States and Britain. (For a very readable treatment of this issue, see McCrum, Cran, and MacNeil 1987; see also Crystal 1997.) In fact, in some non-Western nations that have adopted English, there is a conscious attempt to divorce the English language from British and U.S. culture so that the language will be identified more closely with its new national culture. It could thus be argued that in some situations an English teacher should avoid associating English with the teaching of British or U.S. culture.

More often, however, sensitive incorporation of Western culture into your English courses will benefit both the students and you. One reason is that many situations in which learners use English involve intercultural communication. This might take the form of an African student reading magazines from Britain or a Latin American businessman chatting with a North American client, an Asian watching TV programs or films from Australia or listening to the BBC radio news, a Middle Eastern student writing an application letter to an U.S. university, or a secretary in Hong Kong writing a business letter to a Canadian company. In all of these cases, the learner of English needs to use a foreign language to understand and communicate directly or indirectly with people from a very different culture.

Bringing culture into your courses will also make them more interesting and genuinely communicative, in large part because of the genuine information gap that exists between your cultural knowledge and that of the students. As a native of a Western culture, one of your greatest strengths is your intimate knowledge of a culture that is fresh and new to the students, and students also possess a great fund of knowledge about their culture that they would no doubt be pleased to share with you. By drawing on culture topics, you create opportunities for meaningful sharing of important and interesting information, which helps raise students' interest in communication.

What Is Culture?

The term *culture* is nothing if not broad, and an exhaustive listing of all that it includes would require a book in itself. In a review of various attempts to define the term, Seelye (1993) concludes, "The most widely accepted usage now regards culture as a broad concept that embraces all aspects of human life, from folktales to carved whales. What is culture? It is everything humans have learned" (p. 22; see Damen 1987, 73–74, 85–86, for further discussion). Unfortunately, such a broad definition of culture—correct as it no doubt is—does not provide much direction for teachers who are trying to set an agenda for teaching culture. Thus, at the risk of being less than fully comprehensive, I define culture in a way that is narrower but more helpful to the language teacher. In my view, the essence of a culture lies more in the minds of a group of people than in their physical surroundings and consists primarily of ideas that the group members share. I find it convenient to think of the mental constructs making up a culture as falling into three basic categories:

1. **shared knowledge:** information known in common by group members

2. **shared views:** beliefs and values shared by group members

3. **shared patterns:** shared habits and norms in the ways group members organize their behavior, interaction, and communication

Granted, these three categories overlap to some degree, and most cultural phenomena can and must be analyzed in view of more than one of them. However, this system is fairly simple and manageable yet has enough explanatory force that it helps set an agenda for teaching culture. I examine each of these categories briefly below.

SHARED KNOWLEDGE

Within a culture group, members share a great deal of information, much of which is not familiar to outsiders. Compare, for example, the following two identification tests:

1. (1) Dec. 7, 1941; (2) home plate; (3) Benedict Arnold; (4) Bill Cosby; (5) Niagara Falls

2. (1) May 4, 1919; (2) dragon boat; (3) Yue Fei; (4) Deng Lijun; (5) Dun Huang

Americans with a high school education would no doubt come close to a perfect score on test 1, and even an American with no education would probably get several right answers. However, few Americans would get more than one answer correct on test 2. In contrast, the average Chinese schoolchild would score a clean sweep on test 2 but probably miss most of the items on test 1.[1]

These seemingly isolated bits of information are important in communication because they facilitate the use of top-down comprehension strategies. Consider the following sentences, the opening lines of a (fictitious) novel: "There was a warm gentle breeze blowing on the morning of December 7, 1941. Bob let his thoughts linger on the slim figure and dark eyes of the woman he had met the night before." By the time they finished reading these two sentences, many U.S. readers would already be able to guess a great deal about the story that is to follow. The story is probably set in Pearl Harbor and revolves around the attack. Even the time of day can be guessed with considerable accuracy—it is probably early in the morning, before the attack. Of course, these are only guesses, but they enable a reader to skim forward much faster in the story, checking guesses rather than trying to piece the story together from scratch. In contrast, students of English who didn't know the significance of December 7, 1941, would find little more in these sentences than the aggregate meaning of the words and would be at a disadvantage in comprehending the story.

The other pieces of information included in test 1 could also set the scene for a story, convey an emotion, symbolically suggest values, or simply function as vocabulary. For example, for Americans the mention of Niagara Falls conjures up images of honeymooners and people going over a waterfall in a barrel, and Bill Cosby is associated with images of the family-oriented father and the successful black professional. Finally, Benedict Arnold is synonymous with *traitor* in the United States.

Another reason attention to background information is important in language courses is that students need to learn to be aware of their assumptions about what an audience from another culture does and does not know. Take, for example, a Chinese tour guide who begins his introduction to a temple by saying, "This fine structure was built during the Qin Dynasty." Such an introduction would help a Chinese audience place the temple in a historical context, but it would probably be of no use at all to a group of foreign tourists who don't know what or when the Qin Dynasty was. If the tour guide has some idea what he can and cannot expect his audience to know, he has a better idea what needs to be explained and what doesn't. This enables him to

---

[1] Answer key for test 1: (1) Japanese attack on Pearl Harbor; (2) place where batter stands in baseball; (3) traitor in U.S. Revolutionary War; (4) family-oriented comedian; (5) scenic spot for honeymooners. Answer key for test 2: (1) protests against Japan that mark the beginning of the modern period in Chinese history; (2) boat used yearly in races on Dragon Boat Festival to commemorate the poet Qu Yuan; (3) ancient hero who resisted foreign invaders until betrayed by his own government; (4) pop singer; (5) site where ancient Buddhist manuscripts and cave paintings were found.

provide appropriate clarification when necessary and avoid boring an audience with superfluous explanation when none is needed.

Much of the material that makes up the shared knowledge of a culture is passed intentionally from one generation to the next, often through the educational system or in the home. In modern societies another very important source of shared cultural knowledge is the electronic media (the performing media may have a similar role in more traditional societies). A final source of cultural knowledge is widely shared experiences, such as Little League baseball for boys in the United States or the turmoil of the Cultural Revolution for urban Chinese old enough to have experienced it.

SHARED VIEWS

Within a culture group, people not only know many of the same things, but also believe many of the same things and share many of the same views on a huge spectrum of issues. To some extent, a culture is composed of widely held opinions on such mundane questions as these: What is the best treatment for a cold? Is *ain't* an acceptable word? Who is the world's greatest soccer player? However, a culture is shaped much more by a shared world view consisting of the beliefs and values of a culture, its shared answers to basic questions inherent in human existence, such as these:

- Are there supernatural forces?

- Are humans basically good or evil?

- Who am I/who are we?

- What is my proper relationship to other people?

- How should other people treat me?

- Is my life more defined by what I am like or what I do?

- Should I look more to the future or to the past?[2]

Answers to questions such as these are often found in the dominant religious or philosophical thought of a culture, but they are also embedded in its stories and its models of excellence (e.g., heroes, art, achievements). These beliefs and deeply rooted cultural orientations tend to change slowly, if at all, and play a major role in shaping a culture.

A very practical advantage of understanding the beliefs and values of a given culture is that it improves the ability to accurately interpret what people from that culture do and say. This is of great importance in intercultural communication, where misunderstandings are common and can have serious consequences. Consider the simple example of an Asian student meeting a North American tourist who is obviously floundering in her attempts to shop in an Asian city. The student—partly out of altruism and partly to get English practice—offers to translate and is surprised when the tourist firmly insists that she wants to do things for herself. Students who have some idea of the importance North Americans place on self-reliance are not so likely to be puzzled or offended by this rebuff; students who understand little of North American culture have no recourse but to interpret this refusal in terms of their own culture and may mistakenly assume that the refusal implies a lack of trust or perhaps even sheer prejudice.

A second reason that students should have some knowledge of Western beliefs and values is that it will enhance their ability to express their own ideas, especially in situations where they need to persuade. Take, for example, the problem of application letters. In many countries,

---

[2] Students of cultural anthropology will recognize the influence of Clyde and Florence Kluckhohn's cultural models in my choice of questions. For an easy introduction to their model, see Kohls (2001, 31–38, 150–51).

students study English in part because they hope to study or work abroad, so they must write application letters for jobs, scholarships, and admission to schools. A problem that often crops up in such letters is that students do not understand the fine art of making themselves look good while not seeming boastful. In Asia, I have often seen students make broad assertions about their merits ("I was the best student in my school") without supporting their claims with quantifiable objective evidence. Also, it is difficult for them to gauge what arguments will appeal to a Western employer or admissions officer, and they thus sometimes sound too idealistic ("I wish to devote myself to the construction of my Motherland") or a touch too mercenary ("I hope to get a degree in business and then get rich in the construction industry").

Knowing something of a culture's beliefs and values is especially important in helping students understand why its members act and speak as they do, a level of comprehension that goes beyond the surface meaning of words. An additional benefit of studying this level of culture is that, as students look at the assumptions underlying another culture, the contrast may enable them for the first time to clearly see the assumptions that underlie their own.

SHARED PATTERNS

Not all human activity falls into neat patterns, but a great deal of it follows at least a general pattern, and much of it is rather strictly ordered (see Damen 1987, 142–45, for a discussion of this aspect of culture). More or less clear cultural patterns can be found in a huge range of things, including daily schedules, events of the year, the ordering of events in a meeting, the way people date and find a mate, or even the way a story or article is organized. Sometimes these patterns are cultural habits that have no particular values attached to them, such as the U.S. tendency to shower in the morning rather than the evening or the custom of starting a fairy tale with *Once upon a time.* . . . Often, however, these patterns are evaluative norms, deviation from which is at best odd or impolite and at worst criminal.

Of particular concern to the language learner are the patterns in how a culture deals with communication situations. While conversations don't always closely follow a preordained script, neither is each one improvised entirely anew. Many common functions of language use, such as polite refusals, responses to compliments, and introductions, are fairly conventional. For example, in mainstream U.S. culture a polite refusal to an invitation generally involves an expression of thanks or regret followed by a specific reason why the invitation cannot be accepted (*I would love to, but I won't be in town on that day.*); note that a vague excuse like *I will be busy* is not as polite. When responding to compliments, Americans will often say thank you but follow it by either passing the credit on to someone or something else (*Thank you. My mother taught me how to cook this.*) or using the compliment as a springboard into a conversation topic, hence deflecting attention from the praise given (*Thank you. I bought this shirt on a business trip to Nigeria last year.* . . .).

Obviously, one reason students have a vested interest in studying these aspects of culture is that knowing them will help students communicate more politely and appropriately—or at least avoid unintentionally giving offense. A second and less obvious advantage of knowing these patterns is that it enhances students' ability to predict what they might hear or read. This, in turn, makes comprehension easier. For example, if students can narrow the probable range of responses to a compliment, they are more likely to be able to catch key words even when listening to somebody who talks too fast.

A second set of conventions that are especially important to language students are the genre conventions that shape so much printed and audiovisual communication. Many books, articles, TV shows, films, and other structured forms of discourse tend to follow a formula. For example, romances generally consist of a boy, a girl, and a problem that has to be overcome if the couple is to find happiness. Westerns usually have one or more good guys, a bunch of bad guys, a pretty girl, and a final shootout from which the hero generally rides away more or less intact. Even newspaper news articles are laid out in a predictable pattern, starting with location and date, followed first by the story's main points and then by details in order of decreasing importance. The significance of these formulas for readers and viewers is that once they know which one is being followed, their ability to predict and guess—hence to comprehend—is greatly enhanced. (In the Pearl Harbor example above, even the first two sentences hint strongly that the story is a drama and romance. In fact, I would be willing to bet a week's pay that Bob is a white U.S. soldier; the woman is young, beautiful, and of Japanese ancestry; and the story is about how they will cope with the impact of the attack on their romance.)

A final set of conventions that are especially important to language students are those surrounding written language. Most writing, especially more formal types such as business letters and academic writing, follows rather strict rules as to how ideas are to be organized and presented. Even the layout of the components of a business letter—where to place the date and addresses—is governed by conventions. (These conventions are probably more familiar to most volunteer teachers [VTs] than the genre or behavior patterns mentioned above because the conventions of writing are usually explicitly taught to native speakers in school.)

The point of all this description of different aspects of culture and their roles in communication is that this information is useful to pass on to students so that they see why studying culture is an inherently important part of language study. This does not mean you need to burden students with a series of lectures on the importance of culture in language learning (although this might not be a bad idea if the students' listening skills can handle it), but when you discuss any given point of culture with students, it is helpful to mention why knowing such a point may be beneficial and how it relates to communication. For example, cultural background knowledge is especially important for its ability to enhance top-down comprehension strategies, knowing a culture's beliefs and values improves one's ability to interpret behavior and communication more accurately, and knowing genre patterns enables learners to more accurately predict—hence more easily understand—as they read and view. Knowing how different kinds of culture affect communication will help students see more clearly the connection between language and culture, and the importance of studying culture as well as language.

English—Whose Culture?

As you consider the issue of culture in English courses, you may tend to think first and foremost of U.S. and British culture, but with a little reflection, it is clear that neither of these terms is fully satisfactory as a label for the kind of culture VTs should teach. Even if you consider only those countries in which English is used as the first (and usually only) language, there are several large nations and quite a few more smaller ones. And even within any given English-speaking nation, the culture is hardly uniform; lumping the culture of an ethnic neighborhood in New York City under the same label as that of a rural community in Texas or a retirement community in Florida would be problematic at best. So considering incorporation of culture in English courses means asking exactly whose culture you are going to teach.

Perhaps the best way to approach this problem is by recognizing that culture in English-speaking nations involves at least three general levels: Western culture, national culture, and group culture.

LEVEL ONE: WESTERN CULTURE

Many important aspects of culture are shared not only by the United States, Britain, and other English-speaking nations, but also by other European nations and even non-European nations in which there has been substantial European influence. For example, all Western countries share a considerable portion of their philosophical and religious traditions, a similar approach to law and government, and even much of their literary heritage.

LEVEL TWO: NATIONAL CULTURE

The stratum of culture that people tend to think of most readily is the national level: U.S. culture, Canadian culture, British culture, and so forth. While one cannot assume that all Americans (or Canadians, or Australians) are exactly alike, some cultural characteristics are certainly shared widely within a nation and distinguish it from others. For example, even despite the immediate geographic proximity of Canada and the United States, people of the two nations tend to have rather different views of government, Canadians assuming that it is proper for government to play a greater role in providing medical care and other social services than Americans would expect.

LEVEL THREE: GROUP CULTURE

In casual discussion of culture, working with broad terms like *Western culture* and *U.S. culture* is easier than being more precise about exactly what stream of Western or U.S. culture you are referring to. However, the danger of overusing such terms, particularly in a teaching situation, is that you may obscure the importance of regional, class, religious, ethnic, gender, and occupational cultures. For example, no picture of U.S. culture would be fully complete if it only represented the culture presented often in TV situation comedies—a suburban, middle-class, white family living in a generic community. A complete picture also needs to recognize strong subcultures, such as those of the deep South, the urban poor, evangelical Christians, blacks and Hispanics, women, gays and lesbians, and perhaps even truck drivers.

The question of whose culture to teach is complicated even further by the issue of how much relative weight to give to dominant cultural norms as opposed to minority cultures. In North America, controversy on this point was sparked by Hirsch's (1987) *Cultural Literacy: What Every American Needs to Know,* in which the author argues that there is a core of cultural knowledge that all U.S. schoolchildren need to know and presents a list of names, dates, and terms that he feels represents this cultural core. Most of the controversy about the book arose from Hirsch's list, which was criticized as representing only a dominant white, educated culture and ignoring the existence and importance of a diverse range of minority traditions. (For critiques of Hirsch, see Seelye 1993, 27; Walters 1992, 6; see also Murray 1992.) While this debate primarily concerns the question of what culture should be taught to students in the United States, the larger issue of how much to include regional, ethnic, or other subnational cultures has implications for culture teaching in EFL classes as well.

As you consider how to approach culture in your English classes, perhaps your first goal should be to help students see that different levels of culture are associated with English, in short, that not every point of culture taught in an English class can be neatly labeled *U.S. culture* or *British culture.* By being careful to distinguish between aspects of culture that are shared all over the West, those distinct to a particular nation, and those particular only to a smaller group, you will help students learn an important lesson about the complexity of culture.

With regard to the question of dominant versus minority cultures, I suggest a pragmatic approach. In most of the countries in which you might teach, students often encounter the dominant streams of U.S. and British culture through books, magazines, and the media, so students especially need to learn about this level of culture. However, you do not want to go so far in this direction that students get the impression of the West or your country as a culturally homogeneous entity. You might even make a special point of drawing on your own experience to introduce aspects of group cultures with which you have had experience.

Finally, as to what culture you teach about, you need to find the best possible balance between the culture you know most about (presumably your own) and the culture students can gain the most from learning about. My suggestion is that if you are from one of the larger English-speaking countries, you make that your *target culture* (the culture you will teach about) for many lessons but also bring in other cultures from time to time as a point of contrast and to remind students that your chosen target culture is not the only one they should be concerned with. If you are not from an English-speaking country, or you are from one of the less typical English-speaking nations, you should probably still make your own culture the target for a significant portion of your culture lessons so you can teach about what you know best; however, you should also make an effort to give a fair amount of attention to the cultures of larger English-speaking nations.

Teaching Culture: Methods

As often as possible in language courses, you should try to kill two birds with one stone: have students learn about culture at the same time as they develop their language skills. For example, there is no reason for students to read the story "Harold the Lazy Badger" created by a textbook writer when they could just as well read "The Tortoise and the Hare." By reading the former, students only develop reading skills; by reading the latter, students also become familiar with a story that is known throughout the West. Similarly, a listening exercise in which you call out instructions for a series of meaningless motions is not as rich as one in which you give directions for walking through a wedding or a baseball game. Of course, on some occasions you will need to use material with little cultural content for pragmatic reasons—you can't find an appropriate cultural topic, appropriate materials are not available, and so forth—but genuine cultural topics and issues should be brought into the language classroom whenever possible.

INCORPORATING CULTURE TEACHING INTO LANGUAGE SKILL PRACTICE

Chapters 7–12 mention some of the main ways to incorporate teaching about culture into practicing language skills, but a brief review may be helpful here.

Dialogues as Models of Culture

From the earliest stages of English study, most students are exposed to dialogues in textbooks. If these dialogues are at all realistic, they should provide a model of the normal patterns of social interaction as well as of language use. Thus, when studying dialogues, students should also study how Westerners interact. As pointed out in chapter 8, one way to use textbook dialogues as models of culture is to emphasize the functions (e.g., ways to invite, change a topic, politely disagree). When teaching the dialogue, call attention to the pattern of moves involved, and teach students not only language tools but also how these tools are normally used. You can emphasize this aspect of dialogues by giving students practice assignments that are organized around functions and moves rather than around language per se; simply by presenting dialogues in this way, you will remind students of the patterns of interaction underlying the language.

Culture Talks

The most direct way to approach the teaching of almost any aspect of culture is simply to talk about it. Lecture format allows you to teach students about cultural background knowledge, beliefs and values, and cultural patterns while also giving them listening comprehension practice. You can enhance the richness of lessons based on culture talks by having students respond by talking or writing to you about corresponding aspects of their own culture. (For discussion of procedure, see Talks and Lectures in chapter 7. For specific ideas for culture-based talks, see appendix B.)[3]

Press Conferences

The press conference format allows you to teach about essentially the same range of aspects of culture as the culture talk format does. However, because it is more interactive, this format makes it easier for students to pursue topics they are interested in or puzzled about. This, in turn, increases the chances that you will be able to adequately explain views in the target culture that differ significantly from those in the host culture. (For discussion of the procedure, see Press Conferences in chapter 7. For specific ideas for press conference activities, see appendix B.)

Pair and Small-Group Tasks

Pair and small-group discussion activities are an excellent vehicle for examining many aspects of culture while practicing speaking skills. While the precise way this happens would vary considerably depending on the topic under discussion, the basic formula would be as follows:

1. Choose a topic (or question, or issue) that will allow students to learn more about the target culture and you to learn more about the host culture.

2. Give students a small-group discussion task that requires them to (1) share information and negotiate among themselves and (2) prepare an explanation of the relevant aspect of their culture for you.

3. Have students tell you about the host culture.

4. Respond by telling them about corresponding aspects of the target culture.

(For discussion of this procedure, see Pair and Small-Group Tasks in chapter 8. For specific pair and small-group activities, see appendix B.)

Below I provide a more detailed introduction to three additional types of activities that can be used to teach culture along with language skills, activity types I refer to as mining the media for culture, culture exploration projects, and critical-incident activities.

Mining the Media for Culture

You can almost take for granted that students around the world will be exposed to at least some Western culture, especially U.S. and British, through the printed and visual media. In particular, English language movies are often available, and so are English language books. Use of these resources is discussed in chapters 7 and 9, respectively, as they relate to building listening and reading skills, but such resources are also valuable in a variety of ways as a vehicle for learning about the cultures of English-speaking nations.

First, media products such as films and books can obviously provide a great deal of cultural knowledge input on many aspects of the target culture. To the extent that you have choice in what students read or view, particularly valuable materials include

---

[3] One type of book you may wish to bring with you to the host country is a basic introduction to the culture and society of the country or culture you expect to teach about. Examples for U.S. culture would include those by Althen (1988) and Lanier (1988).

- **material that realistically portrays contemporary daily life and typical social interactions:** Magazines and newspapers, particularly the advertisements in them, are especially rich in daily life realia and cover a range of contemporary culture and social issues. Even when magazine and newspaper articles are too difficult to read (or it is too much trouble to get copies made), they can still be adapted for listening exercises. When available, television programs and films are also an excellent resource.

- **materials that teach the basic background information of Western culture—history, geography, government, economy, and society:** High school textbooks can be a good source of this material (a friend back home may be able to purchase old textbooks for you at a reasonable price). Both printed materials and documentaries are often available at your embassy or consulate in the host country.

- **books or films that tell the well-known stories of the target culture:** These are often inherently interesting and usually raise a rich range of cultural issues. Additionally, they are important to know about simply because they are well known. Traditional Western stories would include the Greek and Norse myths; Bible stories; nursery rhymes; Grimm's and Andersen's fairy tales; and legends surrounding figures such as Ulysses, King Arthur, Joan of Arc, Robin Hood, and Davy Crockett. Modern characters who have moved into legend would include figures like Superman, Helen Keller, Babe Ruth, Marie Curie, Martin Luther King, and even Elvis Presley. Of course, many of these stories can be found in film as well as printed versions, and in many countries simplified readers based on the classic works of Western literature are available.

- **material that tells the story of the target culture:** To some extent, this is the story drawn from the history of the target culture or nation, but it is not a cold, academic rendering of facts. Instead, it is a rather selective account that focuses on people and events that have special significance in defining a culture. In fact, it is often a rather simplified, patriotic version of history. Special attention is usually paid to those people, things, and events of which the culture is most proud—its heroes, victories, great achievements, great creative works, and other models of excellence. This shared cultural knowledge is especially important not only because it is widely known, but also because it plays a significant role in establishing group identity and often offers important clues as to the culture's values. This kind of history is often found in school textbooks.[4]

With regard to how you go about teaching the cultural background knowledge in such materials, the first point is that you should encourage students to study the materials for their cultural content as well as their language. While this might seem obvious, in the context of a language class you often need to make this point explicitly. Keep in mind that in language classes the purpose most salient in students' minds is the learning of language knowledge and skills, so they may be tempted to view odd bits of cultural information they run across in texts or films as clutter that can safely be ignored—especially if they think it will not be tested.

A second important role you should play has to do with helping students assess the value of culture information they encounter. Remember that when students encounter cultural information, they often cannot tell how important or typical it is; for example, they may not know if Thomas Edison is a fictional character, a real but obscure person, or someone who is famous and

---

[4] While this aspect of the target culture is important, it is also potentially sensitive. A nation's identity is often forged in conflict with other nations, so the story may have strong us-versus-them undertones and substantial elements of boosterism. So, while the story should be presented with empathy, it should also be presented with a degree of critical distance.

important. This kind of attention to cultural content may seem unnecessary; one might assume that students would learn this naturally. However, my own experience is that when students run across new names, dates, and events in texts, it is not easy for them to tell whether such bits of culture data are important (or widely known) or not, and students looking for ways to cut corners may ignore names, places, dates, and content in general unless they see good reason to do otherwise.

A third role you should play has to do with helping students sort out how typical or atypical behavior they see in films or books is. While students can learn—and will learn—a great deal about how Westerners behave from books, movies, and so forth, media portrayals of a culture are often not typical, complete, or entirely realistic, and students may not know how much they can generalize based on any particular portrayal of a Westerner's behavior. For example, when they see an American in a Hollywood film behaving in a certain way (e.g., a woman getting upset at a man who holds a door open for her), they may not know whether this particular behavior is typical of the target culture, unusual but still within the normal range, or well within the bizarre zone. So one of your main duties when dealing with media products is helping students evaluate how useful a given text is as a portrayal of culture. While you may not always know precisely how typical or realistic an example of behavior is, you can usually perform the very useful function of letting students know whether it is more or less typical of some stream of culture (and, if so, of which one). Also, simply by calling students' attention to this issue, you will help students form the habit of not simply accepting anything they read or see in the media as the final word on how Westerners behave.

Note also that some of the most interesting patterns that shape a culture are found in the conventions of its genres, the customary patterns into which a culture organizes various kinds of communication. Knowledge of such genre conventions is especially important for advanced-level students in EFL settings because their main opportunity to use English—and main hope for breakthrough—often lies either in reading or in listening to the radio, and knowledge of the genre conventions of whatever material they read or listen to will aid their comprehension.

One approach is simply to point out the formulas underlying whatever texts (e.g., films) students are studying in class. A more interesting alternative in advanced-level classes is to have students try and discover for themselves the formulas of Western texts. I find that this works best if you first prime the pump by having students describe to you the formula for a familiar genre within their own culture. For example, with Asian students, I find that asking them to outline the typical kung fu movie works particularly well; romances are another good option. Then, as students read or view Western texts that are fairly typical of some genre, have them be on the lookout for the underlying formula. Finally, during discussion, ask them to present their theories as to what the formula might be.

Culture Exploration Projects

Over the past few decades, finding out more about other cultures, and even meeting people from those cultures, has become easier and easier for students in many host countries. Library collections have improved in many countries, as has the range of offerings in bookstores, so printed information about other cultures now tends to be more readily available. More foreigners are living in many countries now than ten or twenty years ago, so there are more opportunities to talk with foreigners and learn from them about other cultures. Finally, and perhaps most dramatically, the expansion of the Internet gives many students access to a range of information and contact with people around the globe that would have been unthinkable not so many years ago. All of these changes create the opportunity for students in many host countries to engage in their own research projects, choosing their own questions about the target culture, seeking out their own answers, and then presenting the results in the form of classroom presentations and reports.

Depending on how projects are structured, they can be used to help students build their background knowledge about the target culture, their understanding of the views of people in the target culture, or both. Below I present three basic types of projects that can be used in EFL classes.

CULTURE INFORMATION RESEARCH PROJECTS

The primary focus in this kind of project is on having students gather information through library or Internet resources to gain a deeper and more nuanced understanding of some aspect of the target culture. However, the project also encourages them to be more aware of what their starting point is as they attempt to learn more about the target culture, so that they can also better see how their understanding of the target culture grows and develops. In a culture information research project, you would have students do the following:

1. Choose a topic or question they want to investigate. Fairly specific questions (*How do U.S. university students pay for college?*) tend to result in more interesting projects than broad topics do.

2. List what they already know and think about the topic—a snapshot of their starting point.

3. List specific research questions based on what they don't know about the topic or are not sure about.

4. Write up a simple plan (including the topic, research questions, and ways they will find the answers to these questions), and turn it into you for feedback and suggestions.

5. Research their question(s) using library or Internet resources, or by interviewing people from the target culture (either in person or over the Internet).

6. Prepare a presentation, a report, or both focusing on what they learned—ways in which their understanding moved beyond their original snapshot.

CULTURE PERSPECTIVES INTERVIEW PROJECT

The main focus of this kind of project is on learning more about the perspective members of the target culture have on their own culture. For this project, have students do the following:

1. Choose one or more questions to serve as a focus for the project (e.g., *Why do so many Americans support the idea of easy access to guns?*). For this kind of project, students should investigate aspects of the target culture that they genuinely find strange or difficult to understand (though they should also be careful not to choose topics that their informants might find offensive).

2. Plan how to locate informants and arrange interviews with them.

3. Make a list of specific interview questions. These should focus on inviting informants to say what people in the target culture think as well as to explain why. (You may also ask students to predict and write down what they think informants will say in response to the questions, thus making the interview a kind of reality check.)

4. Find and interview people from the target culture, either in person or via the Internet.

5. Prepare a presentation, a report, or both focusing on what they learned from the informants, especially things that were not what they had expected.

REFLEXIVE CULTURE RESEARCH PROJECT

This project encourages students to more closely examine how people in their culture view the target culture and to get a better understanding of the information sources that shape the views of people in the host culture toward the target culture. (This project is somewhat sensitive in that it invites students to be at least somewhat self-critical with regard to their own culture, so it may not be appropriate for all host-country settings.) Have students do the following:

1. Choose an issue on which they think local people have (strong) opinions about the target culture.

2. Make up a list of specific interview questions asking what the informants think about the issue and from what sources they get their information about it. (As with the culture perspectives interview projects above, it may also be good for students to write down their predictions of what informants will say.)

3. Find several informants and interview them.

4. Using library or Internet resources, study the issue to learn more about it and to check how well informed the views of informants were.

5. Prepare a presentation, a report, or both focusing especially on
    - the views informants expressed about the issue—and how accurate the students' predictions about these views were
    - what students learned about where and how people get their information
    - students' assessment of the quality of information people have and how this may affect their views

Critical-Incident Exercises

Critical-incident exercises (also called *culture-bump stories*) consist of two basic parts: a story in which people of different cultural backgrounds have a communication problem, and a discussion question that invites students to analyze the incident and attempt to arrive at a better understanding of why the problem occurred. These exercises are a good springboard for discussing cultural differences, especially differences in beliefs and values. They also help students develop a number of very basic but important intercultural communication skills and habits:

- They help students become more consciously aware of the processes by which they interpret (i.e., make sense of) the behavior of foreigners.

- They encourage students to pause and think rather than jump rapidly to conclusions.

- They help students build the habit of looking beyond obvious, knee-jerk interpretations of behavior that seems strange or problematic, and of considering alternative explanations.

One possible procedure for using critical-incident exercises in EFL classes is as follows:

1. Present students with an incident in which a person from the students' culture has a puzzling or problematic encounter someone from another culture. For example, *You are applying for an important scholarship, and your American English teacher writes a nice recommendation letter for you. You finally get the scholarship, and feel grateful to your teacher, so you buy her an expensive gift. On the day that you present it to her, after class, she refuses to accept it* (based on an activity in Levine, Baxter, and McNulty 1987; a version can also be found

in Snow 2004). If you present the situation orally, you might check comprehension by quickly asking students questions covering the main points of the situation.

2. In groups, have students come up with at least five possible reasons why the teacher is refusing the gift. (Have one person take notes.) Stress that the goal is not to find one right answer but rather to brainstorm and come up with a variety of interpretations of the teacher's behavior.

3. Have the groups present their theories to the class for discussion. (To allow each group to contribute, it is best to have each group offer just one suggestion while you note it on the board and then move to the next group.)

4. Once the possibilities are listed on the board, ask students to indicate which they think are most and least likely. One way to do this is to have students divide them into categories such as *very likely (VL), likely (L), possible (P), not likely (NL),* and *highly improbable (HI).*

5. After students have categorized the possibilities, it is your turn to provide a reality check from your cultural perspective, commenting on how likely you think each might be and suggesting additional possibilities students might not have thought of. (During this phase, try to give credit to as many suggestions as possible. For theories that are way off the mark, a smile and "Good guess, but no" will usually do the trick without hurting too many feelings.)

Tips

- To compile a good collection of problem situations tailored to your situation, you might listen to stories your friends tell about their cross-cultural encounters or look into your own experience for situations where there were potential or real misunderstandings. (The best situations for use in EFL class are those which allow a number of reasonable interpretations rather than having only one right answer.) Ready-made critical-incident exercises can also be found in a number of resources (e.g., Snow 2004; also see Amity Foundation 2003).[5]

- Critical incident exercises have two goals. One is for students to learn something about the beliefs and values of the culture in question; this is where your responses to students' suggestions are beneficial. The second is to encourage students to think broadly and cautiously about how to interpret behavior across cultural lines, so it is important that students try to think through the issue themselves before you offer your analysis.

- You should try to avoid having the exercise turn into a game in which students try to generate nice but unrealistic explanations or simply try to guess the right answer. The focus should be on discovering as many realistic explanations of the situation (nice and not so nice) as are reasonably possible.

- This kind of exercise is somewhat challenging both conceptually and linguistically, so it is best used with students at intermediate or advanced levels.

---

[5] Fictional stories from films and books, or real stories from newspaper or magazine articles, can sometimes also be fashioned into interesting critical-incident exercises.

Sensitivity in Teaching Western Culture

The main reason English has such a dominant role in so many parts of the world is that, over the past two centuries, English-speaking nations have wielded tremendous economic, political, and military power. One consequence of this fact is that the experience of many countries with the English-speaking nations has been less than entirely positive. Westerners have often been invaders, colonizers, or economic competitors rather than friends, and the desire of many people to learn English is complicated by feelings of resentment toward the power and wealth of the countries that English represents. In some cultures, this resentment is expressed openly; in others, traditions of politeness make these attitudes more difficult for an outsider to detect, but they may nonetheless be present. Thus, the teaching of Western culture, particularly if it presented with strong overtones of Western superiority, may arouse considerable resistance and hostility.

Unfortunately, VTs are not always very sensitive to this problem. While few VTs consciously seek to be offensive, you may well be working in a country that is not as wealthy, efficient, or modern as your home country, and in this situation it is hard not to let a note of pride or superiority creep into your voice when introducing your culture. Most Westerners, Americans in particular, also have no memory of serious oppression by an outside power, so they may underestimate the bitterness with which people in many developing nations view their relationship—historical or current—with the West. A second problem is that the difficulties of adjusting to an unfamiliar culture (culture shock; see chapter 15) often erode VTs' feelings of goodwill toward their host countries, and this makes it more likely that the VT will offend in culture lessons by either explicitly or implicitly suggesting that the host culture is inferior.

Even if you present Western culture in a sensitive way, students may not always be pleased by what they hear. It is not within your power to eliminate all the feelings of local pride or resentment over past injustices that may influence students' feelings toward Western nations, and no matter how sensitively you approach the issue of Western culture, implied comparisons will sometimes reflect negatively on the host culture. However, it is within your power to see that your culture lessons present a model of fair, objective treatment of cultural issues and that they are not unnecessarily offensive. This will help ensure not only that your lessons are well received but also that students will learn to approach culture in the same way themselves.

One strategy that will make your discussion of culture more objective is habitually pointing out that almost every major facet of a culture carries advantages and disadvantages. For example, when discussing the United States' advanced health care system, you should also point out its expense; when discussing the U.S. stress on self-reliance, note that this contributes both to a high level of national productivity and to a willingness to tolerate poverty among people who will not or cannot work hard; when discussing the high rate of U.S. car ownership, mention both the freedom and mobility it allows and the price paid for gas, insurance, and repairs (not to mention the problem of air pollution). This habit of always presenting two sides to an issue may seem somewhat artificial, but it is beneficial because it makes your presentation of issues more objective and because it forces you to think through issues more carefully in order to find two sides. This habit is also, incidentally, good training for you and the students because it reminds you that most aspects of any culture generally do have a good and a bad side, so it is a good antidote to tendencies toward cultural chauvinism.

A second way to avoid being offensive in your presentation of cultural issues is to lean toward politeness more than frankness when talking about the culture of your host country. This does not necessarily mean being dishonest, but it may mean avoiding a question or saying less than you might like to. Remember that your role as a guest in the host country means that you follow rules different from those of host-country nationals. It is not uncommon for newcomers in a host nation to hear host nationals speaking critically of their own country, assume that it is acceptable to chime in with a few criticisms, but then be surprised when even relatively restrained criticisms cause the tone of the conversation to become distinctly chilly. It is a universal human tendency to be more sensitive about criticism coming from outsiders than from insiders, and in most countries the safest initial assumption is that critical comments you make will touch a more sensitive nerve than similar comments made by host nationals.

In general, it is best to behave as a polite guest, especially during the early stages of your sojourn in the host country. Even in your home culture, when invited to someone's home for a meal, you probably try to find something nice to say about the food no matter what it tastes like. A similar policy regarding culture lessons in your host country has much to recommend it.

For Thought, Discussion, and Action

1. **attitudes toward Western culture:** Talk with people from your host culture about the attitudes students are likely to have toward Western culture. How interested are students in studying about Western or other foreign cultures? Which cultures are they most interested in? How much do students already know about Western cultures, and what do they to tend to know and believe about them? From what sources do they get most of their information and ideas about Western culture?

2. **definition of** *culture:* The term *culture* has been defined by many different people in many different ways. Are there ways in which you would revise the definition of culture given in this chapter so as to provide a better guide for your culture teaching?

3. **shared culture knowledge:** This chapter gives several examples of names and dates that have cultural significance. Make a list of other names and dates that have significant symbolic meaning for either your own culture or the culture you plan to teach about.

4. **basic cultural values:** Using the list of questions given in the section Shared Views in this chapter, compare and contrast your culture and your host culture. Then compare notes with natives of the host culture or other foreigners who have extensive experience with the host culture.

5. **genres:** List the major genres of TV programs (or newspaper columns, movies, books, etc.) in your culture. Then analyze each genre and come up with the basic conventions of the genre (in other words, how it is organized and what rules it follows).

6. **culture talks (task A):** Imagine that you are preparing to give a series of talks about your culture (or the target culture). List topics you think it would be good to talk about, and then discuss your list with someone from the host culture to see what suggestions they have.

7. **culture talks (task B):** After you have chosen several topics for culture talks, check the Internet (or library, local bookstore, etc.) for sources of information. Make a list of information sources that you can use for future reference—and that you can exchange with other teachers.

8. **the story of your culture:** Imagine that you are preparing a one-hour talk covering the story of your culture (or of the target culture). List the events, dates, and names that would be most important to include, and consider why each is important.

9. **culture beyond the mainstream:** For the nation whose culture you plan to teach about, list important subcultures (or co-cultures). Then consider how you could incorporate information about these subcultures in your culture talks to provide a point of contrast with mainstream culture.

10. **the problematic points of culture:** For the culture you plan to teach about, list several aspects you think that students in your host culture will find difficult to understand or accept. Then discuss your list with people who are from the host culture or who have extensive experience in the host culture.

11. **literature as a reflection of culture:** List several literary works (e.g., films, novels) in which the characters' behavior reflects important aspects of the target culture and that would be useful in teaching about it. For each work, design a teaching strategy that would effectively exploit the cultural material.

Chapter 14

A Troubleshooter's Guide to the Classroom

This section closes with discussion of a few of the most common problem situations English teachers face overseas. I can't promise solutions—I still face the same problems in my own teaching—but these suggestions may make your load a little more comfortable and manageable.

Overly Large Classes

Class sizes of thirty to fifty students or more are not unusual in many countries. For listening comprehension or reading lessons, such a large class is not an insurmountable obstacle; for speaking and writing lessons, however, large classes present very serious problems. In a speaking class with fifty students, you simply cannot give much individual attention to students, and writing classes of this size mean that you cope either with mountains of compositions or with guilt about assigning students too little writing.

The solution that generally first occurs to language teachers, and that can become a obsessive crusade, is to reduce the class size. Unfortunately, this is often not possible. Large classes are generally a result of necessity (e.g., lack of funds or staff) rather than a philosophy of education; most educators the world over would agree that smaller classes are better and would reduce class sizes if they could. The danger for you in this situation is that if you try to reduce the class size and you fail, you may consciously or unconsciously write off the class as hopeless and go into an embittered survival mode rather than doing what you can to make the class as effective as possible. In some situations, of course, survival is about all that can be expected, but a large class is by no means necessarily one of those situations.

In all but the smallest speaking classes, students will get most of their practice talking to each other rather than to you. The problem presented by a class of fifty is therefore different from that presented by a class of twenty only in degree, not in kind. In both cases, speaking practice should ideally consist primarily of pair and small-group work rather than dialogue between teacher and student. The real problem in large classes is management, specifically, ensuring that students will actually speak English when you are out of earshot. (See chapter 8 for suggestions on encouraging English use in class.)

If most of the students in a class will not speak English unless you are present, the problem becomes much more difficult because the class must be more teacher centered. In such cases, until you solve the attitude problem that keeps students from speaking English in pairs and groups, you may be forced to rely heavily on listening comprehension exercises and teacher-focused question-and-answer exercises. While less than ideal, such use of class time is by no means the end of the world. The development of listening skills contributes to the development of speaking skills, and teacher-focused dialogue can be useful even in a large class if you remember to interact with students in a random pattern so that all of them need to listen and think through responses to questions. Remember, the most difficult part of speaking is the mental process of creating sentences, and any practice that forces students to go through this process under time pressure is valuable for developing speaking skills.

Overly large writing classes are somewhat more problematic in that they almost inevitably require you to work very hard just to respond to a small amount of writing per student. As suggested in chapter 10, in large writing classes it is particularly important to make sure that students edit and polish work as much as possible before you go over it, so in-class self-editing and peer editing are recommended. Putting strict length limits on assignments—as well as emphasizing the virtues of terse writing—can also help. Finally, you can stress activities in which students rather than you are the audience.

The outrageously large writing class is, incidentally, a situation where negotiation with your school has a relatively good chance of being profitable. Most educators can relate very easily to the problem of high stacks of compositions, but they may have an exaggerated idea of how much being a native speaker of English lessens the time it takes to edit a composition. I have known schools to assign all the composition courses in a department to a volunteer teacher (VT) under the assumption that native speakers can correct papers almost effortlessly. Talking to your school administration about how much time you spend working on student papers may result in an attempt to lighten your load. If nothing else, you may get a clear statement of how much time you are expected to devote to composition correction. This, in turn, takes some of the onus (and guilt) from you in situations where you have no choice but to give rare or short writing assignments.

Classes with Disparate Skill Levels

A particularly frequent and annoying problem is having a class in which some students have much better English skills than others. This situation is especially common in night schools and other institutions where students come from a variety of backgrounds, but it is also found in school systems where groups of students move up the educational ladder together as a class. Because of differences in background or simply in the diligence with which students study, you may find that some students already know most of the material you plan to cover while others have fallen completely behind in both mastery of the material and skill development. This situation makes lesson planning difficult because it is hard to meet the needs of students at one level without neglecting those of students at another. It may also produce motivation problems in the class; students toward the top end of the range are bored, while students toward the bottom end are dispirited and confused.

As with the problem of overly large classes, the most obvious response is an attempt to redistribute students into classes of more equal skill levels. An administration that has little experience with language programs might be unaware of the importance of placing students of roughly equal skill levels together, and even an experienced administration may be unaware of the situation in your particular class, so a negotiated solution is worth an attempt. When possible, you might campaign for the use of skill-based placement testing in assigning students to classes, and when this approach works, it is definitely the best solution. However, often little can be done to resolve a situation by moving students, particularly when a term has already started, and then the problem becomes one of how to make the best of things.

In classes with mixed skill levels, the difference between a teacher-centered class and a student-centered one becomes especially critical. The pace and difficulty of activities in a teacher-centered class will necessarily be dictated by the teacher, and this forces students to march together in lockstep. If, for example, all the students in a class must listen to the same story together, students who could understand more rapid speech have to suffer through an overly slow presentation while their weaker classmates are embarrassed to stop you and ask questions or ask for repetition. The same dynamic holds true for whole-class activities such as large-group discussions, in which students with stronger English skills usually set the pace, and many of their classmates have to sit through an activity that is completely inappropriate for their skill level.

In contrast, to the extent that students work alone, in pairs, or in small groups, they are better able to work at their own pace. For example, taped listening assignments done at home allow students with better listening skills to complete the activity quickly and move on to something else; other students can stop and listen to difficult segments as many times as they need to. In small-group discussions, students with weaker speaking skills can express themselves at their own level without as much fear that they will be slowing down other students. Thus, one key to dealing with a class with varied skill levels is to make the class as individualized and student centered as possible.

Another way to approach the issue is through talking about it with the students. Some may resent the effect that other students—stronger or weaker—have on class progress,[1] so you should remind students that this is a normal part of group learning, not a special curse of your language class. Being reminded of this may help students redirect their efforts from complaining about the situation toward trying to productively deal with it. It also helps to stress that the issue is not necessarily one of good students and bad students. Of course, some students wind up with weak English skills through sheer laziness, but the problem can also result from different levels of opportunity or different learning abilities, so remind yourself and the students that skill levels are only that—and not necessarily an indication of a student's intelligence or moral character.

It often helps to do a little special public relations work with the students at the upper and lower ends of the class. Let students with unusually strong English skills know that you recognize their high level of ability, and challenge them by giving them a little extra responsibility (e.g., as discussion group leaders) or some difficult but interesting extra projects. You may also suggest that they have a responsibility to help and encourage others in the class or at least give others a chance to talk. Let students at less advanced levels know that you don't consider their present skill level an indication of lack of ability, but also emphasize that they need to put extra effort into catching up to the rest of the class. Those students who remain below the skill level of the class average will face a constant series of assignments and exercises that are not well suited to their skill level and will not only learn less than will students for whom the level of the activities is more appropriate, but will also find the work difficult and painful. It is therefore worthwhile for them to put in the extra effort necessary to catch up.

All the pep talks in the world are not likely to be of much use to the morale of students at a less advanced level if they are followed by a series of grades that tell students they really are at the bottom of the class. Unfortunately, if all of the class assignments and exercises are graded based on general skill level, and if assignments are all graded on the curve, students at a less advanced level are unlikely to receive much encouragement from their marks. This is one reason it is good to grade at least partly based on progress rather than on absolute skill level. This is also a good argument for including a content component, such as culture, in a course. Students with advanced-level language skills do not necessarily have much more Western cultural background than their classmates at a lower level, so including such an element in a course gives students at a less advanced level at least one opportunity to begin from the same starting point as their classmates.

Even the most student-centered class will have at least some teacher-focused interaction, even if only when you give directions, and in these interactions you need to decide the skill level to which you target your communication. My advice is that you avoid slowing the class down to the pace of the students who are at a less advanced level. While speaking slowly and keeping activities easy may seem to be more humane, in the end it is not. As much as I would like to believe otherwise, the problem with at least some of the weaker students in any class is that they do not put forth as much effort as their peers, and if you slow down the class to the level of the weakest, often the lazier students relax rather than endeavoring to catch up. Even worse, this approach discourages those students who work harder. My suggestion is that you tailor communication to a level slightly higher than that of the average student in the class, thus keeping it within the range of a majority of the students but making it challenging.

---

[1] One potential problem here is *false starters*, that is, students who choose to be placed in a class below their skill level so that they can more easily get a good grade. This problem is less common in EFL settings than in foreign language courses in U.S. universities (where students who have had two years of high school French often sign up for French 101 in order to review and get an easy grade), but when it occurs, it should be taken seriously. The presence of a few false starters in a class skews the curve considerably, and if you do not compensate for this effect, you will be punishing those who are at the level for which your course was intended.

Class Discipline

Unfortunately, some students simply have no interest in learning, and others are just plain mean, and even extensive efforts to bring such students around may come to naught. However, in my experience, most students are willing to give you a fair chance and are generally well disposed toward a teacher who is reasonably pleasant and works hard. The first step toward establishing class discipline is therefore earning students' respect—even their affection.

Elsewhere in this book I touch on a variety of factors involved in earning respect, including diligence in teaching and fairness in evaluation. As Ur (1996, 265) points out, even such basic practices as planning lessons carefully and giving clear instructions can help prevent discipline problems in class. Another factor that may affect students' affection for you is your interest in the host culture and language. An all-too-frequently overlooked reason to study the host language is that it may help you earn the affection of the people you work with; efforts to learn the host language are the most visible and convincing evidence of willingness to identify with the people you work among (see chapter 15). Cultural sensitivity is also a key part of earning respect—a teacher's decisions to flout local norms by doing such apparently irrelevant things as wearing shorts and sandals in class or having a casual sex life may well come back to haunt him or her in the form of inability to win the respect of a class.

However, no matter how ideal a role model you become, it is almost inevitable that you will come across students who do things that you perceive as problematic. An important first step in such situations is to try and determine how members of the host culture perceive such behavior, because some behaviors considered improper in your home country might be considered normal, or at least less serious, in the host country. For example, in many countries class attendance is somewhat optional, and failure to show up for class may not be considered inappropriate. There may also be different standards concerning an appropriate level of attention in class; not all cultures share the assumption that a class should maintain complete silence while a teacher—or especially another student—is speaking. Even such firmly rooted Western taboos as those against burping and farting are not universal. The first time a student loudly burped while I was talking in class in China, I took it as a calculated offense, only to discover later that it was no more intended to offend than a cough or sneeze would have been. (Another important example, copying others' work, is discussed in chapter 10.) It is thus important that you check first with members of the host culture to find out if a behavior that you find unacceptable is also considered a problem behavior within the host culture.

If you determine that the behavior in question is in fact improper, the next step is to find out how such problems are normally dealt with within the culture. Of course, you are not bound to handling the situation the same way a host-country teacher would, but it is important to have an idea of what the normal response would be so that you can gauge whether or not your response might be considered excessive or insufficient. Talking to someone from the host country may be helpful for several reasons. In addition to finding out how he or she might handle the situation, you can get feedback on your planned response, and you may also gain insight into the origins of the problem. (In many cultures, feedback about your behavior may not be direct, so it is important to be on the lookout for apparently irrelevant casual comments—for example, regarding your dress or the amount of homework you are giving— because key information about your own contribution to the problem may be buried within one of these comments.)

Perhaps the most important thing to remember in a cross-cultural situation is to try not to get upset about an issue before getting the facts, and probably not even after. There is a good chance that your interpretation of the situation is not entirely accurate, and the probability that you will handle it inappropriately if you shoot from the hip is even higher.

VTs, many of whom were only recently students themselves, may find it difficult to mentally shift into a class authority role, but it is important to be aware of the need for such a shift. A reality of teaching is that you have a degree of power over students, if only because you determine grades, so the question is not whether or not you should exercise power in class but how well you exercise it. Thus, you should give serious consideration to how you will handle discipline problems, and you may need to consider unpleasant punitive options if the situation calls for them.

With regard to specific responses, it is difficult to do more than make a few very broad, commonsense suggestions—the details depend on the specific problems, personalities, and culture involved. First, before exploding at somebody, fire a warning shot. One possibility is to specifically state the consequences of continued unacceptable behavior—in other words, make a threat. The best threats are those which you can and will carry out; don't threaten to kick a student out of class if you are not prepared to or if it is not within your power to do so. It also helps if threats are very specific so that a student doesn't cross the line due to ignorance rather than intent. "If you copy again, you will regret it!" is not as helpful to a student as "I will make you do the entire paper over again if I find a single phrase in it that is the same as your girlfriend's."

Second, try not to delay too long before clarifying and dealing with a problem situation. Failure to respond may well allow the situation to become worse and may lower the reservoir of respect and support that other students in the class have for you. When your natural desire to avoid seeming like an authority figure tempts you to avoid confrontation, remember that a student's disruptive behavior often influences other members in the class and that you have a responsibility to maintain an environment in which other students can learn. Another problem with long-delayed responses is that they tend to become more spectacular when they finally appear, and there is a greater danger that you will have lost the objectivity and emotional control necessary to handle the situation sensitively and appropriately. An early warning disrupts relationships much less than a blowup a few weeks later.

Finally, loud, public anger is a high-risk strategy for dealing with problems. In many cultures, particularly in Asia, public displays of anger are less acceptable and forgivable than in Western cultures, and the consequences of an inappropriate tirade may be severe and long-lasting. This does not mean that in these cultures nobody ever gets angry in public, but there are very complex rules as to who can get angry at whom, and when and how this is done; a high degree of cultural awareness and finesse is required to prevent the outburst from being a disaster. Even in cultures that are relatively accepting of anger, its use may still do more to damage relationships than to modify behavior. In general, a serious but calm response will be effective in getting your message across and will better preserve your relationship with the wayward student than an angry scolding will.

Students Who Participate Too Much

You are probably familiar with the student who tends to dominate, always being the first to answer a question or offer an opinion. The problem is that such behavior limits the other students' opportunities to participate and may discourage their willingness to try. For you, the problem is how to control the behavior without discouraging the student; the student who participates frequently is, after all, doing what teachers wish most students would do.

One approach is to simply ignore the eager student's hand when it goes up and to direct activity to other members of the class. This approach, however, often makes the eager student more vigorous in efforts to be noticed. Students who talk a great deal tend not be shy or overly sensitive, so more direct approaches may be necessary. One is to speak to these students individually, praising their willingness to participate but asking them to give others a chance. During class then, when the hand pops up again, you might even say, "Jan, I see your hand, but let's see if we can't get someone else to respond first."

Try not to become visibly annoyed with such students. They may already have popularity problems in class (though they may also be class leaders), and your disapproval can give license to other students to be more critical of them. They may also quite understandably feel that chances to practice are not to be wasted and that there is no good reason to let speaking opportunities go to waste if others won't take advantage of them, a view that you should encourage rather than discourage. Your ultimate goal is to encourage other students to participate more rather than to make the overly talkative student participate less, and you may make more progress toward this goal by showing appreciation of the eager student's efforts than by becoming irritated at them.

Students Who Participate Too Little

Teachers often define participation as answering questions or offering opinions during all-class activities, and this kind of participation is generally assumed to be an important part of the learning process. On reflection, however, it should be clear that the few moments a semester students spend speaking in front of the whole class are not a significant part of their total speaking practice time, and students who never volunteer in a large-group setting do not necessarily get much less practice than their classmates. In fact, the only unique benefit of speaking out in front of the whole class is that it trains students to pluck up their courage for speaking in front of large audiences. So I would suggest that failure to speak up in large-group settings should not be considered a serious problem.

In fact, pressuring students to participate unwillingly in whole-class settings may be counterproductive. Most students are, understandably, less than entirely confident of their English skills and already somewhat intimidated in English class. Knowing that they could be called on to publicly perform in front of a large audience increases the level of anxiety, and fear may well become more salient in their minds than interest in learning. If you single out such students by calling on them, the result is tension and wasted class time; the reluctant student often sits in embarrassed panic, unable or unwilling to answer, while classmates become either more nervous or bored. The only thing that such an exercise accomplishes is putting enough fear into students' hearts that they are more likely to do their homework; it achieves little in terms of in-class learning.

The saddest aspect of trial by questioning in class is that it may torment students who are in fact participating—in other words, students who pay attention in class, actively think through responses to questions, and participate actively in pair or small-group activities. These are the most important forms of participation because it is through these activities that students will get the bulk of their English practice. Only a very few highly vocal students will get significant amounts of practice in an all-class forum.

One way to encourage students who speak very little is by providing speaking opportunities that are as nonthreatening as possible, such as pair or small-group activities that don't involve a large audience and that allow students greater freedom to speak at a comfortable English skill level. Another way to help is by seeing that topics are within students' range of competence; some topics, particularly those dealing with a student's daily life, can be discussed at a wide range of skill levels, while others (e.g., capital punishment, constitutional reform) can only be discussed by students who have substantial speaking skills and large vocabularies. A third way you can help is by gently encouraging. A student is more likely to take the plunge and try to say something to a smiling and interested teacher than to a demanding martinet whose primary interest seems to be ensuring obedience to orders.

Ultimately, however, you reach the point where you have done what you can to provide opportunities and encouragement, and then it is up to students to take advantage of those opportunities. One element of treating students with respect is allowing them the freedom to make choices, and beyond a certain point further intervention on your part may do more harm than good by creating fear and tension or simply by wasting time that could have been better spent on other students who are more willing to respond. Make sure that opportunities and communication channels remain open, but don't feel guilty about every student who chooses not to speak up in class.

Students as Friends

For quite a number of reasons, it is not unusual for VTs to discover after a few months in the host country that their social life centers heavily around students and that most of their host-country friends are students. This happens in part because you will see students more regularly than most other people, so there is an opportunity for relationships to develop. Also, it is not uncommon for VTs to be close in age to their students; if you are a recent college graduate, you may be closer in age to the students than to most of your host-country colleagues. Finally, in some settings you will have something very important in common with the students—you are both relatively new and transient in the community. When this is the case, students are more open to new friendships than are other people who are long established in the community.

In some ways, forming close ties with students can be a good thing. As you become closer to students, you will learn more about their background, living and study conditions, and aspirations, not to mention the host culture in general. Having good friends, whether students or not, is also precious in and of itself. However, it can also become a problem if conflict develops between your roles as a teacher and as a friend.

One potential problem is that students with whom you become friends may misunderstand the new relationship. In some cultures it is normal for teachers to choose one or more favored pupils, who then have special privileges; in other cultures no precedent exists for a Western-style friendship between teachers and students. In these cases you may find student friends unintentionally—or intentionally—using their relationship with you in a way that you did not intend.

A second problem is that, as you develop friendships with students, you will inevitably become closer to some than others, which may lead to a perception on the part of other students that you are playing favorites. Often what happens is that you become closest to the students with the best English—these, after all, are the ones who are easiest to talk to—or to those who are most willing to spend time with you. These students are also often the ones most likely to get good grades (and to whom you will feel inclined to give the best grades). So, when grades come out, it is easy for other students to suspect you of favoritism. A third problem is favoritism of the highest order—teacher-student romance. For quite a number of reasons, romances between VTs and students are not uncommon. You will probably be lonely at times in your host country, you may well be very attracted to the host culture and its people, and you may simply have a student who you find to be very attractive. However, a romantic attachment can obviously lead to suspicion of favoritism and may contribute to a souring of relations between the teacher and the other students in the class.

The issue of romances between VTs and students is mentioned in chapter 2, so here I only reiterate my feeling that in most cultural settings this should definitely be avoided (and even in cultures where this kind of relationship is not frowned on, it is still rich in potential for things to go wrong).[2] With regard to friendships with students, I hesitate to suggest that potential problems should deter you because I know too many VTs whose time in the host country has been enriched immeasurably by friendships with students. However, I also know many VTs whose experience in the host country was marred by a student friendship that went wrong. Balancing the roles of teacher and friend, even in your own culture, is not easy, and in a culture where you are not very familiar with the rules, the potential for misunderstandings is substantial. For this reason, a case could be made for exercising at least some restraint in friendships with students, being friendly and enjoying their company but not becoming so close to a special few that they or other students are unclear about roles. The corollary is that you should also try to develop friendships with other types of people in your host community. Friendships with nonstudents may not always sprout and grow as effortlessly as friendships with students often do, but efforts in this direction can result in your building friendships with people who are more naturally your peers.

For Thought, Discussion, and Action

1. **class sizes:** Talk to someone who has taught in your host country, and find out what class sizes are normal for the kinds of courses you will teach. If class sizes are likely to be large, ask what strategies your informants use for dealing with such classes.

2. **disparate skill levels:** Talk to someone who has taught in your host country, and find out how serious the problem of disparate skill levels in class usually is. Also ask how realistic the possibility of redistributing students into classes of comparable skills levels is.

3. **discipline:** Ask someone who has taught in your host country about class discipline issues. What problems are common? To what extent are there school policies that are relevant to these problems? What strategies are normally used in the host country for dealing with these problems? What strategies are most appropriate for a foreign teacher to use in dealing with these problems?

4. **students who talk too much:** Talk to someone who has taught in your host country, and find out what they suggest for dealing with the problem of students who tend to talk too much and dominate in class.

5. **students who don't speak up in class:** This chapter suggests that it is all right not to force each and every student to speak up in front of the whole class. Naturally, however, such an approach has disadvantages as well as advantages. List the advantages and disadvantages of the suggested approach, and then decide what approach you think would be best.

6. **friendships with students:** Ask a host-country teacher about the cultural norms in the host country for relationships between teachers and students.

---

[2] When a VT meets a student who he or she feels is Mr. or Ms. Right, I feel that the most appropriate—and even ethical—approach is to delay the onset of any romantic relationship until the student has graduated from the course and is no longer the VT's student.

PART III

Living Abroad

Chapter 15

Adapting to Your Host Culture

- Adapting comfortably to life in the host country is important for your general well-being and for your teaching.

- Expectations have a great impact on the level of frustration you feel in a new culture.

- Culture fatigue is a common part of the process of adapting to life in a new culture.

- Two of the best ways to speed your adaptation are to learn about the host culture and learn to speak the host language.

The success with which you adapt to life in your host country will have a significant impact on how rewarding your own experience is and will also directly affect your success as a teacher in a number of ways:

1. It will have an impact on your attitude toward the culture in general and hence toward your students and your work. Put bluntly, volunteer teachers (VTs) who don't enjoy life in the host country often find it difficult to maintain enthusiasm for their teaching.

2. It will affect your energy level. The work of VTs who are physically, mentally, and emotionally drained by constant friction with the host culture will almost inevitably suffer.

3. VTs who have a poor attitude toward the host culture often fall into the habit of making hasty overgeneralizations and unfair criticisms. This in turn makes such VTs less than ideal as role models of intercultural communication and understanding. Also, a VT with a negative attitude toward the host culture may do more damage than good in terms of building students' interest in learning English and its culture. Students may pick up on the sense of hostility and respond to it in kind.

4. Finally, VTs who have learned little about the host culture are at a disadvantage as teachers because they will not be able to interact as effectively with students or school staff. Often your ability to teach effectively depends as much on your skills in reaching out to a recalcitrant student—or making friends with the lady who has the key to the audiovisual equipment room—as it does your ability to explain an idiom, and your success in building and maintaining good relationships with people will be directly affected by your success in adapting to the culture.

Of course, life in a new culture has many joys—the delights of friends, new foods, scenic beauty, and the sheer fascination of a new way of life—and it would be a tragedy if anyone were to finish this chapter with the feeling that an experience abroad is a trial to be withstood as stoically as possible. In fact, it may be one of the best experiences of your life. However, here I focus mainly on problems because, in my experience, most people don't need much advice on how to enjoy a good time.

Cultural Adaptation and Expectations

Repeated bouts with frustration and disappointment can eat away at your sense of well-being and make adapting to a new environment a more draining experience. VTs in many countries often experience frustration over low efficiency, disappointment at the slow speed with which friendships with host nationals develop, or many other annoyances. What problems like these all have in common is that the mental and emotional stress they cause is created as much by the expectations you bring with you as by the actual conditions in the host country. Take camping as an illustration. Conditions in a wilderness camp are generally far more primitive than those in most host countries (assuming the camper is backpacking rather than living out of a Winnebago), but campers generally take problems such as the absence of hot showers in stride because the campers don't expect hot showers. If, however, the same campers were to enter a Holiday Inn room and discover that the shower didn't have hot water, the response would probably be less cheerful.

Thus, one important aspect of preparing to enter a new culture, and of adapting to it after arrival, is careful consideration of your expectations. As Weaver (1993) notes about cross-cultural adaptation, "It seems that if we do not anticipate a stressful event we are much less capable of coping with it" (p. 138), and unexamined or unreasonable expectations virtually invite dissatisfaction.

It is not possible to present an exhaustive checklist of all areas in which you might need to check your expectations before venturing into unknown lands, but a brief discussion of a few key areas may highlight some of the kinds of problems VTs often encounter and help get you in the habit of examining the role that your expectations may play in making situations frustrating.

EFFICIENCY

VTs in many host countries fight running battles with their host institutions in an effort to get things done faster. Modern Western culture considers time, hence efficiency, very important and has devoted considerable effort to creating conditions and training people to ensure that things can be done quickly. For a variety of reasons, this will not necessarily be the situation in many host countries. Perhaps the host culture values interpersonal relationships more than efficiency. Perhaps your host country is still in the process of modernization, and even though it now has some of the machines that facilitate work in the West, people may not yet have fully adapted to a work style centered on using and maintaining them. Perhaps the host culture actually works very efficiently, but you have not yet learned how to get things done. For whatever reason, unrealistic expectations vis-à-vis efficiency are a potential source of great frustration for VTs in many host countries.

ORGANIZATION AND DISORGANIZATION

VTs sometimes have unrealistic expectations of how well the host institution has planned for them. It is not uncommon for VTs to think of the people in a host institution as *them,* a monolithic group that presumably thinks as one organic whole. Many VTs also fall into the habit of viewing themselves as the primary focus of the host institution's attention, an assumption that is encouraged by the fact that many host institutions treat their Western teachers as VIPs. It can thus come as a nasty surprise if you discover that different people in the host organization have very different—and perhaps conflicting—expectations of you and that they have not spent the time necessary to come to complete consensus on exactly what your teaching mission is.

APPRECIATION

Many VTs are willing to accept minimal salaries and make other sacrifices because their primary motive for going abroad is a desire to serve the host country (again perceived more or less as a single unit), but they also expect residents of the host country to appreciate the sacrifice they are making. VTs may be disappointed when they encounter people in the host country who don't show much appreciation for their contribution (Stewart and Bennett 1991, 4). Of course, on reflection, many people in any given host country have little or no idea why you are there and may assume that your motives are not in the least altruistic. In addition, host-country nationals may view the help and advice of overseas experts with mixed feelings. In many host countries, your living standard will also be higher than average for a person of your age and experience, a situation that will drastically alter the view many host nationals take of your sacrifice.

A special variation of this problem, sometimes encountered by VTs, arises from a gap in understandings of what their role is. Many VTs perceive themselves not only as language teachers but also as modernizers and reformers. They consider the traditional methods used by their host-country colleagues as less than ideal—if not downright backward—and take it on themselves to correct the situation. Often they are encouraged in this misperception by host nationals who decry the poor quality of local teaching approaches and praise Western methods. However, VTs who launch reform campaigns often meet stiff resistance, and it may be only after considerable frustration that they discover that the school views them as useful mostly because of their native control of English, not because of their credentials in language pedagogy. Praise for Western teaching methods often contains a strong element of politeness and may not indicate much real desire to change.

LIVING CONDITIONS

In poorer host countries, most VTs don't expect all the luxuries of home, and many are pleasantly surprised at how well they are taken care of. However, VTs usually find that some aspects of daily living fall below their expectations. Common problem areas are temperature control, sanitation levels, and food. For example, many Westerners have never had the experience of being uncomfortably cold or hot for long periods of time—and of having no warm or cool place to retreat to. An unfortunately common sight in such situations is an indignant Westerner insisting to a host national that it is too cold (or hot, or wet) for anybody to tolerate, forgetting that the host national may well suffer from the exact same problem every day. (Of course, a VT who is new to difficult conditions may need special treatment in order to keep functioning as a teacher, and martyrdom is not necessarily a virtue. However, the danger is that, if carried too far, this rationale tends to send the message that Westerners think that they deserve better living conditions than host nationals do.)

RELATIONSHIPS

One of the most delightful aspects of life abroad is the opportunity for friendships with people of a different culture. However, in many cultures, significant friendships take longer to develop than they do in the West. North Americans in particular are accustomed to developing close (though often transitory) relationships quite quickly, much faster than close relationships develop in many cultures. One source of frustration for many Westerners can therefore be the slow pace at which friendships develop. A related disappointment often occurs if a friend turns out to have been interested in the gain to be had from a relationship with a Westerner or if it becomes clear that a friendship has very defined and unexpected limits.

ADAPTATION

Many people assume that the hardest part of adapting to a new culture is getting through the initial shock and that adaptation will then get progressively easier. This is not entirely false, but for reasons discussed below, the hardest part often occurs some months after arrival in a new culture. In fact, one of the factors that can contribute to culture burnout is the expectation that things should be getting easier and the frustration when they improve only slowly. A related expectation is that once you are living in the host country, you will pick up the language and culture rather quickly and with a minimal investment of effort, and disappointment results when learning them turns out to require a substantial investment of effort.

It is virtually impossible to approach life in a new culture with no expectations at all. Nor can you be so well informed that all your expectations are accurate. However, it is possible and useful to consider problem situations you may encounter so that you are mentally prepared. Getting as much accurate information as you can about what life will be like in your new culture is also of great value. However, perhaps the most important safeguard is just to be aware of the role expectations play in creating frustration and disappointment. In a frustrating situation, sometimes simply realizing that your expectations are part of the problem is a big step toward improving the situation. The old metaphor of the half-full glass is trite but true: if you focus on the fact that the glass is not full, you will undergo more emotional wear and tear than if you are thankful that there is any water in the glass at all. There may be real hardships and problems in your new life in your host country, and altering the way you look at these problems will not make them all go away, but adjusting expectations can often help reduce your sense of frustration and disappointment.

The Adaptation Process and Culture Burnout

CULTURE SHOCK AND CULTURE BURNOUT

You have probably heard the term *culture shock* and may understand it to refer to the jolting experience of suddenly being thrust into a new culture. This initial impact, however, is not the real problem most people face in adapting to a new culture. There are certainly many new things to adjust to in a new country during the first weeks and months of a stay, but for most people, difficulties during this initial period are more than compensated for by the excitement and joy of being in new surroundings and discovering new things. The more difficult phase for many people occurs later in their stay in the host country, the period after the newness of the experience has rubbed off but before adaptation has progressed very far.

Those who have investigated culture shock explain it in a variety of ways, but there is a growing tendency to view the problem as one of exhaustion and to speak of *culture fatigue* rather than *culture shock*.[1] I assume this view in the following discussion, although I prefer the term *culture burnout* because it seems to better capture the feeling of the experience. The advantage of viewing culture burnout as physical, mental, and emotional fatigue is that it helps people make sense of what is happening to them and implies (correctly, I believe) that the problem is manageable. I find it helpful to describe the problem as one of an empty emotional gas tank resulting from the following formula:

decreased energy intake + increased energy drain = burnout

Decreased Energy Intake

Moving to a new country cuts you off from many of the people and things from which you are accustomed to drawing strength and refreshment. You will no doubt leave behind friends and family members whose loss will deprive you of an important source of comfort. You may also leave behind a job that gave you a sense of self-esteem and confidence in your abilities, a home or possessions that gave you a sense of security, and hobbies or pastimes that provided relaxation. Because you are moving to a place where you probably don't speak the local language, you will be limiting your access to TV, books, movies, and other cultural products that provided both stimulation and recreation. In short, you are drastically cutting down on the number of things in your life from which you draw energy.

The early days of life in a new country tend to be as exciting and interesting as they are draining, so the loss of these old sources of refreshment may not be felt immediately, and ultimately many of these sources of refreshment will be replaced by new ones. However, as you settle in and life becomes more routine, there will probably be a time when the excitement of a new life has worn off but you have not yet found new friends, job satisfaction, hobbies, cultural outlets, or whatever you need to sustain you emotionally. During this period, the energy supplies in your emotional gas tank aren't being replenished as much as they would be at home.

Increased Energy Drain

Until you have gained a comfortable mastery of life abroad, life in your host country will place greater demands on your energy reserves than life at home would. One problem is that you may

---

[1] See Barna (1994), Grove and Torbiorn (1993), and Seelye (1993) for discussion of culture shock as a process of fatigue. For other views, see Kohls (2001) and Weaver (1993).

have to cope with more physical drain, even if only because any move to a new place involves considerable running around in setting up a new home (and this in a place where lower efficiency levels may make getting things done more labor-intensive work than you are used to). People in a new country also tend to get sick more often than they would at home. A second problem is that many of the tasks that you could perform almost unconsciously at home require a lot more thinking in a new country, hence more mental drain. Part of the problem is that you have to relearn many of the basics of living, even for simple tasks like buying food or stamps. Also, if you are in a country where English isn't widely spoken and you don't speak the host language, each effort to communicate involves considerable mental effort.

However, most experts agree that the greatest problem is emotional drain. In a new culture, you are often in uncomfortable situations where you don't fully understand what is going on or don't know what to do. You may also find that in areas of your life where you were previously sure and confident—for example, your work or social skills—you cannot perform at your normal level of effectiveness. Even as simple an act as buying a stamp at the post office can become an emotional trauma if you are afraid that the clerk will say something you don't understand, leaving you unsure of what to do next while at the center of an impatient, pushing crowd. On top of it all, as a novice to the intricacies of etiquette in the new culture, you will probably make a fool of yourself more than once. When these unusual demands on your reserves of energy, patience, and good humor cause them to run low—and when you have not yet found adequate new sources of refreshment—you are afflicted by culture burnout.[2]

SYMPTOMS OF CULTURE BURNOUT

Symptoms of culture burnout vary, but among the most important are these:

1. **decreased patience and increased irritability:** As your energy level decreases, perhaps the most predictable result is that your reserves of patience and good humor become depleted. Over time, rolling with the punches becomes a little harder, and you may find that you are less patient with problems than you were when you first arrived. It is not unusual to subconsciously feel that while you adjust to the host culture, it should be adjusting to you just as much, and that over time you are more justified in a less forgiving response to problems or mistakes.

2. **an increased tendency to be critical of the host culture:** Annoyances that you were initially able to ignore or tolerate often grow over time into more serious grievances. As you are affected by culture burnout, you may also find yourself quicker to leap to negative conclusions when puzzling or unpleasant things happen in your relations with host nationals. These grievances then get passed around in the form of war stories and repeatedly hauled out to prove broader (often negative) generalizations about the host culture.

3. **withdrawal from contact with the host culture into a small community of other outsiders:** It is generally harder to make friends with host nationals than with other foreigners with whom you have more in common, so some VTs tend to drift into self-contained little expatriate communities. At a deeper level, interaction with the host culture may call your ideas, values, and way of life into question, and socializing primarily with a community that does not present these kinds of challenges is generally less exhausting.

---

[2] For a more sophisticated model of the culture fatigue experience, see Grove and Torbiorn (1993).

Unfortunately, complaining about the host country often becomes a staple topic of conversation among ex-pats, and the result is usually reinforcement of negative attitudes.[3]

These symptoms of culture burnout are not only problems themselves; because they tend to separate you from the host culture, they also slow down the speed with which you learn how to function comfortably and efficiently in the host country. These problems are particularly serious for a language teacher because they tend to pull you toward exactly those cross-cultural attitudes that you should be trying to teach the students to avoid. It is thus important to do what you can to prevent culture burnout.

DEALING WITH CULTURE BURNOUT

People have very different experiences with culture burnout. Some are virtually incapacitated, going through a period of extreme withdrawal and hostility toward the host culture; others experience little or no trouble. It seems safest to say that, though the intensity of the problem can vary widely, most people will experience the problem of exhaustion and decreased emotional energy to some degree sometime during their stay abroad. Fortunately, there are steps you can take to minimize adjustment problems.

1. Continue to explore new aspects of your environment. One factor that often contributes to culture burnout is boredom, often caused by routine. It is quite natural during the early stages of adjusting to a new environment to first learn to get by in a limited daily routine of essential places (often consisting of a home–school–dining hall triangle of some kind), and it is not unusual for people to then spend much of their time within this safe, narrow range. This has the advantage of limiting your emotional energy output because life within the routine is easier, but it also tends to become stale after a time, and when that happens, you lose the refreshing and invigorating effects of new discoveries. Even minimal efforts to keep expanding the range of your routine—taking a new route on your walk home, looking for a new store—do much to keep life in your host country interesting and stimulating.

2. Avoid overloading your work and activity schedule, especially with regular commitments. VTs' volunteer spirit often leads them to take on an unreasonable workload of in-class and out-of-class activities during the first few weeks abroad, when they are still fresh and energetic, only to be unable to sustain such a high level of output over longer periods of time. As you calculate the amount of work you expect to do, do not assume that you will be able to maintain the same level of efficiency and output in a new environment that you can in a familiar one. After all, if you later discover that you have extra energy to burn, you can add other commitments; making new commitments is generally easier than breaking existing ones and does not create the bad impression that you do not keep your word.

3. Allow yourself strategic retreats into your own culture. Some people who go abroad do so with the intention of immersing themselves in the host culture, hoping that, by associating only with host nationals and speaking only the host language (except in English class, of course), they will come out of the experience fluent in the language and culture after a fairly short time. This approach works for some people, but it can also be a recipe for burnout. There is much to be said for allowing yourself occasional

[3]See Kohls (2001, 96) for a list of other symptoms.

vacations from the host culture, in the form of afternoons with an English novel or an evening with friends from your home country.[4]

4. Try to maintain a positive attitude and not to give in to the tendency to constantly find fault. Kohls (2001, 102–03) suggests that, rather than complain, you will find it more productive to look for the logic underlying those features of the host culture that seem strange or unpleasant; merely seeing that the host culture is reasonable is a big step toward making peace with it.

Ultimately, the most effective long-term cure for culture burnout is getting to know the people, culture, and language of the host country. Knowing the host country well does not necessarily mean that you will fall in love with it, but familiarity with the language and culture considerably increases the chances that you will find rewards to balance out the trials of your stay. It also makes life easier by reducing misunderstandings and by decreasing your sense of alienation. Finally, study of the culture and language, the topic of the following section, will also help you become a better teacher.

Learning the Culture of the Host Country

As noted in chapter 13, the term *culture* covers a very broad range, from great poets to the local market's closing time, and almost anything that you learn about your host culture will help in your adaptation. However, some kinds of information will be of more immediate value than others.

DAILY-LIFE SURVIVAL INFORMATION

This category needs little discussion: both you and your host institution know you need to learn about such things as eating, shopping, and transportation, so provision is often made for you to get this information.

There is much to be said for trying to become self-sufficient as soon as possible because as your ability to take care of yourself increases, so will your sense of self-confidence and general well-being. Everything may seem overwhelming at first, so you may be more concerned with completing any given task (even just getting a meal or mailing a letter) than with learning how to do it yourself, and you may fall into the habit of relying on helpful friends to do things for you. While there is little harm in this as a short-term expedient, over the long haul it is dangerous because it will make you a burden on those around you and confine you to a restricted routine that may be as stifling as it is safe. As noted above, such a routine is an invitation to boredom and culture burnout.

DOS AND DON'TS OF POLITE BEHAVIOR

The need for knowledge about polite behavior is fairly immediate because from early on in your host-country stay, you want to create the best possible impression. Host-country nationals are unlikely to expect you to have mastered all the intricacies of local etiquette, and numerous faux pas will no doubt be forgiven with good grace. However, every culture has deeply felt taboos that are assumed to be universal standards of decent human behavior, and frequent violation of these

---

[4]Weaver (1993, 153) suggests that associating with other people who have gone through culture burnout is very helpful, provided that the meetings don't degenerate into gripe sessions.

will put considerable strain on your relations with host nationals. In contrast, knowing a few basic rules for handling social situations politely will do much to start your new relationships out on the right foot.

One way to quickly learn a few basic rules of polite behavior is to look in the etiquette sections of books written for tourists. While these books will probably only hit a few of the highlights, this very basic information is what you really need for those first days in your new country. Another way to quickly learn a few of the most important rules is to ask host-country nationals and fellow expatriates. Host-country nationals may enjoy teaching you some of their standards of polite behavior and be favorably impressed by your interest, but they may omit mentioning relatively taboo subjects either because they feel it is rude to discuss them or because they assume you already know. For more taboo issues, you may find the advice of other expatriates more straightforward. Finally, however, the best way to learn how to interact is by becoming a good observer. Learn to pay attention to such things as how people act and speak in formal or polite situations, who is treated with special respect, and how people normally behave in daily life.

THE NATIONAL STORY

As noted in chapter 13, a culture is defined in part by its story—those events, achievements, and people that members of the culture feel to be especially significant. You can easily learn some of this story by reading a little of the history or literature of the host country before arrival. After arrival, you may find it more interesting and more effective to pursue the issue in the company of host-culture friends. Let people take you to museums, historical spots, or cultural events as an opportunity for them to show off their culture to you; the significance of these outings often lies as much in the relationships that are built as in the amount of culture and history that you learn. In many countries, simply expressing an interest in these issues will go a long way toward creating a good impression on people. This is especially true in smaller countries or areas with a strong regional culture because people there don't expect outsiders to take much interest in them and are often doubly pleased when someone does.

BELIEFS AND VALUES

As Kohls (2001) noted, being able to see the logic underlying the host culture is one way to help you come to terms with it and, to this end, study of the beliefs and values of your host culture can be a helpful part of the adaptation process. Insight into why host nationals behave as they do will reduce misunderstanding and enhance your ability to understand and interpret the actions of those around you.

Reading books on the culture of the host culture is one productive approach to this area of study.[5] Another way to learn these beliefs and values is through observation, but it is important to observe carefully over a long period of time lest your conclusions be drawn more from your preconceptions than from the evidence. Perhaps the best approach is to talk with friends or informants in the host culture who will give you a good and reasonably frank explanation of why people do the things they do. Cultivating a friendship that allows the host national to give you good feedback may take a considerable investment of time and patience, but if you can establish such relationships, you will have an unexcelled window into the host culture.

---

[5] See Kohls (2001, 167–79) for a list of information resources about other cultures. Also, the Interacts Series (Intercultural Press) mentioned in chapter 2 is an excellent source of this type of information.

GENERAL BACKGROUND KNOWLEDGE

Knowledge of the history, geography, current affairs, government, society, economy, and politics of your host culture is usually not immediately essential for your daily life there, but over the long run it is helpful to know about these topics if only so that you feel that you understand what is going on around you.

This information is relatively easy to gain access to. Books, museums, newspapers, and magazines are all possible resources. The visual media should also not be ignored; even if you don't understand the host-country language, watching films and TV may be a useful and even enjoyable way to gain insight.

One way to speed up the learning task—and make it more interesting—is to draw on the people around you as resources. Remember that your priority is to learn what host nationals know, so it makes sense to approach a topic first through their eyes. For example, you might approach a topic like history by asking several people about the most important events and people in their history rather than starting with a history book that will tell you far more than even most host nationals remember.[6]

AN AREA OF EXPERTISE

In your study of the host culture, one final possibility to consider is choosing some aspect of the culture as a specialty. Perhaps this might be a hobby like cooking or martial arts, or a special area of knowledge such as the national religion or local history, or learning to play a musical instrument unique to your host country. What makes this kind of study special is that, by focusing in one area, you can gain a degree of mastery in some aspect of the culture, maybe even getting to the point where host nationals respect your accomplishments. The advantage of this—other than the pleasure and recreation that it provides—is an enhanced sense of self-esteem. It simply feels good to know that in some area of life in the host country, you are above average, and having some contact with the host culture that is enjoyable and rewarding can be a helpful antidote to the negative attitudes that may develop as you cope with burnout.

Learning the Host Language

TO LEARN OR NOT TO LEARN: COSTS AND BENEFITS

Many people assume that once they are living in a foreign country, picking up the language will be relatively easy and fast, much less painful than foreign language classes in high school or college were. This is not entirely untrue: studying a language in the country where it is spoken is generally much more rewarding than studying at home, and it certainly offers more opportunities for practice. However, this does not mean that language study will be cost free; even in the host country, learning the language requires a substantial investment of time and effort.

I would argue that, for almost any VT, it is worthwhile to develop at least survival skills in the host language: the ability to shop, deal with social courtesies, ask where things are, use the post office, and so forth. The rewards for achieving this skill level are immediate and significant, and failure to learn at least basic language skills for getting by will leave you in a constant state of dependency on others (or on your ingenuity in nonverbal communication). Over time, the cost this exacts in mental and emotional drain will both diminish the quality of your experience abroad and make emotional survival and adaptation much more difficult.

---

[6] For topic and question lists to serve as an outline for learning about a new culture, see Grey, Darrow, and Palmquist (1975) and Kohls (2001, 153–55). Hess (1997) offers a workbook of activities for learning about a host culture.

However, once you have learned enough of the language to deal with the necessities of daily life, the question of whether or not you wish to continue is a real one. From this point on, the gains made in language mastery are slower and come at a higher price; it doesn't take as much work to go from point zero to survival language skills as it does to go from the survival level to the level where you can carry on social conversation. So, after many VTs reach the survival language level, their language study tends to slow down or even grind to a halt. At this point, you may find yourself asking whether putting in so much additional time and energy is worthwhile.

As argued in chapter 1, one main reason to seriously consider studying toward a greater command of the host language is that as you study it, you will learn a lot about language learning and about effective strategies for language study. All language learners are different to some degree, so study methods that work for you may not be so good for others, but firsthand experience with different learning strategies is still one of the best ways to ascertain how effective they might be, and a teacher who has experience as a language student is generally far more sensitive to these real-world problems than one who has spent little time in the student role. Knowledge of the host language will also directly benefit your teaching by helping you understand why students have some of the problems they do. Not all students' mistakes are related to their native language, but some are, and knowledge of the host language will help you more quickly focus on problem areas common to all of the students in the class.

Speaking a foreign language well enhances your credibility as a language teacher, but the primary issue is not how fluent you become; rather, it is whether or not you have credentials as a language learner. If nothing else, lack of foreign language skills simply looks bad in a language teacher and provides a permanent reason to be defensive. Without credentials as a language learner, you have to apologize too often.

A second significant benefit of continued language study is that it will greatly enhance your chances of successful adaptation to the host culture. Obviously, ability to speak the local language reduces the wear and tear of daily life in your host country by making communication easier. Also, the more you can understand of what is going on around you, the more comfortable and at home you will feel in the host culture. This, in turn, translates into reduced emotional drain from constant uncertainty and confusion. Finally, command of the host language gives you a whole new level of access to the host culture, facilitating friendships and insight that can do much to restore your interest, excitement, and sense that being in the host culture is as rewarding as it is demanding. Over the long run, this is the best single way to counteract culture burnout.

The price of not investing the time and effort to achieve a higher level of skill is permanent alienation from the host culture, and often longer and more severe bouts of culture burnout. This prediction may seem a bit strong, and I recognize that in some host-country situations a monolingual English teacher can survive quite happily for long periods of time. However, even in these cases, satisfaction must be achieved within a limited range because lack of facility in the host language will deny access to some of the population and culture—often most of it—and all too often monolingual expatriates are forced back into a community of other monolingual expatriates.

LEARNING THE HOST LANGUAGE

As suggested above, language study in your host country may be easier in some ways than language courses at home. For one thing, your environment will reinforce your language study and provide ample opportunities to practice. For another, you will have many chances to use what you learn, and in many cultures your attempts to speak the language will be rewarded with praise and enthusiasm.

Trying to learn the host language in many countries involves some special problems, however. The first is that there may be few or no language courses for you to take, especially if you are in an area where there are not many other foreigners, so your study may need to be pursued in less formally structured ways. There may also be few books or other materials available, particularly for intermediate-level study. Finally, you will probably be teaching full-time, and making time for language study may be challenging. In short, language study in the host country will probably require greater initiative and discipline from you than study in a course at home would, but you can also look forward to greater progress and rewards if you find the time to study and practice.

Based on the conditions described above, here are a few suggestions on how to pursue language study in your host country.

Which Language?

One issue you may face is which language or dialect to learn. Many countries have both a national language and a variety of local languages or dialects (which may be completely different from the national language). If you work in an area where a regional language is spoken, you may face a hard choice between the national standard and the regional language.

On the side of the national standard, it will probably be easier to locate study materials, and you will be able to use the language over a wider area. People may also expect you to learn the national standard, and you may meet resistance—or simply confusion—if you don't. On the side of the regional language, this is often what you hear most around you and have more opportunities to practice; in fact, you may have very little chance to use the national standard in your area. The other advantage of learning the regional language in some areas is that people will respond to you more favorably. This is particularly true in areas with a strong regional culture and sense of local pride; in such areas, people may view the national standard with very mixed emotions as a kind of foreign language (perhaps imposed from the outside by force).

My own practice in such situations has been to focus on the national standard but also to pick up a smattering of the local language, but much depends on the local situation and your own language study goals. However, as you consider the issue, don't overlook the attitudes others around you have toward languages because these will have a great impact on how much reinforcement and encouragement you get in your study.

Structuring a Program of Study

One of the main problems of not having an organized language course is that lack of structure—not to mention examinations—makes it easy for your studies to drift off course and eventually dwindle into good intentions. It is therefore especially important to have a clear idea of where you want to go and how you want to get there.

Setting goals is generally not a problem in the beginning because the need to achieve survival speaking and listening skills is so obvious. However, once you reach that skill level, you have harder choices to make. The principles of planning for breakthrough may be helpful to you here (see chapter 3). Assuming that you have limited time, focusing your study efforts on the pursuit of one or two skills will enable you to progress in those areas more rapidly and gain more reward for your efforts. This, in turn, will make it more likely that you keep studying during the intermediate stages, during which rewards are fewer and plateaus more common.

For most people, it is also helpful to have structure in their study program. In foreign language classes, this is generally provided by textbooks and other study materials. In a situation where you do not have a textbook, you may need to rely on a study plan to provide structure. Marshall (1989) suggests a program structured around a *study cycle,* which involves working through a series of steps regularly:

1. Plan the topics and situations you want to learn about.

2. With the help of a mentor (tutor), work up a dialogue for dealing with one of those topics or situations.

3. Have the mentor tape the dialogue, and then you practice it.

4. Go out and practice in the community.

5. Return and evaluate your experience with the mentor.

Such a cycle, or some variation of it, will provide structure for your study and will result in your slowly but surely producing your own language study materials, tailored to your goals and needs.

Materials

As noted above, an advantage of studying a national language is that at least introductory study materials are more likely to be available. For regional languages and dialects, materials may be more difficult to find, though often a dictionary or primer has been written at some point in history by a missionary or scholar. (You may only be able to find these in university libraries at home.)

If you need to make your own materials from scratch, taped materials developed with a tutor's help following the lines suggested above would be useful for beginning- and intermediate-level speaking and listening. For reading, it is good to start out with materials that are of immediate use and provide rapid reward for your efforts, such as maps and signs. To build toward reading more substantial texts, you might work with children's books. Although the content may not always be intellectually stimulating, such materials are relatively easy, often have pictures to help you create context, and may contain widely known stories that will help you build cultural background knowledge. At advanced levels of study, the problem of finding materials is less severe because you can begin working with material intended for adult host-culture audiences.

Tutors

Finding a good language teacher is not always easy. There may not be many people around who have experience teaching the local language to foreigners, so when others help you look for a teacher, they may turn to those whose experience is in teaching the language as rhetoric or literature. They will also probably assume you want someone who will take all of the initiative in presenting lessons for you. Obviously, candidates selected in this way may not be ideal—you may find yourself an audience of one for lectures on schoolbook texts.

Assuming that you want to take control of your own language program, you want someone who will answer your questions, patiently talk with you in the target language, and generally cooperate with you in carrying out your plan. While it is important that your tutor's speech be fairly representative and standard, the qualifications you are looking for may have as much to do with personality and sensitivity as with credentials in language teaching.

One issue that is often sticky is how to pay your tutor. In many cultures, a direct weekly or monthly payment might be culturally awkward. Hence, you will need to seek advice as to what kind of arrangement is culturally comfortable, is fair, and doesn't place you in a greater position of obligation to the tutor than you desire. If direct payment won't work, you might suggest payment through a third party, an exchange of language lessons, occasional gifts from you to your tutor, or some other arrangement. Finding a suitable method of compensation may take some effort and ingenuity, but it has the advantage of not only protecting you from accumulating a huge burden of obligation but also setting your relationship on a clear basis. Arrangements that are more casual have a tendency to drift into irregularity or friendly chatting (often in English).[7]

When to Start Your Study

It is usually best to start your language study as soon as possible, perhaps even before arrival in the host country. One reason for starting early is that language you learn early in your stay will probably be drilled into you permanently by months and years of practice; that which you learn in the last month, you will probably lose. Another reason to have some host-language skills as early as possible is that this will enable you to conduct at least some of your relationships in the host language. One interesting fact of human language behavior is that once two people establish a relationship in one language, they generally continue to communicate in that language. As an English teacher, you will inevitably spend much of your time with teachers and students who will speak to you in English, and it may be hard for you to find opportunities to practice the host language. If you delay your study of the host language for several months, your social life will tend to fill with people who speak to you in English, and host nationals who can't speak English will become accustomed to not speaking to you at all. If, on the other hand, you learn to speak at least some of the host language during the first months of your stay, you are more likely to have some relationships with people who don't speak English or who prefer to speak to you in the host language.

For Thought, Discussion, and Action

1. **expectations:** As best you can, list your expectations with regard to the items in the list below. Then talk to someone from the host culture or who has lived in the host culture and find out how realistic your expectations are.
    *   your living arrangements and conditions
    *   your courses and work assignment
    *   your role in the school or department
    *   availability of goods
    *   ease of developing relationships with colleagues, students, and other people

2. **challenges and rewards:** Find one or more expatriates who have taught in your host culture. Interview them about what they found most difficult and challenging about life and work in the host culture, and what they found most enjoyable and rewarding.

3. **culture shock:** Find one or more expatriates who seem to have adapted successfully to life in your host culture, and ask them what advice they would give you about how to minimize the effects of culture shock as you adapt to the host culture. (Keep in mind that their understanding of culture shock may differ from the one used in this book.)

4. **learning about the host culture:** List questions about one or more of the following issues: (1) daily-life survival information for the host culture, (2) dos and don'ts of polite behavior in the host culture, and (3) the national story of the host culture. Then find one or more informants from the host culture, and interview them.

---

[7] See Marshall (1989, chapter 4) for a more detailed discussion of the problems of working with tutors. Studying Chinese with tutors is also discussed by Snow (2002, 30–45).

5. **developing an area of host-culture expertise:** Make a list of possible areas of expertise (e.g., hobbies, skills) you might consider developing in your host culture. It may help to get ideas from other people who have lived in the host culture.

6. **national/regional languages:** For the area in the host country where you will live, find out what regional languages may be spoken in addition to a national language (if any). In particular, try to find out (1) how different the regional languages are from the national language, (2) how much and in what situations the regional languages are spoken, and (3) what attitudes local people have toward the regional languages and toward the national language.

7. **learning the host language (task A):** Find one or more expatriates who have learned the host language and interview them about their experience. Find out (1) how they did it, (2) what the main challenges and rewards were, and (3) what advice they have for you.

8. **learning the host language (task B):** Make an initial plan for your study of the host language—goals, materials, method, and plan. Then ask someone who has learned the host language to give you feedback on your plan.[8]

---

[8] For a survival skills course in Mandarin Chinese, see Snow (2002).

Chapter 16

Afterword: On Becoming a Professional

Many people who go abroad to teach English do so less out of a burning desire to teach English than out of a desire to experience life in another country. However, many discover that English teaching is an unusually enjoyable profession offering a range of rewards. First, because of the worldwide interest in English, an English teacher can find work and live in a very broad range of countries and cultures (to get an idea of the range of opportunities available, see the job listings in Griffith 2002 and Mohamed 2003). Secondly, English teaching is often an especially fulfilling and meaningful form of work because promoting knowledge of English can make an important contribution to students' personal development and career opportunities as well as to a nation's modernization efforts. Finally, the raw material of the language teaching profession—language, culture, and communication—is inherently interesting. As an English teacher working abroad, you have the opportunity to teach this material and to learn it firsthand through interaction with people of other cultures. Thus, it seems only appropriate to close this book with a few words on steps to take if you find that EFL teaching is a career that you wish to pursue on a professional level.

The first step would be to look into a degree program in language teaching, and a check on the Internet will quickly reveal that a huge range of programs are available in a huge range of countries. (See appendix D for Web sites of major English teaching professional organizations.) One non-Internet resource that deserves special mention is the *Directory of Teacher Education Programs in TESOL in the United States and Canada* (Christopher 2005), which gives detailed descriptions of almost 400 programs in North America.

Obtaining a professional degree in an ESL/EFL-related field makes you eligible for a broad range of English teaching positions, but it certainly does not exhaust the possibilities for professional training. A second highly beneficial way to prepare for a career as a language teaching is through your own continued foreign language study. While such study is recommended by most ESL/EFL degree programs, time limitations mean that it is often not given a great deal of emphasis. As pointed out earlier, experience as a language learner helps you grow in your understanding of language learning strategies, the affective side of language learning, language in general, and English in particular. EFL professionals should make language study a part of preparation for teaching, and—much like coaches or piano teachers—should continue to stay in shape by regularly practicing the skill of language learning. If you learn one language and then rest on your laurels, you may grow stale and forget what it is like to be on the other side of the teacher's desk. It is thus necessary to continue to study, both deepening skills in languages you already know and occasionally going back to the beginning by learning a new language.

A third important area of study and experience that benefits EFL teachers—and arguably ESL teachers as well—is intercultural communication and adaptation. As argued in chapter 13, many if not most of the situations in which the students use English will involve intercultural communication of some kind, so an understanding of the special problems of communicating across cultural lines is very beneficial to a teacher. Also, if you go on to a career as an EFL teacher, you will almost by definition often be living in situations where you need to adapt to a new culture. Furthermore, some students may eventually need to go through the same adaptation process themselves if they go abroad, so your ability to understand and explain the process of adapting to a new culture will be of great value to you as an EFL teacher.

All of this may seem a rather tall order to handle, and it does in fact take years of dedicated work to become prepared in all of the ways mentioned above. The good news, however, is that even in your first year teaching overseas, you will make considerable progress toward learning the skills that will speed you on your road to a professional career. Even for those of you who have no long-term EFL ambitions, the intercultural, language teaching, and foreign language skills that you can develop in a year of teaching abroad will not only make you better prepared for a wide range of careers, but will also enrich your life in ways that you probably cannot now imagine.

The Goals Menu: A Starter Kit for Course Planning

When planning a course, especially one that you have not taught before, you will almost inevitably need to make at least some decisions about the goals of the course. This is most obviously true when you are asked to teach a course for which the stated goals are either very vague or nonexistent (e.g., an evening class for adults for which the only stated goal is to "improve their English"). However, even when teaching courses that have preestablished goals, you will often need to prioritize the goals and make them more specific so that they give you—and the students—clearer guidance in deciding how to make best use of class time, how to allocate study time outside of class, and so forth.

The following menu is intended to give you some ideas for goals you might select for your English courses.[1] By necessity, it is general and is intended as a starting point rather than a final plan. A few reminders from chapter 3:

- It is good to have both short-term and long-term goals for a course. The former are limited goals that can be accomplished during the course; the latter are ultimate goals toward which students will have to work over a long time.

- You should have both content and proficiency goals for most courses. In other words, students should improve both in what they know and in what they can do. (One natural source of content in English courses is Western culture.)

I. General Goals for All Levels and Kinds of Courses

A. Encourage students' interest in English study

B. Help students begin to take a more active approach to language study, setting their own goals and choosing their own study approaches

C. Help students develop discipline in language study

D. Build students toward a good balance of English skills. What makes up a good balance depends greatly on the situation, but for many learners it would look something like this:

1. Stronger in listening than speaking

2. Stronger in reading than writing

3. Larger receptive vocabulary than productive vocabulary

4. Stronger knowledge of vocabulary than of grammar

II. Speaking Goals

A. General (all levels): help students improve in

1. Ability to express meaning

2. Flexibility and creativity in dealing with communication problems (e.g., finding another way to say something when you don't know the right word)

3. Vocabulary

4. Grammatical accuracy

5. Fluency

6. Accuracy in pronunciation

7. Interpretation (English to host language or vice versa)

8. Ability to interact in culturally appropriate ways

---

[1] In drawing up this menu, I am indebted to the *ACTFL Proficiency Guidelines* (American Council on the Teaching of Foreign Languages 1999; see the note in chapter 4), although the system I propose above is simpler than ACTFL's. While the *ACTFL Guidelines* are not goals in themselves, they provide a helpful basis for considering instructional goals.

B.   Beginning level: help students learn to

1.   Deal with predictable classroom communication

2.   Handle simple courtesies

3.   Ask and answer basic information questions

4.   Use vocabulary to talk about themselves, family, school, environment, and daily routine and activities

5.   Use basic grammar structures (e.g., *wh-* questions, basic verb tenses, plurals)

6.   Construct short simple sentences with a fair degree of accuracy

7.   Achieve intelligible pronunciation

C.   Intermediate level: help students learn to

1.   Deal creatively with daily communication situations (going beyond use of memorized material)

2.   Sustain a conversation

3.   Tell stories, express an opinion, explain something

4.   Cope with communication problems through clarification or circumlocution

5.   Use vocabulary for discussion of
     • daily-life needs (e.g., shopping, health, transport)
     • personal information (e.g., history, plans)
     • their home, town, city, region, country
     • their profession, topics of personal interest

6.   Use vocabulary accurately and appropriately

7.   Accurately construct short or simple sentences

8.   Construct more complicated sentences that are intelligible (though perhaps not always entirely accurate)

9.   Develop sufficient fluency to sustain rhythm of daily conversation

10. Develop clear (though probably accented) pronunciation

11. Handle common social interactions in linguistically and culturally appropriate ways

D.   Advanced level: help students learn to

1.   Handle most normal communication situations fluently

2.   Explain, persuade, and negotiate proficiently

3.   Produce sustained (paragraph-length) discourse

4.   Resolve misunderstandings or communication problems through clarification or circumlocution

5.   Handle unexpected situations, especially problematic intercultural situations

6.   Use vocabulary for discussion of
     • current affairs, news, and social issues
     • professional topics
     • their own culture and Western culture

7. Use vocabulary properly (in level of formality, connotation, grammar)

8. Make few grammar errors that impede comprehension

9. Achieve clear (though probably still accented) pronunciation

10. Handle a broad range of situations in culturally appropriate ways

11. Find opportunities to practice speaking outside class

III. Listening Goals

A. General (all levels): help students improve in

1. Comprehension of oral English

2. Ability to guess

3. Ability to determine meaning from language clues (bottom-up) and from context and background knowledge (top-down)

4. Comprehension of fast or unclear speech

5. Interpretation (English to host language or vice versa)

6. Vocabulary (receptive)

7. Ability to hear and derive meaning from grammatical structure

8. Cultural background knowledge

B. Beginning level: help students learn to

1. Follow classroom instructions

2. Understand measured, clear speech

3. Comprehend aurally material learned visually from the textbook

4. Comprehend simple information questions (*wh-* questions, yes/no questions)

5. Use vocabulary for understanding
   - classroom language
   - social pleasantries
   - discussion of themselves and daily routine

6. Hear (notice) and understand basic grammar structures (e.g., past tense endings, plural endings)

7. Use knowledge of common cultural patterns to understand and deal with common social interactions (e.g., classroom activities, greetings, leave-takings)

C. Intermediate level: help students learn to

1. Understand clear speech at normal speeds in face-to-face communication

2. Aurally comprehend material learned first visually from textbooks

3. Develop skills for clarifying in conversation when they don't understand

4. Use vocabulary for understanding
   - daily social interactions (e.g., shopping, transport)
   - questions about themselves

- discussion of their own culture and the target culture
- discussion of their profession and personal interests

5. Hear (notice) and understand basic grammar structures

6. Use context clues to guess (top-down strategies), particularly when listening to more difficult language

7. Use knowledge of common cultural patterns to understand and deal with a wide range of social interactions

D. Advanced level: help students learn to

1. Understand native speech at normal speeds

2. Understand nonstandard speech (e.g., accents, unclear pronunciation, reduced forms)

3. Understand discussion not directed to themselves (e.g., overheard conversation)

4. Understand radio programs, TV, and films in English

5. Understand and take notes on lectures

6. Use vocabulary for comprehension of a broad range of topics, including current events and their own profession

7. Develop cultural background knowledge assumed by media news (e.g., place names, names of famous people, historical knowledge)

8. Understand nuances and implied meanings in conversation (e.g., sarcasm, hints)

9. Understand cultural patterns—hence expectations—for common types of discourse (e.g., lectures, stories, news programs, various film and TV genres)

10. Find enjoyable opportunities to listen in English (e.g., radio programs, TV, films)

IV. Reading Goals

A. General (all levels): help students improve in

1. Intensive reading, that is, carefully extracting maximum meaning from a text

2. Extensive reading, that is, quickly getting the gist of a text

3. Skill in using top-down strategies to increase depth of comprehension, including implied meanings, bias, and tone

4. Translation (English to host language or vice versa)

5. Vocabulary (receptive)

6. Grammar comprehension

7. Reading speed

8. Ability to guess vocabulary from context

9. Ability to guess around unfamiliar vocabulary (so they can continue reading without stopping to look words up in a dictionary)

10. Knowledge of cultural background information

B.   Beginning level: help students learn to

1.   Recognize letters of the alphabet

2.   Recognize spelling-sound correspondences

3.   Read short, simplified texts (often from a textbook) slowly (using bottom-up strategies)

4.   Make preliminary guesses as to what a text may be about (using top-down strategies)

5.   Recognize and use vocabulary as found in the textbook

6.   Comprehend and use grammar for reading classroom materials and other simple texts

7.   Use a dictionary

C.   Intermediate level: help students learn to

1.   Read relatively simple material quickly while still understanding and retaining main ideas

2.   Slowly decode more difficult texts

3.   Start building a large receptive reading vocabulary

4.   Attend to vocabulary use (e.g., level of formality, connotation, grammar) when reading intensively

5.   Decode grammatically complex sentences

6.   Predict and guess using knowledge of the world and knowledge of discourse structures (using top-down strategies)

7.   Skim

8.   Effectively use dictionaries

9.   Guess around unfamiliar vocabulary using context clues

10. Develop basic knowledge of Western literary culture (e.g., myths, Bible stories, other well-known stories)

11. Develop basic factual knowledge about Western history, society, and culture

12. Find and read Web sites

D.   Advanced level: help students learn to

1.   Read a broad range of material (e.g., magazines, novels, general interest books, books related to their profession) with little or no dictionary use

2.   Read relatively unimportant or easy material quickly, skimming where desirable

3.   Extract main ideas, flow of thought, and logical organization from a text

4.   Build a large receptive vocabulary

5.   Attend to vocabulary use when reading intensively

6.   Decode grammatically complex sentences

7.   Read actively—predicting before and while reading, guessing from context, and skimming over unimportant material

8.   Understand Western literary culture

9.   Understand Western history, society, and culture

10. Research topics using library resources and the Internet

11. Enjoy and develop the habit of reading material in which they are interested

V. Writing Goals

A. General (all levels): help students improve in

    1. Ability to communicate in writing

    2. Range of vocabulary

    3. Accurate usage of vocabulary

    4. Grammatical accuracy

    5. Translation (English to host language or vice versa)

    6. Ability to edit and revise

    7. Ability to write quickly

    8. Knowledge of proper forms for written communication

    9. Knowledge of cultural knowledge, beliefs, and assumptions of Western audiences

B. Beginning level: help students learn to

    1. Write down spoken language—dialogues, messages, personal letters, lists (material that requires little formal organization)

    2. Do dictation exercises

    3. Use proper conventions of writing (capitalization, spelling, punctuation)

    4. Fill in forms

    5. Develop adequate vocabulary for writing about themselves and their immediate environment

    6. Check word usage and spelling in a dictionary

    7. Understand and use basic grammar

C. Intermediate level: help students learn to

    1. Use proper forms for letters—personal and business

    2. Write journal entries

    3. Write personal narratives

    4. Write creatively

    5. Organize expository paragraphs and short compositions

    6. Take notes

    7. Use vocabulary for above

    8. Check word usage, spelling in a dictionary

    9. Accurately use most common grammar structures

    10. Proofread for errors

11. Revise compositions to improve organization and general effectiveness of communication

12. Write with sufficient speed and fluency to produce multiparagraph texts in a relatively short time

13. Use word-processing programs and tools for writing and revising

D. Advanced level: help students learn to

1. Use expository writing skills for academic and business purposes

2. Write for professional purposes

3. Write narratives

4. Write creatively

5. Write longer (multipage) compositions

6. Develop and use vocabulary for the above

7. Organize texts clearly, develop points effectively, write in ways that are coherent

8. Find and correct most grammar errors

9. Adjust explanation or persuasion to take into account knowledge and beliefs of target audience (Western or other)

10. Find opportunities to practice writing in English outside class (e.g., correspondence with friends by mail or Internet chat rooms, writing for publication)

Culture-Topic Activity Ideas for Oral Skills Classes

This appendix consists of culture-based activities[1] that can be used by volunteer teachers (VTs) for teaching oral skills courses or culture courses. Use of such topics can be a valuable addition to your courses for several reasons. First, cultural differences between you and your students provide a natural information gap that can drive genuinely communicative language use as you teach students about your culture and students teach you about theirs. Second, the cultural information that you and the students can learn from each other by talking about such topics is useful in and of itself. Third, one of main things that students need to be able to do in English is explain their culture to people from other cultures, and discussion of culture-related topics allows them to practice explaining their culture in English.

---

[1] These activities were originally written for teachers working in China through the Amity Foundation's Teachers Project. For the original, China-specific (and sometimes more detailed) versions of the activities, see the Teaching Resources section of the Amity Foundation's English language Web site (http://www.amityfoundation.org/).While the activities here are geared toward oral skills courses, they can also be adapted for use as writing assignments or for other language skill areas.

There is, however, another reason that structuring a conversation or culture course in an organized way around a set of culture-related topics will benefit students. We often think about improvement in speaking skills as a question of fluency but forget that fluency is determined by topic as much as it is by a student's general skill level in oral English; students can normally discuss some topics much more fluently than they can others. Improvement in oral skills is thus in large part an issue of how broad a range of topics students can talk about fluently in English. You might think of such improvement as a widening circle in which students first become comfortable talking about themselves and their immediate environment, then learn to talk about life issues with which they and those around them have direct experience, and finally learn to talk about broader, more abstract social issues that may be farther removed from their daily experience. The topics covered by activities in this appendix are organized so that you can help students expand the range of culture-related topics they have experience talking about.

Using This Appendix

The activity ideas in this appendix are organized into modules corresponding to broad areas of culture. In turn, each module is divided into units organized around more specific topics. Finally, each unit consists of specific in-class activity ideas. Within each unit, the first three activities are presented in some detail, including suggested goals, detailed procedure notes, and suggested language points the activity might be used to teach or rehearse. The remaining activities in each unit are presented only as bare-bones ideas that you will need to flesh out by setting goals and planning specific steps.

While the activities in each unit do not need to be used in the order listed, I have tried to sequence the first three activities in a logical progression.

All units contain activities of varying levels of difficulty, but on the whole, the earlier modules (Daily Life, The Cycle of Life, and Relationships) are somewhat closer to students' daily lives and therefore somewhat easier to handle conceptually. I assume that you will modify activities as necessary so that they are appropriate to your students' skills levels.

This appendix can be used as a grab bag to provide supplementary material for your courses. However, the modules can also serve as the core outline for all or part of a course. If you choose the latter option, you can give the course more coherence and validity in students' eyes by providing students with a syllabus or course plan that lets them know in advance the range of topics they will practice talking about. Without such a syllabus or plan, the course may seem like a random series of disconnected activities; with such a plan, students can more clearly see that they are developing skills in discussing a defined and coherent slice of culture and human life.

GOALS

All of the activities in this appendix have three general underlying goals:

1. build students' speaking and listening skills in general

2. build students' ability to talk about and understand conversation about the topic areas covered

3. enhance students' knowledge about the target culture and the teacher's knowledge of the host culture

You will probably want to set more specific goals for each activity, for example, building vocabulary related to a certain topic, practicing sentence patterns used for giving advice, and so on.

Students should be told the specific goals of activities and be frequently reminded of the general underlying goals. (For activities that are described in detail, I suggest one or more specific goals under *specific goal ideas*.)

ACTIVITY TYPES

For each topic-based activity, I suggest one or more specific activity types (e.g., survey, dictocomp) you can use to turn culture topics into activities that are useful in a foreign language class. These activity types are all discussed in more detail in chapters 7 and 8, so you may review what those chapters have to say about each. For many topics, activity types other than those suggested here might work just as well. For example, pair and small-group tasks may also work as debates, and vice versa. Survey, interview, and cocktail-party activity types are often interchangeable, and talks can often be redesigned as press conferences, focused listening, or even dictocomp or dictation activities.

In suggesting a format for each activity, I have tried to consider where the main information gap lies. Where there may be a significant information gap between students as well as between student and teacher, I have suggested activities that emphasize discussion between students; where the main gap would seem to be between students and teacher, I have suggested activities that highlight conversation between students and teacher.

In the activities, I use the term *target culture/country* to refer to the culture or country you are teaching students about. In many cases, this will be your own culture or country. However, VTs from large English-speaking countries like the United States and United Kingdom may at times wish to teach about other cultures and countries in order to remind students that the English-speaking world is not confined to those two nations. Likewise, VTs who are not from the United States or United Kingdom may need to teach, at least some of the time, about these two large English-speaking nations and cultures.

A word of caution: Some of the topics below may be quite sensitive in some host cultures, so be sure to check with local colleagues before embarking on an activity that you think might be overly sensitive.

Module 1: Daily Life

GETTING TO KNOW YOU

Getting to Know Me (Press Conference, Chapter 8)

Specific goal ideas: Allow students to get to know you a little; find out how well students work in groups and how willing they are to speak in class; have students practice actively asking questions as a strategy for learning about another culture; have students practice *wh-* questions (*who, what, where, when, how, why*).

1. Tell the students you want to introduce yourself to them but would like to respond to questions rather than just talking.

2. Divide students into groups of three or four, and have each group list questions they want to ask you—ones they are really interested in. As students list questions, help them with proper question form; also put sample question structures on the board as necessary.

3. Conduct the interview following the procedure in Press Conferences (chapter 8).

4. Closure suggestion: Check comprehension by asking students what your answers to their questions were.

Getting to Know Each Other (Interview, Chapter 8)

Specific goal ideas: Help students get to know each other better; have students practice asking and answering questions; have students practice *wh-* questions.

1. Tell the students you want them to interview a classmate they don't know well and find out one or more interesting things about that person. Also tell them they should practice using correct question forms.

2. Have the students choose and interview a partner—in English.

3. Closure suggestion: Have each student briefly report an interesting fact they learned about the person they interviewed.

This activity could also be conducted in cocktail-party format.

Advice on Learning the Local Language (Pair or Small-Group Task, Chapter 8)

Specific goal ideas: Learn about the students' ideas on language learning; have students practice giving advice (*You should . . .* , *Always . . .* , *Never . . .*); teach vocabulary related to language study.

1. Tell the students that you would like to learn some of the local language while in their country and that you want their advice.

2. Ask groups of students to list five important pieces of advice for you on how to learn their language. Tips should be as specific as possible. For example, *Practice listening* is not as helpful as *You should listen to tapes every night before you go to bed.* (Have groups that finish early prioritize their lists, deciding which tip is most important.)

3. Have each group report one piece of advice; then allow everyone to chime in with other tips. Write these on the board as they are reported, using the proper form for advice. Then have the students discuss which tip is most important and why.

4. Closure suggestion: Have the students teach you a few words or phrases in their language.

Other Activity Ideas

*   Pictures (show and tell): Bring some pictures of your life to class, and talk a little about them.

*   Life Story (interview): Have the students interview a partner about his or her life story. Closure suggestion: Ask a few students what the most interesting thing they discovered about their partner was.

*   Childhood Memories (survey): Have the students survey several classmates about some of their earliest childhood memories.

*   My Life (press conference): Tell the students they are newspaper reporters who need to interview you about your life in order to write a story for the local newspaper; then have them prepare questions and interview you. (If some questions are too personal, tell the students before the interview.)

*   Special Memories (cocktail party): Ask the students to think of the most exciting (or dangerous, or wonderful) thing that ever happened to them. Then have everyone get up,

find a partner, and ask about his or her story. Closure suggestion: Ask a few volunteers to report on a good story they heard.

DAILY SCHEDULES

My Ideal Schedule (Survey, Chapter 8)

Specific goal ideas: Warm up; have students practice asking and answering hypothetical questions (e.g., *What would your ideal schedule be? I would . . .*); teach schedule-related phrases (e.g., *I would get up at 9:00.*).

1. Have the students quickly consider what their own ideal schedule would be, for example, when they would get up or go to bed.

2. Have the students survey each other about what their ideal schedule would be.

3. Closure suggestion: Have several students report the most interesting ideal schedule they heard.

Typical Target Culture Daily Schedules (Dictocomp, Chapter 7)

Specific goal ideas: Teach terms for making generalizations (e.g., *usually, in general, generally*); teach terms for making approximations (e.g., *around, approximately*).

1. Write out a passage in which you describe a typical daily schedule for people in the target culture. (You may need to be specific about what kind of people you are talking about.) Include terms and sentence patterns for making generalizations and approximations.

2. Present the passage to students using the dictocomp procedure.

3. Review language points you want to call attention to by asking students to tell you about typical schedules in their culture.

4. Closure suggestion: Ask the students to point out differences between typical schedules in their culture and the target culture.

Late and Early (Pair or Small-Group Task, Chapter 8)

Specific goal ideas: Have students practice specifying situations (e.g., *for a date, for business meetings*); have students practice explaining rules for being on time (e.g., *You should never be more than . . . late or more than . . . early.*).

1. Explain that one of the main differences between cultures lies in the rules for what is considered too late and too early. (In virtually all cultures, it is acceptable to arrive at an appointment either before or after the exact time specified—the question is how much flexibility is allowed in each direction.)

2. Ask the students to prepare to tell you the rules for being on time in their culture. For each of the following engagements, have them tell you how early is too early and how late is too late: a business appointment, a dinner, a date, others.

3. Closure suggestion: Based on what students tell you, comment on any differences between their culture and yours in the rules for being early and late.

Other Activity Ideas

- Early to Bed and Early to Rise (pair or small-group task): Introduce the saying *Early to bed and early to rise makes a man healthy, wealthy, and wise.* (Or introduce the saying *Time is money.*) Then have the students decide whether they think this is true or not and be ready to explain why they think so.

- What's Nice about Our Schedule? (pair or small-group task): Have the students list three good things about the average schedule in their culture (or in the target culture) and three things that are not so ideal.

- Should Students Have Class on Saturday? (debate): Have the students debate the merits of requiring students to have classes on Saturdays.

- What Is Their Day Like? (classroom chat): Ask the students to describe the normal daily schedule for people of different professions—workers, farmers, students, officials, teachers, and so forth.

- When Do You Eat? (classroom chat): Ask the students what a normal schedule is for eating meals in their country (when, what, and how much).

- When Do You Sleep? (classroom chat): Ask the students what the normal pattern is for sleeping in their culture.

- Do I Always Have to Be on Time? (pair or small-group task): Ask the students to list situations in their culture in which it is acceptable—or even polite—to be late.

- When Is the Best Time to Study? (survey): Have the students survey several classmates on the best time of day for studying.

FOOD

Typical Western Meal Contest (Pair or Small-Group Task, Chapter 8)

Specific goal ideas: Have students practice making generalizations; have students practice use of the plural form for countable nouns when discussing things in general (e.g., *eggs, potatoes*); teach food-related vocabulary.

1. Have the students list what foods they guess a typical breakfast (lunch, or dinner) would consist of in the target country. Foods should be listed so they fit grammatically into *Forians[2] eat . . . for breakfast.*

2. Have each group write its list on the form, being careful to use proper grammatical form.

3. Go over the lists, providing a reality check and correcting any problems.

4. Closure suggestion: Lead a round of applause for the group(s) whose guesses were closest.

---

[2] I use *Foria* as my generic term for the target nation/culture and *Forians* for the people and language.

Restaurant (Activity)

Specific goal ideas: Have students practice ordering meals; teach vocabulary for types of Western restaurants and names of foods; teach phrases for ordering meals (e.g., *I'll have . . . ; Do you have any . . . ?*).

1. On the board, list typical types of restaurants found in the target culture (e.g., steakhouses, hamburger joints, Chinese restaurants) and common phrases used for ordering meals. Introduce these to the students as necessary.

2. Have groups of students choose a type of restaurant and—as best they can—create an English language menu appropriate to that type of restaurant. As students work on this, go from group to group and assist as necessary.

3. Choose half of the groups to display their menu and open their restaurant. Give fake money to the other students, and set them loose to read the menus, choose a restaurant, and order a fine meal using the phrases listed on the board.

4. Have everyone switch roles and repeat.

5. Closure suggestion: Review newly introduced words and phrases. Then have the students vote on which was the best menu or restaurant.

Banquet Etiquette (Pair or Small-Group Task, Chapter 8)

Specific goal ideas: Have students practice stating possibilities (e.g., *Maybe . . . ; Perhaps . . . ; You might . . .*); have students practice explaining etiquette and customs; teach vocabulary related to dining.

1. Tell the students you want to know how to behave properly if invited to a banquet in their country.

2. Have the students list problems you may encounter as a foreigner and tips on what you should and shouldn't do.

3. As each potential problem is reported, follow up with questions to make sure you understand what the problem is. Then, when a solution is suggested, check with other students to see if they agree with the tip.

4. Closure suggestion: Thank the students for their advice, and comment on especially valuable tips.

Other Activity Ideas

- Food Contest (pair or small-group task): Have the students list as many fruits (or meats, vegetables, or other foods) in English as possible within three to five minutes. The words must fit grammatically into the blank in *I love to eat . . .* , and students should be able to pronounce the words correctly. When you call time, have each group count up their list, and see which group has the most. Then have that group read the list as you write on the board. If the students make any mistakes (e.g., in grammar or pronunciation), they lose their chance, and you move to the group with the next largest number.

- What Do You Eat? (classroom chat): Ask the students what they normally eat for breakfast, lunch, or supper.

- My Favorite Eats (show and tell): Bring in pictures of a few of your favorite foods, and describe how to make them.

- A Memorable Meal (talk, dictocomp): Tell a story about a memorable meal you had in your host country or at home.

- What Is Your Favorite Food? (survey): Have the students survey each other on their most (or least) favorite foods.

- What Foreign Foods Have You Had? (survey): Have the students survey several classmates on what, if any, foreign foods they have had and what they think of them.

- What Would You Feed a Foreigner? (pair or small-group task): Have the students decide what (local) dishes they would prepare if they were going to prepare a banquet for a foreign guest. If necessary, they should be prepared to explain to you what these dishes are.

- If Yan Can Cook . . . ! (pair or small-group task): Have the students describe to you step-by-step how to make some wonderful local dish. As each group reports, allow other groups to comment (and critique).

- A Food for Every Season (pair or small-group task): Have the students list advice regarding what should or should not be eaten in the winter (or summer).

- Fast Food (survey): Have the students survey each other on this question: What do you think of the spread of Western fast food?

- Health Foods (pair or small-group task): Have the students list five especially nutritious (local) foods and what they are good for.

- Local Delicacies (pair or small-group task): Have the students list the most famous dishes of their region and be ready to explain what makes them special.

- You Want Me to Eat That? (pair or small-group task): Have the students teach you several culturally appropriate strategies for how to politely avoid eating something you don't want to eat at a banquet or dinner.

- The Dinner No-No (pair or small-group task): Have the students list five things they would tell a foreign visitor never to do at a meal in their culture and be ready to explain why.

- Toasting 101 (pair or small-group task): Have the students prepare to explain to a foreigner the local rules for toasting.

- Can I Say No? (pair or small-group task): Have the students list and describe the circumstances (e.g., who? what situation?) under which it is hard to refuse to drink.

- Should There Be a Drinking Age? (debate): Have the students debate whether there should be a set drinking age below which it is illegal to buy or drink alcoholic beverages.

CLOTHING

What Do You Like? (Survey, Chapter 8)

Specific goal ideas: Have students practice explaining preferences; have students practice describing clothing; teach clothing-related vocabulary—styles, materials, clothing items, colors, and patterns.

1. Have the students interview several classmates, asking them what they like most in current local fashion and why (e.g., *I love leather jackets because . . .*) and what they hate most and why (e.g., *I hate pink shoes because . . .*).

2. Have the students report an opinion on fashion they heard that they especially agreed with. They need to clearly explain what fashion trend they are talking about, what the opinion about it was, and why they agree with that opinion.

3. Closure suggestion: Share some of your own apparel preferences. Also review any new vocabulary that came up.

Fashion Show (Pair or Small-Group Task, Chapter 8)

Specific goal ideas: Have students practice describing clothing; have students practice making flattering comments about clothing (and have some fun in the process); teach clothing-related vocabulary describing styles, materials, clothing items, colors, and patterns; teach complimentary adjectives related to clothing (e.g., *stylish, gorgeous, chic, glamorous*).

1. Pair students and have them decide who will be the model and who the announcer. Then have them prepare a fashion-show-style presentation in which the announcer describes—in flattering terms—what the model is wearing while the model calls attention to whatever is being announced. Ideally, students should actually stand up and rehearse a bit before the show.

2. Have the fashion show. (Music, applause, gasps of admiration, and so forth would add to the atmosphere.)

3. Closure suggestion: Give awards for the best models and announcers, decided by the class as a whole, a panel of judges, or you.

What Should I Wear (or Not Wear)? (Pair or Small-Group Task, Chapter 8)

Specific goal ideas: Have students practice giving advice on how to dress; teach phrases for giving advice (e.g., *You should . . . ; Never . . .*); have students practice specifying situations (e.g., *for a date*); teach clothing-related vocabulary.

1. Tell the students you are newly arrived in their country, and this coming week you have a busy schedule of events to attend, including a formal banquet, a job interview, a class you will teach, a walk in the park with a local friend, and a visit to the house of an official for dinner. For each event, you want to dress as appropriately as possible according to local custom, and you don't want to seem too foreign, so you want their advice on how to dress properly for each event.

2. Have the students list tips on how you should dress for each of the occasions listed above (or others you choose). Tips should be quite specific, and each should be stated as a piece of advice (e.g., *For a job interview, you shouldn't wear tennis shoes.*). Students should also be prepared to explain why dressing in a certain way is more or less appropriate.

3. Have the students report one situation at a time, and have several groups offer their advice on how to dress for each occasion. Discuss as appropriate.

4. Closure suggestion: Talk with students about how similar or different dress would be in the target culture for the occasions in question.

Other Activity Ideas

- What's New in Local Fashion? (classroom chat): Ask the students about the latest trends in local fashion—what's in and out. (Alternative: Ask how fashion has changed over the past ten years.)

- Changes in Fashion (talk or dictocomp): Give a short talk for students about changes in Western fashion during the past few decades, especially changes you have seen within your lifetime. As closure, have the students tell you about changes in local fashions over the past several decades.

- Dressing for Winter (pair or small-group task): Tell the students that you have heard it is very cold in their country in the winter (or hot in the summer), and you are worried about how to dress so that you will be as comfortable as possible. Of course, you have some idea about how to dress, but they probably know some things you don't know, so you would appreciate their advice. Then have pairs or groups of students list suggestions for you, stating each suggestion as a bit of advice (e.g., *Be sure to wear a hat when you sleep at night*). Tip: If necessary, first introduce vocabulary and sentence patterns for giving advice.

- What Should a . . . Wear? (pair or small-group task): Have pairs or groups of students describe the proper dress for different kinds of people (e.g., teachers, business people, officials).

- Can You Judge a Book by Its Cover? (classroom chat): Tell the students that in your own country, you can sometimes guess a lot about people from the way they dress. Ask the students to give you some tips on how to make guesses about the backgrounds (e.g., profession, social class, region, income level) of people in their country by the way they dress.

HOMES, BUILDINGS, AND SPACE

My Dream House (Interview, Chapter 8)

Specific goal ideas: Have students practice describing dwelling layouts; have students practice describing space relations (e.g., *in front of, to the left, in the rear*); teach house or apartment-related vocabulary (e.g., *living room, bedroom, kitchen*).

1. Have the students interview each other in pairs, asking *If you could build your dream house (apartment), what would the layout be like?* Students can draw pictures of the layout but also need to practice describing the layout in English. As students talk, wander and assist with vocabulary, putting new words on the board.

2. Before having students report, go over any new words on the board.

3. Have one or more students describe the layout of their partner's dream house as you draw the layout on the board, following their description. Ask why students would lay the house out as they did.

4. Closure suggestion: Lead into Blueprint.

Blueprint (Pair or Small-Group Task, Chapter 8)

Specific goal ideas: Have students practice describing dwelling layouts; have students practice describing space relations (e.g., *in front of, to the left, in the rear*); teach house and apartment-related vocabulary (e.g., *living room, bedroom, kitchen*).

1. Have the students prepare in pairs or groups to describe to you the most typical layout of a house or apartment in their country.

2. When the students are ready, ask one group what the general outline of the apartment (exterior walls) would be like and then where the kitchen would be. As they describe, draw the blueprint on the board. Then ask a different group to tell you where the next room is, and so on. (Going from group to group like this will almost certainly generate good-natured confusion—no two groups will have drawn exactly the same layout. This will force them to practice clarifying instructions and repairing miscommunications.)

3. Closure suggestion: Give a prize to the group that gave you the clearest instructions.

Buying a House (Talk, Chapter 7; Dictocomp, Chapter 7)

Specific goal ideas: Have students practice focused listening and note-taking; teach vocabulary and phrases related to home purchasing and financing (e.g., *realtor, classified ads, mortgage*).

1. Prepare a talk in which you describe—step by step—the typical process of finding and buying a new dwelling in the target country. Include issues such as how to find available homes, what factors to consider, how to choose, and how to finance.

2. Before giving the talk, list the number of steps on the board (and, if necessary, some clues as to what each step might be), and tell the students they will need to be able to report the steps back to you. Then give the talk.

3. Closure suggestion: Have the students repeat the steps back to you. Also ask what in your talk was new to them. (Alternative: Lead into Moving House.)

Other Activity Ideas

- Moving House (pair or small-group task): Have the students prepare to describe to you, step by step, how they would go about finding and getting a new place to live in their country. (Tip: Rather than having each group describe the whole process, ask each group what the first step would be, establish a consensus, and write it on the board. Then move to the second step, and so on.)

- My Office (survey): Have the students survey each other on the following question: *If you had your own office and could arrange it any way you wanted to, how would you arrange the furniture, and why?* (Variation: Have the students ask how they would arrange a living room, bedroom, or kitchen.)

- A Typical Apartment (talk): Describe a typical apartment in the target country. (Caution: If housing in the target country is much nicer than the host country, try to be sensitive. It may be better to describe a modest apartment than an individual house.)

- Housing Options (talk): Give a talk describing different housing options in the target country (e.g., apartments, condos, homes) and the relative advantages and disadvantages of each.

- Receiving Guests (classroom chat): For receiving guests in a living room (meeting room, etc.), ask the students what the best way to arrange chairs is.

HEALTH AND HYGIENE

Health Proverbs (Pair or Small-Group Task, Chapter 8)

Specific goal ideas: Have students practice translating; teach proverbs; teach health-related vocabulary.

1. Write several proverbs and sayings about health on the board (e.g., *an apple a day keeps the doctor away; an ounce of prevention is better than a pound of cure; early to bed, early to rise makes one healthy, wealthy, and wise.*)

2. Have the students guess at the proverb's meaning and say whether they agree with the wisdom contained in the proverb or not.

3. Have the students in pairs or groups think of similar health sayings in their language and translate them into English.

4. Have the groups report. Different groups will probably have translated the same sayings, so you can compare the translations.

5. Closure suggestion: Choose the translation that seems closest to idiomatic English.

Health in My Country (Dictocomp, Chapter 7)

Specific goal ideas: Have students practice listening and note-taking; have students practice using grammar knowledge to reconstruct the passage; teach vocabulary related to health.

1. Prepare a talk about one or more of the health topics (fads) that are prominent in the target country (e.g., weight and dieting; aerobic exercise, cholesterol, vegetarianism; health food, vitamins, and other diet supplements).

2. Preteach any necessary vocabulary.

3. Give the talk following the procedure for a dictocomp exercise.

4. Closure suggestion: Review new vocabulary with students.

Eating for Health (Pair or Small-Group Task, Chapter 8)

Specific goal ideas: Have students practice giving and explaining advice; have students practice considering what might or might not need to be explained to a foreigner.

1. Have the students list five bits of advice for a foreigner on what to (or not to) eat and drink in order to develop and maintain good health in their country. In particular, they should try to think of tips that a foreigner might not already know and might benefit from knowing.

2. As each tip is reported, give feedback on whether foreigners might already know what is suggested and whether they would be able to understand the tip.

3. Closure suggestion: Give special praise to tips that would be genuinely useful to a foreigner and are stated clearly enough to be readily understandable.

Other Activity Ideas

- A Healthy Diet (talk, dictocomp): Give a short talk about what Westerners think makes up a healthy diet, in other words, what people should and should not eat. Allow time for questions. Closure suggestion: Have the students tell you which points in your talk most people in their country would agree with and which many might disagree with.

- Cold Remedies (pair or small-group task): Have the students list what you should eat and drink if you have a cold. Closure suggestion: Tell the students about some of the folk remedies used in the target country.

- Living a Long Life (pair or small-group task): Have the students list the five most important things people can do to ensure that they remain healthy and live a long life.

- A Healthy Menu (pair or small-group task): Have the students design a healthy, week-long meal plan for you, using food available in the town you are living in. (Alternatively, have them design an exercise plan.)

- Teach Your Children (pair or small-group task): Have the students list—in order of importance—the five most important things parents should teach children about hygiene.

- Night or Morn? (debate): Is it better to bathe (shower) in the morning or evening?

WORK

Occupations (Game)

Specific goal ideas: Teach vocabulary for names of occupations; practice pronunciation for names of occupations; teach that in English the norm is to use the same parts of speech for all items in a list.

1. In small groups, give students exactly three minutes to list the names of all the occupations they can think of in English (e.g., *driver, farmer, teacher*). All occupations must be stated in as the same part of speech.

2. Call time, and ask each group to count the occupations on their list.

3. Have the group with the longest list read it out as you write it on the board. If they make a mistake, move on to the next group.

4. Closure suggestion: Read over the list with the class for pronunciation.

Part-Time Jobs (Game)

Specific goal ideas: Teach about tendency to create names of occupations by turning verb phrases (e.g., *paint houses, flip burgers*) into occupation names (e.g., *house painter, burger flipper*).

1. Tell the students how many part-time (summer, regular, etc.) jobs you have had, and then ask them in groups to guess what those jobs might have been. Each guess must be stated as a noun. (This exercise assumes you have had part-time jobs such as *lawn mower* or *dish washer*. If not, modify the task, e.g., by asking students to guess a list of common part-time jobs.)

2. Have each group present one guess at a time. If they guess one of the jobs on your list, they get a point. The group with the most points at the end wins.

3. If students do not guess some of the jobs, allow them to ask questions for clues until they do guess.

4. Closure suggestion: Talk about some of the more unusual part-time jobs you have had (or have heard about).

The Best and Worst Occupations (Pair or Small-Group Task, Chapter 8)

Specific goal ideas: Have students practice explaining advantages and disadvantages; teach vocabulary—especially adjectives—related to the virtues and disadvantages of different occupations (e.g., *rewarding, lucrative, boring, dangerous*).

1. Have the students list—in order—the three best occupations and the three worst in their country, and be ready to explain why these occupations are good or bad. (The definition of *best* and *worst* is intentionally left vague here—students will need to decide what criteria they use to decide whether a job is good or bad.)

2. For student reports, have different groups each nominate their choice for best and worst, and explain their reasons. This can open into discussion or debate.

3. As students report, note appropriate adjectives on the board.

4. Closure suggestion: Tell the students what you think the best and worst occupations are in the target country and why. Also review any new vocabulary.

Other Activity Ideas

- What Is Most Important in a Job? (survey): First have the class as a whole list the rewards a job can have (e.g., status, salary, satisfaction, challenge, opportunity to learn). Then have the students survey several other classmates by asking: What is most important in a job? (Alternative: Have the students try to reach consensus in small groups on which rewards are most important and on a prioritized list.)

- My Working Life (talk, dictocomp): Give a talk about different jobs you have had in your life, including part-time jobs you had during adolescence.

- Part-Time Jobs for Students? (debate): Should students be allowed to take part-time jobs?

- And What Do You Do? (cocktail party): Using fictional identities and professions, have the students meet, greet, and interview each other about their work.

- Starting a Business (survey): If you were going to start a business, what kind would it be?

- How Do You Like Your Job? (interview, survey): Have the students survey or interview each other on their feelings about present or future jobs.

- How Do You Find a Job? (classroom chat): Ask the students how they go about finding jobs after graduation.

- Finding a Job (pair or small-group task): Have the students describe the steps in finding and getting hired in a new job. (Alternative: Have the students decide on the three best ways to get a job.)

- When They Grow up . . . (survey): What are the top three jobs you would want your child to have?

- To Be in Business? (pair or small-group task): Have the students list the advantages (or disadvantages) of business as a career.

- To Start a Business (pair or small-group task): Have the students discuss how one goes about starting a business.

- Big Firm or Small? (pair or small-group task): Have the students discuss the relative advantages of working in a big versus a small company.

- Getting Ahead (pair or small-group task): As a series of tips, have the students list the rules for success in business.

- Back to Nature? (pair or small-group task): Have the students list the advantages and disadvantages of life as a farmer.

RECREATION AND ENTERTAINMENT

What Do You Do for Fun? (Survey, Chapter 8)

Specific goal ideas: Have students practice asking and answering questions about likes and dislikes; have students practice stating activities as gerunds (e.g., *hiking, swimming, listening to music*).

1. Ask a few students what they like to do when they have free time. Put answers on the board as infinitives (*I like to sleep*), gerunds (*I like sleeping*), or both.

2. Have the students survey each other on what they normally like to do if and when they have free time.

3. Have the students report some of the more interesting answers they heard from class-mates. Make sure the answers are correctly formed.

4. Closure suggestion: Encourage students to ask you about what you like to do.

Entertainment (Talk, Chapter 7)

Specific goal ideas: Have students practice listening and note-taking; teach vocabulary related to the form of entertainment you chose to talk about.

1. Prepare a short talk on one of your favorite forms of entertainment and the reasons you like it. (Alternative: Give a talk on popular forms of entertainment in the target culture.) Also list vocabulary you will need to teach before the talk.

2. Teach the new vocabulary items, then give students a chance to hear the new words in sentences.

3. Give the talk, and have the students take notes.

4. Check comprehension using one of the approaches in Talks and Lectures (chapter 7).

5. Closure suggestion: Review the new vocabulary.

A Hobby for the Teacher (Pair or Small-Group Task, Chapter 8)

Specific goal ideas: Have students practice explaining and justifying opinions; teach vocabulary for names of hobbies; teach vocabulary for describing virtues of hobbies (e.g., *healthy, educational*).

1. Tell the students you would like to learn a typical local hobby or pastime but don't know what to chose.

2. Have the students decide which hobby or pastime to recommend to you and why it would be good for you.

3. Closure suggestion: Tell the students which of the hobbies they recommended sounds most appealing to you and why.

Other Activity Ideas

• My Hobby (show and tell or press conference): Take something to class that is related to a hobby of yours, and chat a little about your hobby. Then tell the students they have been asked to write an article about your hobby for the local newspaper, and have them prepare questions and interview you. Close by asking a few students whether your hobby sounds interesting to them or not, and why.

• How to . . . (talk): Teach students how to do some aspect of one of your hobbies.

• Hobbies Galore! (pair or small-group task): Have the students list as many hobbies as they can think of in three to five minutes.

• The Strangest Hobby (pair or small-group task): Have the students decide which hobbies are the three best (most fun, most useful, strangest, or most dangerous).

• The Most Popular Hobby (survey): Have the students survey their classmates to find out which is the most popular hobby (or travel location, etc.) and why.

• Enough Holidays? (pair or small-group task): Have the students decide how many holidays (i.e., days off from work) a country should ideally have each year, and be ready to explain their decision. (Alternative: Have the students decide whether their country needs more or fewer holidays.)

- Fun Galore! (pair or small-group task): Have the students list (mainly using gerunds like *playing basketball* and *drinking tea*) the most popular leisure activities in their country.

- Party Types (pair or small-group task): Have the students list the most common kinds of parties (or social gatherings, or activities) in their country and be ready to describe what happens at each.

- Work or Play? (debate): Have the students debate this question: Is it better to work a lot and have more income, or work less and have more vacation?

- Top Tourist Attractions (pair or small-group task): Have the students list their county's top tourist attractions and the virtues of each.

- Weekend Fun (survey): Have the students survey each other on the best way to spend a weekend.

- Pets? (survey): Have the students ask whether keeping pets is a good hobby.

- Gardening for Fun? (survey): Have the students survey each other on whether they think gardening sounds like an appealing hobby or not.

- Can a Green Thumb Be Taught? (pair or small-group task): Have the students list five rules for raising healthy plants.

SPORTS AND GAMES

What Is Your Favorite Sport? (Survey, Chapter 8)

Specific goal ideas: Have students practice explaining; teach vocabulary for names of sports.

1. Have each student interview several classmates, asking: What are your three favorite sports, and why are they your favorites?

2. Have the students call out the names of sports their informants mentioned; write these on the board.

3. After the sports are listed, ask the students to report why the informants said these were favorites.

4. Closure suggestion: Mention a few sports that are missing from the list, and ask the students about these.

A Foreign Sport (Talk, Chapter 7; Dictocomp, Chapter 7)

Specific goal ideas: Teach sports-related vocabulary, especially words and phrases that have come to be often used outside their original sports context (e.g., American baseball: *strike out, throw someone a curve*).

1. Prepare a talk introducing a sport that plays a major role in the life of the target country (e.g., baseball, [U.S.] football, rugby, cricket). Introduce both the sport itself and vocabulary and phrases from the sport that are widely used in society.

2. Have the students take notes as you give the talk, making special note of the new words.

3. Closure suggestion: Have the students try making sentences with the new words and phrases. Let students know whether they have used the new items correctly and appropriately.

Teaching a Local Sport (Pair or Small-Group Task, Chapter 8)

Specific goal ideas: Have students practice giving directions; teach vocabulary related to sports.

1. Have the students pick an interesting local game or sport—one that is not very familiar to foreigners—and draw up simple directions in English explaining how to play it.

2. Have the students explain their game or sport to you. (This is more fun if you try to walk through the motions as the group explains.)

3. Closure suggestion: Compare the local sports with similar ones in the target country, if there are any.

Other Activity Ideas

- Learning to Play a Sport (total physical response): Walk students through some of the basic aspects of a sport you want to teach, either in the classroom or outside. Bring to class the items needed for the sport, or some creative substitutes (e.g., a wad of scrunched-up paper generally serves well as a ball for indoor use).

- Monopoly (show and tell): Bring in Monopoly or some other typical game from the target country to show and explain to students.

- Popular Sports (pair or small-group task): Have the students list the five most popular sports in their country in order of popularity.

- If the Target Country Were a Sport . . . (pair or small-group task): Have the students decide what sport best symbolizes their country and be ready to explain why.

- Children's Games (pair or small-group task): Have the students list five popular children's games in their culture and be ready to teach you one.

- Party Games (classroom chat): Ask the students if adults in their culture play party games and, if so, what they are.

SHOPPING

Teaching the Teacher to Bargain (Pair or Small-Group Task, Chapter 8)

Specific goal ideas: Have students practice explaining strategies; have students practice describing steps in a process (e.g., *first, next, finally*); teach vocabulary related to bargaining (e.g., *offer, counteroffer*).

1. Tell the students you want them to teach you—a newcomer—an effective strategy for bargaining in a local market.

2. Have the students list the steps you should follow. Help the students by putting new vocabulary they need on the board.

3. Have groups report their strategies. As groups suggest strategies, do a market role play with a willing student, literally following the students' advice. (If your role-play partner has any gumption at all, the advice won't work as smoothly as promised—to everyone's amusement—which gives you an excuse to ask advice from the next group.)

4. Closure suggestion: Praise the best strategy, or offer one of your own.

How We Buy and Sell in My Country (Talk, Chapter 7; Focused Listening, Chapter 7)

Specific goal ideas: Have students practice listening and note-taking; teach vocabulary for kinds of stores.

1. Prepare a short talk about stores and shopping in the target country: what kinds of stores there are and what goods they sell. Also comment on issues such as what kinds of stores allow self-service, when bargaining is allowed, different ways you pay for goods, what kinds of stores allow returns, and so forth. Include new vocabulary items related to shopping. (Focus objectively on how the target culture deals with shopping rather than on how many goods are available in the target country; try to avoid creating the impression that your intent is to compare availability of goods in your home country unfavorably with availability in the host country.)

2. Give the talk and check comprehension following the procedure for Talks and Lectures (chapter 7).

3. Closure suggestion: Review new vocabulary.

Selling Bikes (Pair or Small-Group Task, Chapter 8)

Specific goal ideas: Have students practice persuasion; teach vocabulary related to products.

1. Have the students create and prepare to present a short advertisement in English—about one minute—for one brand of bicycle (computer, etc.). As new vocabulary emerges, put it on the board.

2. Have each group perform its ad for the class while one student keeps time. Threaten to charge for extra airtime if a group's ad goes over one minute.

3. Closure suggestion: Ask the class to vote on which ad was best. Also review new vocabulary.

Other Activity Ideas

- What Did It Cost? (game): Bring to class a few inexpensive items that you have purchased locally or at home. Try to find items for which students may not easily guess the price. In class, show students an item and allow them to ask a few yes/no questions to get clues. After you have answered several questions, make everyone announce a guess.

- Which Bike Is Best? (classroom chat): Ask the students which brand of bicycle (computer, motorcycle, etc.) they think is best and why. Encourage good-natured debate. List brand names on board as they are suggested, and close with practice pronouncing them.

- Language in Advertising (pair or small-group task): Tell the students that you have noticed that, even in their country, the packaging of many goods has English on it. Ask the students why this is so. Then tell the students that they work in the sales department of a packaging company, and they must decide which language to use on the packaging of many goods. Have the students list products under three categories: those which should only have the host language on them, those which should have mostly or all English, and those which should have about half and half. They should be ready to explain why.

- Buying and Selling in a Store (activity): Assign half of the students to be sellers and half to be customers. Set the sellers up as a certain type of store (e.g., shoe store, fast food restaurant) and show them normal procedure in that kind of store. Then turn the customers loose. Variation: Set up a shopping mall (with many kinds of stores).

- Buying and Selling in a Market (activity): Set up a market to practice bargaining, and assign some students to be sellers and some to be customers. Give each seller an object (or picture of something) to sell, and give each buyer a limited amount of fake money. See which sellers can earn the most for their products and which buyers can get the most for their money.

- Get Rich! (pair or small-group task): Have the students make a plan for getting rich in business. They should decide what would they sell, to whom, where, and so on.

- I Want My Money Back! (activity): Divide students into two groups: merchants and customers. Each customer needs an item, which he or she will try to return to the merchant for a refund, and should prepare to explain why he or she should be allowed to return the item; the merchant explains why not to give a refund. (Either have the students bring in items, or you prepare some items.) If time permits, switch roles or partners. Closure suggestion: Ask volunteers to share the best explanations (excuses) they heard.

- Returns (classroom chat): Ask the students about customs vis-à-vis returning items to stores in their country.

- Do the Math (game): Call out math problems. Have the students do the problems and write or read out answers. Increase the speed as appropriate. (This is intended to build fluency in listening to numbers.)

- Where Can I Get . . . ? (classroom chat): List a few things you would like to buy in the host country, and then ask the students, "Where can I go to buy . . . ?" or "Where is the best place to buy . . . ?"

- Store Genres (pair or small-group task): Have the students make a list for a foreign visitor describing the different kinds of stores in their country and what one would buy there.

- Stores (show and tell): Show pictures of different kinds of stores in the target country.

TRANSPORT AND TRAFFIC

Road Safety (Pair or Small-Group Task, Chapter 8)

Specific goal ideas: Have students practice trying to think from the perspective of an outsider; have students practice giving advice; teach vocabulary and phrases related to traffic (e.g., *stay in your own lane, look before you pass*).

1. Tell the students that the traffic patterns in their country are still a little unfamiliar to you, and you need advice on how to stay safe when biking (driving, etc.) on crowded streets.

2. Have the students list the five most important safety tips they think you would need.

3. As students report, as appropriate ask them to explain why each tip is important.

4. Closure suggestion: Let students know which of the tips you think would be the most useful for a foreigner.

Improving Transport (Pair or Small-Group Task, Chapter 8)

Specific goal ideas: Have students practice making a case and stating a rationale; teach vocabulary for kinds of transport (e.g., *subway system, bus system*).

1. Have students call out forms of (urban) transport as you write them on the board.

2. Tell the students the local government has recently been given a significant loan for the purpose of improving local transport.

3. Have the students decide which form of transport they think should be promoted the most and make a proposal for how to use the loan money to promote that form. Each group should be prepared to explain why its proposal is the best one.

4. Have the students present their proposals and rationales. As each group reports, the others should take notes.

5. Discuss and debate the proposals.

6. Closure suggestion: Have everyone vote on which is the best proposal.

Should More People Get Cars? (Survey, Chapter 8)

Specific goal ideas: Have students practice justifying opinions; teach vocabulary related to car ownership (e.g., *maintenance, insurance, convenience*).

1. Start by having students survey each other on this question: *Would it be a good thing if most people could have their own car? Why or why not?*

2. Have the students report the results of their surveys.

3. Lead into a debate on the merits of promoting car ownership.

4. Closure suggestion: Point out any advantages and disadvantages of car ownership you can think of and that the students haven't mentioned.

Other Activity Ideas

- Rules of the Road (pair or small-group task): Have pairs or groups of students list and prepare to explain to a foreign teacher the most important local traffic rules.

- Which Rules Are Really Important? (pair or small-group task): Tell the students they have been asked to give their city recommendations for the revision of its traffic rules. Ask the students to place the rules in the following categories: rules police should strictly enforce, rules that should be revoked, and rules that should be kept on the books but not strictly enforced.

- Getting a License (pair or small-group task): Have the students list and explain the steps for getting a driver's (car, motorcycle, bicycle, etc.) license.

SOCIAL LIFE

Gifts (Pair or Small-Group Task, Chapter 8)

Specific goal ideas: Have students practice explaining local customs to a foreigner; teach vocabulary related to gift giving and gift-giving occasions.

1. Tell the students that, as a newcomer to their country, you don't know what occasions call for gifts and what gifts are best for each occasion.

2. Have the students list occasions on which gifts would normally be given and what kinds of gifts you should give.

3. Ask the students to list the occasions as you write them on the board. Then, going through the occasions one by one, have the students explain what gifts would be appropriate and why. Ask for clarification as necessary.

4. Closure suggestion: Ask the students how much a foreigner would be bound by the local rules for gift giving.

Gift Giving in the West (Dictocomp, Chapter 7; Talk, Chapter 7)

Specific goal ideas: Help students become more comfortable with guessing; have students practice clarification questions (e.g., *What does . . . mean? How do you spell . . . ?*).

1. Prepare a dictocomp passage on gift giving in the target country, including what occasions call for giving gifts and what gifts are appropriate for each occasion. Make sure to include a few—but only a very few—words you think students won't know.

2. Present the passage following the dictocomp procedure.

3. After the students have tried to recreate the passage, allow them to ask about any unfamiliar words.

4. Closure suggestion: Review the clarification questions that were used in the lesson.

Refusing an Invitation (Pair or Small-Group Task, Chapter 8)

Specific goal ideas: Teach strategies for turning down invitations; have students practice stating excuses (e.g., *I would love to come, but . . . .*).

1. Tell the students to imagine that they have been invited to a banquet or some other social occasion that they don't want to attend.

2. Ask the students to list the excuses most commonly used in their culture for turning down (or not accepting) an invitation.

3. Have the students report the excuses to you and explain why these excuses are often used—that is, why these excuses and strategies are good in this particular culture.

4. Closure suggestion: Comment on how well the suggested excuses would work if offered to someone from the target culture. Also introduce some of the commonly used excuses in the target culture, and tell how they are used.

Other Activity Ideas

- What Should We Talk About? (pair or small-group task): Have the students list the five most common topics people in their country chat (or gossip) about when making small talk.

- How Do I . . . ? (model-based dialogue): Write and teach a dialogue that provides a typical model (in language and culture) of how people in the target culture carry out the following social interactions. To close, have the students prepare to explain to a foreigner the rules for these forms of social interaction in their culture.
  — introducing people
  — making invitations, accepting invitations, and (politely) refusing invitations
  — striking up conversations with strangers (appropriately)
  — apologizing, including how and when one apologizes
  — giving and responding to compliments, including how and when to do so
  — excusing oneself, including when and when not to
  — disagreeing (politely)
  — giving advice, including when it is appropriate to give advice
  — interrupting others, including when it is or is not acceptable to interrupt
  — accepting and refusing gifts politely, including when you should you say no to a gift

Module 2: The Cycle of Life

BABIES AND CHILDREN

Should Children Be Given Chores? (Survey, Chapter 8)

Specific goal ideas: Have students practice expressing and explaining opinions; have students practice describing chores as gerunds.

1. Briefly explain what chores are, and list names of typical chores on the board. (These are usually stated as gerunds, e.g., *cleaning your room, washing the dishes.*)

2. Have the students survey each other on this question: *Should children in their culture be given household chores? Why or why not? If yes, what chores would be appropriate?*

3. Have the students report.

4. Closure suggestion: Talk about what chores are typically given to children in the target country, the target culture, or both, and why.

Lessons I Learned as a Child (Interview, Chapter 8)

Specific goal ideas: Have students practice preparing interview questions; have students practice talking about the past and using past tense verbs.

1. Tell the students you are interested in what lessons their parents (grandparents, etc.) taught them as children and how these lessons were taught.

2. Have each student prepare to interview a classmate by making a list of interview questions (e.g., *What are some of the lessons you remember being taught as a child? Who taught these lessons? How?*).

3. Pair students, preferably with classmates they don't know very well, and have them interview each other.

4. Have a few volunteers report on interesting lessons and teaching methods they were told about (but first have them ask the permission of the person whose memories are being publicly shared).

5. Closure suggestion: Share a few memories of your own.

What Is a Mother (or Father) to Do? (Pair or Small-Group Task, Chapter 8)

Specific goal ideas: Have students practice stating and justifying strategies.

1. Have the students list the best strategies for dealing with a child who is misbehaving and be ready to explain why these strategies are best.

2. Have groups report their strategies and rationales.

3. Closure suggestion: Comment on how, from the target culture's perspective, you would view their suggestions.

Other Activity Ideas

- Advice for Pregnant Women (pair or small-group task): Have the students list rules in their culture for pregnant women—what they should and should not do. Each can be written as a sentence completion: *Pregnant women should . . . . Pregnant women should not . . . .* Closure suggestion: Respond with a corresponding list of rules in the target culture for pregnant women.

- My First Baby (talk): If you are a parent, tell the story of the day your first (second, or other) child was born. Walk students through the events of the day.

- Having Babies Western-Style (press conference): Tell the students their local newspaper has assigned them to interview a Westerner and then write a story on how Westerners typically handle childbirth. Have them prepare interview questions in groups. Then have them interview you and take notes. Closure suggestion: Ask the students what the most surprising discovery was.

- Having Babies Our Way (pair or small-group task): Have the students list and be ready to explain customs in their culture surrounding birth.

- Birthdays (pair or small-group task): Have the students describe how birthdays are celebrated in their culture.

- Taking Care of Babies (pair or small-group task): Have the students describe how babies are fed and taken care of in their culture. Closure suggestion: Describe corresponding customs in the target culture.

- My Mama Taught Me . . . (talk): Tell the students about some of the lessons your own parents taught you during childhood and the way they were taught.

- Spare the Rod? (debate): Is it better to err on the side of strictness or leniency with children?

- Who Should Take Care of the Kids? (pair or small-group task): Have the students decide who should be primarily responsible for taking care of children: The wife? The husband? Grandparents? Relatives? A day-care center?

- Teach Your Children Well (pair or small-group task): Have pairs or groups of students decide on the five most important lessons parents should teach young children at home.

- The Best Years? (pair or small-group task): Have the students decide whether or not they think childhood is the best time of life and be ready to defend their decision.

- How Tight Should the Apron Strings Be? (pair or small-group task): Have the students decide whether, on the whole, children should be trained to be more obedient or more independent.

ADOLESCENCE

The Difficult Years (Focused Listening, Chapter 7)

Specific goal ideas: Teach vocabulary related to adolescence (e.g., *maturing, dating, puberty, growth spurts*).

1. Prepare a brief talk in which you explain why Westerners consider the early years of adolescence, especially junior high school age, the difficult years. Discuss some of the changes students are going through at that point.

2. Before giving the talk, list questions for which you want students to listen for the answers (e.g., *Why are the early years of adolescence considered difficult years? What are some of the changes young people are going through?*).

3. Give the talk, and have the students listen for and note down answers to the questions.

4. Check using one of the methods suggested in Talks and Lectures (chapter 7).

5. Closure suggestion: Ask the students whether the same age is difficult for young people in their culture or whether another age period might be considered the difficult stage.

Independence? (Pair or Small-Group Task, Chapter 8)

Specific goal ideas: Have students practice stating and justifying opinions.

1. Tell the students that one main issue in adolescence in the West is how much independence adolescents should be allowed.

2. Have the students prepare to answer questions about how much independence they think adolescents in their own culture should be allowed (e.g., *How much should adolescents have to tell their parents about what they do and where they go? How late should they be allowed to stay out at night? How much say should parents have in who their adolescent children are friends with?*). They should be ready to explain and justify their opinions.

3. Have the students report.

4. Closure suggestion: Talk with students about the range of answers one might encounter in the target culture to the above questions, and share your own opinions.

To Date or Not to Date (Pair or Small-Group Task, Chapter 8)

Specific goal ideas: Have students practice stating and justifying opinions.

1. Have the students decide at what age they think it is appropriate for young people in their country to start dating or having a boyfriend or girlfriend, and be ready to explain their position.

2. Have the students report.

3. Closure suggestion: Comment on the various views held on this topic in the target country.

Other Activity Ideas

- Western Adolescents (press conference): Tell the students their school newspaper has assigned them to interview a Westerner and write an article on how much freedom parents allow young people in the West. Have them prepare interview questions and then interview you. Closure suggestion: Ask the students which answers they found most different from those someone from their culture would give.

- Coming of Age (classroom chat): Ask the students when someone becomes an adult in their culture. In other words, what marks the passage from being an adolescent (child) to an adult?

- Youth Culture (classroom chat): Ask the students about youth culture in their country.

- Generation Gap (classroom chat): Ask the students to tell you whether there is a generation gap in their culture. If so, what are some of the differences between the generations?

DATING AND CHOOSING A MATE

The Steps of the Dating Process (Pair or Small-Group Task, Chapter 8)

Specific goal ideas: Have students practice explaining local culture; teach vocabulary related to dating.

1. Have the students write down one by one the steps through which a typical couple in their country goes from first meeting to marriage. They should make a special point of noting what signals and events indicate that the relationship is getting more serious.

(Tip: This may be easier if the class first creates an imaginary typical couple of a certain age, job, education, area, etc.)

2. Have the groups report.

3. Closure suggestion: Comment on differences between the process the students describe and what is typical in the target country.

The Advantages and Disadvantages of Matchmaking (Pair or Small-Group Task, Chapter 8)

Specific goal ideas: Have students practice stating advantages and disadvantages.

1. Tell the students that in virtually every culture some people seem to like matchmaking. Quickly ask how common this is in their country.

2. Have the students list the advantages and disadvantages of matchmaking as a way to help single people find mates.

3. Have the students report.

4. Closure suggestion: Talk a little about how people make matches in the target culture.

Advice Columns (Problem-Solving Situation, Chapter 7)

Specific goal ideas: Have students practice focused listening; have students practice giving advice.

1. Find (or write) a short letter from a personal advice column in a magazine or newspaper (e.g., Dear Abby, Dear Clare Rayner).

2. Read the letter to students, and have them take notes on the situation described so that they can respond to it.

3. Have the students play the role of advice columnist in groups and jointly write a response.

4. Have each group read its response to the class.

5. Closure suggestion: Present the advice actually given by the source from which you got the original letter and see how it matches any of the students' suggestions. You might also collect the students' written responses and give feedback on the language and content.

Other Activity Ideas

- Meeting Your Mate (pair or small-group task): Tell the students you have heard that the dating process is different in their country than in yours and that you are curious. Have the students list, in order of frequency, how couples in their country usually first meet. Closure suggestion: Based on what the students tell you, comment on differences you see between their country and yours.

- What Is Love? (pair or small-group task): Ask the students to explain what *love* really means (in their context). Give them a few minutes to think and jot down notes. Then have the students share their ideas and try to come to agreement. Each group should be ready to present an explanation all members (more or less) agree on. Closure suggestion: Comment on differing views of love in the target culture.

- The Ideal Boyfriend or Girlfriend (pair or small-group task): Divide the class into small groups composed of either all women or all men. Have the women list the characteristics of the ideal boyfriend; have the men do the same for the ideal girlfriend. Then have the women report their top five characteristics, have the men report their top five, and ask how each group feels about the expectations of the other.

- What Is Courting Like in the Target Country? (press conference): Have the students interview you about the typical steps by which couples meet and move toward marriage in the target culture.

- Cupid Tricks (pair or small-group task): Have the students list clever ways to introduce two people who would make a good couple.

- My Love Story (Story): If you are married and wouldn't mind, talk about how you met your mate. The students would probably love it.

- How Much Say Should They Have? (pair or small-group task): Have the students decide how much influence parents should have in deciding who their children marry.

- Who Makes the First Move? (pair or small-group task): Ask the students to decide whether it should be acceptable for women in their culture to invite men out.

- Blind Dates? (pair or small-group task): Explain what a *blind date* is, and then have the students list the advantages and disadvantages of blind dates.

- Problems in Finding a Match (classroom chat): Have the students tell you what the most common problems are in finding (choosing, winning) a partner in their country.

- Mr. Right? (pair or small-group task): How do you know which person is Mr. Right or Miss Right? Have the students list the most important signs.

MARRIAGE

Wedding Pictures (Show and Tell, Chapter 7)

Specific goal ideas: Teach wedding-related vocabulary (e.g., *bride, groom, bouquet*).

1. Bring wedding pictures to class—your own or those of someone you know. Plan vocabulary you can teach as you show the pictures.

2. In class, show the pictures, chat with students about them, and introduce vocabulary as appropriate.

3. Closure suggestion: Lead into Mock Wedding.

Mock Wedding (Total Physical Response, Chapter 7)

Specific goal ideas: Teach wedding-related vocabulary and phrases (e.g., *If anyone has any objections, let them speak now or forever hold their peace; Do you take this man/woman . . . ?*).

1. Tell the students you want to teach them about weddings in the target culture by walking them through one.

2. Assign roles to everyone in the class (or have them draw roles from a hat), and explain everyone's duties. Put key phrases and vocabulary on the board. (You might even dictate some of the key phrases.)

3. Arrange the furniture in the room as best you can, and walk everyone through the rehearsal—you give directions and students respond by following instructions.

4. Close by having the wedding; maybe even take pictures.

Tips on a Happy Marriage (Pair or Small-Group Task, Chapter 8)

Specific goal ideas: Have students practice viewing issues from another's perspective.

1. In same-sex groupings, have the students list tips on what wives and husbands should or should not do in order to have a happy marriage. Men list tips they think women would suggest; women list tips they think men would suggest. You might want to have the students use sentence completion (e.g., *Men would say that wives should always . . . .*).

2. After women suggest a tip they think men would suggest, have the men comment on whether the tip is one they would actually give; in other words, how well the women understood their perspective. Then do the reverse. List tips on which consensus is reached on the board.

3. Closure suggestion: Praise the group that seemed best able to see things from the other's viewpoint.

Other Activity Ideas

- Weddings Local-Style (pair or small-group task): Have the students in pairs or groups list the usual steps in the process of getting married in their country. When they report, put *step 1, step 2,* and so forth on the board. Then have one group tell you what the first step is, write it on the board, and so forth. Discuss disagreements. Closure suggestion: Use this activity as a lead-in to the Mock Wedding activity above.

- To Marry or Not? (pair or small-group task): Divide class into A and B teams. (If the class is large, divide A and B into smaller teams.) Have the A teams list the advantages of being single and the disadvantages of being married; have B list the opposite. Then tell the class they are going to play Ping-Pong with their ideas. In Ping-Pong, one player serves the ball and the other has to hit it back; when one player cannot return the ball, the other player scores a point. In this game, one side "serves" an idea to the other side; the other side must then "hit" the idea back with a reply. When one side cannot directly reply to the other side's ideas, then the other side scores a point. Then a new idea is served. You keep the score on the blackboard. For example,
  A: If you are single, then you can keep all the money you earn for yourself.
  B: But if you are married, you will have two salaries, therefore twice the money.
  A: But what if your wife doesn't work?
  B: (Here team B cannot reply, so team A scores one point.)

- Please Can I Marry Him or Her? (pair or small-group task): What do you do if you want your parents' approval to marry someone they don't like? Have the students list strategies.

- Weddings in My Hometown (talk): Give a talk about weddings in the target country.

- A Memorable Wedding (story): Tell the students about a particularly memorable (entertaining, disastrous, unusual, etc.) wedding you attended.

- Making It All Legal (classroom chat): Have the students explain to you what legal procedures one normally goes through to get married in their country.

- The Ideal Mate (pair or small-group task): Have the students list the most important characteristics of the ideal wife or husband.

- Should Cutting the Knot Be Easy? (pair or small-group task): Have the students decide whether it should be easy (with regard to law and procedure) to get a divorce and list reasons for their position.

ADULTHOOD AND CAREERS

Getting a Promotion (Pair or Small-Group Task, Chapter 8)

Specific goal ideas: Have students practice explaining strategies and their relative advantages; teach vocabulary and phrases related to career advancement (e.g., *promotion, good relations*).

1. Begin with a quick survey, having students ask each other what job they want after graduation (or already have). As they report, ascertain the job that most seem interested in.

2. Using a job that many students seem interested in, have them list strategies that are commonly used in their country for getting a promotion. (Alternative: List strategies for getting a raise.) Each needs to be clearly explained.

3. Have the students report.

4. Have the students discuss the relative advantages and disadvantages of the strategies suggested.

5. Closure suggestion: Comment on which of these are most common in the target country.

Saving for the Future (Pair or Small-Group Task, Chapter 8)

Specific goal ideas: Teach vocabulary related to savings (e.g., *bank account, investments*).

1. Ask the students what advice they would give to a couple—married, about thirty-five years old, with one child—about how much of their income they should be saving. What percentage of their income should the couple try to save, and what they should do with that money (e.g., invest it? put it in a bank?).

2. Have the students come up with a plan, stated as advice to the couple (e.g., *They should try to save . . . each month*).

3. As the students report, have them discuss the relative merits of their plans.

4. Closure suggestion: Talk to students a little about the savings and investing habits of people in the target country.

Success (Pair or Small-Group Task, Chapter 8)

Specific goal ideas: Have students practice discussing and justifying priorities; have students practice stating criteria (factors) as nouns.

1. Have the students list factors that might be used as criteria for deciding whether one is successful or not (e.g., *wealth, health*).

2. In groups, have the students decide—in order of priority—which three criteria are most important and give their rationale for each choice.

3. Have each group report the criteria they ranked as most important, and discuss.

4. Closure suggestion: Share your own ideas on what factors are most important in defining whether someone is a success or on which factors people in the target country would tend to rank highest.

Other Activity Ideas

- The Best Age for Having Children (pair or small-group task): Have the students decide what the best age is for couples to have a child. They should be ready to explain the advantages of that age.

- To Have Kids or Not? (debate): Have the students debate the relative advantages of having versus not having children. (Be sure to check whether this topic is culturally appropriate in your host country.)

- Career or Home? (debate): Which is more important: career or home life?

- Life Insurance, Anybody? (pair or small-group task): Have the students decide whether or not it is good for married couples (or people in general) to buy life insurance.

RETIREMENT

What Do You Look Forward to Doing When You Retire? (Survey, Chapter 8)

Specific goal ideas: Have students practice the *look forward to + gerund* pattern; teach vocabulary for retirement activities.

1. Ask a few students: *What do you look forward to doing when you retire?* Put their responses on the board as gerunds (e.g., *watching lots of TV, sleeping in*).

2. Have the students survey each other on the same question.

3. Have the students report as you list responses on the board—as gerund phrases if possible.

4. Closure suggestion: Share a few of your own retirement dreams.

Retirement (Press Conference, Chapter 8)

Specific goal ideas: Have students practice actively asking questions as a strategy for learning about another culture; teach retirement-related vocabulary (e.g., *pension, investments, retirement community*).

1. Tell the students they are reporters writing a story on postretirement life in the target country, especially what living arrangement options are typical and where retirement income comes from. Have them prepare a list of interview questions—especially interesting ones.

2. Conduct the interview following the press conference procedure.

3. Closure suggestion: Praise the most interesting questions asked.

Should Retired Parents Live with Their Grown Children? (Pair or Small-Group Task, Chapter 8)

Specific goal ideas: Have students practice stating advantages and disadvantages.

1. Have the students list the advantages and disadvantages of retired parents living in the same home with their grown children and decide whether or not the advantages outweigh the disadvantages.

2. For reports, divide the board into two columns labeled Advantages and Disadvantages. Have each group report one advantage or disadvantage.

3. Closure suggestion: Comment on the question from your perspective.

CULTURE-TOPIC ACTIVITY IDEAS FOR ORAL SKILLS CLASSES

Other Activity Ideas

- Retirement Benefits (show and tell): Take documents related to retirement (e.g., social security cards) to class and show students the documents. Talk a little about how the system works in the target country, and what its pros and cons are.

- When You Retire . . . (survey): Have the students survey several other classmates, asking: *After you retire, what do you expect from your children?* (What should they give you or do for you?) Give everyone a minute to think about the question before the survey starts. Closure suggestion: Have a few students report results.

- If I Were a Rich Man . . . (classroom chat): Ask the students what they would do for retirement if they were rich.

- Saving for Retirement (talk): Give a talk on how people in the target country typically plan and save for retirement.

- Should Granny Teach the Kids? (pair or small-group task): Have the students discuss the advantages and disadvantages of having retired parents take care of and teach their grandchildren.

- Should There Be a Set Retirement Age? (pair or small-group task): Have the students discuss the advantages and disadvantages of having a set age at which people (in a given profession) are required to retire. If there is a set retirement age, what should it be?

- How about a Retirement Home? (survey): Have the students survey each other on whether they would be willing to live in a retirement home when they get old.

PASSING THE TORCH[3]

Looking Back (Survey, Chapter 8)

Specific goal ideas: Have students practice using the future perfect tense.

1. Ask a few students: *When you are eighty years old looking back on your life, what will you most want to see?* (What would you want to have accomplished or become?) Help them state the response correctly using the future perfect verb tense, and put a few examples on the board (e.g., *I hope I will have had a successful career. I hope I will have been a good parent*).

2. Have the students survey each other using this question.

3. Have the students report the most interesting answers they heard—being sure to use the proper verb tense.

4. Closure suggestion: Tell the students your hopes.

Euphemisms (Dictocomp, Chapter 7)

Specific goal ideas: Introduce the concept of euphemisms; teach vocabulary and phrases related to death.

1. Prepare a passage introducing and explaining some of the euphemisms for death used in English. Include both more genteel and sensitive terms (e.g., *pass away, gone*) and others that are more colloquial, informal, and even a bit humorous (e.g., *kick the bucket, croak, six feet under pushing up daisies*) and make it easier to talk about an awkward topic.

---

[3] Students in the host country may find talking about death uncomfortable or even offensive, so be sure to check before deciding whether or not to use material in this section.

2. Explain that people in the West, like people in most cultures, are somewhat uncomfortable talking about the end of life, so instead of talking about death, people often use indirect, euphemistic terms.

3. Conduct the dictocomp exercise.

4. Closure suggestion: Ask the students whether similar euphemisms exist in their language.

Funerals (Talk, Chapter 7)

Specific goal ideas: Teach vocabulary related to funerals.

1. Prepare a talk on the procedures and customs for funerals in the target country, including necessary vocabulary.

2. Introduce vocabulary students will need for the talk.

3. Give the talk.

4. Closure suggestion: Ask the students to tell you similarities and differences they notice between the customs you describe and those in their culture.

Other Activity Ideas

- Causes of Mortality (talk): Give a talk listing and explaining the leading causes of mortality in the target country.

- Where There's a Will . . . (talk): Give a talk explaining wills and inheritance procedures and laws in the target country.

- Remembering Those Who Have Gone Before (talk): Give a talk on how the departed are remembered in the target culture, especially any holidays or special occasions devoted to that purpose. Have the students tell you about corresponding commemorations in their culture.

- And the Cycle Goes On (talk): Give a talk about some of your ancestors, focusing especially on some of the more interesting facets of your ancestry. If possible, bring pictures.

Module 3: Relationships

FAMILY

My Family Tree (Press Conference, Chapter 8)

Specific goal ideas: Have students practice actively asking questions as a strategy for learning about another culture; teach vocabulary for relatives.

1. Prepare a family tree for your own family (or a fictitious one), including people you normally consider when you think of relatives.

2. In class, draw the start of your family tree on the board—perhaps just you and your parents (enough to get the idea across but not the entire tree). Include people's names and their relationship to you. Then tell the students their goal is to get you to fill out your family tree by asking questions (e.g., *Do you have any sisters? How about brothers?*).

3. Closure suggestion: Review the vocabulary for kinds of relatives.

Family Members (Interview, Chapter 8)

Specific goal ideas: Teach vocabulary for relatives.

1. Ask the students to find a partner they don't know well. Partner A should interview partner B about his or her family and then draw B's family tree.

2. When the students are finished, ask them what relatives they normally view as being part of their family. Is the pattern similar to that in the target culture? Is the range of relatives with whom they interact larger than in the target culture? Or is it more restricted?

3. Closure suggestion: Review terms for relatives.

Extended Family? (Debate, Chapter 8)

Specific goal ideas: Have students practice stating and justifying views; teach vocabulary for different types of family patterns (e.g., *nuclear family, extended family*).

1. Following the procedure for debates, have the students debate the issue: *Is it better to live in nuclear families (just parents and children) or extended families?*

2. Closure suggestion: Note especially good points made during the debate, and explain why you thought they were good.

Other Activity Ideas

- My Aunt Minnie (talk): Give a talk introducing one of the more interesting members of your family and his or her career—the more entertaining, the better.

- My Family (show and tell): Bring pictures of family members to class. Show the pictures and talk about the people. Having students come up and circle around your desk makes it easier for them to see small pictures; this also creates a more informal atmosphere.

- The Ideal Family (pair or small-group task): Ask the students to decide in groups what the ideal family household would consist of (e.g., two parents and one child? two parents, one child, and grandparents?).

- Who Does What? (classroom chat): Ask the students what tasks various family members (e.g., father, mother, grandparents, children) are usually responsible for in a countryside or urban family in the host country.

FRIENDS

The Perfect Friend (Survey, Chapter 8)

Specific goal ideas: Have students practice using adjectives to describe the characteristics of people (e.g., *honest, kind, entertaining*); teach vocabulary related to virtues of friends.

1. Ask one or more students: *What are the characteristics of the perfect friend?* and write the answers on the board in the correct part of speech. The answers will probably be something like *The perfect friend is* + adjective (e.g., *faithful, entertaining*).

2. When students have the idea, have them survey each other on what the characteristics of the perfect friend are. Students should take notes and be ready to report.

3. As students report, list the characteristics on the board in the correct form to fit the pattern *The perfect friend is . . . .*

4. Closure suggestion: Mention a few more characteristics that you think are important but have not been mentioned, and teach the necessary words.

Making Friends in the West (Dictocomp, Chapter 7)

Specific goal ideas: Teach vocabulary for places where people meet others (e.g., *school, workplace, clubs, churches, synagogues, mosques, bars*).

1. Prepare a dictocomp passage on how and where people in the target country typically find and make their friends.

2. In class, start by pointing out that in some Western cultures, especially North America, people move many times during a lifetime, so they need to make many friends during their lifetimes. Then conduct the dictocomp exercise.

3. Closure suggestion: Ask the students to tell you where people in the host culture typically make most of their important friendships.

How Can I Make Friends? (Pair or Small-Group Task, Chapter 8)

Specific goal ideas: Have students practice explaining aspects of the local culture.

1. Have the students list tips on how you as a foreigner should go about making friends with people in the host culture.

2. As each group reports their suggestions, respond with follow-up questions until the idea is fully explained.

3. Closure suggestion: Thank students for their ideas, and mention one or two you might try.

Other Activity Ideas

*   Where Did You Meet Your Friends? (classroom chat): Ask the students to quickly think of a few of their best friends and maybe even write their names down. Then ask a few students where and how they met these friends. Try to learn how people usually meet and make friends (or best friends) in the host country.

*   My Best Friends (talk, show and tell): Give a short talk about a few of your best friends, where and how you met, and so on. If you have pictures, so much the better.

*   Friend or Acquaintance? (classroom chat): Talk about the difference between *friend* and *acquaintance* in the target culture.

*   What Is a Friend? (pair or small-group task): Have the students write a definition of *friend*.

*   A Friend in Need . . . (pair or small-group task): Have the students list the kinds of help you should always be able to expect of a friend and the kinds of help you cannot necessarily expect of friends.

MEN AND WOMEN

Housework according to Gender (Pair or Small-Group Task, Chapter 8)

Specific goal ideas: Have students practice explaining opinions; teach vocabulary for household chores.

1. Have the students call out the various housework tasks that need to be done in a typical home in their country. Write these on the board.

2. Have the students divide the tasks into three categories—those more appropriate for women, those more appropriate for men, and those equally appropriate for both. They should be ready to explain their choices.

3. Have the groups report and explain. Ask follow-up questions, and encourage discussion.

4. Closure suggestion: After the students report and discuss, comment on the list from the perspective of your own culture. Also review the chore-related vocabulary.

Gender and Jobs (Pair or Small-Group Task, Chapter 8)

Specific goal ideas: Have students practice trying to see things from someone else's perspective; teach vocabulary for occupations.

1. Divide students into all-male and all-female groups.

2. Have the students make two lists—one of occupations that are more suited for women and one of those more suited for men.

3. Then ask the groups to make a second pair of lists. Men should list the jobs they think the women said were more suited for men and for women; women should list the jobs they think men listed for men and women. In other words, the men try to guess what the women wrote, and the women try to guess what the men wrote.

4. Have the men share their guesses on what the women wrote, and vice versa. Encourage discussion.

5. Closure suggestion: Reward the side that most accurately guessed the perspective of the other.

Do Women and Men Think Differently? (Survey, Chapter 8)

Specific goal ideas: Teach vocabulary related to ways of thinking (e.g., *logical, sensitive*).

1. Have the students survey each other on whether they think there is a difference in the way men and women think.

2. Have the students report what they were told, and then discuss.

Other Activity Ideas

- Should Both Men and Women Work Outside? (pair or small-group task): Have the students discuss the relative advantages and disadvantages of having both members of a couple work outside the home. Is it better to have one stay at home?

- Mars and Venus? (pair or small-group task): Have the students decide: *Is it more difficult for women to communicate with men (and vice versa) than with other women?*

HOSTS AND GUESTS

The Perfect Guest (Survey, Chapter 8; Pair or Small-Group Task, Chapter 8)

Specific goal ideas: Have students practice discussion skills for working toward consensus; have students practice explaining and justifying priorities; teach vocabulary related to the virtues of guests.

1. Have the students survey each other on what the characteristics of the ideal guest are. These could be stated as sentence completions (e.g., *The ideal guest is . . . .*)

2. As students report, list the characteristics on the board—as adjectives, if possible.

3. Introduce basic discussion skills for working toward consensus (e.g., make sure each person expresses an opinion, ask clarifying questions if you don't understand, try to find points you agree on).

4. Have the students discuss in pairs or groups which five characteristics are most important and in what order. They should try to work toward a consensus.

5. Have the groups report and explain their choices.

6. Closure suggestion: Ask groups whether or not it was difficult to come to consensus, and why or why not.

The Perfect Host (Pair or Small-Group Task, Chapter 8)

Specific goal ideas: Have students practice discussion skills for working toward consensus; have students practice explaining and justifying priorities; teach verb phrases to describe duties of hosts (e.g., *bring tea, make conversation, suggest interesting conversation topics*).

1. Have the students list (in order of importance) the three main duties of the ideal host in their culture. These could be stated as sentence completions (e.g., *The ideal host should . . . .*). Have each student take notes on what the group decides.

2. After each pair or group has a list, redivide the class so that each student is now with different partners. Each student should explain what his or her previous group decided and why; the new groups should then try to come to a consensus.

3. Have the groups report.

4. Closure suggestion: Ask the students whether it was difficult for the (new) groups to come to consensus, and why or why not.

Hosting a House Guest (Press Conference, Chapter 8)

Specific goal ideas: Have students practice checking guesses; have students practice actively asking questions as a strategy for learning about another culture.

1. Have the students imagine that a friend of theirs is planning to go to the West for several weeks on an exchange program, and will be living with a Western host family. He doesn't know what this will be like so has come to them for advice. They have some guesses about what to suggest, but want to check their guesses.

2. Have the students in pairs or groups list their guesses about what a Western host generally expects—and doesn't expect—to do for a house guest and what a Western host generally expects of a house guest.

3. Introduce sample sentence patterns for checking guesses (e.g., *Is it true that . . . ? We think that . . . . Is this true?*).

4. Have the students interview you using the press conference procedure.

5. Closure suggestion: Ask the students which of the answers you gave was most unexpected, and why.

Other Activity Ideas

- The Unexpected Guest (classroom chat): Ask the students: *According to the norms of their culture, if a friend stops by to visit, is it ever OK to turn the friend away? If so, under what circumstances is it OK?*

293

- Hosting (pair or small-group task): Have the students list for you the things you should do in order to be a good host according to the norms of the local culture.

- Who Would You Invite to the Party? (problem-solving situation): Tell the students you are having a party and there are five acquaintances you would consider inviting, but you only have enough room to invite three guests. Introduce each of the five acquaintances and give reasons you do and don't want to invite each. Then have the students discuss the problem, give you recommendations, and explain them.

STRANGERS

Stranger in a Strange Land (Interview, Chapter 8)

Specific goal ideas: Encourage students to imagine what feelings might affect someone in a foreign culture; teach vocabulary for feelings (e.g., *isolated, confused, excited*).

1. Ask the students to think of an experience they had where they were a stranger in an unfamiliar place.

2. Have them interview one or more classmates about the experience of being a stranger, especially how they felt.

3. After the interviews, ask volunteers to report some of the feelings they heard others mention. As you put these on the board, make one list for adjectives (e.g., *lonely, fascinated*) and another for other phrases (e.g., *It seemed very new and strange.*).

4. Closure suggestion: Talk about what it feels like to be a foreigner in a new culture—both the good and the bad aspects. Also, go over the feelings mentioned and make sure students can use them properly in sentences. (They may tend to confuse the nouns and adjectives.)

To Help or Not? (Pair or Small-Group Task, Chapter 8)

Specific goal ideas: Have students consider how value-based choices are made and what factors affect such decisions; have students practice stating conditions and criteria (e.g., *I would . . . if . . . .*).

1. Start by telling students, "We have all had the experience of passing strangers on the street who seem to need help. Sometimes we decide to offer help; other times we pass on by. The question is, How do you decide whether or not to stop and offer help?"

2. Have the students list—in order of importance—the criteria that would influence their decision whether or not to help. You might have them do this as a sentence completion, such as *I would stop if . . .* (e.g., *the stranger seemed to be in serious difficulty, I wasn't in a big hurry*).

3. Have the students report their criteria and discuss.

4. Closure suggestion: Share your own thoughts.

You Should Never Trust a Stranger (Debate, Chapter 8)

Specific goal ideas: Encourage students to be more aware of decisions about whether or not to trust strangers and the factors that affect these decisions; practice stating conditions and criteria (e.g., *I would . . . if . . . .*).

1. Following the procedure for debates, have the students debate the proposition *You should never trust a stranger.*

2. Closure suggestion: Ask the students to discuss how they would decide whether or not to give a stranger the benefit of the doubt.

Other Activity Ideas

- The Stranger on the Train (classroom chat): Tell the students that in the West it is not unusual for people on planes (trains, long-distance buses, etc.) to get into conversations with strangers in which they wind up talking about personal problems or issues, perhaps telling the stranger things they wouldn't tell their friends or family. Ask the students if the same phenomenon occurs in their culture as well. If so, have them discuss why it happens.

- Interesting Encounters (cocktail party): Have the students share stories of interesting encounters they have had with strangers.

- To Trust or Not? (pair or small-group task): Have the students list criteria they would use in deciding whether or not to trust a stranger.

- Never Talk to Strangers? (pair or small-group task): Have the students decide: *Should we teach children not to talk to strangers?* and list the advantages and disadvantages.

- Lonely or Alone? (survey): Have the students survey each other on this question: *Do you enjoy being a stranger in a place where no one knows you?*

- Obligation (debate): Have the students debate whether or not people have as much obligation to help strangers as they have to help people they know.

- Local Golden Rules (pair or small-group task): Have the students list five golden rules for foreigners on being polite in their country.

- Foreign Golden Rules (pair or small-group task): Have the students list tips they would give to a friend who was going to travel in the target culture, a list of golden rules for how to be polite. After students share their lists, comment from the perspective of the target culture. (Or have the students list five rude things a foreigner should never do in the target country.)

BOSSES AND EMPLOYEES

The Ideal Boss (Survey, Chapter 8)

Specific goal ideas: Have students practice stating characteristics as verb phrases; teach vocabulary related to qualities of bosses (e.g., *fair, friendly, well organized*).

1. Have the students survey each other on the characteristics of the ideal boss.

2. As students report, have them state the responses they heard as completions for the sentence *The ideal boss . . .* (e.g., *treats employees nicely, is easy to talk to*).

3. Closure suggestion: Tell the students what people in the target country think would characterize the perfect boss—and comment on similarities and differences between what they said and what people in the target country would probably say.

Motivating the Staff (Pair or Small-Group Task, Chapter 8)

Specific goal ideas: Encourage students to think about how motivation relates to language study; have students practice discussing motivation.

1. Tell the students that a friend of theirs has just been made manager of a shoe company. The friend has never been a manager before and comes to them for advice on how to motivate the company's employees.

2. Have the students list ways the new manager can motivate employees to work hard and enthusiastically.

3. Have the students report.

4. Closure suggestion: Ask the students to what extent similar strategies would work for motivating students to learn English.

If I Had My Own Company . . . (Cocktail Party, Chapter 8)

Specific goal ideas: Have students practice explaining motivations; teach vocabulary for kinds of companies.

1. Introduce the procedure for cocktail-party activities.

2. Have the students do a cocktail-party activity using the following question: *If you could be the boss of any kind of organization (e.g., company, institution, agency) in the world, what would you want to be boss of, and why?*

3. Have volunteers report on what kinds of companies they heard others mention. List these on the board. Also ask the students what people's motivations were.

4. Closure suggestion: Have the students list some of the headaches they might wind up with if their wishes were granted.

Other Activity Ideas

- Bosses and Employees in My Country (talk): Give a talk on what management-employee relations are normally like in companies in the target culture.

- The Ideal Employee (pair or small-group task): Have the students list the characteristics of the ideal employee.

- My Best Boss (talk): Give a talk on the best (or worst) boss you ever had.

- How Should a Boss Boss? (pair or small-group task): Have the students discuss and decide: *What is the best way for bosses to make decisions? Consult? Put issues to a vote? Decide by themselves?*

- One Rule to Rule Them All? (pair or small-group task): Have the students discuss: *Should leaders and bosses always be bound by the same rules as employees?*

- If I Were the Boss . . . (survey): Have the students survey each other on this question: *If you were the leader of your organization (school, company, agency, etc.), what changes would you make?*

- One of the Gang? (pair or small-group task): Have the students list the advantages and disadvantages of an office situation where the boss tries to treat everyone as equals.

HUSBANDS AND WIVES

The Ideal Spouse (Pair or Small-Group Task, Chapter 8)

Specific goal ideas: Have students practice seeing an issue from someone else's perspective; have students practice stating characteristics as adjectives, verb phrases, or both.

1. Divide students into all-men and all-women groups. Then ask each group to make two lists, one of the characteristics of the ideal husband and one of the ideal wife. These can be set up as sentence completions; for example, *The ideal husband . . .* (e.g., *always comes home on time, is handsome*). (Alternative: Have groups make lists of what they think the other group will list as the characteristics of the ideal wife or husband.)

2. When it is time for groups to report, first have the men present their list of characteristics of the ideal husband, and then have the women compare what the men said with their list. Then reverse the process. Encourage good-natured disagreement and debate.

3. Closure suggestion: Comment on some of the characteristics people in the target culture would agree with and some on which the general view in the target culture would be quite different.

Who Should Wear the Pants? (Debate, Chapter 8)

Specific goal ideas: Have students practice explaining and justifying arguments.

1. Start by explaining the expression *wear the pants in the family.*

2. Divide students into groups, some to argue that women should wear the pants and some to argue that men should.

3. Conduct the debate following the procedure in chapter 8.

4. Closure suggestion: After the debate, comment on which of the arguments presented you found most compelling.

Separate Vacations? (Pair or Small-Group Task, Chapter 8)

Specific goal ideas: Have students practice seeing two sides of a (possibly strange) aspect of a foreign culture; have students practice stating advantages and disadvantages.

1. Tell the students that some Westerners feel that husbands and wives should take separate vacations so that they get a little break from each other. Have the students list the advantages and disadvantages of such a custom.

2. Have the students report.

3. Closure suggestion: Point out that while some Westerners do this, this is not necessarily typical (i.e., not all couples do this). Then talk a little about other approaches to vacationing in the target culture.

Other Activity Ideas

- The Power of the Purse (debate): Have the students debate: *Who should manage family finances?*

- Keeping the Flame Burning (survey): Have the students survey several classmates, asking *What should husbands and wives do to keep romance alive in their marriage?* Closure suggestion: Have the students vote on the most efficacious or cleverest strategy.

- Shall We Overcommunicate? (pair or small-group task): Tell the students that some Westerners feel it is best if wives and husbands overcommunicate with each other, in other words, make an effort to communicate in words as much as possible of what they think and feel. Have them list the advantages and disadvantages of such an approach. (Alternative: Have the students decide approximately how much time husbands and wives should spend talking to each other alone each day.)

- Raising the Kids (pair or small-group task): Have the students decide which roles husbands and wives should each play in raising the children.

- He's Always . . . ! (pair or small-group task): Have groups of men list the most common complaints they think women in their culture have about husbands, and have the women list the complaints they think men most often have about wives. Then have groups share their lists—to be critiqued by groups of the other gender.

PARENTS AND CHILDREN

Golden Rules for Raising Children (Pair or Small-Group Task, Chapter 8)

Specific goal ideas: Have students practice making and qualifying generalizations (e.g., *most people think that . . . ; people usually believe . . .*); have students practice explaining and justifying opinions; teach vocabulary related to child raising.

1. Have the students list five common (typical) beliefs people in their country have about what parents should and should not do to raise children well (e.g., *Most parents think that they should make their children study very hard.*). If necessary, put a few sample generalizations on the board.

2. When a group reports a generalization, check with other students to see if they think it is fair and accurate as it is or should be qualified to make it more accurate.

3. After the generalizations are on the board, have the students discuss whether or not they also hold these beliefs, and why or why not.

4. Closure suggestion: Lead into Child Raising in My Country.

Child Raising in My Country (Focused Listening, Chapter 7)

Specific goal ideas: Have students practice focused listening; teach vocabulary related to child raising.

1. Prepare a talk on common ideas and beliefs about child raising in the target country (e.g., *Children should be given the chance to learn from their own experiences.*).

2. Before you give your talk, introduce any relevant new vocabulary. Also tell the students their task is to listen for and take notes on beliefs people in the target country hold on child raising. Then give the talk.

3. After you finish the talk, allow students to ask questions.

4. Ask them to list the beliefs you mentioned. Then check their work.

5. Closure suggestion: Ask the students which of these beliefs would be shared by many people in their country and which would not be.

Allowances (Pair or Small-Group Task, Chapter 8)

Specific goal ideas: Have students practice looking for two sides of a (possibly strange) cultural custom; teach vocabulary related to chores and allowances.

1. Tell the students that in Western countries, children are often paid for doing chores like mowing the lawn, babysitting, and even cleaning their rooms. They may either be paid for each chore, often at some set rate, or given a regular allowance that is contingent on performance of set chores (a kind of contract).

2. Have the students discuss and list the advantages and disadvantages of this custom.

3. Have the students first report the advantages and disadvantages. Then open the floor to discussion of whether this system is—overall—a good idea or not.

4. Closure suggestion: Comment on how this custom fits into the overall cultural values of the target culture.

Other Activity Ideas

- My Childhood (show and tell): Bring some pictures of your own childhood (or, e.g., your children, nieces, and nephews) to class.

- Chores When I Was Young (talk, dictocomp): Give a talk about chores you were given as a child and whether or not you were paid in some way for them. You might also comment on the idea of chores as a part of a child's education.

- Were Your Parents Strict or Lenient? (classroom chat): Ask the students if their parents were strict or lenient. Ask for examples of behavior that illustrate their opinions. Closure suggestion: Use this as lead-in to the activity Strict or Lenient? below.

- Strict or Lenient? (survey): Have the students survey several classmates on whether it is worse for parents to be too strict or too indulgent toward children.

- Allowances (debate): Divide students into affirmative and negative groups, and have them debate whether or not the custom of giving regular allowances is a good idea.

- Adoption (survey): Have the students survey each other on whether they think adoption is a good thing.

- Adoption (talk): Give a talk on adoption in the target country—how common it is, how they process works, what attitudes toward it are, and so forth.

- My Upbringing (talk): Give a talk about how you were raised—what was best about it and what you wish might have been different. (Clearly, this is could be a somewhat personal topic, but you don't need to make it any more personal than you and your class are comfortable with.)

SIBLINGS

Sibling Rivalry (Classroom Chat, Chapter 8)

Specific goal ideas: Introduce the concept of sibling rivalry; teach vocabulary related to relations between siblings (e.g., *competition, rivalry, parents' affection*).

1. Explain what the term *sibling rivalry* means, and note that Westerners tend to believe that this is quite common. Provide any examples you can think of, and introduce any necessary vocabulary that arises.

2. Ask the students whether or not sibling rivalry occurs in their culture, and ask for examples.

3. Closure suggestion: Review newly introduced vocabulary.

The Joys of Siblings (Pair or Small-Group Task, Chapter 8)

Specific goal ideas: Have students practice stating advantages and disadvantages as noun phrases.

1. Have the students list the advantages and disadvantages of having siblings and of being an only child. This could be done as a sentence completion, such as *One advantage of having siblings is . . .* (e.g., *you have someone to borrow money from*).

2. Have the students report.

3. Closure suggestion: Share your own thoughts.

Duty toward Siblings (Pair or Small-Group Task, Chapter 8)

Specific goal ideas: Have students practice explaining aspects of culture; have students practice stating duties as verb phrases.

1. Have pairs or groups of students list the duties that people in their culture expect siblings to have toward each other. This could be done as a sentence completion, such as *Siblings should always . . .* (e.g., *financially support brothers and sisters who are in school*).

2. Have the students report.

3. Closure suggestion: Comment on which duties people in the target culture would also expect from siblings and on any differences you note in expectations.

Other Activity Ideas

• To Be an Only Child? (survey): Have the students survey several classmates, asking *Do you think it is better to have siblings or be an only child?*

• My Siblings (show and tell): Bring pictures to class, and tell the students about your siblings.

• You Must Be a Second Child (pair or small-group task): In the West, people sometimes assume that oldest children, second children, and so on have certain characteristics. Have the students discuss whether this is true in the host culture.

• The Eldest Child (classroom chat): Ask the students whether in their culture the eldest child has any special duties and responsibilities (e.g., toward parents or younger siblings).

• The Family That Stays Together (pair or small-group task): Is it best for siblings to live in the same town? Have the students list advantages and disadvantages.

• Better by the Dozen? (pair or small-group task): Have the students list the advantages and disadvantages of having a family with many children.

RELATIVES AND ANCESTORS

Where Are Your Ancestors From? (Classroom Chat, Chapter 8)

Specific goal ideas: Introduce the idea of ancestors' origins as a conversation topic; teach vocabulary for names of countries. This activity is appropriate mainly for teachers from the United States, Canada, Australia, and New Zealand.

1. Explain that in many English-speaking countries, most people's ancestors came from some other country, often only one or two generations ago. List the countries from

which immigrants to the target country (or the target country) came. Note also that in these countries asking about one's ancestors is a common conversation topic.

2. Encourage students ask about the origins of your ancestors.

3. Closure suggestion: Review the pronunciation of country names you have mentioned.

Was Your Grandfather Really a Pirate? (Interview, Chapter 8)

Specific goal ideas: Build relations within the class; have students practice explaining relationships.

1. Have the students interview a classmate they don't know well, asking the classmate to tell them about an ancestor they are especially proud of or one who is especially interesting (famous, accomplished, noteworthy). Interviewers should take notes on why the ancestor was notable and on how he or she was related to the person being interviewed.

2. Ask a few eager students to tell about an interesting ancestor they heard about and to explain how that ancestor was related to the interviewee.

3. Closure suggestion: Talk about an interesting ancestor of yours.

My Relatives (Talk, Chapter 7)

Specific goal ideas: Teach vocabulary for relatives.

1. Prepare a talk on how much or little you normally have contact with your relatives (outside the immediate family) whom you have contact with, and how you go about maintaining ties. Also comment on how typical this pattern is or is not for the target culture.

2. Give the talk.

3. Closure suggestion: Ask the students to tell you how they go about maintaining ties with their relatives.

Other Activity Ideas

- Terms for Relatives (classroom chat): Have the students call out for you all the English terms they know for relatives as you list these on the board. Make sure they know what each means. Then ask them to try to explain to you the corresponding terms in their language. (In many cultures, these are considerably more complicated than their English semi-equivalents, so this may quickly descend into good-natured confusion.)

- Godparents (classroom chat): Explain what godparents are, and ask the students to tell you about any corresponding role in their culture.

- Family Tree (talk): Introduce your family tree, perhaps also talking about whether genealogy is popular in the target country.

- Family Ties (classroom chat): Chat with students about the kinds and degrees of obligation relatives in their culture and yours feel to help each other.

- Family Reunions (classroom chat): Ask the students whether they often have family reunions in their culture. If so, when and how?

- Keeping the Family Together? (debate): Have the students debate whether it is most important for family members (or relatives) to live near each other (even at the cost of giving up job or career opportunities) or whether one should move to where job opportunities are best.

- Passing on the Story (survey): Have the students survey each other on this question: *How are memories of ancestors passed on in your family?*

Module 4: Our Nation

VISITING MY COUNTRY

If You Could Go Anywhere in the Target Country . . . (Survey, Chapter 8)
Specific goal ideas: Teach vocabulary related to popular destinations and to why they are popular.

1. Have the students survey their classmates, asking *If you could visit anywhere in the target country for one day, where would you go and why?*

2. Have the students report on the places and reasons they heard about. As students report reasons, list relevant vocabulary—especially adjectives—on the board.

3. Closure suggestion: Review the new vocabulary.

You Absolutely Must Visit . . . (Focused Listening, Chapter 7)
Specific goal ideas: Have students practice focused listening for reasons and explanations; teach vocabulary for names of famous places.

1. Prepare a short talk introducing the main tourist attractions in the target country, why people like to go there, and what significance they have for your history or culture.

2. Tell the students they should listen for place names, why these places are popular, and what cultural significance they have. Then give the talk.

3. Closure suggestion: Check comprehension.

Five Top Attractions (Pair or Small-Group Task, Chapter 8)
Specific goal ideas: Have students practice explaining local tourist attractions in English; teach vocabulary for virtues of tourist locations.

1. Have the students list the five best places in their country for a foreign visitor to travel to and the reasons these are the best ones. (Variation: Have groups decide which city or place in their country would be best for a foreign teacher to work in and why.)

2. Have the students report and explain their choices.

3. Have the students discuss the suggested options and try to agree on a top-five list.

4. Closure suggestion: Express interest in visiting some of the places students recommend.

Other Activity Ideas

- The Trip of a Lifetime (pair or small-group task): Tell the students they have an unlimited supply of money for three weeks of travel. Have them plan where they will go and what they will do.

- What Kinds of Places Do You Like? (survey): Have the students ask each other what kinds of places they like to visit (e.g., temples, rivers).

- Tour Planner (pair or small-group task): Have the students plan a ten-day trip for a foreign visitor in their country. The plan should be as detailed as possible, including information on mode of travel, accommodations, and so forth.

GEOGRAPHY

National Geography (Classroom Chat, Chapter 8)

Specific goal ideas: Teach vocabulary for geographic and spatial terms; teach vocabulary related to geography and topography.

1. Draw a rough outline map of your host country on the board, or have a student do it for you. Do not include details; just sketch an outline of the outer boundary.

2. Have the students tell you where major geographic features of their country (e.g., rivers, mountains, cities) are while you draw them on the map, following the students' instructions literally.

3. As students give you directions for where to draw, have them use either geographic terms (e.g., *in northern . . . , west of . . .*) or spatial terms (e.g., *a little to the left, further down*). Teach these terms and write them on the board as necessary.

4. Closure suggestion: Lead into My Country's Geography below.

My Country's Geography (Pair or Small-Group Task, Chapter 8)

Specific goal ideas: Teach vocabulary for geographic features and place names.

1. Draw an outline map of the target country on the board.

2. Have the students prepare to tell you where to draw the major geographic features of the target country (as they did for their own country in National Geography above).

3. As students tell you what features to mark and where, put them on the outline map.

4. Closure suggestion: Make any necessary corrections to the picture students provided, and add important features they missed.

Regions of My Country (Talk, Chapter 7)

Specific goal ideas: Encourage students to be more aware of the diversity in the target country; teach vocabulary related to features of various regions.

1. Prepare a talk on the main regions of the target country and how they differ from each other. Consider things such as topography, climate, history, economy, special features, and special problems.

2. Before the talk, introduce necessary vocabulary. A big map for students to look at would also be helpful.

3. Give the talk, then check comprehension following the procedure in Talks and Lectures.

4. Closure suggestion: Have the students tell you about the major regions and regional differences in their country.

Other Activity Ideas

- The Best Place (pair or small-group task): Have the students decide which region of their country is best to live in and why. As groups report their opinions, encourage good-natured debate.

- My Home Region (show and tell): Bring photos or artifacts from your region to show your class.

- Your Province or State (classroom chat): Ask the students to tell you about the geography and topography of their province or state.

- Geography and Me (pair or small-group task): Have the students list ways in which the geography of their province (region, etc.) affects life there.

- Economic Regions (classroom chat): Ask the students to describe the different economic regions of their country.

- Famous Peaks (classroom chat): Ask the students about the most famous land features (e.g., mountains, rivers, deserts) in their country. Also ask which of them are important symbols of the country.

- By Land or by Sea? (pair or small-group task): Have the students list advantages, disadvantages, or both of living near the seacoast, in the mountains, and so forth.

THE CLIMATE

The Local Climate (Classroom Chat, Chapter 8)

Specific goal ideas: Have students practice describing the local climate and weather in English; teach vocabulary related to climate and weather.

1. Ask the students what the climate is like in different regions of their country and which areas have the best and worst weather.

2. As useful vocabulary emerges—especially adjectives for describing weather—put it on the board and teach it.

3. Closure suggestion: Review the new vocabulary.

The Rain in Spain . . . (Talk, Chapter 7)

Specific goal ideas: Teach vocabulary related to climate and weather.

1. Prepare a talk on the climate in different parts of the target country. Make special note of unusual or extreme climates.

2. Introduce any necessary vocabulary. Then give the talk.

3. Closure suggestion: Review newly introduced vocabulary.

Extreme Weather (Focused Listening, Chapter 7)

Specific goal ideas: Have students practice focused listening; teach vocabulary relating to storms.

1. Prepare a talk in which you introduce the types of storms and extreme weather experienced in the target country.

2. On the board, list the names of different types of storms you will discuss. Ask the students to take notes as they listen, and be prepared to explain what these different kinds of storms are and how they differ from one another.

3. Give the talk.

4. Closure suggestion: Ask the students to tell you the difference between the different kinds of storms, using the pattern *The difference between . . . and . . . is that . . . .*

Other Activity Ideas

- The Perfect Storm (survey): First have the students list as many kinds of storms and natural disasters as they can think of. Then have the students survey each other on which of these natural disasters they think is most frightening and why. Closure suggestion: Tell the students which of these you would least—or most—like to experience.

- To Every Season (classroom chat): Have the students tell you how the climate varies from season to season locally.

- It's All in the Climate (pair or small-group task): Have the students list ways the climate of their country influences its culture.

- The Perfect Climate (survey): Have the students interview each other asking what they think the perfect climate would be. (Alternatives: What is the best season of the year? What is the most perfect weather? The worst?)

- Staying Cool (pair or small-group task): Have the students list five tricks for staying cool in the summer. (Alternatives: have them list tips for staying warm in winter; coping with high humidity; coping with very dry climates; or staying safe in a typhoon, blizzard, etc.).

- Weather Porn (pair or small-group task): Tell the students that in many Western countries, documentaries about extreme weather and other natural disasters are a common—and popular—form of TV programming. Have them discuss why this might be so and list possible reasons.

ANIMALS AND PLANTS

Useful Creatures (Survey, Chapter 8)

Specific goal ideas: Have students practice using the plural form of countable nouns when discussing something in general; teach vocabulary for animal names.

1. Ask one or more students to tell you what animals are most useful (dangerous, interesting, friendly, etc.) Note that the correct response should generally be in the plural (e.g., *dogs, cats, tigers*).

2. Have the students survey each other on this question: *What animals are most useful (most dangerous, nicest, etc.)?* As they respond, they should use the plural form when the animal name is a countable noun.

3. Have the students report some of the more interesting responses they heard.

4. Closure suggestion: As necessary, go over the names of animals for pronunciation and plural form.

Dirty as a Pig (Pair or Small-Group Task, Chapter 8)

Specific goal ideas: Have students practice explaining aspects of the local culture in English; practice stating qualities as adjectives; teach vocabulary for qualities and animal names.

1. Note that animals are often associated with different qualities, and list examples from the target culture (e.g., *pigs = dirty; lions = brave; foxes = crafty*).

2. Have the students list animals and the qualities which their culture associates them, and be ready to explain why.

3. Have the students report. Ask the students to explain any associations that are not immediately obvious to you.

4. Closure suggestion: Review vocabulary related to qualities that arose during the activity. Make sure students know the proper part of speech for each quality. (For this situation, this would normally be the adjective form.)

Flora and Fauna (Pair or Small-Group Task, Chapter 8)

Specific goal ideas: Have students practice explaining local plants and animals in English; teach vocabulary related to plants and animals.

1. Prepare to take students through a short nature walk in the target country using pictures (e.g., photographs, Microsoft PowerPoint slides).

2. Have the students imagine they are going to lead a group of foreign tourists on a nature hike to introduce the main plants and animals that are important in their country. (This hike could be set in a city park, the local countryside, or a national park.) They should be prepared to name and introduce these plants and animals in English.

3. Have each pair or group report by naming a plant or animal, describing it, and saying something about why it is interesting (important, dangerous, etc.).

4. Closure suggestion: Take students through your target-country nature walk.

Other Activity Ideas

• As Tough as Hickory (pair or small-group task): Have the students list five plants (e.g., trees, flowers) and what they symbolize in their culture.

• Local Plant Life 101 (pair or small-group task): Have the students list five plants (e.g., trees, flowers) that everyone in their country would recognize and that every visitor to their country should recognize. Have them be ready to describe the plants and why it is important to recognize them.

HOLIDAYS

My Favorite Holiday (Survey, Chapter 8)

Specific goal ideas: Introduce the topic of holidays; teach the English names of local holidays.

1. Have the students survey each other on this question: *Which is your favorite holiday and why? Which is your least favorite holiday and why?*

2. As students report, list the names of holidays on the board in their best-known English translation.

3. Closure suggestion: Tell about your own favorite holiday and the reasons you like it.

The Top Ten Holidays (Pair or Small-Group Task, Chapter 8)

Specific goal ideas: Have students practice explaining and justifying opinions; teach holiday-related vocabulary.

1. Have pairs or groups of students list their culture's ten most important holidays in order of importance and be prepared to justify the rankings they give.

2. Have each group report their first choice, and then discuss as necessary until consensus is reached. Then move on to the second most important, and so forth.

3. Closure suggestion: Ask the class to tell you more about the holidays that are unfamiliar to you or seem particularly interesting.

Listing Holidays *(Pair or Small-Group Task, Chapter 8)*
Specific goal ideas: Teach holiday names and holiday-related vocabulary.

1. Make sure you know the major target-country holidays, when and how they are celebrated, and what the origins are.

2. Put a graph on the board with columns for the following: *Holiday Name, Date, How Celebrated, Origin.*

3. Have the students list as many of the holidays of the target country as they can think of and fill in the graph as best they can.

4. Tell groups they get one point for every box in the graph they have filled in. Have them count up their scores and report.

5. Starting with the group that reports the highest score, choose one holiday (preferably a relatively obscure one) and have the students report what they put in each box they claimed points for. If they get anything wrong, praise their courage, disqualify them, and move onto the next group. If a group gets everything right, that group wins.

6. Ask the students which holidays they knew least about, and hold a question-and-answer session about them.

7. Closure suggestion: Review holiday names.

Other Activity Ideas

- What Do You Know about . . . ? (pair or small-group task): First have the students quickly list what they already know about a major holiday in the target country and how it is celebrated. Then have each group report one item of information while you take notes on the board. If the students are not clear on some points, mark them with question marks. Follow up with a press conference activity in which students interview you about the holiday.

- Holiday Pictures (show and tell): Bring to class pictures of celebrations for Christmas or some other holiday. Show the pictures and talk about them.

- Our Holidays (talk, dictocomp): List several holidays of the target country on the board, and have the students take notes as you explain when the holiday is and what it celebrates.

- What Is a Maypole For? (pair or small-group task): Introduce a custom of a holiday in the target country that students probably don't know the origin of (e.g., Christmas trees, Maypoles). Have groups of students discuss the issue, make one guess as to the origin, then present the guess. Award one prize for the closest guess, one for the most original, and so on (a piece of candy per group member would be suitable). To close, briefly explain the origin.

- We Need a New Holiday (pair or small-group task): Have the students invent a new holiday for the host country and plan how to celebrate it. Closure suggestion: Have each group present its proposal, and have the class choose the best (the most creative, the most fun, etc.) new holiday.

HISTORY

What Events Shaped Your History Most? (Pair or Small-Group Task, Chapter 8)

Specific goal ideas: Have students practice explaining local history in English.

1. Tell the students you are interested in the history of their country and want to learn more.

2. Have the students list the five events that shaped their history most, in order of importance, and be ready to explain each to you. (If you want to avoid contemporary politics, restrict the period of the events to pre-1900.)

3. Have each group report an event, explain it, and suggest a ranking. Move eventually into discussion of the relative importance of each.

4. Closure suggestion: Give students some idea of how much of what they told you would be general knowledge among foreigners in their country and what would be less familiar (and hence require more explanation).

History Time Line (Pair or Small-Group Task, Chapter 8)

Specific goal ideas: Have students practice imagining how people in the target culture would view their own history; teach vocabulary related to the target culture's history.

1. Have the students list as many major events in the history of the target country as they can think of in approximate chronological order. (Exact dates are not necessary.) As groups work on this, assist them with vocabulary as needed.

2. Draw a long horizontal line on the board, possibly marked with years (e.g., 1500, 1600, 1700, 1800, 1850, 1900, 1950). Then have groups contribute events one at a time as you write them in on the time line.

3. Have the students choose the five events that they think people in the target country would probably list as being the five most important in their history. Comment on their choices.

4. Closure suggestion: Tell the students which events in their history people in the target culture are probably most familiar with. (Be sensitive to the potential problem that, given the tendency of bad news to travel especially fast and far, what people in the target culture know about the host country's history may be heavily weighted toward bad news.)

Our History as We See It (Talk, Chapter 7)

Specific goal ideas: Help students gain a better understanding of how people in the target country view their own history; teach vocabulary related to the target country's history.

1. Prepare an overview talk on the history of the target country as the average person in the target country sees it.

2. Introduce new vocabulary as necessary, then give the talk and ask the students to take notes on any new information.

3. Closure suggestion: Ask the students what information in the talk was new to them.

Other Activity Ideas

- Proudest Moments? (pair or small-group task): Have the students list the achievements in history their people are proudest of. (Alternative: Have them list their country's achievements of the past ten years.)

- Back to the Future? (debate): Have the students debate this question: *Does a country's past determine its future?*

- Those Who Do Not Study the Past . . . (survey): Have the students survey each other on these questions: *Is it important to study your own country's history? Why or why not? How about the history of other countries? Why or why not?*

- Ten Years from Now (pair or small-group task): Have the students decide what their country might be like ten years from now.

CONTACT WITH OTHER COUNTRIES

Who Shaped Us? (Talk, Chapter 7)

Specific goal ideas: Encourage students to see the target culture in part as the product of cultural borrowing; teach vocabulary related to the influence of other cultures on the target culture.

1. Prepare a talk on which nations have influenced the culture of the target country most and how.

2. Introduce any necessary vocabulary, then give the talk and have the students take notes.

3. Closure suggestion: Lead into Borrowing from the Neighbors.

Borrowing from the Neighbors (Pair or Small-Group Task, Chapter 8)

Specific goal ideas: Have students practice explaining aspects of the local culture in English; teach vocabulary related to (borrowed) aspects of culture.

1. Have the students list elements (e.g., customs, artifacts, institutions, technology) other cultures have borrowed from their culture and elements their culture has borrowed from other cultures.

2. First have the students report the elements other countries and cultures have borrowed from theirs, explaining what was borrowed, who borrowed it, and how. Then have them report on what their culture borrowed from others.

3. Closure suggestion: Make the point that as long as there is interaction between cultures, cultural borrowing is natural and virtually inevitable.

Neither a Borrower nor a Lender Be? (Pair or Small-Group Task, Chapter 8)

Specific goal ideas: Have students practice explaining and justifying opinions.

1. Start by giving some examples of English words that were borrowed from other languages (e.g., *lariat*—Spanish; *beef*—French; *quorum*—Latin; *vodka*—Russian; the list is endless).

2. Ask the students to give you examples of words in their language that are borrowed from English.

3. Have the students discuss and decide: *When borrowing new words from English, is it better to borrow words directly in their original form (transliteration)? Or should new vocabulary always be translated into the host language?*

4. Have the students explain and support their conclusions.

5. Closure suggestion: Summarize the advantages and disadvantages of each approach that students mentioned, and add any others that you can think of.

Other Activity Ideas

- The World Out There (pair or small-group task): Have the students list the ways in which people in their country learn about foreigners.

- The People in My Country (talk, dictocomp): Give a short talk about the different ethnic (social, etc.) groups in the target country. (Alternatives: Talk about the different social classes in the target country or regional differences in the people.)

- What Makes One a Utopan?[4] (pair or small-group task): Have the students list the features that make them distinctive and different from the people of other countries. Have them do this as a set of sentence completions: *A Utopan is someone who . . .* (e.g., *likes Utopan food*).

FAMOUS PEOPLE

How Many Famous People Can You Think of? (Pair or Small-Group Task, Chapter 8)

Specific goal ideas: Teach vocabulary for names of famous people.

1. Have the students quickly list—in English—the names of as many famous people from the target country as they can think of. Tell them that this is a race and that they will only have a few minutes.

2. When the time is up, have groups count the number of names on their list and announce how many they have. Then pick one group—probably the one that claims to have the most—and have members call out the names on the list one by one as you write them on the board. As each name is called out, ask the rest of the class to say whether they got the name right or not (e.g., whether they pronounced it properly and whether the person is actually from the target country). Then decide if this group should festively be declared the winner, or if another group should be given a chance.

3. Closure suggestion: Go over the list on the board, and see if everyone knows who these people are and why they are famous. Explain as necessary.

Our Most Famous (Focused Listening, Chapter 7)

Specific goal ideas: Have students practice mapping out what they already know about a topic and spotting unanswered questions as a focus for listening; teach vocabulary related to the person being introduced.

1. Prepare a talk on one of the target country's most famous people (e.g., leaders, thinkers). Tell the story of this person's life, why he or she is famous, and what impact he or she had on the target country.

2. Before the talk, ask the students to list what they already know about the person you will talk about. Then, have them list—as questions—the things they don't know about that person.

3. Teach any necessary vocabulary, and then ask the students to listen for answers to their questions as you give the talk.

4. Closure suggestion: Ask the students what their questions were and whether or not the talk answered the questions. If they say they did get an answer, have them report what they learned. If not, answer the question for them (as best you can).

---

[4] For lack of a better term, I use *Utopa* as a generic term for host nations and *Utopan* for the people and language.

Utopa's Most Famous (Pair or Small-Group Task, Chapter 8)

Specific goal ideas: Have students practice explaining the local country's history in English.

1. Ask the students to list—in order of importance—the ten people from their country they think foreigners should know about and be ready to explain why each of these people is important in their history. (If you want to avoid contemporary political issues, restrict the list to people born before 1900 or even 1850.)

2. Have each group add one person to the list and introduce that person. Keep going from group to group until the students run out of candidates. (This should result in a list of more than ten on the board.)

3. Have the class discuss which people should be on the top-ten (or top-five) list until they come to a consensus.

4. Closure suggestion: Tell the students what people from the target country would typically already know or not know about these famous people and what would need to be explained.

Other Activity Ideas

- A Famous Person (press conference): Read up on a famous person from the target country (e.g., Abraham Lincoln, Winston Churchill, Audrey Hepburn, Michael Jordan) so that you can play that person for an interview; if possible, also come up with a bit of a costume. Then have the students interview you as that person for their local newspaper. Closure suggestion: Ask the students what discovery surprised them most during the interviews. (If you were forced to improvise answers to some of the questions, you might also let students know which answers were real and which ones you made up.)

- Beyond the Spotlight (talk): Give a talk about a lesser known but interesting person from the target country you think students should know about.

- Fame? (survey): Have the students survey each other on this question: *Would you want to be famous? If so, for what?*

- Famous Women (pair or small-group task): Have the students list the most famous women (e.g., leaders, scientists, soldiers) in their country's history.

- Listing the Leaders (pair or small-group task): Have the students list as many of the target country's leaders (e.g., presidents, prime ministers, kings) as they can.

HEROES AND VILLAINS

Heroes (Pair or Small-Group Task, Chapter 8)

Specific goal ideas: Have students practice explaining the local country's history in English; teach vocabulary for virtues.

1. Suggest that a hero is someone admired for being courageous physically and morally and for bravely persisting in the face of difficulties and obstacles.

2. Have the students list the top ten heroes (not just famous people) of their country and be ready to explain why each is considered a hero. (You can make the task more challenging by restricting the list to, for example, people who are still alive or those who lived before modern times.)

3. When groups are ready to report, have each group contribute one or more names to the list. If you do not know who the person is or why he or she is famous, have the group explain.

4. Once a list of candidates is compiled, have the students discuss who should be the top three and why.

5. Closure suggestion: Have the students analyze what virtues the suggested people embody, and have them discuss what the list suggests about the virtues their culture especially values.

Heroes of the Target Country (Pair or Small-Group Task, Chapter 8)

Specific goal ideas: Have students practice imagining how people from the target culture view their own culture.

1. Prepare by making a list of the most famous heroes and villains of the target country.

2. Have the students list the five greatest heroes and villains of the target country and tell why they think these people are considered heroes or villains.

3. Have each group write its list on the board. Then ask the students to explain any choices you are curious about.

4. Comment on the lists from your cultural perspective.

5. Closure suggestion: Offer your own list.

My Hero! (Focused Listening, Chapter 7)

Specific goal ideas: Have students practice focused listening; teach vocabulary for virtues.

1. Prepare a talk introducing the life of one or more of your favorite heroes and explaining what qualities made this person a hero to many in the target country.

2. Introduce any necessary vocabulary (but not words for the virtues you will speak about). Tell the students you want them to listen for the qualities that made this person considered a hero. Then give the talk.

3. Closure suggestion: Check comprehension by having students list the qualities that made this person a hero.

Other Activity Ideas

- Makers of History (pair or small-group task): Have each student write down, according to their own opinion, (1) the name of the greatest person who ever lived, (2) the most important event in the last century, and (3) the most important invention. Then have the students compare their lists in groups. Have the students explain and justify their answers to other members of the group and try to reach consensus. After students report, if time permits, discuss what criteria may be used to make a choice within each of the above categories.

- A Scene from History (activity): Have small groups prepare and perform a brief skit involving a hero in a famous scene from history or folklore. Allow them to prepare props as well.

NATIONAL SYMBOLS

Our Flag (Classroom Chat, Chapter 8)

Specific goal ideas: Have students practice explaining aspects of the local culture in English.

1. Ask the students to tell you about their nation's flag. Have them explain what the various parts symbolize and whatever they know about the flag's history.

2. Closure suggestion: Introduce the flag of the target country.

Our National Anthem (Pair or Small-Group Task, Chapter 8)

Specific goal ideas: Have students practice translating into English; have students practice explaining aspects of the local culture in English.

1. Have the students translate their national anthem (or perhaps only the first verse) into English for you. (Before doing this activity, check to make sure that most people in the host country know the national anthem and its lyrics.)

2. Have one group dictate a line to you as you put it on the board; then work on it as a class. Repeat the process with the remaining lines.

3. Closure suggestion: Ask the students to tell you about the anthem's story and significance. You might also ask them to sing it for you—in the original language.

My National Anthem (Talk, Chapter 7; Dictocomp, Chapter 7)

Specific goal ideas: Teach words from the national anthem.

1. Prepare a talk telling how your national anthem was written and why it was chosen for its national role.

2. First introduce any necessary vocabulary. Then dictate the anthem (or its first verse) to the students using dictation or dictocomp procedure.

3. After students have and understand the lyrics, give a talk about the background of the anthem.

4. Closure suggestion: Sing or play the anthem for students.

Other Activity Ideas

- My Flag (talk, dictocomp): Tell the story of the target country's flag.

- The National Animal (classroom chat): Ask the students what animal best symbolizes their country and why. If the target country is associated with a certain animal, explain why.

- The National Flower (classroom chat): Ask the students what flower or plant best symbolizes their country and why.

Module 5: Society

CITY AND COUNTRYSIDE

Urban or Rural Life? (Survey, Chapter 8)

Specific goal ideas: Have students practice explaining advantages; teach vocabulary related to urban and rural life.

1. Have the students survey each other on which location they think is best to live in and why: village, small town, or city.

2. Have the students report on which setting most of their classmates preferred, perhaps even keeping a tally on the board.

3. As students report why their classmates preferred a given setting, note the main advantages of each setting on the board.

4. Closure suggestion: Go over useful vocabulary and phrases that emerged during the activity.

Trouble in River City (Talk, Chapter 7; Pair or Small-Group Task, Chapter 8)

Specific goal ideas: Have students practice explaining local social issues; have students practice comparing cultures to identify both similarities and differences; teach vocabulary related to urban issues.

1. Prepare a talk introducing the main issues and problems facing cities in the target country.

2. Introduce necessary vocabulary, and then give the talk following the procedure in Talks and Lectures.

3. In response to your talk, have the students list and explain for you the major social problems facing cities in their country.

4. Closure suggestion: Review new vocabulary. Also ask the students to comment on how similar or different the issues facing cities in their country are from those facing cities in the target country.

Trouble on the Farm (Talk, Chapter 7; Pair or Small-Group Task, Chapter 8)

Specific goal ideas: Have students practice explaining local social issues; have students practice comparing cultures to identify similarities and differences; teach vocabulary related to rural issues.

1. Prepare a talk introducing the main issues and problems facing rural areas in the target country.

2. Introduce necessary vocabulary, and then give the talk following the procedure in Talks and Lectures.

3. In response to your talk, have the students list and explain for you the major social problems facing rural areas in their country.

4. Closure suggestion: Review new vocabulary. Also ask the students to comment on how similar or different the issues facing rural areas in their country are from those facing rural areas in the target country.

Other Activity Ideas

- Urban versus Rural (pair or small-group task): Have the students list the advantages and disadvantages of living in a town (city) as opposed to the countryside (village, small town).

- Town and Country, My Style (talk, dictocomp): Give a talk in which you compare country-side and city life in the target country, noting the relative virtues of each. Show photos if you have any.

- The Place to Be (survey): Have the students ask each other which city in their country they think is best to live in.

- Our Most Important Cities (classroom chat): Ask the students which cities in their country are the most important and what the characteristics of each are.

- Your Biggest City Is . . . ? (pair or small-group task): Have pairs or groups of students list (in order of size) the cities they are familiar with in the target country and what they know about them.

- Playing Mayor (pair or small-group task): Have the students imagine that they are a committee that has been appointed to give the mayor of their city advice on how to improve life there. Have them list and be ready to present proposals for debate in an expanded council meeting (i.e., a whole-class discussion).

- From Our Perspective (pair or small-group task): Have the students list and explain differences in outlook (aspirations, goals) between urban and rural people in their country.

GOVERNMENT AND POLITICAL LIFE

How the Target Country Government Works (Pair or Small-Group Task, Chapter 8)

Specific goal ideas: Have students practice explaining government structures; teach vocabulary related to government.

1. Prepare to introduce the government system of the target country.

2. Have the students quickly write down as much as they know about the structure of the target country government—what its main parts are and what each does.

3. Have the groups report.

4. Tell the students to listen for information that fills in holes in their picture of the target country's government system. Then give a talk introducing the main government bodies, what each does, and how the system works. Focus especially on areas students didn't know about or were confused about. (To avoid creating the impression that you are comparing the host government system unfavorably with that of the target country, be sure to mention disadvantages as well as advantages of how the system works.)

5. Closure suggestion: Have the students report on what information in the talk was new to them.

How Our Government Works (Pair or Small-Group Task, Chapter 8)

Specific goal ideas: Have students practice explaining the local country's government structure in English; teach vocabulary related to government.

1. Have the students prepare a brief introduction to their government's system in English. They should introduce the main government bodies and what each does.

2. When students report, have each group introduce and explain one body. Ask for further clarification and explanation as necessary.

3. Closure suggestion: Review for students what you have learned, and ask them to check whether you got it right.

Taxing Matters (Press Conference, Chapter 8)

Specific goal ideas: Have students practice actively asking questions as a strategy for learning about another culture; teach vocabulary related to taxes.

1. Have the students quickly write down what they already know about taxes in the target country (e.g., *What kinds of taxes are there? Who needs to pay? How is the amount determined? How are taxes collected?*). Then have them write down questions about what they don't know or are not sure about.

2. Have the students ask questions following the press conference procedure.

3. Closure suggestion: Ask the students to tell you about the tax system in their country.

Other Activity Ideas

- Levels of Government (classroom chat): Ask the students to explain the administrative levels and setup of their government system to you. Chart out the system on the board as they explain, in part so they can check to see if you have understood. Follow up by finding out where the students are from (e.g., cities, county towns, villages).

- Wanna Be Mayor? (survey): Have the students survey each other on this question: *Would you want to be a mayor (president, general secretary, etc.)? Why or why not?*

- The Pains of Power (pair or small-group task): Have the students list the joys and headaches of being a mayor (president, prime minister, etc.).

- The Other Kind of Party (talk): Introduce the main political parties in the target country and the differences between them.

- How We Pay Taxes (pair or small-group task): Have the students prepare to describe their country's tax system to you, including what taxes there are, who needs to pay them, how the amount is determined, and how taxes are collected.

- A Better Tax (pair or small-group task): Have the students design the ideal tax system. (Alternatives: Have the students discuss and decide these questions: *What is the best way to tax? How much—what percentage of income—is it fair to tax? Should the tax system be used to redistribute wealth?*)

- Elections (talk): Describe the election process in the target country and how it works—warts and all.

- IDs (show and tell): Bring one or more of your important ID documents (e.g., passport, driver's license) to class and go over it with students. Follow up by asking them about basic IDs in their country.

ECONOMIC LIFE AND DEVELOPMENT

Bringing in New Industry (Survey, Chapter 8)

Specific goal ideas: Have students practice stating names of industries as nouns (e.g., *tourism, mining, shipbuilding*); teach vocabulary for names of industries.

1. Have the students survey each other on this question: *If you could establish a new industry in your area, what kind would it be, and why?*

2. As students report, write names of industries on the board (generally as nouns).

3. Closure suggestion: Go over the industry names, and add others to the list.

Reeling in the Clients (Pair or Small-Group Task, Chapter 8)

Specific goal ideas: Have students practice making and justifying recommendations; teach vocabulary related to industry.

1. Tell the students that they have been asked to advise their local government on how to attract outside companies to set up joint venture enterprises locally, creating more jobs and helping the local economy.

2. Have the students come up with recommendations for what kind of industry the local government should try to attract and how to go about it. (Each recommendation could be stated as a sentence completion, e.g., *Our first recommendation is that . . .*).

3. Have the students present and justify their recommendations; then have the students discuss the relative merits of the recommendations.

4. Closure suggestion: Have the students vote on the best recommendation.

What Keeps Our Local Economy Afloat (Talk, Chapter 7)

Specific goal ideas: Have students practice (carefully and mindfully) drawing lessons from the experience of other countries; teach vocabulary related to economic life.

1. Prepare a talk on the economic life of the target country (region, etc.). Introduce the main products, services, industries, and sources of employment. Mention both strengths and weaknesses of the economy.

2. Teach any necessary vocabulary. Then give the talk.

3. After the talk, have the students discuss what—if any—relevant positive or negative lessons they can draw about their own economy from the experience of the target country.

4. Closure suggestion: Comment on any interesting insights you have gained about economic issues through your experience in the host country.

Other Activity Ideas

- Do We Want to Reel the Clients in? (pair or small-group task): Tell the students that they have been asked to advise their local government on whether it is a good idea to attract foreign companies to set up joint venture enterprises locally in order to create jobs and help the local economy. Have them come up with a recommendation.

- Our Industries (classroom chat): Ask the students to tell you what the most important national and local industries are.

- A Development Strategy (pair or small-group task): Have the students create an economic development strategy for their province (county, etc.).

- On the Farm (classroom chat): Have the students tell you about the main agricultural products produced in their area, the normal schedule of the farming year, and the steps for planting and harvesting the main local crop.

- Opportunity Knocks (classroom chat): Ask the students: *If a business person from another country asked you what investment opportunities there were in your home area, what would you say?*

- Creating Jobs (survey): Have the students survey each other on this question: *What is the best way to create jobs for the local economy?*

- Controlling Inflation (survey): Have the students survey each other on this question: *What is the best way to control inflation?*

- Made in Utopa (classroom chat): Ask the students to list and describe the products exported by their home area.

- WTO or No? (debate): Have the students debate whether membership in the World Trade Organization (WTO) is a good thing for their country.

- How Good an Idea Is Industrialization? (pair or small-group task): Have the students list the advantages and disadvantages of industrialization and be ready to explain whether they think their country should industrialize further.

MONEY AND BANKING

No Wooden Nickels (Show and Tell, Chapter 7)
Specific goal ideas: Teach vocabulary related to money.

1. Bring in money from the target country, and explain what denominations of coins and bills the target country uses. Teach any relevant vocabulary.

2. Closure suggestion: Review the terms for various denominations of money.

Investment Tips (Talk, Chapter 7)
Specific goal ideas: Teach vocabulary related to investment.

1. Prepare a talk on investment in the target country—the main options and the advantages and disadvantages of each.

2. Teach any necessary vocabulary, then give the talk.

3. Closure suggestion: Ask the students to compare what you said about the target country with investment options in their country, noting similarities and differences in how people go about investing money.

Spare Change (Pair or Small-Group Task, Chapter 8)
Specific goal ideas: Give students practice in explaining aspects of the local economy in English; teach vocabulary related to investment.

1. Ask the students the following: *If you were unexpectedly given an extra sum of money and wanted to invest it for the future, what would be the best thing to do with it?*

2. Have the students list the main options that would be available, choose the option they think would be best, and prepare to explain why.

3. Have the students report, and have them discuss the relative merits of different options they suggest.

4. Closure suggestion: As the students report, note anything that is not entirely clear to you. Close by asking the students to clarify those points to you.

Other Activity Ideas

- Opening a Bank Account (talk, dictocomp): Describe for the students the steps for opening a bank account in the target country.

- Financing a Home (talk): Explain how one normally goes about financing a home in the target country. (Alternative: Talk about financing a child's university education.)

- Borrowing Money (classroom chat): Ask the students how one normally goes about borrowing money in their country, and for what purposes people are most likely to borrow money.

- Credit Cards (debate): Have the students debate whether wide use of credit cards is good or bad for a society.

MEDICAL CARE

Health Problems (Focused Listening)

Specific goal ideas: Teach vocabulary related to health problems.

1. Prepare a talk on common health problems in the target country.

2. Before the talk, introduce necessary vocabulary. Also put a list of questions on the board that will guide students' listening during the talk.

3. Give the talk.

4. Check whether students were able to catch the answers to the questions.

5. On the board, list the terms for health problems mentioned in your talk. Then ask the students what some of the most common health problems are in their country, and add new terms to the list.

6. Closure suggestion: Review the health problem vocabulary.

Improving the System (Pair or Small-Group Task, Chapter 8)

Specific goal ideas: Have students practice explaining health care issues; teach vocabulary related to health care.

1. Tell the students to imagine that they have been appointed to a blue-ribbon panel of experts asked to make recommendations for improving the health care system in their country. (Some funding is available to implement the recommendations, but the funding is limited, so not all recommendations can be funded.)

2. Have the students decide what recommendations they will make. They should be ready to explain both the recommendation itself and why they made it.

3. Before the reports, tell the students that they will eventually be asked to vote on which recommendations should be funded (and they cannot vote for their own).

4. As students report, encourage other groups to ask follow-up questions; you may also want to ask follow-up questions on anything you think needs further explanation.

5. Closure suggestion: Vote on which proposals should be funded.

Health Care in My Country (Press Conference, Chapter 8)

Specific goal ideas: Have students practice explaining health care issues; teach vocabulary related to health care.

1. Have the students prepare to interview you about health care in the target country (e.g., common health problems, how health care is paid for, advantages and disadvantages of the current system). Ask the students to try to think of the most interesting questions they can.

2. Conduct the press conference.

3. Closure suggestion: Have everyone vote on which questions were the most interesting.

Other Activity Ideas

- Seeing a Doctor (classroom chat): Ask the students to explain the steps involved in seeing a doctor at a clinic or hospital in their country.

- Medical Insurance (show and tell): Bring medical insurance forms or records to class to show the students.

- Home Remedies (classroom chat): Ask the students about home remedies their parents or grandparents use to cure various ailments.

- To Tell the Truth (debate): Is it better to tell dying patients who have incurable diseases the truth about their condition or to encourage them to believe that they might recover?

- Staying Alive (pair or small-group task): Have groups decide on the five most important health tips they would give to a foreigner visiting their country.

- Cure for the Common Cold (survey): Have the students survey each other on the best steps to take if you have a cold, a fever, or a stomachache.

- No Smoking? (debate): Have students debate the question: *Should smoking be restricted? If so, how?* (Variation: Have the students debate whether access to alcohol should be restricted and, if so, how.)

LAW AND ORDER

Crime and Punishment (Classroom Chat, Chapter 8)

Specific goal ideas: Teach vocabulary for crimes and punishments.

1. Ask the students to call out as many names of crimes as they can think of. List these on the board (using the noun form). Add names for other common crimes that students don't know.

2. Do the same for names of punishments.

3. Closure suggestion: Teach the new words on the board, then erase it. Then have the students write down as many of the crime and punishment names as they can remember (in noun form). Finally, check their work.

Improving Public Order (Pair or Small-Group Task, Chapter 8)

Specific goal ideas: Have students practice explaining crime control measures; have students practice making recommendations.

1. Tell the students that they are law enforcement experts who have been asked by local government to come up with a plan for reducing crime in the area.

2. Have the students make plans that include (1) an assessment of what the most serious local crime problem is and (2) several recommendations for what should be done about it.

3. When students report, first ask each group what they think the most serious problem is. Try to reach consensus on the order of importance. Then, starting with the most important, elicit recommendations, and have the class discuss the merits of each.

4. Closure suggestion: Share your thoughts on the most serious crime problems in the target country and what you think should be done about them.

Order in the Court! (Talk, Chapter 7)

Specific goal ideas: Teach vocabulary related to trials.

1. Prepare a talk explaining the main steps of a typical trial in the target country (e.g., charging the suspect, making opening statements, cross-examining witnesses, making closing statements). Also prepare to introduce and teach some of the key terms and phrases used in trial procedure (e.g., *I object, innocent until proven guilty, defendant, prosecutor*).

2. Give the talk.

3. (Optional: Have the students role-play a trial, following the steps you outlined.)

4. Closure suggestion: Review new vocabulary and phrases.

Other Activity Ideas

*   Keeping the Peace (talk): Give a talk introducing the various law enforcement agencies in the target country and what they do. Closure suggestion: Ask the students to tell you about the law enforcement agencies in their country and their duties.

*   The Death Penalty I (pair or small-group task): Have the students list advantages and disadvantages to society of having capital punishment.

*   The Death Penalty II (debate): Have the students debate whether it is good for a society to have capital punishment.

*   Behind Bars (talk): Give a talk about prisons in the target country.

*   A Lawyer-to-Be? (pair or small-group task): Have the students list the advantages (or disadvantages) of a career as a lawyer (policeman, judge, etc.).

*   Behind Bars? (pair or small-group task): First have the students list alternatives to prison as approaches to dealing with criminals. Then have them list the advantages and disadvantages of each approach.

SCIENCE AND TECHNOLOGY

If You Were a Scientist . . . (Survey, Chapter 8)

Specific goal ideas: Teach vocabulary for scientific fields and kinds of scientists.

1. Have the students survey each other on this question: *What kind of scientist would it be most . . . to be?* (e.g., *interesting, dangerous, boring, profitable*).

2. As students report the results of their surveys, make a list of the names of scientific fields and kinds of scientists.

3. Closure suggestion: Review the vocabulary lists, especially for pronunciation.

The Down Side of Technology? (Pair or Small-Group Task, Chapter 8)

Specific goal ideas: Have students practice explaining benefits and unfortunate effects of technological developments.

1. As a whole class, list several important examples of technological development that have affected their country (or the whole world) in recent years.

2. Have the students in groups list the benefits and disadvantages of these technological developments.

3. Have the groups report.

4. Closure suggestion: Briefly discuss whether societies should try to control the implementation of technological advances in some way.

Should Ideas Be Patented? (Debate, Chapter 8)

Specific goal ideas: Have students practice arguing points.

1. Introduce the concept of intellectual property rights, and point out that opinions differ on the degree to which intellectual property rights should be protected through means such as copyrights and patents.

2. Organize students into teams, and have them prepare to argue either that intellectual property rights should be protected as much as possible or that people should have as much freedom as possible to borrow and use the ideas of others.

3. Follow the procedure for debates.

4. Closure suggestion: Rather than choosing a winner, have everyone list and review the advantages and disadvantages for their society of promoting protection of intellectual property rights.

Other Activity Ideas

- A Famous Scientist (talk): Give a talk about a famous scientist (inventor, etc.) from the target country.

- Cultivating Scientists (pair or small-group task): Tell the students that their local government is exploring ways to promote technological innovation in order to boost the local economy and wants advice on how to train young people so that more of them will become good scientists, inventors, and technicians. Then have pairs or groups of students come up with a set of recommendations for their local government. Closure suggestion: Have the class decide on which are the three best recommendations.

- How We Train Scientists (talk): Give a talk on training scientists and technicians in the target country.

- Research (classroom chat): Ask the students how and in what kinds of institutions scientific research is carried on in their country, and what the most famous centers of scientific research and learning are in their country.

- Is Technology Necessarily a Good Thing? (pair or small-group task): Have the students list the advantages and disadvantages of society's becoming more technologically oriented.

- A Better Mousetrap (survey): Have the students survey each other on this question: *If you could invent one new thing, what would it be?*

- A Scientist-to-Be? (pair or small-group task): Have the students list the advantages (or disadvantages) of a career as a scientist.

- Famous Scientists (pair or small-group task): Have the students list several of the most famous and important scientists in their country—past and present—and be ready to explain to you who these people were and why they are important.

- Cell Phones (debate): Have the students debate whether the increasing use of mobile phones is more advantageous or more disadvantageous for society.

- The Magic Bullet? (survey): Have the students survey each other on this question: *Can technology solve most of society's problems?*

- Star Trek? (pair or small-group task): Start by noting that more and more countries are developing a space program. Then have groups list the advantages and disadvantages for a country of having a space program. Finally, have them decide whether the costs are greater than the benefits.

COMPUTERS AND THE WEB

Bill Gates II (Survey, Chapter 8)

Specific goal ideas: Have students practice explaining types of software; teach vocabulary related to software.

1. Have the students survey each other on this question: *If you wanted to get rich by designing computer software, what kind would you design?*

2. Have the students report and explain the best ideas they heard. Introduce new vocabulary, and put it on the board as appropriate.

3. Closure suggestion: Have the students vote on which idea is most likely to make money.

Computers and Wealth (Pair or Small-Group Task, Chapter 8)

Specific goal ideas: Have students practice explaining and justifying opinions.

1. Have the students decide whether they think the increasing use and availability of computers will tend to increase or lessen the gap between the rich and the poor. Ask them to try to reach consensus and be ready to explain their position.

2. Have the students report and justify their positions.

3. Closure suggestion: Ask for suggestions on what could be done to minimize wealth gap problems that might be created by the increasing reliance on computers.

The World of Local Web Sites (Classroom Chat, Chapter 8)

Specific goal ideas: Teach vocabulary for types of Web sites.

1. Ask the students to tell you about what kinds of Web sites are available in their language. As they explain, introduce necessary vocabulary and put it on the board.

2. Closure suggestion: If possible, have the students show you one or more popular local language Web sites.

Other Activity Ideas

- Computers in Local Life (classroom chat): Ask the students to tell you about the role of computers in their country today (e.g., How easy is it to buy one? How much do they cost? Are there places you can use one? How many people have computers? How prevalent is computer knowledge? How fast is computer use growing?).

- Giving Computer Directions (pair or small-group task): Have the students prepare to explain to you in English—from turning the computer on—how to write and send an e-mail message (visit a Web site, etc.). As they prepare, help them with computer-related vocabulary. When the first volunteer group reports step by step, stand in front of the class, and do exactly what the group tells you to do. If you have a computer that can serve as a visual aid, fine. If not, pretend. As new computer-related words come up, write them on the board and explain how they are used. Closure suggestion: Review the new words, and have the students use them in a sentence. (Note: Before this activity, check to see whether the students know enough about the relevant computer operation to do the activity.)

- Word Processing (classroom chat): Ask the students to explain to you how to do word processing in their language.

- A Bad Computer Day (talk): Tell a story about an amusing or disastrous experience you had with computers. Closure suggestion: Review computer-related vocabulary from the story.

- Computers—Blessing or Bane? (pair or small-group task): Have the students list the advantages and disadvantages for society of the increase in computer availability and use. (Alternative: Discuss advantages and disadvantages of the growing use of the Internet.)

- Computers in Kindergarten? (pair or small-group task): Have the students decide whether schools should teach children to use computers and, if so, starting at what age.

- Shareware? (pair or small-group task): Have the students decide whether computer software should be freely available to the public (shareware) or whether people should be required to pay for it.

NEWS AND INFORMATION

A Typical TV News Broadcast (Classroom Chat, Chapter 8)

Specific goal ideas: Encourage students to view culture as patterned behavior; teach vocabulary for types of TV news items.

1. Point out to students that TV news broadcasts tend to follow a formula; there is usually a fairly clear pattern for what kinds of stories are presented in what order.

2. Ask the students to tell you what the normal elements of a typical TV news broadcast are in their country and what order they appear in.

3. Closure suggestion: Respond by telling students about the typical kinds of and order of items in a TV news program in the target country.

What's in a Newspaper? (Pair or Small-Group Task, Chapter 8)

Specific goal ideas: Encourage students to view culture as patterned behavior; teach vocabulary for types of newspaper articles, pages, and columns.

1. Have the students introduce to you the typical organization of a popular newspaper in their country. They should first list the kinds of pages (e.g., *news page, sports page*) and then list what kinds of items are normally found on each.

2. As students work, provide them with necessary vocabulary.

3. When the students report, first have the class come to a consensus on what the main kinds of pages are, and then deal with the kinds of articles, columns, and items that are usually found on each.

4. Compare the students' description with newspaper organization in the target country.

5. Closure suggestion: Ask the students which pages they usually read first, which they like most, and which they tend to skip. Respond by revealing the same about your own newspaper-reading habits.

Car Wreck on Route 66 (Pair or Small-Group Task, Chapter 8)

Specific goal ideas: Have students practice explaining and justifying opinions.

1. Start by noting that in many Western countries, reports on local car accidents, crimes, and other unfortunate occurrences are a staple of local TV news.

2. Have groups of students list the advantages and disadvantages of giving such stories prominent coverage in the news.

3. Have the students report and explain.

4. In follow-up discussion, have the class try to generate guidelines for a local TV news station producer on how to handle such news items. Questions to consider would include where they should be placed in the broadcast, how long the stories should be, and what the video should and should not show.

5. Closure suggestion: Compare what the students suggest with what local TV stations in the target country actually tend to do.

Other Activity Ideas

- The Daily News (talk): Give a talk about the news industry in the target country. What are the main outlets for news? What kind of news does each tend to focus on?

- Local Newspapers (classroom chat): Have the students tell you what the various newspapers are in your host city and describe what is special about each.

- Our Local Papers (talk): Give a talk about the different kinds of newspapers in the target country or community, and describe what is special about each kind.

- How Do You Stay in Touch? (survey): Have the students survey each other on how they normally get their news (e.g., TV, newspapers, word of mouth).

- All the News That's Fit to Print? (pair or small-group task): Have the students list—in order of priority—the five most important kinds of information that should be printed in newspapers and five kinds of information that should be given minimal coverage.

RELIGION AND PHILOSOPHY

Great Thinkers (Classroom Chat, Chapter 8)

Specific goal ideas: Have students practice explaining traditional philosophical ideas in English; teach English names of local philosophical figures.

1. Ask the students to tell you the names of the major thinkers (e.g., philosophers, religious figures) in their country's history. List these on the board, in their English form if possible.

2. For each person listed, ask the students to explain to you one philosophical idea that the thinker is famous for. Help with vocabulary as necessary.

3. Closure suggestion: Repeat back to students what they have told you to see if you got it right.

Religions and Values (Pair or Small-Group Task, Chapter 8)

Specific goal ideas: Teach vocabulary for values (e.g., *patience, hospitality*).

1. Have the students choose one of their culture's traditional religions (or schools of thought) and prepare to explain several ways in which it influences the values of their culture. As students prepare, help them with relevant vocabulary.

2. As students report, ask follow-up questions on points that are not clear to you. Also list values (in noun form) as they are mentioned.

3. Closure suggestion: Review the list of values in their noun form, and then have the students generate the adjective forms.

Religion in My Country (Talk, Chapter 7)

Specific goal ideas: Teach vocabulary related to religion in the target culture.

1. Prepare a talk on religious life in the target country. What religions are represented? What are the basic beliefs and practices of each? What role do they play in society?

2. Before giving the talk, provide students with necessary vocabulary. Also assign them to respond to the talk with one or more follow-up questions.

3. Give the talk.

4. Follow up with questions and answers.

5. Closure suggestion: Review new vocabulary.

Other Activity Ideas

- The Legacy of the Sage (pair or small-group task): Have the students discuss how much impact one or more of the important thinkers of their country's past has on their culture today.

- Local Religions 101 (pair or small-group task): Have the students prepare to explain to you the main religions in their country and the main beliefs of each.

- A Traditional Religion (pair or small-group task): Have the students prepare to introduce in detail one of their country's main traditional schools of thought to you.
- Traditional Religion Today (classroom chat): Have the students tell you about the impact on culture and daily life of traditional religion in their country.

LANGUAGES AND DIALECTS

Your Next Language (Survey, Chapter 8)

Specific goal ideas: Teach names of languages; encourage additional language learning.

1. Have the students survey each other on this question: *If you were to learn another language, what would it be and why?*

2. As students report, list the (English) names of the languages on the board.

3. Follow up by asking students whether they have any plans to actually learn additional languages and, if so, how. Also share any desires or plans you have for your own continued foreign language study.

4. Closure suggestion: Review the names of languages, perhaps adding other important language names that were not mentioned.

Languages in My Country (Talk, Chapter 7)

Specific goal ideas: Have students practice guessing new vocabulary; teach vocabulary related to languages.

1. Prepare a talk on the language situation in the target country, dealing with questions such as these: What languages are spoken, where, and by whom? How much difference is there between one part of the target country and another in terms of accent, vocabulary, and other aspects? How much can you tell about people from their speech?

2. Before giving the talk, tell the students to listen for new vocabulary, make note of what the unfamiliar words sound like, and try to guess what the unfamiliar words mean. Each student should locate at least one new word.

3. Give the talk.

4. After the talk, have the students ask about any unfamiliar word by first telling you what it sounded like and what their guess about its meaning was. Then teach the word, affirming anything in their guess that was right.

5. Closure suggestion: Move into the activity Our Languages and Dialects below.

Our Languages and Dialects (Pair or Small-Group Task, Chapter 8)

Specific goal ideas: Have students practice explaining the host-country language situation.

1. On the board, have a student draw an outline map of the host country.

2. Have the students prepare in groups to explain to you what different languages (dialects) are spoken in their country and where. They need to be ready to explain—in English—where on the map these language or dialect areas are, and tell you something about each of them and how similar or different they are from each other.

3. As students report, fill in the map on the board according to what they tell you. Ask follow-up questions as necessary to clarify the explanations.

4. Closure suggestion: Review your understanding of the situation and check with students to see if you have it right. Also review new words that emerged during the course of the discussion.

Other Activity Ideas

- What Is in a Dialect? (classroom chat): Have the students explain to you what dialect differences exist in their country and how great these are. Are there only small accent differences? Does vocabulary differ? How easily can people from different regions communicate with each other?

- English Only? (talk): Give a talk about a current language-related issue in the target country (e.g., bilingual education, English-only versus multilingualism).

- Local Language Policy (classroom chat): Have the students introduce the language policies of their country to you. Is a national standard language promoted? If so, how? Is there more than one official language?

- High School French (talk): Tell the students about which foreign languages students in the target country most often learn and why.

- A Social Language Map (pair or small-group task, in multilingual host countries): Have the students list the situations in which people would normally speak the country's standard or national language and the situations in which they would normally speak some other language or dialect. (To describe a setting, have the students consider who is speaking to whom, where, under what circumstances, and on what topic.)

SOCIAL PROBLEMS

A Litany of Social Ills (Survey, Chapter 8)

Specific goal ideas: Teach vocabulary related to social problems (using noun forms, e.g., *poverty, unemployment*).

1. Have the students survey each other on which is their country's most serious social problem.

2. As students report, write the names of the social problems on the board, all in noun form.

3. List some of the main social problems facing the target country (also in noun form).

4. Closure suggestion: Move into the activity Whatever Shall We Do?

Whatever Shall We Do? (Pair or Small-Group Task, Chapter 8)

Specific goal ideas: Have students practice asking follow-up questions; have students practice explaining social issues.

1. Put a list of social problems on the board (or use the one students came up with in A Litany of Social Ills above).

2. Assign each pair or group one problem, and have each produce a plan for dealing with it. They should also be ready to state the main advantage of their plan and its main drawback or problem.

3. As each group reports its plan, have the other groups listen and come up with a follow-up question that helps clarify the plan or its advantages and disadvantages.

4.   Follow up with general discussion of the merits of the plans.

5.   Closure suggestion: Praise especially good (well-explained) plans and especially insightful follow-up questions.

A Social Problem (Talk, Chapter 7)

Specific goal ideas: Encourage students to generate follow-up questions; teach vocabulary related to social problems.

1.   Prepare a talk on one of the main social problems facing the target country (e.g., drugs, poverty, crime, unemployment). Be ready to explain the causes of the problem and the efforts being made to deal with it.

2.   Before giving the talk, introduce any necessary vocabulary (or ask the students to listen for unfamiliar vocabulary and be prepared to ask about it). Also require students to think of at least one good follow-up question to ask about your talk.

3.   Give the talk.

4.   Have the students ask their follow-up questions.

5.   Closure suggestion: Say which follow-up questions you thought were best and why.

Other Activity Ideas

*   The Best Way to . . . (survey): Have the students survey each other on the following questions:
    — What is the best way to combat drug use and addiction?
    — What is the best way to deal with juvenile crime?
    — What is the best way to combat illiteracy?
    — What is the best way to alleviate poverty?
    — What is the best way to prevent children from dropping out of school?
    — What is the best way to deal with unemployment?

ENVIRONMENT AND ECOLOGY

Pollution (Talk, Chapter 7)

Specific goal ideas: Teach vocabulary for types of pollution.

1.   Prepare a talk on pollution in the target country. Talk about what kinds of pollution there are, what measures have already been taken, and what challenges and problems still await solution.

2.   Before giving the talk, tell students to listen for and be ready to ask or tell you about each kind of pollution mentioned. They should also generate at least one follow-up question about your talk.

3.   Give the talk.

4.   Have the students tell you what kinds of pollution they heard mentioned, and answer any questions they have about these.

5.   Have the students ask their follow-up questions.

6.   Ask the students what kinds of pollution are a problem in their country.

7.   Closure suggestion: Review the names of pollution types and any other new vocabulary.

Who Should Pay? (Pair or Small-Group Task, Chapter 8)

Specific goal ideas: Have students practice analyzing advantages and disadvantages; have students practice explaining pollution-related issues, especially with regard to costs.

1. Point out that everyone is in favor of eliminating pollution; the problem is that stopping pollution and cleaning it up is usually expensive, at least in the short run.

2. Have the students decide who should bear the main costs of cleaning up pollution—national government, local government, or the producers of the pollution. They should be ready to explain (1) who should pay, (2) why, and (3) what the main disadvantages of their choice are.

3. Have groups report and explain their positions.

4. Review the disadvantages of each choice, and then move to the advantages.

5. Closure suggestion: Praise especially good points students made as they analyzed the problem.

The Spotted Grubil (Problem-Solving Situation, Chapter 7)

Specific goal ideas: Have students practice analyzing and explaining costs and benefits; teach vocabulary related to ecology and development.

1. Prepare (flesh out) a problem situation along the following lines: The local government of Sylvania (a mythical country) wants to build a dam on a river in a poor, mountainous region of the country as a way to generate clean, inexpensive electric power that may help the region develop economically. However, within the region there is currently no immediate need for the extra power the dam will generate, and it is not clear whether cheap power alone will attract industry to the region. Also, the resulting lake that grows behind the dam will destroy the habitat of the spotted grubil, a rare (mythical) rodent, and will almost certainly result in the extinction of this endangered—and largely unstudied—animal.

2. Present the problem to the students orally, and have them take notes.

3. Have the students first analyze and list the potential costs and benefits of building the dam, and then decide whether or not the dam should be built. They should be ready to explain and justify their position.

4. Have groups present their cases and discuss.

5. Closure suggestion: Praise any especially insightful comments students made as they analyzed the possible costs and benefits of the proposed dam.

Other Activity Ideas

- To Dam or Not? (pair or small-group task): Have the students list the advantages and disadvantages of building dams on major rivers.

- Don't Be a Litterbug (pair or small-group task): Have pairs or groups of students come up with a plan for an antilitter campaign.

- Global Warming (pair or small-group task): Have the students decide whether or not they think global warming is really a serious problem and why.

- The Last of the Tigers? (pair or small-group task): Is it really important to protect endangered species? If so, why? If not, why not? Have the students discuss and prepare a response.

- Development or Environment? (debate): Have the students debate which is more important—economic development or environmental protection. Closure suggestion: Discuss the following question: *Is there is necessarily a trade-off between economic development and environmental protection? Can a society have both? Or can environmental protection only be made a priority after a society becomes fairly wealthy?*

- Jobs or Clean Air? (debate): Have the students debate this question: *Should polluting industries that will bring in jobs be encouraged?*

Module 6: Arts, Entertainment, and Media

MOVIES

Local Movies (Classroom Chat, Chapter 8)[5]

Specific goal ideas: Have students practice translating film titles; have students practice explaining plot lines.

1. Ask the students to list popular local films—with the titles translated into English. Then have the students tell you a little about the plot of each.

2. Follow up with more general questions about the local film industry. How many films are made each year? How popular are they?

3. Closure suggestion: Lead into the activity Kinds of Movies.

Kinds of Movies (Pair or Small-Group Task, Chapter 8)

Specific goal ideas: Teach vocabulary for kinds (genres) of movies.

1. Have the students list the different genres (kinds) of movies that are made locally (e.g., love stories, war films, mysteries). They should also come up with one or more examples of films that fall into each genre. As they work, assist them in coming up with good English terms for the genres they describe.

2. Have the students report—and, if necessary, explain—the genres on their list as you write the names on the board. Try to generate good names for any genres that do not already have widely used English terms.

3. Closure suggestion: Point out which of the genres are the same in the target culture, and introduce genres in the target culture that aren't the same.

The Formula for Success (Pair or Small-Group Task, Chapter 8)

Specific goal ideas: Encourage students to look for similarities and differences in the patterns by which different cultures organize things; have students practice explaining genre conventions.

1. Point out that, in a culture, a given kind of film often follows a rough formula (i.e., genre conventions). Give an example, such as the conventions followed by a Hollywood comic romance.

2. Ask the students to list and describe the formula for a popular film genre in their culture.

---

[5] This activity will work best in countries that have a local film industry.

3. Closure suggestion: If the genres students describe are similar to genres in the target culture, ask questions to find out any subtle ways in which the local formula differs from the one in the target culture.

Other Activity Ideas

- What Is Your Favorite Movie? (survey): Have each student ask several others what their favorite movies are. (If they only know the film title in their first language, they should do their best to translate it into English.) Closure suggestion: Have a few volunteers report, and as films are mentioned, have the rest of the class rate them with a quick voice vote.

- What Kinds of Films Does the Teacher Like? (press conference): Have the students interview you about your favorite films.

- Movie Stars (pair or small-group task): Have the students list their country's top movie stars and be prepared to explain to you why each is popular.

- My Idol (talk): Give a talk about one or more movie stars you really like and why.

MUSIC

Your Favorite Kind of Music (Survey, Chapter 8)

Specific goal ideas: Teach vocabulary for kinds of music.

1. Have the students ask each other what their favorite kinds of music are.

2. As students report, list the kinds of music on the board. If students don't know how to say a certain kind of music in English, ask them to do their best to explain it, and you can then help with necessary vocabulary.

3. Review and clarify the terms for kinds of music.

4. Closure suggestion: Have the students rate how much they like each kind of music with a quick voice vote.

Is Music a Necessary Part of Education? (Pair or Small-Group Task, Chapter 8)

Specific goal ideas: Have students practice explaining the impact of music.

1. Start by telling students that in Western education, music is sometimes viewed as less important than other kinds of courses. (When funds are short, music programs are often among the first to be cut.) This raises the question of how important it is to teach music in public education programs.

2. Have the students decide whether not primary and secondary education in their country should include some training in music, whether such music education should be required or optional, and what music training should be provided. They should be ready to explain and justify their positions

3. Have the students report, explain, and justify their decisions. Ask follow-up questions as necessary to clarify their views. Follow up with general class discussion.

4. Closure suggestion: Tell the students about the role of music in primary or secondary school education in the target country.

What Would You Like to Learn to Play? (Survey, Chapter 8)

Specific goal ideas: Teach vocabulary for musical instruments.

1. Have the students call out the English names of as many musical instruments as they can think of; fill in with others. Don't forget to include local instruments (which may or may not have English names).

2. Have the students survey each other on this question: *If you could magically learn to play one instrument brilliantly, what instrument would you pick and why?*

3. Have the students report what they found out.

4. Closure suggestion: Have the students tell you more about any local instruments mentioned that you are not familiar with.

Other Activity Ideas

*   Music Education (pair or small-group task): Have the students design a curriculum for music in elementary (or middle) schools. They should decide things such as what kind of musical training students should be given (e.g., singing, instruments, or music appreciation); whether musical training should be required or optional; where and how music would be taught in the curriculum (e.g., outside class or in a special music class); and how much time each week should be devoted to music.

*   Music in Local Schools (classroom chat): Ask the students about music education in local schools.

*   Local Musical Instruments (classroom chat): Ask the students to tell you about traditional folk instruments in their culture.

*   Piano Lessons (talk): Give a talk describing experiences you—or someone you know—had learning to play a musical instrument.

*   Funding for the Arts? (debate): Have the students debate the following question: *Should classical (or traditional) music be financially supported by the government?*

*   A Folk Song (pair or small-group task): Have the students prepare to teach you a local folk song in English. They will need to translate the song—or perhaps the first verse—into English. Closure suggestion: Have the class decide which group's translation is most aesthetically pleasing.

*   Local Classical (classroom chat): Have the students tell you about the most famous pieces of classical (traditional) music in their culture. Also ask how popular traditional (classical) music is in their culture now.

*   Should Pop Rule the Roost? (debate): Have the students debate the following question: *Is the growth of an international, modern pop style of music a good thing?*

TELEVISION

Local TV Shows (Classroom Chat, Chapter 8)

Specific goal ideas: Teach vocabulary for genres of TV programs.

1. Ask the students what genres of TV programs are most popular in their country. If a genre clearly corresponds to one that has a widely used English term, put the term on the board. If the genre does not seem to have a corresponding English term, work with students to come up with one.

2. Follow up by introducing the genres common in the target country.

3. Closure suggestion: Review the terms for TV program genres.

TV Show Formulas (Pair or Small-Group Task, Chapter 8)

Specific goal ideas: Encourage students to think about what they would and would not need to explain to a foreigner about the host culture; have students practice explaining genre conventions.

1. Point out that, in a culture, a given kind of TV program often follows a rough formula (i.e., genre conventions). Give an example, such as the conventions a situation comedy follows.

2. Have the students prepare to describe the formula of a type of TV show popular in their country. They should choose a genre they think foreigners might be less familiar with, and in their explanation they should emphasize points they think foreigners might not be aware of.

3. As students report, ask follow-up questions as necessary.

4. Closure suggestion: Comment on what genres foreigners would generally be less familiar with and on points students made that would be especially helpful to foreigners in understanding the genre being described.

TV—the Boob Tube? (Debate, Chapter 8)

Specific goal ideas: Have students practice explaining and justifying views; teach vocabulary related to the impact of TV.

1. Point out that the advent of TV has had a major impact on societies and cultures all around the world, and that—as is often the case with major technological innovations—the impact has been both positive and negative.

2. Have the students list the positive and negative effects increased TV viewing has had in their country. These should be stated as sentences (e.g., *It has reduced the amount of time children spend playing with their friends.*).

3. As students report, make sure each idea is explained adequately—in other words, that it is clear why the effect is positive or negative.

4. Divide the class into teams, and have them debate whether the overall impact of TV on their society has been more positive or more negative.

5. Closure suggestion: Comment on especially good points made during the debate.

Other Activity Ideas

- Your Favorite TV Programs (survey): Have the students ask each other what their favorite TV programs are. If they don't know how to say the name of a program in English, they should try to explain it.

- TV Viewership (classroom chat): Ask the students how much TV most people in the host country watch and who watches most.

- Lock on the Box? (debate): Have the students debate whether parents should limit the amount of time per day children watch TV. (Alternative: Discuss whether parents should put limits on the kinds of shows children are allowed to watch.)

ADVERTISING

An Effective Ad (Survey, Chapter 8)

Specific goal ideas: Teach vocabulary for qualities (as adjectives); teach vocabulary related to advertisements.

1. Start by asking a few students what qualities they think make an advertisement effective. Write the responses on the board (probably as adjectives that would fit into the sentence *A good advertisement should be . . .*).

2. Have the students survey each other on this question: *What are the key qualities of an effective advertisement?*

3. As students report, list the qualities mentioned on the board.

4. Review any new vocabulary.

5. Closure suggestion: Comment on what qualities people in the target culture tend to like—or not like—in advertisements.

New and Improved! (Pair or Small-Group Task, Chapter 8)

Specific goal ideas: Have students practice trying to think from the target culture's perspective; have students practice persuasion.

1. Tell the students that a newly opened local soap factory has asked them to design an ad campaign for a new brand of soap in the target country market.

2. Have the students design and prepare to perform a one-minute advertisement. Encourage them to be creative and entertaining.

3. Have the students perform their ads.

4. Closure suggestion: Comment on how effective the various strategies students tried are likely to be in the target culture.

Ads on TV (Pair or Small-Group Task, Chapter 8)

Specific goal ideas: Have students practice explaining and justifying opinions; teach vocabulary related to broadcasting.

1. Point out that in some countries TV broadcasting is paid for by the state; in others, it is supported mainly by advertising.

2. Have the students decide which approach they think is better and be ready to explain why.

3. After each group reports, have the students in other groups ask follow-up questions to clarify (and perhaps call into question) the position of the reporting group.

4. Comment on the issue from the perspective of the target culture.

5. Closure suggestion: Praise groups that ask especially good questions or respond especially effectively to questions, and explain why you thought these questions and answers were especially good.

Other Activity Ideas

- Your Favorite Ad (survey): Have the students survey each other on this question: *What are your favorite advertisements? What ads do you like least?*

- Ad Genres? (pair or small-group task): First have the students list the most common types (genres) of advertisements in their country. Then have them choose one, analyze it, and be ready to explain how it works.

- Can You Trust an Ad? (debate): Have the students debate this question: *Are advertisements totally untrustworthy?*

SPORTS

Sports Galore (Pair or Small-Group Task, Chapter 8)

Specific goal ideas: Teach vocabulary for names of target country sports.

1. Give groups five minutes to correctly list the English names of as many sports they can think of that are popular in the target country.

2. For reporting, let each group add one sport to the list. In order for the group to get a point, the sport must be spelled and pronounced (more or less) correctly. Keep going from group to group until all the sports are on the board. Then see which group has the most points.

3. Briefly introduce any sports that students did not think of.

4. Closure suggestion: Go over the list to make sure that students have some idea of what each sport is and know how to pronounce it.

Curling (Talk, Chapter 7)[6]

Specific goal ideas: Teach sport-related vocabulary.

1. Prepare a talk on a sport from the target country that is not widely known in the host country. Discuss aspects such as who plays it, where and when it is played, what the rules are, and what its history is.

2. Introduce any necessary vocabulary; then give the talk.

3. Check comprehension.

4. Closure suggestion: Check to see whether students think this sport has the potential to be successful in their country.

The Winning Team (Pair or Small-Group Task, Chapter 8)

Specific goal ideas: Have students practice persuasion; have students practice explaining how the art of persuasion works in the host culture.

1. Tell the students that they are famous sports coaches who have been approached by the national government for advice on how to train the national football (soccer) team for the next Olympics.

2. Have the students come up with a plan for creating a winning team. The more creative it is, the better.

3. Have each group present the plan and its virtues.

4. Have the students vote—from the perspective of their own culture—on which plan they think is best.

---

[6] *Curling* is a shuffleboard-like winter sport played with brooms on the ice in the northern climes of North America.

5. Closure suggestion: Ask the students to explain why they voted as they did and what kinds of appeals would be especially effective in their culture.

Other Activity Ideas

- Your Favorite Sport (survey): Have the students survey classmates on which sports they enjoy playing—or watching—the most.

- Super Bowl (talk): Give a talk about a famous sporting event in the target country. Explain the event's role in society as well as the nuts and bolts of the competition itself.

- Popular Sports Back Home (press conference): Have the students interview you about what sports are popular in the target country.

- The Home Team (talk): Give a talk about how sports teams are trained in the target country.

- A Good Spectator Sport (pair or small-group task): Have pairs or groups of students decide—in order of importance—what the key elements of a good spectator sport are.

- Phys Ed or Just Playing Around? (pair or small-group task): Have the students decide whether or not it is important for schools to stress sports—especially during school time.

- Pay for Play? (debate): Have the students debate whether or not the government should financially support sports teams for the Olympics or whether they should find private funding.

THEATER

Theater and Language (Focused Listening, Chapter 7)

Specific goal ideas: Teach expressions related to the theater.

1. Prepare a short talk about expressions in English that derive from theater (e.g., *the show must go on, break a leg, the final curtain, in the limelight, stage fright*). Explain the expressions and how they are used.

2. Tell the students to listen for and take notes on such expressions and their explanations. Then give the talk.

3. After the talk, check to see whether students understood the expressions and explanations.

4. Closure suggestion: Ask the students to tell you about expressions in their language that derive from the theater.

Traditional Opera (Classroom Chat, Chapter 8)

Specific goal ideas: Have students practice explaining local performing art forms.

1. Ask the students in groups to choose a local, traditional performing art that Westerners may find hard to appreciate, explain to you what the art form is, and tell you why it was traditionally popular. Encourage the students to mention as many reasons as they can think of.

2. As groups present their introductions, ask follow-up questions for clarification.

3. Closure suggestion: Ask the students how they themselves now feel about the performing art in question.

School Plays (Pair or Small-Group Task, Chapter 8)

Specific goal ideas: Have students practice explaining and justifying opinions.

1. Tell the students that schools in the West often sponsor school plays as part of their programs, especially in secondary school. Ask whether or not this is true in the host culture.

2. Have the students decide whether or not schools should put on plays involving students as part of students' education and be ready to explain why or why not.

3. Have the students present their positions and rationales. Follow up with discussion of the merits of the positions suggested.

4. Closure suggestion: Tell the students about any experiences—positive or negative—you had with school plays and any feelings you have about them as a result.

Other Activity Ideas

- Plays or Films? (survey): Have the students survey classmates on whether they think it is better to watch movies or plays, and why.

- Famous Plays (classroom chat): Have the students introduce their culture's most famous plays to you.

- Theater in My Country (talk): Give a talk on theater in the target country.

- An Actor's Life (survey): Have the students survey each other on these questions: *Would you want to be a professional actor? Why or why not? Would you want your child to become an actor?*

- Stage or Silver Screen? (survey): Have the students survey each other on this question: *If you were an actor, would you rather do plays or films?*

DANCE

The Best Kind of Dance (Pair or Small-Group Task, Chapter 8)

Specific goal ideas: Have students practice explaining and justifying opinions; teach names of dance types.

1. Have the students call out all the different kinds of dances they can think of in English while you list these on the board (e.g., *ballet, square dancing*).

2. Have the students in groups rank these kinds of dances according to beauty and be ready to explain their rankings.

3. Have each group state the kind of dance members think is most beautiful and their reasons. After each group reports, let other students respond using applause (loud or soft) to indicate how much they agree or disagree.

4. Have each group state the kind of dance members ranked as least beautiful and why. Allow others to respond as above.

5. Closure suggestion: Share your own opinions, and see how much applause they get.

Learning to Dance (Total Physical Response, Chapter 7)

Specific goal ideas: Teach vocabulary related to dance movements.

1. Prepare to teach a dance (perhaps a simple folk dance from the target country) in class using verbal explanation. (This may take some preparation, as the normal inclination is to show rather than explain verbally.)

2. Teach students the dance as a total physical response activity: you give verbal instructions, and students respond by doing what you tell them to. Try as much as possible to explain what students should do rather than showing them.

3. If time allows, follow up by having students prepare in groups to teach a dance they know—preferably one that not all the other students know—using the same approach.

4. Closure suggestion: Review new vocabulary that emerged during the activity.

Why Would Anyone Want to Dance? (Pair or Small-Group Task, Chapter 8)

Specific goal ideas: Have students practice explaining and justifying opinions.

1. Point out that, in some ways, dancing could be considered a rather strange activity—after all, it involves movements that are quite unusual and different from one's daily movements. Yet, all around the world, virtually every human culture has developed dances.

2. Have the students discuss the question *Why do people dance?* Have the students list possible reasons and be ready to explain them.

3. Have groups offer their explanations.

4. Closure suggestion: Comment on any explanations you thought were especially ingenious or insightful.

Other Activity Ideas

- Do You Like to Dance? (survey): Have the students survey each other on this question: *Do you like to dance? If so, what kind of dancing do you like?*

- Dancing in My Country (talk): Give a talk about the different kinds of dancing that are popular in the target country.

- Shall They Dance? (pair or small-group task): Have the students try to reach a consensus on whether children should be taught in school to dance. Closure suggestion: Tell the students about the role of dance in public education in the target country.

READING AND LITERATURE

Utopa's Greatest Literary Hits (Pair or Small-Group Task, Chapter 8)

Specific goal ideas: Have students practice translating book titles; have students practice explaining the host country's literary culture.

1. Have the students list—in order of greatness—their country's greatest works of literature, and be ready to introduce them to a foreigner (you). They should translate the titles into English and be ready to explain what makes these works great.

2. After the groups report, have the class try to agree on a prioritized list; then move on to the question of what makes these works great.

3. Follow up by asking students what values are promoted, upheld, and reflected in these works and what the popularity of these works says about the culture.

4. Closure suggestion: Ask the students to tell you the titles of famous literary works in English they are familiar with (perhaps as you list these on the board). Then comment on which of these—plus any others—you consider to be the greatest.

Books for the Countryside (Pair or Small-Group Task, Chapter 8)

Specific goal ideas: Have students practice explaining and justifying a proposal.

1. Point out that in most countries, people in cities have much better access to reading material than people in rural areas do, especially because libraries are usually found in cities. So a problem governments face is how to make reading material and information available to people in remote areas.

2. Have the students design the most practical and cost-effective plan possible for making books and other reading material more available in rural areas of their country, especially small remote villages. They should be ready to explain and justify their plan.

3. Have the students present their plans and their rationales. Follow up with discussion of the relative merits of the plans.

4. Closure suggestion: Comment on any solutions to this problem used in the target country (e.g., bookmobiles).

That Special Book (Interview, Chapter 8)

Specific goal ideas: Encourage students to read—both in English and in general.

1. Have the students interview each other about the book they have read that has had the most influence on their life and why it had so much influence.

2. Have a few students report on books they wish to recommend to others in the class. (These can be books they read themselves, not necessarily books their interview partner read.)

3. Closure suggestion: Recommend a number of books in English that you think students might be interested in reading (preferably those to which they also have access).

Other Activity Ideas

- What Do You Like to Read? (survey): Have the students survey others about what they like to read and why.

- Where Can I Get a Magazine? (classroom chat): Ask the students about the different places where people in their country buy books, magazines, newspapers, and other reading matter, and what kind of reading matter each place sells. (The answers may be somewhat different than in the target country.) Also ask where you could find reading matter in English.

- What Makes Great Great? (pair or small-group task): Have the students list, in order of priority, the criteria for determining whether a work of literature is great.

- Traditional Story Characters (classroom chat): Ask the students about their country's most popular traditional stories and their characters.

- The Funniest Book (survey): Have the students survey each other on the funniest (most boring, etc.) book they have ever read.

- You've Got to Read This (pair or small-group task): Have the students decide on an answer to this question: *If you could recommend one book to a foreigner who wants to learn about the host country, what would it be and why?*

- Books You Must Know (classroom chat): Ask the students what works of literature virtually every person in their country would know about.

- Famous Story (talk): Tell—or read aloud—a famous story from the target culture. (Alternative: Tell about famous characters from novels.)

- What Sells? (classroom chat): Ask the students what kinds of books are most popular—that is, sell best—in their country.

- Formula for Success (pair or small-group task): Have the students describe the formula for a popular genre of book (e.g., detective stories, romances).

ART

Types of Art (Survey, Chapter 8)

Specific goal ideas: Teach names of art forms (e.g., *painting, sculpture*).

1. Have the students quickly call out in English as many (visual) art forms as they can think of (e.g., *painting, sculpture*) while you list these on the board using noun or gerund forms. (Use a very broad definition of *art form*.)

2. If necessary, discuss which items on the board should be considered art. (There may be considerable room for discussion on this point.)

3. Have each student survey several classmates on what their favorite form of art is and why.

4. Have volunteers report their findings.

5. Closure suggestions: Tell the students about your own preferences. Also comment on what people in the target country would normally include—and not include—in the category of art forms.

Our Most Famous Artists (Pair or Small-Group Task, Chapter 8)

Specific goal ideas: Have students practice explaining aspects of local culture.

1. Have the students decide who their country's three most important (or famous) artists are and prepare to introduce these people to you, telling you a little about them and why they are considered great.

2. For reports, have each group introduce one artist who hasn't been mentioned yet by another group.

3. Follow up with discussion of who should be on the top three list and why.

4. Closure suggestion: Thank students for their introduction, then review for them what they have told you, partly so they can see if you got it right and partly to show you were listening and trying to understand.

Is Art Just in the Eye of the Beholder? (Pair or Small-Group Task, Chapter 8)

Specific goal ideas: Have students practice explaining and justifying criteria.

1. Note that people often argue about whether there are objective criteria for judging whether a work of art is great or not. Is it just a question of personal opinion? Is greatness established by community approval and popularity?

2. Have pairs or groups of students list the three most important criteria they think should be used in determining whether a work of art is great or not. (The criteria might be stated as a completion of the sentence *A great work of art is one that . . . .*) Each pair or group should try to reach consensus. They should be ready to clearly explain the criteria they chose and to justify their choices.

3. Have the students report and justify their criteria. Move into general discussion, and try to work toward a class consensus on the issue.

4. Closure suggestion: Share your own opinion and prevailing views in the target country.

Other Activity Ideas

- My Least Favorite Art Form (survey): Have the students survey each other on what form of art they find least interesting and appealing, and why.

- Art for Art's Sake? (debate): Have the students debate this question: *Should the value of art be determined primarily on the basis of its social impact (art for the sake of serving society) or its artistic merits (art for art's sake)?* Closure suggestions: Share your own opinion or the prevailing views in the target country.

- The Making of an Artist (talk): Describe how artists are trained in the target country.

- To Make an Artist (pair or small-group task): Have groups discuss what the best way to train artists is and come up with a plan.

Module 7: Teaching and Education

GETTING AN OVERVIEW

The School System in My Country (Press Conference, Chapter 8)

Specific goal ideas: Teach vocabulary related to education.

1. Tell the students they are reporters assigned to interview you and write an article on education and schools in the target country. Have the students prepare questions, either individually or in groups.

2. Have the students interview you. As new vocabulary emerges, put it on the board.

3. Closure suggestion: After the talk, have the students tell you differences and similarities they noted between education in the target country and theirs.

Problems in Education (Pair or Small-Group Task, Chapter 8)

Specific goal ideas: Have students practice explaining educational issues.

1. Have the students list, in order, the five major problems and challenges faced by schools in the host country.

2. As students report, ask follow-up questions to make sure you understand the problem they are describing.

3. Through class discussion, try to reach consensus on how the problems should be ranked.

4. Closure suggestion: Introduce the main problems faced by schools in the target country.

The Role of English (Classroom Chat, Chapter 8)

Specific goal ideas: Get a better understanding of the role of English in the host-country education system.

1. Prepare a list of questions on the role of English in their country's education system (e.g., *Is English study optional or required? How many years of English study do most students have? At what age does English study usually start? How is English usually taught? What kinds of English tests do students have to take? How do scores on English examinations affect students?*).

2. Chat with students about these questions in class.

3. Closure suggestion: Tell the students about the role of foreign language education in the target country.

Other Activity Ideas

- Utopa's School System (classroom chat): Ask the students to introduce the school system in their country, starting with kindergarten (or the equivalent) and then moving on up. You might chart the system and put new vocabulary on the board.

- My School (show and tell): Bring pictures of one or more schools you have attended. For a more balanced picture of schools in the target country, bring in pictures of other (nice and not-so-nice) schools as well.

- Do You Like Language Learning? (survey): Have the students survey each other on this question: *What do you like most (least) about language study?*

- What Is the Best Way to . . . ? (pair or small-group task): Have the students list the five best tips they can think of for how to
  — learn a language
  — improve listening, speaking, reading, and writing
  — improve grammar in writing and speaking
  — improve reading speed and comprehension
  — study for a test
  — memorize vocabulary
  — learn about a foreign culture

PRIMARY SCHOOL AND BEFORE

Preschool (Classroom Chat, Chapter 8)

Specific goal ideas: Teach vocabulary related to preschool education.

1. Ask the students to tell you about preschool education options in their country (e.g., day care, nursery schools, kindergartens). As new vocabulary emerges, put it on the board.

2. Closure suggestion: Tell the students about similar options in the target country.

What's the Point of Preschool? (Pair or Small-Group Task, Chapter 8)

Specific goal ideas: Have students practice stating goals.

1. Have the students list what they think the main goals of preschool education should be. These might be done as sentence completions (e.g., *The main goal of preschool education should be to . . .* [e.g., *get kids used to being in school*]).

2. Have the students report and explain their ideas on goals.

3. Try to reach class consensus on which goals are most important.

4. Closure suggestion: Comment on this issue from the perspective of the target culture.

How Much Homework? (Debate, Chapter 8)

Specific goal ideas: Have students practice explaining and justifying positions.

1. Divide students into teams and have them prepare to argue one of the two following positions: (1) *Primary school children should be given very little or no homework,* or (2) *It is all right to give primary school children homework.*

2. Conduct the debate.

3. Closure suggestion: Note especially good points made during the debate and why you thought they were good. Also, comment on the issue of homework for primary school students in the target country.

Other Activity Ideas

- Parents' Choice? (pair or small-group task): Start by asking students what, in their country, determines which primary school a student will go to. Then have the students discuss the following questions: *Should all children just go to the closest school? Or should parents have some choice as to what school their child goes to?* The groups should try to arrive at consensus and be ready to explain their view to the class.

- Learning to Read (classroom chat): Ask the students to tell you how children in the host country are taught to read. (This question is especially in interesting if your host country uses a writing system that is unfamiliar to you.)

- English in Primary School? (pair or small-group task): Have the students decide whether they think children in the host country should start learning English in primary school.

SECONDARY SCHOOL

A Student's Day (Pair or Small-Group Task, Chapter 8)

Specific goal ideas: Find out what students know about school life in the target culture; have students practice stating and checking guesses.

1. On the board, list a number of questions about the typical day of a high school student in the target country. These might include *What time do students go to school? How many class periods do they have? What courses are required? What elective course options do they have? What extracurricular activities are available, and how popular are they? When do classes end? How much homework do students usually have?*

2. Have the students write down educated guesses about the questions.

3. Question by question, have the students present their guesses about each question; then provide your response.

4. Closure suggestion: Clear up any misimpressions students seem to have about student life in the target country, and affirm their accurate guesses.

Should Schools All Use the Same Books? (Debate, Chapter 8)

Specific goal ideas: Have students practice stating and supporting arguments.

1. Have the students prepare to argue either for or against this proposition: *All schools throughout a given country should use the same textbooks for the same courses.*

2. Conduct the debate.

3. Closure suggestion: Comment on how books and other teaching materials are selected and distributed in the target country.

Getting into University (Pair or Small-Group Task, Chapter 8)

Specific goal ideas: Have students practice stating and explaining strategies.

1. Have the students list, in order of importance, the strategies that a teacher in the last year of secondary school should use to prepare students for university admission. They should be ready to explain and justify these strategies.

2. When groups report, ask one group to suggest the strategy members think is the most important. Then ask if other groups agree, and discuss as necessary. Once there seems to be adequate agreement on something, write it on the board as number one, and move on to the next group and its suggested strategy.

3. Closure suggestion: Talk with students about the process of applying for university admission in the target country.

Other Activity Ideas

- A Typical Student's Day (pair or small-group task): Tell the students you want to learn more about the lives of students in their country, and ask them to write out a typical daily schedule for a secondary school student. When groups report, have the first group suggest the first item of the day and approximate time for it. Quickly check this with the rest of the class. Then have the next group report the next item of the day, and so on. Write this composite schedule on the board as students report.

- Secondary School My Way (Talk): Tell the students what courses are typically offered in middle schools in the target country. Points to comment on might include how much choice students have in what courses they take, whether they can choose majors, and what the requirements of a typical course are.

- The Curve (classroom chat): Ask the students to tell you what a typical grade curve looks like in a secondary school in their country.

- Courses (classroom chat): Ask the students to list the courses usually offered in a secondary school curriculum in their country and tell you which are considered most important.

- After-School Activities (classroom chat): Ask the students what extracurricular activities schools in the host country usually offer.

- How Much Homework Is Reasonable? (pair or small-group task): Have the students decide how much homework per night they think is reasonable for secondary school students. Closure suggestion: Ask the students what kind of homework is most important and useful to secondary school students.

- The Exams (classroom chat): Ask the students what kinds of standardized examinations and other tests students in the host country face. Also ask how teachers typically go about evaluating students.

- Heading off Failure (pair or small-group task): First ask the students how a teacher in their country normally handles a situation in which a student is headed toward failing a course. Then have them decide in groups whether they think this is the best approach. If so, why? If not, what would be better?

- School Fees (classroom chat): Ask the students to list for you the costs involved in secondary school education.

- After Secondary School? (pair or small-group task): Have the students list the options for students at the end of secondary school and be ready to explain each. They should also be ready to tell you roughly what percentage of students take each option and how it is generally viewed (i.e., how desirable it is). Closure suggestion: Summarize what the students have told you so they can tell you if you got it right or not.

UNIVERSITY

Liberal Arts (Talk, Chapter 7)

Specific goal ideas: Teach vocabulary related to university courses.

1. Prepare a talk on what a typical undergraduate university program in the target country is like. You might approach this by choosing one or more majors that you are familiar with and describing the program of a student in those majors—for example, what courses they would be required to take, what elective courses they might have to choose from, how courses would generally be taught, how courses would be assessed, and whether or not a final thesis is required.

2. Warm up by having students list the names of all the university majors they can think of as you list them on the board. Also introduce any other necessary vocabulary.

3. Give the talk, then check comprehension.

4. Review new vocabulary.

5. Closure suggestion: Ask the students to comment on differences between what you described and what undergraduate university education is like in their country.

Advance Warning (Press Conference, Chapter 8)

Specific goal ideas: Have students practice imagining what challenges life in the target country might pose; teach vocabulary related to university teaching.

1. Tell the students they have been asked to teach their language at a university in the target country for two years. Before they go, they need to interview you to get more information on how they should teach courses in a Western university.

2. Have the students list questions. (You might suggest some examples to get them started, e.g., *What is the grade curve in the target country like? How much homework should I give? How should I evaluate students' performance? What should I do if students cheat or don't do their homework?*)

3. Have them interview you.

4. Closure suggestion: Share with students a little of what worried you most about coming to teach in a foreign country and what you have enjoyed most.

How Much Choice Should Students Have? (Pair or Small-Group Task, Chapter 8)

Specific goal ideas: Have students practice stating and supporting arguments.

1. Point out that universities need to decide how much, if any, choice to allow students in the courses they take. Should the department decide on all the courses? Or should students be free to take whatever courses they want? Should the policy fall somewhere in between? If so, where?

2. Ask the students to list the advantages and disadvantages of university departments' deciding most or all of students' courses for them, and then to do the same for students' being allowed to choose many of their own courses. The students should also decide which they think is preferable and be ready to explain why.

3. Have the students present the advantages and disadvantages of each approach.

4. Have them present and explain their views. Follow up with discussion.

5. Closure suggestion: Ask the students whether they think university faculty would hold the same views they do, and why or why not.

Other Activity Ideas

- A Typical College Day (classroom chat): Ask the students to describe the typical day of a college or university student.

- The Class Curve (classroom chat): Ask the students what a typical college or university grade curve looks like in the host country and what happens if students get failing grades.

- What Does an English Major Really Need? (pair or small-group task): Have the students make a proposal for an English department on which courses should be required and which should be elective. They should be ready to justify their ideas.

- Getting into College (talk): Explain the process in the target country for choosing and getting into a college or university.

- Continuing Education? (classroom chat): Ask the students to tell you what continuing education opportunities exist in the host country.

- Guide to Getting into College (pair or small-group task): Have the students prepare to describe to you, step by step, the process for choosing and getting into a college or university in the host country.

- Beyond the Major (classroom chat): Ask the students how many and what courses students are generally expected to take outside their major.

- College Football? (pair or small-group task): Have the students decide what role they think sports should play in university life. Should there be college teams for intercollegiate competition? Should there be only intramural sports? Or should the college sponsor no sports at all?

- Are Tests the Best? (pair or small-group task): Have the students decide which methods university teachers should use to evaluate students. Are tests the best way?

- Getting into Graduate School (classroom chat): Have the students explain to you the process for getting into graduate school in the host country.

- Paying for College (press conference): Have the students interview you about the costs involved in university or graduate school education and how students generally pay these costs. Closure suggestion: Have the students tell you how this is handled in the host country.

TEACHERS

My Best Teacher (Survey, Chapter 8)

Specific goal ideas: Have students practice stating qualities.

1. Tell the students about one of the best teachers you ever had and why you thought he or she was a great teacher. Ask the students to summarize the good qualities your teacher had. (These will probably be stated as adjectives, e.g., *friendly, encouraging.*)

2. Have the students survey each other about the best teachers they ever had. What made those teachers good? What did they learn from them? As students listen to each other, they should note down qualities that they hear.

3. Have the students report the qualities that they heard about as you write these qualities on the board as adjectives (if possible).

4. Closure suggestion: Have the students generate the antonyms of each of the positive qualities listed on the board.

The Teaching Profession (Talk, Chapter 7)

Specific goal ideas: Have students practice stating advantages and disadvantages; teach vocabulary related to teaching.

1. Prepare a talk on the joys and challenges of being a teacher in the target country.

2. Introduce any necessary vocabulary; then give the talk.

3. Have the students respond to the talk by listing the advantages and disadvantages of teaching as a profession in their country and comparing these with what you have said about teaching in the target country.

4. Closure suggestion: Ask the students whether any of them are considering teaching as a profession and, if so, why.

Getting Ahead (Pair or Small-Group Task, Chapter 8)

Specific goal ideas: Have students practice explaining the teaching profession.

1. Have the students list for you, in order of importance, the things that a university (secondary school) teacher in the host country needs to do in order to get promoted.

2. When groups report, have one group suggest what they consider to be the most important factor. Then see if other groups agree, and discuss if necessary. Once the class agrees, list it as number one on the board, and move on to a candidate for the number two position. Continue ranking the factors.

3. Closure suggestion: Compare what students said about their country with the teaching profession in the target country.

Other Activity Ideas

- A Good Teacher (pair or small-group task): Have the students list—in order—the most important characteristics of a good teacher.

- My Teacher (talk): Give a talk about one of the best teachers you ever had and what you think was so good about him or her. (Or about one of the worst teachers you ever had—if you can make it amusing.)

- Getting Ahead as a Teacher (press conference): Have the students interview you on how teachers in the target country get promoted.

- The Big Class (pair or small-group task): Ask the students to imagine they are giving advice to a Western English teacher who has never taught a large class (fifty to eighty students) before. In groups, they should prepare a list of advice, each given as a sentence completion: *You should . . . . You should not . . . .* Have them be ready to present their advice and explain why it is important.

- To Be Strict or Lenient? (pair or small-group task): Have the students list the advantages and disadvantages of teachers being strict and of teachers being lenient. Then have each group decide whether it is better to err on the side of being too strict or too lenient.

Books for
Further Reading

This appendix lists books I would recommend to volunteer teachers (VTs) for an EFL minilibrary. Given the large and growing number of excellent books available on various aspects of English teaching, I have expanded this appendix considerably in this second edition of *More Than a Native Speaker*. Recommendations are based both on my own experience and on suggestions from other English teachers. In general, these books are easily available and accessible to the general reader; also, I have tried to recommend books that are appropriate to an EFL setting and relevant to the kinds of courses VTs are most likely to teach.

Books are listed by general category, and within each category most books are listed alphabetically by author. However, in cases where I feel certain books are especially deserving of recommendation, I have marked them with asterisks and provided brief annotations.

Language Teaching

*Brown, H. D. 2001. *Teaching by principles: An interactive approach to language pedagogy.* 2nd ed. New York: Longman. Brown's book is an effective and readable introduction to how theory relates to language teaching.

Graves, K. 1999. *Designing language courses: A guide for teachers.* Boston: Heinle and Heinle.

Harmer, J. 1997. *How to teach English.* London: Addison Wesley Longman.

*———. 2001. *The practice of English language teaching.* Harlow, England: Pearson ESL. Harmer offers an accessible yet comprehensive introduction to English teaching.

*Scrivener, J. 1994. *Learning teaching: A guidebook for English language teachers.* New York: Macmillan Education. This is a brief, accessible, and very practical introduction to language teaching.

Ur, P. 1996. *A course in language teaching: Practice and theory.* Cambridge: Cambridge University Press.

Language Learning

*Lightbown, P., and N. Spada. 1999. *How languages are learned.* 2nd ed. Oxford: Oxford University Press. This book is a reader-friendly introduction to second language acquisition.

*Rubin, J., and I. Thompson. 1994. *How to be a more successful language learner.* 2nd ed. Boston: Heinle and Heinle. This book is a good, brief introduction to language learning strategies and the nature of language.

*Scovel, T. 2001. *Learning new languages: A guide to second language acquisition.* Boston: Heinle and Heinle. Scovel offers an entertaining yet scholarly overview of second language acquisition.

Speaking/Oral Skills

Bailey, K., and L. Savage, eds. 1994. *New ways in teaching speaking.* Alexandria, VA: TESOL.

Hadfield, J., and C. Hadfield. 2000. *Simple speaking activities.* Oxford: Oxford University Press.

Keller, E., and S. Warner. 1988. *Conversation gambits.* Hove, England: Language Teaching Publications.

*Klippel, F. 1984. *Keep talking: Communicative fluency activities for language teaching.* Cambridge: Cambridge University Press. This is an excellent cookbook of speaking activities.

Paul, D. 2004. *Communication strategies.* Stamford, CT: Thomson Learning.

———. 2004. *Further communication strategies.* Stamford, CT: Thomson Learning.

*Ur, P. 1981. *Discussions that work: Task centered fluency practice.* Cambridge: Cambridge University Press. This introduction to conducting discussions includes lots of good activity ideas.

Collections of Activities/Miscellaneous

Baker, J., and H. Westup. 2000. *The English language teachers' handbook: How to teach large classes with few resources.* New York: Continuum.

Clark, R., P. Moran, and A. Burrows. 2004. *The ESL miscellany: A treasury of cultural and linguistic information; The new 21st century edition.* Brattleboro, VT: Pro Lingua Associates.

Fragiadakis, H. 1993. *All clear: Idioms in context.* Boston: Heinle and Heinle.

Huizenga, J. 2000. *Can you believe it? Stories and idioms from real life.* Oxford: Oxford University Press.

Kress, J. 1993. *The ESL teacher's book of lists.* Norwich, England: Centre for Applied Research in Education.

Pollard, L. 1997. *Zero prep: Ready-to-go activities for the language classroom.* Burlingame, CA: Alta Book Center.

Pollard, L., N. Hess, and J. Herron. 2001. *Zero prep for beginners: Ready-to-go activities for the language classroom.* Burlingame, CA: Alta Book Center.

Shameem, N., and M. Tickoo, eds. 1999. *New ways in using communicative games in language teaching.* Alexandria, VA: TESOL.

Sion, C. 1984. *Recipes for tired teachers.* Reading, MA: Addison-Wesley.

————. 1991. *More recipes for tired teachers.* Reading, MA: Addison-Wesley.

Ur, P., and A. Wright. 1992. *Five-minute activities: A resource book of short activities.* Cambridge: Cambridge University Press.

Wharton, S., and P. Race. 1999. *500 tips for TESOL teachers.* London: Kogan Page.

Woods, E., D. Howard-Williams, and M. Tomalin. 2004. *Instant lessons: Intermediate.* Harlow, England: Pearson ESL.

Pronunciation

Baker, A. 1981. *Ship or sheep? An intermediate pronunciation course.* 2nd ed. Cambridge: Cambridge University Press.

Baker, A., and S. Goldstein. 1990. *Pronunciation pairs.* Cambridge: Cambridge University Press.

Gilbert, J. 1993. *Clear speech: Pronunciation and listening comprehension in North American English.* Cambridge: Cambridge University Press.

Grant, L. 2000. *Well said.* 2nd ed. Boston: Heinle and Heinle.

Hancock, M. 1995. *Pronunciation games.* Cambridge: Cambridge University Press.

Hewings, M., and S. Goldstein. 1998. *Pronunciation plus student's book: Practice through interaction.* Cambridge: Cambridge University Press.

Kelly, G. 2001. *How to teach pronunciation.* London: Longman.

Listening

Hadfield, J., and C. Hadfield. 1999. *Simple listening activities.* Oxford: Oxford University Press.

Nunan, D., and L. Miller, eds. 1995. *New ways in teaching listening.* Alexandria, VA: TESOL.

White, G. 1998. *Listening.* Oxford: Oxford University Press.

Grammar

*Azar, B. 1998. *Understanding and using English grammar.* 3rd ed. Englewood Cliffs, NJ: Prentice Hall Regents. Azar's grammar books contain straightforward explanations of grammar structures, accompanied by charts, examples, and a multitude of exercises, some of which are set up so that they can be done orally. The book is a good resource both for learning and teaching grammar.

Batstone, R. 1994. *Grammar.* Oxford: Oxford University Press.

Elbaum, S. 2000. *Grammar in context 1.* 3rd ed. Boston: Heinle and Heinle.

————. 2003. *Grammar in context 2.* 3rd ed. Boston: Heinle and Heinle

Firsten, R., and P. Killian. 2002. *The ELT grammar book: A teacher-friendly reference guide.* Burlingame, CA: Alta Book Center.

Parrott, M. 2000. *Grammar for English language teachers.* Cambridge: Cambridge University Press.

Rinvolucri, M. 1985. *Grammar games.* Cambridge: Cambridge University Press.

*Ur, Penny. 1988. *Grammar practice activities: A practical guide for teachers.* Cambridge: Cambridge University Press. A conveniently referenced collection of activities for grammar practice. Many of the activities are communicative ones that could serve as a useful supplement in speaking/listening classes. Note: This book does not teach grammar to the teacher.

Writing

Boardman, C., and J. Frydenberg. 2002. *Writing to communicate: Paragraphs and essays.* 2nd ed. Harlow, England: Pearson Education.

Broukal, M. 2003. *Weaving it together: Connecting reading and writing, 1.* Boston: Heinle and Heinle.

Folse, K., A. Muchmore-Vokoun, and V. Solomon. 2004. *Great paragraphs.* Boston: Houghton Mifflin.

Hadfield, J., and C. Hadfield. 2000. *Simple writing activities.* Oxford: Oxford University Press.

Raimes, A. 1983. *Techniques in teaching writing.* Oxford: Oxford University Press.

Reid, J. 1984. *The process of paragraph writing.* Harlow, England: Pearson ESL.

———. 1999. *The process of composition.* 3rd ed. Harlow, England: Pearson ESL.

Ruetten, M. 2002. *Developing composition skills: Rhetoric and grammar.* Boston: Heinle and Heinle.

Smalley, R., M. Ruetten, and J. R. Kozyrev. 2000. *Refining composition skills.* 5th ed. Boston: Heinle and Heinle.

White, R., ed. 1995. *New ways in teaching writing.* Alexandria, VA: TESOL.

Culture and Intercultural Communication

Davis, L. 2001. *Doing culture: Cross-cultural communication in action.* Beijing, China: Foreign Language Teaching and Research Press.

DeCapua, A., and A. Wintergerst. 2004. *Crossing cultures in the language classroom.* Ann Arbor: University of Michigan Press.

Fantini, A., ed. 1997. *New ways in teaching culture.* Alexandria, VA: TESOL.

*Kohls, L. R. 2001. *Survival kit for overseas living: For Americans planning to live and work abroad.* 4th ed. Yarmouth, ME: Intercultural Press. A brief but readable and insightful discussion of learning to live in another country. The various lists in the book, including the list of culture topics in chapter 14 and the list of U.S. values in chapter 8, are also very handy as teaching resources. Despite the explicit U.S. focus, most of the general principles would apply to anyone from a Western background.

Snow, D. 2004. *Encounters with Westerners: Improving skills in English and intercultural communication* (Student text and teacher version). Shanghai, China: Shanghai Foreign Language Education Press.

*Stewart, E., and M. Bennett. 1991. *American cultural patterns: A cross-cultural perspective.* Rev. ed. Yarmouth, ME: Intercultural Press. While slightly technical, this short volume is a good introduction to the values and assumptions of U.S. culture, and is very helpful in thinking through the issue of what a culture is.

Assessment

Bailey, K. 1998. *Learning about language assessment: Dilemmas, decisions, and directions.* Boston: Heinle and Heinle.

Brown, J. D., ed. 1998. *New ways in classroom assessment.* Alexandria, VA: TESOL.

McNamara, T. 2000. *Language testing.* Oxford: Oxford University Press.

English and Language

Bauer, L., and P. Trudgill, eds. 1998. *Language myths.* London: Penguin Books.

*Crystal, D. 2003. *English as a global language.* 2nd ed. Cambridge: Cambridge University Press. Crystal gives an overview of the rise of English to its current position as the world's most widely used international language.

Trudgill, P., and J. Hannah. 2002. *International English: A guide to varieties of standard English.* 4th ed. London: Edward Arnold.

Internet Resources for Teachers and Learners

There is a virtually limitless—and ever-growing—body of material on the Internet for English teachers and students. Given the fluid nature of the medium, by the time this book reaches your hands some of the information in the following list (current as of early 2006) will no doubt be out of date, but presumably many of these sites will be up and running for some years to come, so this list should help get you started.

English Teaching

The Amity Foundation (Teachers Project). http://www.amityfoundation.org/. Teaching resources available under Teachers Program.

Boggle's World. http://www.bogglesworld.com/. Loads of activities; a job search site.

Capital Community College Foundation. *Guide to grammar and writing.* http://grammar.ccc.commnet.edu /grammar/. Grammar and writing resource.

Dave's ESL Café. http://www.eslcafe.com/. Teaching ideas and information on job opportunities.

EFL/ESL Games. http://teflgames.com/. Word games.

EFL Tasks. http://efltasks.net/. Activities for beginning-level students.

E. L. Easton. http://eleaston.com/. Aids for teaching English and other languages.

EnglishClub.com. http://www.englishclub.com. Lesson plans, jobs, discussion forums, and other resources.

English Language Teachers' Forum. http://www.eltforum.com/. A range of materials on English teaching.

ESL Lounge. http://www.esl-lounge.com/. Lesson plans, teaching aids, flash cards, role-play cards, book reviews, and more.

ESLnotes: The English Learner Movie Guides. http://www.ESLnotes.com/. Plot summaries, vocabulary, and discussion questions for a long list of films.

everythingESL. http://www.everythingESL.net/. Lesson plans, activities, and other resources; more ESL than EFL focused.

Gateway to Educational Materials. http://www.thegateway.org/. Search engine for lesson plans in many areas, including EFL.

John's ESL Community. http://www.johnsesl.com/. Worksheets, activities, and other teaching resources.

Karin's ESL Partyland. http://www.eslpartyland.com/. Lesson plans, materials, chat rooms, job information, and other resources.

Longman English Language Teaching. http://www.longman.com/. Resources for teachers and students, but also advertisements for Longman publications.

Macmillan. One Stop English. http://www.onestopenglish.com/. A wide range of resources, from lesson plans to culture information.

Purdue University. The OWL Family of Sites. http://owl.english.purdue.edu/. An abundance of resources, especially handouts for different aspects of writing, and links to other sites.

Rubistar. http://rubistar.4teachers.org/. Aids for creating grading templates (rubrics) for oral and written assignments.

Sites for Teachers. http://www.sitesforteachers.com/. Links to a many Web sites for teachers.

Sounds of English. http://www.soundsofenglish.org/. Information, activities, exercises, links, and other resources dedicated to the pronunciation of American English.

Teaching English. http://www.teachingenglish.org.uk/. Teaching ideas, downloads, and other resources from the BBC and British Council.

Teachingfish.com. http://www.teachingfish.com/. Games, activities, EFL/ESL resources, and job-search links.

TEFL China Teahouse. http://teflchina.org/. Support for English teachers in China; articles, lesson plans, and informal tips and discussion by Chinese and other teachers.

TEFL Net. http://tefl.net/. Resources, discussion forums, links, jobs, and other resources.

TEFL Professional Network. http://www.tefl.com/. Listing of English teaching job opportunities worldwide.

Wordskills.com: Services in Education and Training. http://wordskills.com/. A variety of resources, including book recommendations, level tests, and mini–grammar lessons.

Journals and Magazines

Asia Journal of English Language Teaching. http://www.cuhk.edu.hk/ajelt/. Research-oriented journal on topics relevant to teaching in Asia; published by the Chinese University of Hong Kong.

Asian EFL Journal. http://www.asian-efl-journal.com/. Academic articles on English teaching in Asia; information on conferences in the region.

English for Specific Purposes World. http://www.esp-world.info/. Web-based journal with academic articles from around the world on teaching English for specific purposes.

English Teaching Forum Online. http://exchanges.state.gov/forum/. Quarterly journal on EFL teaching published by the United States Information Agency; articles by teachers around the world.

English Teaching Professional. http://www.etprofessional.com/. Selected articles from the print magazine.

ELT Asia. http://www.eltasia.com/. Online journals and discussion lists for English teaching in Asia.

ESL Magazine. http://www.eslmag.com/. Bimonthly magazine serving ESL/EFL professionals worldwide.

Essential Teacher. http://www.tesol.org/. Quarterly magazine of the TESOL association, including columns, articles, and reviews.

Humanising Language Teaching. http://www.hltmag.co.uk/. Interesting variety of articles and features for language teaching.

IATEFL Newsletter. http://www.iatefl.org/, under Newsletter. Newsletter of the International Association of Teachers of English as a Foreign Language, an organization based in the United Kingdom.

The Internet TESL Journal. http://iteslj.org/. Monthly Web journal started in 1995; includes articles, research papers, lesson plans, teaching techniques, book reviews, links, and more than 500 quizzes students can take to test their knowledge of grammar, vocabulary, and idioms.

Journal of the Imagination in Language Teaching and Learning. http://www.njcu.edu/cill/journal-index.html. Pretty much what title says.

The Language Teacher. http://jalt-publications.org/tlt/. Monthly publication of the Japan Association for Language Teaching; readable and practical articles. See also *JALT Journal,* linked from this site.

The Reading Matrix. http://www.readingmatrix.com/. Journal focusing on reading issues; other reading-related resources.

SEAMEO Regional Language Centre. http://www.relc.org.sg/. Under Publications, articles on language teaching in *RELC Journal.*

TEFL Web Journal. http://www.teflweb-j.org/. Quarterly magazine for teachers.

TESL-EJ: Teaching English as a Second or Foreign Language. http://www-writing.berkeley.edu/TESL-EJ/. Quarterly journal offering articles on a wide range of teaching topics.

TESL—Hong Kong. http://www.tesl-hk.org.hk/. Journal, based at City University of Hong Kong, publishing articles on English teaching in Hong Kong.

Professional Organizations

Asian Association of Teachers of English as a Foreign Language. http://www.asiatefl.org/. Based in Asia.

British Council. http://www.britishcouncil.org/. Based in the United Kingdom.

International Association of English Language Teachers of English as a Foreign Language (IATEFL). http://www.iatefl.org/. Based in the United Kingdom.

International Society for Language Studies (ISLS). http://www.isls-inc.org/. International association with a focus on critical studies.

Teachers of English to Speakers of Other Languages (TESOL). http://www.tesol.org/. Based in the United States.

Text and Other Reference Collections

Absolutely All Free Clipart. http://www.allfree-clipart.com/. Clip art and graphics; links to other clip art and graphics sites.

Alex Catalogue of Electronic Texts. http://www.infomotions.com/alex/. Collection of public domain electronic books.

Bartleby.com: Great Books Online. http://www.bartleby.com/. Free access to a large range of great literary works, dictionaries, encyclopedias, and almost anything else you would expect to find in the reference collection of a Western library.

BookBrowse. http://www.bookbrowse.com/. Excerpts from and reviews of books.

CoolCLIPS.com. http://www.coolclips.com/. Clip art.

Drew's Script-o-rama. http://www.script-o-rama.com/. A large collection of movie scripts.

FreeFoto.com. http://www.freefoto.com/. A wide variety of photographs.

Google Images. http://images.google.com/. Search engine for pictures.

Internet Public Library. http://www.ipl.org/. Collection of links organized like a library.

Library of Congress. http://www.loc.gov/. Web site of the U.S. Library of Congress.

JoBlo's Movie Scripts. http://www.joblo.com/moviescripts.php. Links to sites with movie scripts.

Picsearch. http://www.picsearch.com/. Search engine for photographs.

Project Gutenberg. http://www.gutenberg.net/. Collection of 13,000 free electronic books, mostly older books in the public domain.

Wikipedia: The free encyclopedia. http://en.wikipedia.org/. Online, multilingual encyclopedia with entries on about everything you could ask for.

yourDictionary. http://yourdictionary.com/. Online dictionary and grammar resource; a variety of other language-related resources, including a section on endangered languages.

Sites for English Language Learners

1-language.com. http://www.1-language.com/. English study resources and chat rooms.

Aardvark's English Forum. http://englishforum.com/. Many resources.

Activities for ESL Students. http://a4esl.org/. Quizzes and activities.

Advanced Composition for Non-Native Speakers of English. http://eslbee.com/. Resources for learning and teaching advanced-level composition writing.

AskOxford. http://www.askoxford.com/. Dictionary resource from Oxford University Press.

Centre for Independent Language Learning, Hong Kong Polytechnic University. http://elc.polyu.edu.hk/cill/. Wide range of resources.

Churchill House School of English Language. http://www.churchillhouse.com/english/. Quizzes, games, and advice on grammar.

Dave's ESL Café. http://eslcafe.com/. Language information, quizzes, and other resources.

English Club. http://www.englishclub.com/. Games, quizzes, chat rooms, and other resources.

EnglishLearner.com. http://englishlearner.com/. Lessons, quizzes, pen-friends, and links.

English Listening Lounge. http://www.Englishlistening.com/. Listening practice; Chinese language version available.

ESL Resource Center. http://www.eslus.com/eslcenter.htm. Lessons for students.

Interesting Things for ESL Students. http://www.manythings.org/. Games, puzzles.

John's ESL Community. http://www.johnsesl.com/. Exercises, quizzes, games, and other resources.

Karin's ESL Partyland. http://www.eslpartyland.com/. Quizzes, discussion forums, and other resources.

Learn English. http://www.tolearnenglish.com/. Placement tests, lessons, exercises, and other resources.

Listening on the Net. http://AD.Walker.org/listening.htm. Student guide to listening to English (e.g., radio programs) on the Internet; links included.

Randall's ESL Cyber Listening Lab. http://www.esl-lab.com/. Listening exercises and quizzes.

Repeat after Us. http://repeatafterus.com/. Listening and pronunciation practice.

Sounds of English. http://www.soundsofenglish.org/. Activities and exercises for English pronunciation.

Topics: An Online Magazine for Learners of English. http://www.topics-mag.com/. Features written by and for learners of English.

World News Review. http://webs.wichita.edu/ielc-lab/wnr/. News stories to listen to and read in English.

References

Abbott, G., and P. Wingard, eds. 1981. *The teaching of English as an international language.* Glasgow, Scotland: Collins.

Althen, G. 1988. *American ways: A guide for foreigners in the United States.* Yarmouth, ME: Intercultural Press.

American Council on the Teaching of Foreign Languages. 1999. *ACTFL proficiency guidelines—speaking.* http://www.actfl.org/files/public/Guidelinesspeak.pdf.

Amity Foundation. 2003. *Amity teachers toolkit 2003.* http://www.amityfoundation.org/page.php?pagc=247.

Bailey, K. 1998. *Learning about language assessment: Dilemmas, decisions, and directions.* Boston: Heinle and Heinle.

Bailey, K., A. Curtis, and D. Nunan. 2001. *Pursuing professional development: The self as source.* Boston: Heinle and Heinle.

Barna, L. 1994. Stumbling blocks in intercultural communication. In *Intercultural communication: A reader,* 7th ed., ed. L. Samovar and R. Porter, 337–46. Belmont, CA: Wadsworth.

Bowen, J. D., H. Madsen, and A. Hilferty. 1985. *TESOL: Techniques and procedures.* 2nd ed. Rowley, MA: Newbury House.

Brown, H. D. 1991. *Breaking the language barrier.* Yarmouth, ME: Intercultural Press

———. 2001. *Teaching by principles: An interactive approach to language pedagogy.* 2nd ed. Reading, MA: Addison Wesley Longman.

———. 2002. English language teaching in the "post-method" era: Toward better diagnosis, treatment, and assessment. In *Methodology in Language Teaching: An Anthology of Current Practice,* ed. J. Richards and W. Renandya, 9–18. Cambridge: Cambridge University Press.

Byrd, D., and I. Clemente-Cabetas. 2001. *React interact.* 3rd ed. Harlow, England: Pearson Education.

Carrell, P., and J. Eisterhold. 1987. Schema theory and ESL reading pedagogy. In *Methodology in TESOL: A book of readings,* ed. M. Long and J. C. Richards, 218–32. Rowley, MA: Newbury House.

Carruthers, R. 1987. Teaching pronunciation. In *Methodology in TESOL: A book of readings,* ed. M. Long and J. C. Richards, 191–200. Rowley, MA: Newbury House.

Christopher, V., ed. 2005. *Directory of teacher education programs in TESOL in the United States and Canada, 2005–2007.* Alexandria, VA: TESOL.

Cohen, A. 1998. *Strategies in learning and using a second language.* Reading, MA: Addison Wesley Longman.

Cross, D. 1991. *A practical handbook of language teaching.* London: Cassell.

Crystal, D. 1997. *English as a global language.* Cambridge: Cambridge University Press.

Damen, L. 1987. *Culture learning: The fifth dimension in the language classroom.* New York: Addison-Wesley.

DeCarrico, J. 2001. Vocabulary learning and teaching. In *Teaching English as a second or foreign language,* 3rd ed., ed. M. Celce-Murcia, 285–99. Boston: Heinle and Heinle.

Dörnyei, Z. 2001. *Teaching and researching motivation.* Harlow, England: Pearson Education.

Eisenstein, M. 1987. Grammatical explanations in ESL: Teach the student, not the method. In *Methodology in TESOL: A book of readings,* ed. M. Long and J. C. Richards, 282–92. Rowley, MA: Newbury House.

Farber, B. 1991. *How to learn any language.* New York: Citadel Press.

Fotos, S. 2001. Cognitive approaches to grammar instruction. In *Teaching English as a second or foreign language,* 3rd ed., ed. M. Celce-Murcia, 267–84. Boston: Heinle and Heinle.

Fox, L. 1987. On acquiring an adequate second language vocabulary. In *Methodology in TESOL: A book of readings,* ed. M. Long and J. C. Richards, 307–11. Rowley, MA: Newbury House.

Gairns, R., and S. Redman. 1986. *Working with words: A guide to teaching and learning vocabulary.* Cambridge: Cambridge University Press.

Goodwin, J. 2001. Teaching pronunciation. In *Teaching English as a second or foreign language,* 3rd ed., ed. M. Celce-Murcia, 117–38. Boston: Heinle and Heinle.

Gower, R., and S. Walters. 1983. *Teaching practice handbook: A reference book for EFL teachers in training.* Portsmouth, NH: Heinemann.

Grey, B., K. Darrow, and B. Palmquist. 1975. *Transcultural study guide.* 2nd ed. Stanford, CA: Volunteers in Asia.

Griffith, S. 2002. *Teaching English abroad: Talk your way around the world.* 6th ed. Oxford: Vacation Work.

Grove, C., and I. Torbiorn. 1993. A new conceptualization of intercultural adjustment and the goals of training. In *Education for the intercultural experience,* 2nd ed., 73–108. Yarmouth, ME: Intercultural Press

Guangdong Bureau of Higher Education. 1991. *A guide to the revision of college English, vol. 2.* Guangzhou, China: Guangdong Bureau of Higher Education.

Harmer, J. 2001. *The practice of English language teaching.* Harlow, England: Pearson Education.

Hedge, T. 2000. *Teaching and learning in the language classroom.* Oxford University Press

Hendrickson, J. 1987. Error correction in foreign language teaching: Recent theory, research and practice. In *Methodology in TESOL: A book of readings,* ed. M. Long and J. C. Richards, 355–72. Rowley, MA: Newbury House.

Hess, D. 1997. *Studying abroad/learning abroad.* Yarmouth, ME: Intercultural Press

Hirsch, E. D. 1987. *Cultural literacy: What every American needs to know.* New York: Vintage Books.

Hughes, A. 1989. *Testing for language teachers.* Cambridge: Cambridge University Press.

Kohls, R. 2001. *Survival kit for overseas living.* 4th ed. Yarmouth, ME: Intercultural Press.

Lanier, A. 1988. *Living in the USA.* 4th ed. Yarmouth, ME: Intercultural Press.

Larsen-Freeman, D. 2001. Grammar. In *The Cambridge guide to teaching English to speakers of other languages,* ed. R. Carter and D. Nunan, 34–41. 2001. Cambridge: Cambridge University Press.

Levine, D., J. Baxter, and P. McNulty. 1987. *The culture puzzle: Cross-cultural communication for English us a second language.* Englewood Cliffs, NJ: Prentice Hall.

Lewis, M. 1993. *The lexical approach: The state of ELT and a way forward.* Hove, England: Language Teaching Publications.

Littlewood, W. 1984. *Foreign and second language learning: Language acquisition research and its implications for the classroom.* Cambridge: Cambridge University Press.

Madsen, H. 1983. *Techniques in testing.* Oxford: Oxford University Press.

Marshall, T. 1989. *The whole world guide to language learning.* Yarmouth, ME: Intercultural Press.

McCrum, R., W. Cran, and R. MacNeil. 1987. *The story of English.* London: Faber and Faber.

McKay, S. 1987. *Teaching grammar: Form, function, and technique.* Englewood Cliffs, NJ: Prentice Hall International.

Mohamed, J. 2003. *Teaching English overseas: A job guide for Americans and Canadians.* 3rd ed. Cypress, TX: English International.

Morley, J. 2001. Aural comprehension instruction: Principles and practices. In *Teaching English as a second or foreign language,* 3rd ed., ed. M. Celce-Murcia, 285–99. Boston: Heinle and Heinle.

Murray, D., ed. 1992. *Diversity as resource: Redefining cultural literacy.* Alexandria, VA: TESOL.

Nunan, D. 1989. *Designing tasks for the communicative classroom.* Cambridge: Cambridge University Press.

———. 1997. Designing and adapting materials to encourage learner autonomy. In *Autonomy and independence in language learning,* ed. P. Benson and P. Voller, 192–203. New York: Longman.

Omaggio Hadley, A. 2001. *Teaching language in context.* 3rd ed. Boston: Heinle and Heinle.

Oxford, R. 1990. *Language learning strategies: What every teacher should know.* New York: Newbury House.

———. 2001. Language learning styles and strategies. In *Teaching English as a second or foreign language,* 3rd ed., ed. M. Celce-Murcia, 359–66. Boston: Heinle and Heinle.

Paige, M., ed. 1993. *Education for the intercultural experience.* 2nd ed. Yarmouth, ME: Intercultural Press.

People's Publishing House. 1984. *English: Senior I.* Beijing, China: People's Publishing House.

Raimes, A. 1983. *Techniques in teaching writing.* Oxford: Oxford University Press.

Richards, J. 1990. *The language teaching matrix.* Cambridge: Cambridge University Press.

Rubin, J., and I. Thompson. 1994. *How to be a more successful language learner.* 2nd ed. Boston: Heinle and Heinle.

Scarcella, R., and R. Oxford. 1992. *The tapestry of language learning: The individual in the communicative classroom.* Boston: Heinle and Heinle.

Seelye, N. 1993. *Teaching culture: Strategies for intercultural communication.* 3rd ed. Lincolnwood, IL: National Textbook.

Snow, D. 2002. *Survival Chinese.* Beijing, China: Commercial Press.

———. 2004. *Encounters with Westerners: Improving skills in English and intercultural communication.* Shanghai, China: Shanghai Foreign Language Education Press

Spence, J. 1984. *The memory palace of Matteo Ricci.* New York: Viking.

Stewart, E., and M. Bennett. 1991. *American cultural patterns: A cross-cultural perspective.* Rev. ed. Yarmouth, ME: Intercultural Press

Stevick, E. 1988. *Teaching and learning languages.* Cambridge: Cambridge University Press.

———. 1996. *Memory, meaning, and method.* Boston: Heinle and Heinle.

Taylor, B. 1987. Incorporating a Communicative, Student-Centered Component. In *Methodology in TESOL: A book of readings,* ed. M. Long and J. C. Richards, 45–60. Rowley, MA: Newbury House.

Underhill, N. 1987. *Testing spoken language.* Cambridge: Cambridge University Press.

Ur, P. 1981. *Discussions that work: Task-centred fluency practice.* Cambridge: Cambridge University Press.

———. 1984. *Teaching listening comprehension.* Cambridge: Cambridge University Press.

———. 1996. *A course in language teaching: Practice and theory.* Cambridge: Cambridge University Press.

Walters, K. 1992. Whose culture, whose literacy? In *Diversity as resource: Redefining cultural literacy,* ed. D. Murray, 3–25. Alexandria, VA: TESOL.

Weaver, G. 1993. Understanding and coping with cross-cultural adjustment stress. In *Education for the intercultural experience,* 2nd ed., ed. M. Paige, 137–68. Yarmouth, ME: Intercultural Press.

About the Author

Don Snow holds an MA in ESL from Michigan State University and a PhD in East Asian language and culture from Indiana University. He has taught language, culture, and linguistics in the United States, Taiwan, mainland China, and Hong Kong, and has worked with a number of organizations that send volunteer teachers abroad. At present he teaches in the graduate program of the English Department of Nanjing University, seconded to that university through the Presbyterian Church USA. In addition to writing about language teaching, he researches Chinese dialects, and his *Cantonese as Written Language: The Growth of a Written Chinese Vernacular* was published by Hong Kong University Press in 2004.